A Rage for Order

A Rage for Order

Black/White Relations in the American South Since Emancipation

JOEL WILLIAMSON

New York   Oxford
OXFORD UNIVERSITY PRESS
1986

Oxford University Press

Oxford   New York   Toronto
Delhi   Bombay   Calcutta   Madras   Karachi
Petaling Jaya   Singapore   Hong Kong   Tokyo
Nairobi   Dar es Salaam   Cape Town
Melbourne   Auckland

and associated companies in
Beirut   Berlin   Ibadan   Nicosia

This book is an abridged edition of *The Crucible of Race: Black-White Relations in the American South Since Emancipation* (Oxford University Press, 1984)

Copyright © 1986 by Joel Williamson

Published by Oxford University Press, Inc.
200 Madison Avenue, New York, New York 10016

Oxford is the registered trademark of Oxford University Press

Library of Congress Cataloging-in-Publication Data
Williamson, Joel.
A rage for order.
"An abridged edition of The crucible of race"—
T.p. verso.
Bibliography: p.
Includes index.
1. Afro-Americans—Civil rights—Southern States.
2. Southern States—Race relations.
3. Afro-Americans—Southern States—History.
I. Williamson, Joel. Crucible of race.   II. Title.
E185.61.W7382   1986   305.8′96073′075   85-31946
ISBN 0-19-504024-4
ISBN 0-19-504025-2 (pbk.)

Printing (last digit): 9 8 7 6 5 4 3 2 1

Printed in the United States of America
on acid-free paper

For
Joelle, William, Alethea

Preface

Black-white relations in America is a problem that will not go away. In politics, in economics, in every phase of our national life, race continues to be a divisive issue. This book is an attempt to understand how this came to be.

In America we find a white world on one side and a black world on the other. Each has its own beauty, its special integrity, and its difficulties. In important ways we share the good things that each world offers the other—music, language, cuisine. But there are other areas in which we have given one another great pain—in slavery and slave rebellions, in violence and the threat of violence. But the use and abuse of one race by the other is primarily the sin of the whites in that it is they who have had, ultimately, the power to determine the character of race relations in the land. It is a power that they have not failed to use, sooner or later. It is white America that decided that black folks and no others among the post-Columbian migrants to this land would be denied full admission to American society—denied not just for one generation or two or three, but, thus far, for a whole dozen generations. It is, indeed, ironic that black people are among the first Americans, but of all the ethnic groups that have migrated in great numbers to this land, none has been so totally and perpetually excluded from full membership in the social body.

The exclusion of blacks proceeds, and the price is very high. In the time of slavery, race was made to pay: blackness was married to slavery, and slavery was a paying institution. With emancipation the picture began to change radically, and white America in the twentieth century has generally evinced a willingness to pay for its racism. The exclusion of blacks from full participation in the educational, medical, economic, political, and cultural centers of American life has been costly, not only to blacks but to whites as well. White America pays the price, not happily to be sure, but readily enough obviously—pays it in a comparatively retarded rate of economic growth, pays it by filling its prisons with black people at a yearly per person cost that exceeds the cost of sending a student to Harvard University for a year, pays for it by way of the welfare rolls, and, most of all, will continue to pay through the lifetimes of millions of black children who today live below the poverty line. In the turn-of-the-century years other great powers in Western civilization were making racism pay. In South Africa today some six million white people living on top of the tightly organized labor of some twenty-four million black and colored people still make it pay. But white Americans, clearly, are willing to foot the bill for their racism.

This book is informed by the idea that the primary roots of race relations in modern America can be found in the Southern past, particularly in the turn-of-the-century decades, a time and a place called "the crucible of race" in the study of which this volume is an abridgment. Blacks and whites have met in the North and West, of course, as well as in the South, and those streams too have fed into the river of race relations in America. But over the whole of American history most black experience has taken place in the South and so has the greater part of relations between blacks and whites. Indeed, going into the second decade of this century, very nearly 90 percent of all black Americans lived in the South, and a large proportion of them lived in the lower South—that is, south and west of North Carolina. The out-migration began with World War I, and sometime in the 1960s the balance was struck, where it has remained, with roughly half of black America living in the South and half out. Still, even with the shift, it seems that the black heartland remains in the South, more especially in the deep South, where the state of Mississippi is almost half black, where Booker T. Washington reigned at Tuskegee, where Martin Luther King was born in Atlanta, gained power and fame in Montgomery and Birmingham, and died in Memphis.

The human geography and the attitudinal climate of race relations in the South are varied and complex. There are many Souths and many Southerners, and each has a special history of race relations. One might study race relations in the South by states, or by sub-regions, politics, or economics. Or one might follow William Faulkner's lead and feature a combination of race, sex, and class. It happened that in this book, and in its parent book *The Crucible of Race*, we came to the same ordering as did Faulkner. This book tells the story of race relations in the South as a play among these three elements. It finds that the South in the last century and a half has been in a significant measure ruled by a white elite—continuous not so much in blood lines as in mentality. This elite has managed to maintain hegemony over black and white masses rather clearly separated from each other. Sex roles have been integral in that process. And so, too, has violence: the physical violence of Ku Kluxers—sheeted and unsheeted—of lynchers—legal and illegal—and even more importantly the quiet violence of poverty, hunger, and disease.

There is a Southern story to be told in race relations, and it can be told with a relatively narrow focus on the South. Also, it can be told as the Southern portion of a national story. Ultimately, however, it must be told as a part of a global story. The South is and has been no island in race relations. Once tied to the world by threads of cotton, more recently it is tied by the hard politics of global confrontation.

Obviously there are many elements involved in the complex of race relations in the South, and we can touch representatives of only the most important of these. In the black world we have recast Booker T. Washington and W. E. B. DuBois, but also we have found an extraordinary black working man in the person of Robert Charles. Charles was fiercely proud, a "race man," and an uncanny marksman who defied the police, the militia, and a mob of some 2,000 white men in a New Orleans shootout in 1900. In Rebecca Felton, the first woman to sit in the United States Senate, we offer a white woman of the elite element whose life and world view was, in important ways, strikingly different from that of the men in her class. We feature race, sex, and class in our organization, but these occur, as we all know, in the matrix of a broad and ongoing world.

This book is not in any major way an intellectual history. It does not much concern itself with "high thought." But it is deeply concerned with "thinking" and with the sources of thinking. It is no less concerned with the action that is related to thinking. Unabashedly we seek to walk a mile in their shoes, and to think what they thought. How else can we ever meet what happened then? There is no model offered to relate thought and action in a mechanical way. Rather it seems in our study that every situation was unique—thought and action interplaying to produce some certain result. Whatever we do with models in this book we do with humility, with respect for the infinite complexity of human kind. We assume that these are constructs made as aids to navigation in our pursuit of understanding and deserve respect only as possible means toward that end.

Our chronology is chosen to fit our case. We might begin with the first blacks arriving in Jamestown in 1619. Or we might begin in the Caribbean before then, or in Africa, or with the Crusades in the Near East. It is, indeed, all continuous. But we chose to begin with Nat Turner in 1831 because his rebellion signaled unmistakably the black response to subordination. In one way or another, it is the response with which white America still contends.

Johns, North Carolina   J. W.
December 5, 1985

Contents

A Rage for Order

CHAPTER I

Slavery and After: Building the Organic Society, 1831–1889

BETWEEN TWO WORLDS

It is possible to construct an interpretation of the experience of the African in British America and subsequently the United States upon the assumption that black life has oscillated between two extremes of perfect separation and perfect integration. At one extreme, blacks might have found themselves practically outside of personal contact with white Americans—for instance, detached and settled upon a reserve that included South Carolina, Georgia, Alabama, and Mississippi. At the other extreme, they might have found themselves in a world in which no cultural distinction was attached to skin color, and they were melting physically and mentally into the white world. However, the nature of the society in which blacks have found themselves in America has prevented them from achieving the relative stability promised by either extreme. Rather has it cast them into a perpetual motion, moving first toward the one and then toward the other. Like some giant pendulum, the weight of black existence swings with a rush through a center line between separation and integration, but even as it moves beyond, the forces pulling it back increase with geometric rapidity.

The fluctuation between a perfect integration and a perfect separation began in the middle of the sixteenth century when white men from an aggressively expanding England came by sea to meet blacks south of the Sahara. Through enslavement, through the crossing of the Atlantic in the infamous "middle passage," and in the careful system of acculturation called "seasoning" in which the African was married to the plantation system and learned to survive in the New World, the process of depriving black people of their natal culture and of force-drafting them into Euro-

3

pean, English, and English-American culture proceeded very far, even in the first generation of those taken. But when the very first black child was conceived, and born, and bred in America, a cultural mutation occurred. That child, and the brothers and sisters who came after, were lost to Africa far more than were their parents. No child can know precisely what its parents knew, and the life experience, the consciousness of a black born a slave in America was vastly different from that of an African born free. Each succeeding generation in America, by its very birth, moved a quick half-step farther away from the primal culture of Africa.

From the beginning, simple economics made it necessary that whites educate blacks into plantation living and, in some minimal degree, into life in the British-American world. But after about 1750, when the first great waves of African migrations had passed, there was no broadly concerted and highly effective attempt by the owners or the authorities to acculturate the African. Rather did the African in America seem to experience a kind of cultural neglect born of white indifference. Even so, as the generations passed, black Americans probably drifted rather vaguely toward whiteness.

Among white people, the Revolutionary generation was the first to pause and squarely face the broad issue of what was to be the future of black people in America. Generally speaking, they decided with relative ease that they were against slavery. But they evinced a profound and persistent ambivalence about black people, the great majority of whom were slaves. One could end slavery by legislative fiat, but blackness was another and much less tractable problem. What did the blackness of these people signify in cultural terms? Could black people once freed join the cultural communion of whiteness? And what did their blackness mean for the future of the new nation? In the North, emancipation was made easier by the relatively low proportion of Negroes in the total population. The same fact made freed blacks less threatening. In the South, large numbers of Negroes made both slavery and blackness very difficult problems. In the upper South, meaning North Carolina and points west and north to Mason's and Dixon's line (the southern border of Pennsylvania), the Revolutionary generation of Jefferson, Madison, and Monroe responded to the problem with a focus that their ancestors had lacked. They did so, in part, because theirs was the first generation in that part of America who knew what it was to be born white in small seas of black humanity. In the lower South, where the black population often outnumbered the white, the Revolutionary generation hardly recognized any problem with slavery. For them, slavery itself was the solution to the problem of blackness.

Black people had come to the South early, in 1619, close upon the heels of the English who settled at Jamestown in 1607. Slavery, too, came early and was fairly well defined in practice, concept, and law within fifty years of the arrival of the first blacks. But in this formative period, British America remained vastly white, even in the South. In 1648 in Virginia, for instance, only 300 blacks lived among 15,000 English. As late as 1681, blacks comprised only some 4 percent of the total population in this first settled British North American colony. The great majority of "bound" labor in the seventeenth century consisted not of black slaves, but of white people held to work for a fixed term of several years under the system of "indentured servitude," essentially a device for exchanging work for passage across the Atlantic to the New World. It was only in the early eighteenth century, about 1715, that Africans existed in such massive numbers as to stir the imagination, and the anxieties, of the already solidly entrenched whites. When blacks did come in great numbers in and after the 1690s, they came, of course, to the South, into Maryland and Virginia and the eastern portions of the Carolinas and Georgia. In Maryland and Virginia the black population rose to roughly 30 and 40 percent of the total by the middle of the eighteenth century. In South Carolina blacks outnumbered whites as early as 1708.[1]

Much of the leadership of Revolutionary Virginia was born amid waves of black migration and to parents wealthy in slaves. Thomas Jefferson's first remembrance was of being carried on a pillow held by a slave mounted on horseback from Albemarle, in western Virginia, to the plantation Tuckahoe, near Richmond. His father had undertaken the management of Tuckahoe for one of the Randolphs, his landed and slave-rich kinsman by marriage. There young Thomas grew up white and favored among a black slave population so numerous as to require seven overseers. Thomas Jefferson shared a color-conscious youth with many of the leaders of the Revolution in the South. He and they grew to manhood with a perspective on blackness that their parents born to whiter worlds could not have known.[2]

Nation-building compelled leaders in the Revolutionary generation to study slavery and black people with unprecedented intensity. The Founding Fathers were forced to think deeply and deliberately, as people not often do, about the far future of a whole people that was yet to be. Slavery emerged as a difficulty susceptible to solution. Both economics and Revolutionary ideology militated against it. In the upper South by the 1750s labor-intensive tobacco culture was rapidly losing ground to the cultivation of cereals, and the demand for slave labor was declining. At the same time, the idea of the natural rights of man was gaining currency, and that principle did not explicitly except black people from its rule. Jefferson himself, in 1776, drew the approval of his colleagues in the Continental Congress by beginning the Declaration of Independence with the ringing assertion that "all men are created equal, that they are endowed by the Creator with certain unalienable Rights, that among these are Life, Liberty and the pursuit of Happiness." Furthermore, in first drafting that document, he had indicted King George III for disallowing colonial laws attempting to halt the further importation of slaves, an item that was later deleted.[3] In 1784 Jefferson proposed, in an ordinance for the governance of western territories ceded to the national government by the states, that slavery be prohibited after the year 1800 west of the Appalachian Mountains. That proposal was defeated in the Confederation Congress by a vote of seven states to six.[4] However, in 1787 the Northwest Ordinance did pass. It prohibited the further introduction of slavery north and west of the Ohio River, and thus the whole of that vast territory from Indiana to Wisconsin was set in the direction of freedom at home and, when the struggle came, antislavery in the nation.[5]

Revolutionary society as a whole reflected Jefferson's antislavery inclinations. In 1776 slavery existed in each of the thirteen colonies. However, the "First Emancipation" began in New England with the beginning of the Revolution and proceeded southward over the next generation as state after state down through New Jersey and Pennsylvania either abolished slavery immediately or implemented some plan of gradual emancipation.[6] Antislavery sentiment by no means stopped at Mason's and Dixon's line. Indeed, there were more antislavery societies in the South in the 1820s than there were in the North, even though there seems to have been no organized antislavery movements in South Carolina and Georgia. Where slavery was not abolished, the various states, at least for economic if not for ideological reasons, acted independently to prohibit the importation of slaves from abroad. In 1794 no state licensed such additions to its black population. South Carolina and Georgia soon reversed themselves, but in 1808 Congress exercised the option offered by the Constitution and outlawed the further importation of slaves from abroad. Thus the total effect of the Revolutionary generation's actions on slavery was to press the institution southward below Mason's and Dixon's line and to push it into an isolation that led finally to extinction.

In the sense that slavery was ultimately eradicated by Americans themselves, it became a manageable problem. Blackness, on the other hand, proved to be perpetually unmanageable. Thought in the Revolutionary era tended against slavery, but it decided practically nothing about the meaning of blackness.[7] The perplexity of the Founding Fathers is fully understandable. To that generation and for at least a century afterward, culture was tied directly to color and blood. Inevitably they saw in the physical mixing of white and black a dilution of superior European culture. Shortly many of them thought that they saw precisely that phenomenon occurring in Latin America. To them the vital question of race relations was what color the complexion of the future American would be, and it was a question that gave them serious pause. Would future Americans be purely white by dint of excluding blacks from their society? Or would they be a mixture of white and black, a mongrel breed in a mongrel nation? What followed by way of answer were a few fretful starts, a rising hesitancy, ambivalence, indecision, and then drift. For a time after 1817, with the foundation and support of the American Colonization Society by such eminents as John Jay, Thomas Jefferson, and James Monroe, the resettlement of blacks abroad, particularly Africa, seemed a possible solution. The idea of inducing masses of people voluntarily to export themselves across the seas seemed not unrealistic to a white population that had so recently shipped itself to America by the tens of thousands. Liberia, a child state created by America in Africa in the 1820s, began to be peopled by Americanized blacks. Liberia survived and grew, but only slowly, and it did not flourish, primarily because the great majority of American blacks simply refused to go.[8] America, to them, was home.

In the long, hot summer of 1831 the drifting suddenly ceased. In August in southside Virginia, Nat Turner led a band of rebel slaves to slaughter, in the most horrible way with knives, axes, and crude guns, some fifty-seven whites and to be slaughtered themselves. The whites thus killed were nonslaveholders as well as slaveholders, kind slaveholders as well as unkind, women and children was well as men. The single clear condition that held all the massacred together was that they were white— a fact not lost upon contemporaries of the same color.[9] The message of the Turner insurrection was that when blacks rebelled, all whites died. There had been large-scale insurrections and insurrectionary plots in the United States and abroad before, and whites were never totally free of the fear. But for nearly a century any real plots in the South had been nipped in the bud. Before the advent of Nat Turner reasonable people could believe that it could not happen here, that the American South was different, and that fears of servile insurrection were for the faint-hearted who overreacted to plots and rumors of plots. Turner's rebellion had one transcendent result: massive slave rebellion in the South was lifted from the realm of possibility and conjecture and placed with terrific bluntness in the realm not only of the possible, but of the probable. With that great traumatic convulsion, the broad current of race relations in the South was wrenched up and out of its former channel. Like a great river disrupted by some giant earthquake, it poured out over the land in a rushing search for a new bottom, a new place to flow smoothly in the natural order of things.

THE HARD-SOFT PERIOD OF SLAVERY

The signal response of the white South to Nat Turner's insurrection came in the meeting of the Virginia legislature in the winter of 1831–32. Virtually the whole of that session was devoted to a great debate on slavery. Antislavery Virginians insisted upon facing the issue of what the state should do about that institution. While no vote was taken upon the precise question of whether to end slavery or not, a vote was taken on a motion that is often considered to have been an effective test of the question. If that assumption is warranted, emancipation in Virginia was defeated by a very narrow margin of 65 to 58.[10]

It would appear, then, that at times before Nat Turner there was a fair chance that Virginia would go the way of New England and the Middle States and become a free state. Had it done so, it is very possible that the Civil War would not have occurred, and the Southern nation that existed from 1861 to 1865 would never have come to be. In 1830 nearly a quarter of the 2,000,000 slaves in America lived in Virginia.[11] Without slavery in Virginia there would have been far fewer slaves to supply the slave frontier to the southwest, to help make cotton a self-crowned king to defy the world. Without slavery the state's political weight would have been thrown into the balance with the free states in the face of threats of secession and civil war from the lower South. Without Virginia, Robert E. Lee, a host of able generals and other officers, and more than 200,000 soldiers would have been denied to any future Southern Confederacy and their numbers added to those against the rebels. Without it, the war would have been fought, if there had been a war at all, in South Carolina and south and west of that testy state, and it would have been a very abortive affair. One can, of course, exaggerate the importance of Nat Turner's insurrection, the Virginia debates, and of Virginia itself at this juncture. There was rebelliousness among the slaves before 1831 and a response among whites. There was always dissent against slavery among whites in the South. Always some people opposed the evil, and some of these spoke out against it. Nevertheless, the Turner insurrection and its sequel marked the last time that slavery was seriously challenged in Dixie by both blacks and a powerful combination of Southern whites. Thereafter, there would be no more slave rebellions in the South approaching such magnitude, and organized antislavery action would become an exclusively Northern phenomenon.

The debates in the Virginia legislature and their result were a signal, an indicator of how the upper South in the post-Revolutionary generation was going to respond to slavery. In 1834 Tennessee and in 1835 North Carolina held constitutional conventions in which they followed Virginia's lead. In the end, the upper South decided that it could not dismount from the tiger of slavery. It must, therefore, take the animal by the ears and ride. That decision was one of the critical turning points in the creation of a distinctive Southern people and in the genesis of a racial universe within which we in America still struggle today.

After the Virginia debates and during the last generation of slavery, a paradox occurred in race relations in the South. Even as white society came to impose a more rigid police control over black people, it also moved across the race line to touch blacks with unprecedented intimacy. This era may well be called the "hard-soft" period of slavery. On the one hand, white society elaborated and tightened the laws dealing with blacks, both slave and free, and revamped the police system for enforcing those laws. On the other side, white people went among black people in a new style. Whites strove hard to make a place for black people in the white-dominated world, to integrate them, as it were, into a harmonious order—almost to make them white. Ultimately what had begun as an effort to change blacks ended in the reconstitution of white society itself. Out of the labor of race control was born an altered Southern character. That character and the culture that supported it grew in the face of a North that at first saw and repudiated William Lloyd Garrison and a passion for immediate emancipation but finally came, by 1861, with its 22,000,000 people, to deny slavery and the Southern order the right to expand beyond the limits then imposed upon them.

After Turner's insurrection and the decision that they must ride the tiger, Southern states generally enacted more stringent laws for the control of black people, both slave and free. For example, black people were not allowed to assemble together in any considerable numbers, even to worship, without a white person present. It became universally illegal in the South to teach slaves to read or write for fear that they would use those skills to foment insurrection. Slaves were not, of course, allowed to have weapons; but they were also not to have drums or trumpets that might be used to pass signals, nor to work in pharmacies where they might have access to poisons. The curtailing of the rights of free Negroes was also striking. In North Carolina after 1835 free Negroes were not allowed to vote. In South Carolina restrictions upon their worship were so tight that the African Methodist Episcopal Church felt constrained to close its doors and withdraw from the state.[12] Finally, new laws regulated more closely the behavior of white people in relation to blacks. For instance, a Richmond ordinance of 1859 imposed a fine of up to twenty dollars upon any white person who beat a slave unlawfully, and inflicted lashes or a fine upon any free person of color who did so.[13]

In addition to special slave laws, brought together from time to time in the so-called slave codes, blacks were regulated by the master's rules on the plantation itself. Those rules, built around a desire to utilize the labor of the slave to the maximum, closely fixed such details as hours of work and rest, feeding, and care of tools and clothing. The law of the plantation left few hands idle for the devil's use. Above the slave codes were provisions in the general laws of the states that paid special attention to blacks. For instance, criminal codes often prescribed lashes for blacks and fines for white people, and the crimes for which a black person might be punished by death far outnumbered those for which a white person might suffer the same fate. There were also national laws that impinged especially upon black people. The federal government itself guaranteed the rendition of fugitive slaves and, in its commitment to suppress "domestic insurrection," was bound to put down slave revolts. In the revamping of the fugitive slave law in 1850 to facilitate the return of runaway slaves and in the ready repression of John Brown's rebellion in 1859, the federal government showed itself not remiss in honoring these commitments.

Effective police control of Southern blacks was a function of both white numbers and white alertness. In the black belts of the South where slaves were heavily concentrated and in a majority, vigilance was the crucial element. Antebellum Southern whites knew well enough that eternal vigilance was the price of slavery as well as freedom—and the price, too, of the security of their own lives and property. The local police, the state militia, and, ultimately, the armed forces of the United States stood ready to control the slaves. But the immediate instrument by which white society as a whole consciously and officially kept black people in check was the "patrol." The patrol was the front line of defense in what was, in essence, an undeclared war between the races.

The patrol began as early as the seventeenth century, and it varied in constitution and function from state to state and from time to time. In the colonial period it was usually made up of masters and overseers, people with a direct stake in slavery who banded together with full legal authority to enforce the laws of slavery. In the nineteenth century the constitution of the patrol shifted; its essential feature in this new phase was that, typically, every white male of military age and capacity—not only masters and overseers—was required to serve, sometimes without pay. Increasingly the patrol assumed the aspect of a *posse comitatus* enlisted by the state in an emergency. It savored of the power of the government to command the services of its citizens in cases of fire, flood, or foreign invasion. The patrol had authority not only over slaves, but over free blacks as well, and over any white person who might be suspected of conspiring with blacks in illegal activities. It was, in short, a system in which virtually all white men came together to enforce the racial establishment. In the patrol every white man was a policeman in the face of every black person. In the institution of the patrol in the years before the Civil War, one can see the racial system meshing smoothly into the slave system. Slavery was no longer simply a matter of economics, nor of masters controlling slaves in a somewhat separated segment of society. It had become a matter of all whites controlling all blacks . . . a matter of race.

Particularly, it was the duty of the patrol to ride the highways and byways at night while the masters slept. In effect, patrols were courts on horseback. They arrested blacks away from their plantations without passes, searched their persons and cabins for arms and stolen goods, and broke up meetings. Patrols were often made up of three, six, nine, or a dozen men; they were juries or fractions of juries with the power to try, judge, sentence, and punish offenders on the spot. These were summary courts over which masters had little immediate control. Most especially the patrol enforced the laws regulating blacks, but the design of those laws and the raison d'être of the patrol were very clearly to stop insurrections before they began. So central to the concerns of white people in the black-belt states was the problem of racial control that the very term applied to the area for which a patrol was responsible, the "beat," came to be applied to the smallest area of civil administration. What was a "township" in New England and the Northwest and a "community" or a "parish" in other areas, in the deep South was a "beat." In South Carolina the term "beat" was replaced by "township" only in 1868 after the carpetbaggers assumed control, and in Alabama and Mississippi to this day "beat" remains the designation for the smallest governmental and political subdivision in rural areas. The persistence of the term in these three states is but indicative of the lastingly high ratios of blacks to whites, the danger to which white lives and limbs were subjected, and the intensity of racial feelings there.[14]

The militant South, the military South prone to shoot first and answer questions later, did and still does exist. It sprang from the necessity of controlling a potentially explosive black population. In the nineteenth-century South the key to control lay in possessing all the guns and the mobility that horses afforded. Given blacks armed only with knives, axes, and hoes, it was very possible that a single white man could match twenty slaves. On the other side, Negroes were well aware of the facts of life, and of death, and of the odds against them in an insurrection. It is pos-

sible that every major insurrectionary plot from the Stono affair in South
Carolina in 1739 to John Brown's raid in Virginia in 1859 included some
plan for seizing an arsenal, and it is certain that whites saw that red thread
woven into every scheme for slave rebellion. The fact that John Brown
struck at the federal arsenal at Harper's Ferry was an awfully accurate
testimony to Southerners of the deadly seriousness of the threat he
represented.

White Southerners were alert to rebelliousness among their slaves,
and they by no means relaxed between open outbreaks. They were fearful
of the insidious attacks of arsonists and poisoners; and they took anything
less harmless than a childlike face and manner among blacks as an open
threat to peace and good order. In one sense they were too fearful, but in
another they could hardly be fearful enough. Masters and mistresses were
terribly vulnerable, in themselves and vastly more so through their loved
ones. They could not long forget the tortuously precarious way of their
lives. After 1830, as Southerners saw themselves threatened by the North
from the outside, their fears of the enemy within increased. They took
small comfort in John Brown's defeat by United States Marines under
Colonel Robert E. Lee when every night might hide the infiltration of
dozens of other John Browns into the South. Secession offered some protection, but even secession itself was accompanied by a great well-poison-
ing scare that swept eastward from Texas through the lower South in
1860 and 1861. Indeed, there seemed to be no safe place, and armed sur-
veillance the best and only refuge.

The military personality that we call Spartan arose in an ancient society where a master class confronted a slave population some twenty times
its size. The South was not another Sparta, but it was Spartan-like, and
from a comparable necessity. The message of the South to its young men
in the last decades of slavery was to be, perhaps, more Spartan than the
Spartans. If people are told early and late, and often and long, that they
are the very sons of Mars, if their rewards and pleasures—night and day,
before whites and blacks, men and women, fathers and mothers, powerful
and powerless—tend to come from striking the military pose, then they
will strike it. And if they play the martial role long enough, intensively
enough, and without relief, then they tend to become precisely what they
play.

The martial spirit in the South was further advanced by the fact that
the militia in the various states was inextricably bound up with the patrol
system. Every state supported a militia in which every white male of military capacity was enrolled. Typically the militia was organized by counties, each county supplying one or more regiments. The county was sub-
divided into districts that supplied the men for a company. These were

usually townships, parishes, communities, or "beats." Whatever the civil designation, the beat of the patrol, the area of its responsibility, was exactly the same one that supported the militia company. Usually the county sheriff or the county court was responsible for organizing the patrol. Immediate supervision most often was assigned to the company officers of the militia. The militia captain was also the captain of the patrol, and the same men served in both organizations under the same officers. Consequently, the South was a social order in which every able-bodied white man was a trooper in the service of the racial state. The antebellum South was military-minded, and it was full to overflowing with military titles, not only with colonels but with a plethora of majors and captains as well. Those titles sprang from a central and vital function—race control. They were not ludicrous, or empty, or even merely honorific. When one Southerner addressed another as "Cap'n," it did mean something.

It was no accident that the Southern landscape was dotted with preparatory schools run rigidly along the military model and that various states established military academies in the style of West Point. In 1859 when Louisiana recruited William Tecumseh Sherman to open its State Seminary and Military Academy, Braxton Bragg, a fellow West Pointer who had become a successful Louisiana planter, advised him that "every plantation is a small military establishment—or it ought to be." It was not slaves as soldiers that he had in mind, but rather management. "Give us well-disciplined masters, managers, and assistants," he urged the commandant, "and we shall never hear of slave insurrections."[15] Louisiana was late in starting, but the Virginia Military Institute (1839) and South Carolina's academy, The Citadel (1842) in Charleston, had for nearly a generation produced officers who did not need to blush deeply in the presence of graduates of the United States Military Academy.

Black-belt white Southerners of military age were conditioned to leap into the saddle at the mere suspicion of a black revolt, and, apparently, after Nat Turner they had an abundance of exercise in that drill. Young Southerners understood that a large part of their mission was to avoid large and disastrous outbreaks by suppressing small ones quickly and with exhibitory ruthlessness. "Overkill" was a way of interracial life in the South. An insurrection, a threat of insurrection, or a presumption of insurrectionary intent was a mandate to chase, seize, search, lash, and to scar psychologically as much as physically, to squelch the rise this time and to deter its happening again. White men also understood that divisiveness among whites in the face of the enemy had to be minimized, and that they ought to be as ruthless against deviation among whites as among blacks. It was literally a living fact in the world of the antebellum South that every white man, ideally, had to be more than a man to face the rising enemies both within and outside the walls of the peculiar institution. It is probably true that most Southerners conditioned to martial postures by the travail of slavery and by a generation of militancy really believed, in 1861, that one of them could lick ten Yankees.

Even as they were moving to enforce a more stringent slavery upon blacks, Southern whites were also moving to reach across the race line to contact black people in a softer style. Most clear in this regard were the activities of the churches, and especially those of the evangelical sects. In South Carolina in 1858, for example, Baptists counted 22,000 blacks among their formally enrolled members. In addition they probably ministered separately to several times that number without having enlisted them in the white-dominated congregations. In 1860 Methodists in the Palmetto State carried 42,000 Negroes on their rolls, and the Presbyterians counted 5,000 blacks in a membership that totaled only 13,000. Interestingly the Presbyterians in South Carolina offered both some of the most ardent and effective proslavery protagonists, such as James Henley Thornwell, sometime president of the South Carolina College, and some of the most conscientious laborers among black people, such as Dr. J. L. Girardeau. In 1850 Girardeau organized Zion Church in Charleston with special provision for a Negro membership that grew to several hundred. The church building itself, designed to seat 2,000, became the frequent meeting place of the liberated Negro community after the occupation of the city by the Union Army early in 1865. The Episcopalians were also influential in reaching across the race line into the Negro world. On the eve of the Civil War they claimed some 3,000 Negro members. Given the facts that the churches regularly touched more people than they took in as members and that the entire black population in South Carolina numbered about 400,000 including children, a formal enrollment of some 72,000 was indeed impressively large.[16] The indications are that South Carolina was not unique, that in and after the 1830s all over the South the movement of white churchmen into black worlds proceeded with purposeful vigor.[17] In fact, in the last generation of slavery many eminent churchmen earned their fame as missionaries to the slaves. It was, for a time, the frontier of Southern religion, and ambitious young clerics went there to seek their fortunes.

In the last three decades before the Civil War, Southern churchmen were also in the vanguard of those who constructed what came to be called the proslavery argument. In its beginning, this was a defense of slavery that drew upon every aspect of thought and art from theology to science to literature. The argument was based, ultimately, upon race. The truth was, it asserted, that black people were creatures inferior to white people. God had made black people precisely to be slaves, and it was the genius of white Southerners to recognize that fact. Thus, racism was finally turned fully to the service of slavery. It was, in effect, married to slavery, and as the marriage matured race became the junior partner in the union. At its crest, the proslavery argument was so vital, so dynamic that it reached out to anticipate, for its own peculiar purposes, evolutionary science and sociology. It was fantastically imaginative, informed by masses of research, and profoundly and intricately worked out. On the eve of conflict it was a weirdly beautiful flower, the black orchid of antebellum Southern intellectual culture.[18]

Elaborate as it was, the proslavery argument was only a small part of a larger effort involving a tremendous outpouring of energy. Whites worked diligently, desperately, and, given their particular lights, one must say brilliantly to build a place for black people in their economy, their religion, politics, philosophy, literature, and even in their families. They were amazingly successful in this vast endeavor, and their success was still growing when the war came.

Out of the mix of mind and matter involved in the evolution of Southern culture, whites in the last decades of slavery began to build a stereotypical image of the black person as simple, docile, and manageable. They labored hard to see all blacks as, essentially, perpetual children. In time, that image of the Negro came to be labeled "Sambo." Sambo, the name given to the second son in some African cultures, was one of the several most popular among male slaves in the South. In colonial times there had been no single ruling image of black people in the white mind. Indeed, slave traders and buyers had closely marked the differences between Africans because the traits, real or imagined, of various peoples were directly related to their prices as slaves. It was only in the last generation of slavery that all blacks came to look alike in the eyes of Southern whites, and the person they chose to see was Sambo. The Sambo of imagination was a child adopted into the white family, an adult black body with a white child's mind and heart, simultaneously appealing and appalling, naturally affectionate and unwittingly cruel, a social asset and a liability. Sambo had within him, then, two terrific and opposite capacities. Improperly cared for, he became bestial, an animal in human form and all the more dangerous because of his human capabilities. Properly managed, on the other hand, he was like a white child—and dear.

Seen from the black side, playing Sambo was simply a way to survive. When local whites panicked into color-coded hysteria (which they did recurrently), Sambo was a mask behind which black people might survive the holocaust. Downcast eyes, shuffling feet, soft uncertain words, and a totally pliant manner were white-invented signals to be used by a black person to say that this individual was no threat. The role sometimes saved blacks. Indirectly, it also sometimes saved whites themselves from the wild and murderous behavior that did damage to their flattering image of themselves as protecting parents to these childlike people.

The Sambo role also worked toward building up a social structure designed to afford stability and security to all. In the role, black people were called upon to perform like white people, but to stop short of being totally white. In the role, black people were here to stay, perpetually, as slaves. No longer did Southerners talk of recolonizing all American blacks in Africa, the Caribbean islands, or out West among the displaced Indians. The positive inducements offered to black people to become like whites were great. To be Christian, to labor well and faithfully in their place within the slave system, to be family people, in brief to be "civilized," was to gain a certain measure of respect and security from the whites that slaves might value. At the living level, survival for slaves depended upon their seeming to be white-like, as well as upon their not being too white to threaten the whites. It seems that many things conspired in those last three decades of slavery to cause black people to learn the ways of the white world and to practice them, even as they evolved a consciousness of the great chasm that separated them from a happy entry into that world.

In reality, of course, Sambo was a creature purely of the white mind, a device by which white slaveholders day by day masked a terror that might otherwise have driven them over the edge of sanity. In time, however, the Sambo role functioned to build white egos. The role was, after all, beautifully fitted to flatter the white man's image of himself. He was the superior, the Spartan warrior and the winner. The Negro was the subordinate. The white man was the Christian, civilized gentleman carrying the message to the heretofore heathen and savage black. He was doing God's work in the Southern world, and it was a labor that would earn him grace in the hereafter. The slaveholder's women were worthy and willing helpmates in that effort. If Sambo came to have a role with certain moves to make on the Southern stage and certain lines to speak, so too did his masters.

Black people probably did not much internalize the Sambo role because it was ultimately unflattering.[19] It seems clear enough that they had the strength to resist that role, to wear it as a mask when necessary and to set it aside at will. Tight as it was, the slave system was simply not tight enough to force blacks to become the Sambos they played. Negroes were not always under the eyes of the whites. There were some blacks who were not slaves, and even the slaves could build other roles for themselves in the woods and swamps, in the cabins at night, and even in the fields by day. Moreover, in song, dance, religion and folk tales they lived through metaphor beyond the ken of whites.[20]

THE ORGANIC SOCIETY

White people could not prescribe and enforce a precise role upon black people without prescribing and enforcing a precise role upon themselves. If blacks were to be held in place, white people would have to assume a place to keep them there. In brief, if there were to be Sambos, there would have to be Sambos' keepers, and the keeper role, being superior, had to be even more firmly fixed than the role of the kept. In practice, of course, there would have to be a broad range of Sambos (male and female, house servants, artisans, drivers, field hands, adults and children) and a broad range of keepers (masters, mistresses, overseers, nonslaveholders, physicians, merchants, and ministers). But the varieties, obviously, were not nearly so important as the species.

The movement to reform the late Old South into an ideal, unitary order of masters and slaves, whites and blacks, was a drive to achieve what might be called an "organic" society. In that order there would be various parts in the social body, and every part would have its place and function. In that society everyone would have a role to play. To use the image that prevailed in late-medieval Western civilization, the head would not want to be the heart, and the hand would not pine to be the head. Rather each would function contentedly in its place according to its nature. In the organic society, people would know their own places and functions and those of others around them. They would govern themselves in those places with keen awareness of the approval of others within their circle. As a personality, the individual would be "other directed" rather than "inner directed."[21] His or her values would be relative and fluid in response to society rather than fixed and absolute. Diversity would be the complement of unity; conscious individuality and power within the accepted circle of society would be its strength. This ideal world would need many different parts, each with distinct functions, but each would mesh smoothly with the others into one harmonious whole. When things had found their places, real dissent from within was inconceivable, and criticism from without would become inconsequential.

In the organic society idealized by the Old South the key people were the men and women of the white elite. They were, one might say, the head and the heart of society. Their roles were rather precisely prescribed. The white elite was dominated by the large slaveholders. In 1860 there

were some 10,000 individuals who possessed fifty or more slaves whom
they worked on tobacco, rice, sugar, and cotton plantations from Maryland down to Florida and across into Texas and Arkansas.[22] Since the
average family in that period contained about five people, this meant that
some 50,000 men, women, and children belonged to the planter elite.
Some lesser planters belonged to the elite because of birth, education, or
manner. Planters themselves often served as leading ministers, lawyers,
merchants, politicians, professors, and physicians; at other times these
special functions were performed by their faithful allies. In the organic
society, Southern men of the higher order were supposed to play a paternalistic role. They were to behave as fathers not only to blacks, but also
to white women and children of their own sort and to the lower orders
of whites of both sexes.

The roles of upper-class men and women in the Old South were generally reinforced and given specific form by Victorian concepts of the
family. Essentially the Victorian family was the early-nineteenth-century
creature of the industrial revolution and a Romantic reaction against the
extreme rationalism of the Enlightenment. The Victorian family cast men
as the physical protectors of society, and women as its moral conservators. It was specially the function of each man to protect physically and
provide materially for his wife and children. It was he who was to venture
forth into the harsh world to succeed and "bring home the bacon." It was
the function of the wife to be submissive to her husband and to make the
home morally strong and physically comfortable. At home every evening
the husband would find physical ease and, most important, moral sustenance after a hazardous day in a world of open competition. Most of all,
women were to be the conservators of piety. Pious and pure, domestic
and submissive, they were the veritable angels of the earth, God's agents
in human form. As such, it was the wife and mother who was most
responsible for the spiritual education of the children.[23] The Victorian
world thoroughly loved the idea that "the hand that rocks the cradle rules
the world." Thus the chain of command, the flow of moral energy so to
speak, ran from God to mother, to boys and girls, to men, and through
men out into the world and back home again to women for spiritual
regeneration every evening, weekend, and holiday. The family, the
hearthstone, the heavenly sanctioned and harmonious union between
husband and wife, was the very center of earthly good.

Victorian ideas were imported into the North just as they were into
the South. The difference was that in the South the roles were intensified
to an extraordinary degree because all roles among Southern whites had
to be deeply internalized and earnestly played in order to keep Sambo in
his place. White women and white men in the South became something

that their contemporaries in the North did not. Southern men had to be gentlemen, or aspire to be, and all women were ladies. In the South in and after the 1830s Victorian prescriptions of role were woven firmly into fabrics of male and female identity already reshaping themselves to meet the black threat.

Threads of high feudalism were also woven into the culture of the late Old South. The relishing, for instance, of the idea of men as chivalrous knights and women as castellated ladies was not merely coincidental, nor was it frivolous. On the contrary it was immanent and deadly serious. The concept of the organic society is, of course, ancient, but its modern phase is late medieval in origin. It sprang from the centuries around 1200 when a rather desperate Western society, having barely survived invasions by the barbarians, then the Moslems, and at last the Vikings, drew itself together into rather rigid orders of churchmen, royalty, nobles, serfs, and, finally, townspeople. Everyone recognized by the society was fixed in place and function. The purpose of such fixedness was no less than the survival of Western civilization against external threat and internal dissolution.

Before the nineteenth century, the late medieval period was also the last great age of idealism, revolving, of course, around Christian idealism. During the Renaissance the philosophical center began to shift toward realism, a process that continued with the scientific revolution and led to the Age of the Enlightenment in which rationalism and realism were virtually enshrined. In the minds of many people in the West, the bloody chaos of the French Revolution and the subsequent rampage of the beast Napoleon became associated with an excess of realism. In a sense, when Napoleon went down at Waterloo, so too did the philosophy of the Enlightenment. After 1815 the center of thinking shifted again, this time back in the direction of idealism. By the 1830s, when Victorianism came to America, the reaction was in full swing, and America imported along with Victorianism a heavy cargo of idealism. Idealism saw truth in the idea of the thing rather than in the thing itself. Ideas of the monarchy, of the church, and of man and woman were the realities. Truth was approximated best not by natural laws, but by such ideas as love, duty, and honor, piety, purity, and motherhood. Idealism, like Victorianism, flooded the North as well as the South. In the North it helped give rise to Emerson, Thoreau, and the Transcendentalists. In the South it rendered legitimate the abstraction of ideas of slavery, gentility, and paternalism. Again there was no difference between the idealism that came into the North and that which came into the South. What differed was the use each made of it. In the South it was turned to the support of slavery, and it was woven into the cultural fabric being created out of old threads and new. The new threads were the roles of black and white, the Victorian roles of men and women, and of knights and ladies with their retainers.

Thus a process of change that had begun with a readjustment to the presence of menacing blacks and resulted first in the creation of a Sambo role for blacks and a paternalistic role for whites, now added roles drawn from the Victorian order, roles that were reinforced by overtones that smacked of the high feudal ages—all overlaid by a template of idealism in the form of its post-Napoleonic Western revival. There remained to be infused into the reconstructed Southern order one more vital element, that of Romanticism.

Romanticism went with idealism and Victorianism, like, one might say, a soft hand in a velvet glove. The Romantics sought truth through feelings rather than reason. They raised emotions, intuition, faith, and sentiment from the level of the despicable to the divine. Romanticism was primarily a mood, verbalized most succinctly in the words from Keats's "Ode on a Grecian Urn":

> "Beauty is truth, truth Beauty."—that is all
> Ye know on earth, and all ye need to know.

—probably the most quoted lines in the nineteenth-century South. When the South adopted Romanticism, it had abandoned Thomas Jefferson and the Age of Reason. In time the North would move through Romanticism and into other things, but in the South Romanticism and its allies would persist long after the cause of its being there had died.

At the height of the Romantic era in the mid-nineteenth century, Western civilization looked admiringly back to that seemingly static and secure age of high feudalism as some beau ideal. It appropriated for itself the chivalric image in which the best men were knights who donned their armor and went out to fight for noble, and indeed holy, causes. It also absorbed the courtly manners ascribed to that era. Gentlemen respected ladies of proper birth, and relations between gentlemen and ladies were governed by precise and well-understood rules. The United States at large shared in the Romantic revival of the chivalric ideal. The South, however, not only accepted the basic formula, it elaborated upon and practiced it to an extraordinary degree. Elite Southerners knew about Richard the Lion-Hearted, they knew about Eleanor of Aquitaine, and they emulated what they understood to be their styles. *Ivanhoe* (1820), one of Sir Walter Scott's knightly stories, was the most popular novel in the South before the Civil War. Southerners actually engaged in tournaments in which men on horseback "jousted" with relatively harmless lances and played other knightly games. The victor won the right to name the "Queen," often styled the "Queen of Love and Beauty," who "reigned" with her ladies-in-waiting at the evening ball that followed the tournament. The winner's prowess was thus dedicated to her honor. During the "combat" he carried her handkerchief hidden in his clothes at his bosom, and that was his real reward—to battle for her. Publicly, his victory was gladly surrendered to her triumph. It was all very Romantic, very idealistic, and very Victorian, even as it seemed very medieval. Knightly combat between gentlemen often enough passed beyond social games into games that were deadly serious. In the South the code *duello* persisted as a way of life among gentlemen unmatched in intensity elsewhere in America.

Placeness was the key word in the organic society, and thus in the social order of the Old South. Inevitably placeness included hierarchy. Some parts of the body are more vital than others. A hand is expendable, a head is not. Andrew Jackson's revolution notwithstanding, the elite in the Old South on the eve of the Civil War was not democratic in its attitudes. It believed in an aristocracy of talent and that talented people should rise. But it did not believe that all men were equal or ought to be treated equally. Some people were better than others, it declared, and a proper society, a proper ordering of persons, would recognize that fact. Southern law itself was not blind to color, frankly unequal, and seemed not vastly disturbed by the split-level justice it meted out. Black people, slave and free, got lashes and white people got fines. And above and beyond the written law was the "code," the private law by which gentlemen organized relations among themselves and with others. A gentleman owed it to his honor to respect himself and to respect others in their proper places. If anyone got out of place and offended, a gentleman had clearly prescribed methods for rectifying the situation and "satisfying" his honor.

In private law, as in public law, different punishments were meted out to different sorts. The last resort in a difference with another gentleman was the duel, which constituted a penultimate recognition of equality between gentlemen. Disagreements with men of the lesser sort were to be settled by means less honorable to the offender, by horsewhipping, beating with a stick, or even by having someone else administer the punishment in behalf of the gentleman offended. The perfect illustration of the latter is the famous Sumner-Brooks affair. When Massachusetts Senator Charles Sumner made a speech on the floor of the Congress in 1856 in which he alluded to the fact that South Carolina Senator Andrew Butler expectorated when he talked, which that elderly gentleman did, he forfeited any claim to gentility by referring to an unfortunate, unavoidable personal infirmity. By the code, the task of exacting justice from Sumner fell to Butler's proximate kinsman, the very physical Congressman Pres-

ton Brooks. After due deliberation and in a seemingly calm mood, Brooks
selected a walking cane of proper heft. He walked onto the Senate floor
where Sumner sat at his desk writing. Brooks called Sumner's name.
When Sumner turned to face him, Brooks struck him over the head.
When Sumner tried to stand, Brooks struck him again and continued to
strike him until the cane shattered and Sumner fell to the floor bleeding
profusely. It was two years before Sumner returned to the Senate cham-
ber, and all over the South gentlemen made up purses to buy Brooks new
canes, usually with highly complimentary inscriptions. These men understood precisely what Brooks had done. He had punished a man of the
lower orders for an offense against the honor of an aged kinsman who
was physically too infirm to exact justice for himself. He did not give
Sumner a gentleman's chance to defend himself, and he did not simply
shoot him. He chastised Sumner, ignominiously, calmly, without putting
his hand upon him, almost as he would whip a rebellious dog.[24]

By their acts Southerners of the upper orders frankly repudiated any
Jeffersonian inclination to treat all men equally. They went rather with
John C. Calhoun, who exalted the inequality of men, and they sought to
organize society hierarchically to accommodate their various capacities.
It was precisely fitting that the Confederacy should elect Jefferson Davis
as its president. The essential facts of his life are nearly perfectly symbolic
of the evolution of Southern culture. Davis was born of farmer stock in
Kentucky in 1808, ironically not a hundred miles from the place where
Abraham Lincoln was born a year later. Both were born in modest material circumstances, but each was vastly rich in talent. By 1861 Davis was
wealthy in Mississippi land and slaves, but, more important to the South,
he was a paragon of the gentlemanly ideal, the living representative of
the potential high elegance of Southern culture. Jefferson Davis was
named for Thomas Jefferson, but his very life had marked the travels of
the South away from Jeffersonian ideals.[25] By the time of the Civil War
the elite in the South saw itself as aristocratic, and they saw Northern
leadership as plebeian. Abe Lincoln as the "common man" in the White
House might have had great appeal in the North and West, but in the
South he was an anathema. His election struck incisively at one great
difference between Northern and Southern culture. The ruling elite in the
South was bending strongly in the direction of a hierarchic social universe, while the North was tending democratic.

The idealized organic society of the Old South featured placeness in
time as well as function. In that increasingly structured society, there was
a time for every event and a procedure for carrying it through. Courtship,
marriage, birth, death, and social relations of all kinds had their forms,
as they do in all societies. But in the South, the forms were more impor-

tant, and they were very closely prescribed. Behavior after marriage, for example, was specified in detail, especially for women. The demeanor of ladies, the behavior of gentlemen, the lower orders of whites, and blacks all came to be increasingly ritualized. Forms of address denoted station. Hats on heads or off and yielding walkways established order in personal encounters all the way up and down the social pyramid. As young people grew up in this system, they behaved almost as if they had been drilled in a military fashion in the rituals of human interaction. Behavior came to be delivered as promised in the contract implied by accepting membership in the social order, namely, by being born there.

"The principals are to be respectful in meeting and neither by look or expression irritate each other," South Carolinian John Lide Wilson instructed the would-be duelists who read his 1838 booklet on the etiquette of maintaining one's honor. "They are to be wholly passive . . . ," he continued, moving beyond a prescription for behavior to one for mood. The pistol, he directed, is to be handed to the duelist in a certain way, and the duelist grasps it "midway the barrell." As in a play, even the words of the participants are prescribed. When the first pair of shots has been fired, the second of the challenged party approaches the second of the challenger and says: "Our friends have exchanged shots, are you satisfied, or is there any cause why the combat should be continued?" One could hardly imagine more precise instructions and a stricter ritual.[26]

Duels were tied to honor, and honor very often involved women; James Marion Sims, a pioneer gynecologist, declared that he was "educated to believe that duels inspired the proprieties of society and protected the honor of women."[27] It was then, perhaps, no accident that Wilson edited the Southern edition of the romantic tale of Cupid and Psyche, and also authored the manuals for sword and artillery drills for the South Carolina militia. Psyche might well have been the genteel Southern lady. In mythology Psyche was mortal, but fairer than Venus. Though cursed by the jealous goddess and afflicted with the frailties of humankind, Psyche strove and, with the help of the gods (particularly Jupiter), triumphed.[28] *Psyche,* the Greek word for "butterfly," was also the word for "soul." The butterfly represents a height in beauty achieved out of the lowly and earthly caterpillar, a loveliness that has a brilliant moment in the sun and dies. Soul is the essential reality, the ultimate truth of God as given to man. Sweet ephemeral beauty and lasting truth was the Southern woman. All else were but aspiring shadows, and all found life through her. Put on a pedestal, enshrined like a holy object, woman was to be approached only through a set ritual. Cupid is a handsome young god, the son of Venus and Jupiter, and Psyche's lover. Ironically, he brings love with an instrument of death. He smites the intended through the heart with an arrow. Love begins with a wound, open and bleeding.

"Upon the word swords being given," John Lide Wilson instructs the South Carolina militia soldier in one of his manuals, "direct the eyes to the sword hilt, bringing the right hand with a brisk action across the body and seize the hilt, at the same time seize the scabbard with the left hand; draw the sword about four inches, and wait in that position for the next word of command."[29] Swords and pistols, love, sex, and violence, women, blood, and death, were all becoming inextricably mixed in that Southern world before the Civil War. It was a world in flux and under pressure, and rituals gave the planter elite a feeling of order, a sense that certain acts, certain words, and even certain emotions ought to and did follow one another with predictable, reassuring regularity.

Southerners had cast off from the ideals of the Revolutionary generation, and they were moving into a separate culture that was both like and increasingly unlike that of other Americans. It was as if they took the common qualities of Western civilization, the qualities that all Americans shared, and exaggerated them terrifically. Occasionally the exaggeration approached the point of caricature, constructs that might seem humorous were they not so dangerous. If upper-class women in Western civilization generally were being pedestalized, in the South the pedestal was higher and rising. If private violence was legitimate in America, it was more legitimate in the South. If American men had individual honor, Southerners saw themselves as having more of it. It was a strung-out, tension-laden society where vast energies were spent simply holding one's self together. The tension was there because the blacks were there. In a real way, the Southern white was the person black people made simply by being in the South in such numbers and in such manner as they were. That manner was recurrently rebellious—in the fields, in the kitchens, and in the cabins—and it made of Sambo's keepers a peculiar people.

The drive for a harmonious, unitary culture produced an outpouring of intellectual energy in the Old South that is no less than astounding. The proslavery argument—horrible in its purpose of enforcing perpetual bondage upon a whole race of people—was yet an impressive example of how gymnastic, how muscular, how imaginative and driven the human mind can be under pressure. Nourished in the rich soil of economic prosperity, warmed by the sun of social necessity, the black flowers of the proslavery argument thrived marvelously in the Old South. As there had been an earlier flowering of genius in New England, now there was a flowering in the South. But there the flowers turned their faces heliotropically toward slavery, and they drew life from that false, that brilliant and bogus sun.

Although it could be said that this drive began negatively for the purpose of keeping black people under control by a total and perfectly rationalized slavery, by the late 1850s Southern thought and culture were beginning to transcend that narrow goal by assuming that it was already nearing accomplishment. What had begun as a movement to keep the Negro down ended by raising the white man and Southern culture up. Slavery was the "mudsill" upon which a societal superstructure marvelous for the time was to be constructed. Slavery was not the end of Southern society, it was rather the beginning. On the very eve of conflict, Southern culture—as seen by itself—was attaining flight speed and about to soar. Southerners were fully aware of the necessity of slavery and generally convinced of its beauty. But it was not slavery itself that exhilarated them. It was the sense of moving up and out in a limitless ascent where none had been before. Southern culture was risingly self-confident and aggressive. Southerners felt that they knew who they were, and they had images of what they were becoming. They were expansive—in the West, in Latin America, and in the Caribbean—because they thought they had found a new and better order for humanity and felt that that order should spread.[30]

Practically speaking, to realize the unitary society the planter elite had to move into place three great classes of people, each more or less dissident: Negroes, nonslaveholding whites, and women—among the last, particularly plantation women.

Of these, the problem of Negroes, free as well as slave, was most critical. A more stringent system of control and a Sambo image worked for the slaves, but the quarter-million free Negroes scattered across the South posed a more delicate problem. Free Negroes were a contradiction in an organic world in which whites were free and Negroes were slaves. In the last generation of slavery, the controlling whites exerted tremendous social pressure, largely successfully, either to drive free Negroes out of the South or else reduce them practically to slavery and thereby de facto integration into the organic society.[31]

Mulattoes also constituted a threat to the organic society. In the lower South, three-quarters of the free Negroes were mulattoes, and their claims to whiteness were often deeply disturbing to the social order. On the other side, the number of slaves who were seen as mulattoes increased tremendously in the years from 1850 to 1860. While the number of blacks in slavery rose in that decade only 20 percent, the number of mulattoes in slavery rose an astounding 67 percent. Slavery was undoubtedly getting lighter—indeed, some slaves were indistinguishable from whites—and yet , as South Carolina judge William Harper indicated in 1835, "a slave cannot be a white man." Slavery and whiteness were incompatible. Whites could drive free mulattoes out of the South and devalue those who remained, but it soon became clear that they could not halt the alarming proliferation of mulattoes among slaves. In the end, they did in their imagination what they could not do in reality. In the last years of slavery, the white South generated a great mythology about people of mixed blood. One concept in the myth, an idea that took firm root and flourished in the twentieth century, was that one drop of black blood made a person all black. Thus, a slave could seem to be as white as snow and yet be essentially black. Another idea, one that faded and died early in the twentieth century, was that such hybrids could not last. Like that other ubiquitous Southern creature, the mule, mulattoes could not bear children or would do so only poorly. Mulattoes were weak, effete, delicate, and failing things who would soon wither away and die. Although clearly visible to the eye, in the mind of the South mulattoes were already seen as dead, and, hence, unthreatening.[32]

There were no Nat Turners in the 1850s, but there were other disturbing indications that elements in the institution of slavery needed correction. For instance, slaves in the cities and slaves who hired out their own time were tending to break down the system.[33] In 1859 Edward A. Pollard, a young Virginian who had just returned from travels in which he actively supported a briefly successful attempt by Southerners to gain control of Nicaragua and who was later to win eminence by explaining the Civil War as essentially a constitutional debate, most famously in a book entitled *The Lost Cause* (1866), was outraged by the sleek, well-fed, well-dressed "slave gentry" in the cities and on the large plantations who condescended to notice and make slurs about the untutored whites of the lower orders. He ardently sought the reduction of all blacks to "the uniform level of the slave." On the other side, seemingly few things afforded Pollard and other Southerners more pleasure than the image of the black man playing the Sambo role. Returning home to Virginia from wanderings that took him to the California gold fields and the Orient, Pollard grew ecstatic over the first venerable black uncle that he saw. "I love the simple and unadulterated slave," he rhapsodized, "with his geniality, his mirth, his swagger, and his nonsense. . . ."[34]

Similarly, the organic society of the Old South concerned itself with finding a place for the great mass of nonslaveholding whites. It was, perhaps, least effective in that area. When the war came, Southern leadership was groping simultaneously toward two solutions. Either nonslaveholding whites would be instituted as a squirearchy in support of the aristocratic knighthood of the South, or they would be dissolved by a universal elevation of all whites into the upper class through slaveholding. In pursuit of the latter end, some Southerners pressed for the reopening of the international slave trade so that every white family might partake of the liberating and elevating effects of the peculiar institution. As Pollard indicated, the purchase of a slave for $150 would allow a poor man to "at once step up to a respectable station in the social system of the South."[35] The alternative was to fix the white mass as a dependent and loyal class. The role finally handed to nonslaveholding whites was that of willing and permanent squires to the knightly order. Plain folk but genteel, they were to accept the values of the upper class and emulate the manners of the aristocracy in so far as their means allowed. In the organic society, nonslaveholders were to have an honorable place somewhere between the earth of Sambo and the sky of aristocracy, but certainly closer to the former.

Although the Southern elite was less than totally effective in its drive to integrate the lower orders of whites, it had already developed a capacity for defusing potential rebelliousness by preempting leadership talent as it emerged in the lower orders. In South Carolina, for instance, rather clearly there was a multi-layered "aristocracy" consisting of successive appropriations of new leadership. It began when the royal governors allied themselves with those who gained affluence in the rice-indigo culture, and later added those who rose through the cultivation of long-staple cotton in the Sea Islands, and finally the barons of the short-staple fleece. In the South at large on the eve of the Civil War, ruling elite whites were properly anxious about their capacity to control the lower order. There were men in the South like Andrew Johnson, the Tennessee senator, and Albert Gallatin Brown, the governor of Mississippi, who preached democracy and behaved rather mulishly in what was supposed to be a stable of exclusively fine horses. Still the people at the top managed well enough and, on the whole, successfully. For every Andy Johnson there were dozens of Jefferson Davises who rose into the elite from somewhere and accepted its values, and the leadership did manage to carry a constituency of about seven million nonslaveholding whites into the Confederacy and to put well over a million of those into butternut gray.

Southern women, and especially some of those plantation women who lived with their families closest to large numbers of slaves, were also restless under the rising regime of the slave-based society. The wives and mothers of slaveholders had probably long been anxious about their men in the midst of a village of subordinate if not submissive dark women. However much they might relish and want to believe in a world in which superbly loyal Negro women existed only to nourish fondly their own white children, the fact was that numbers of mulatto children were constantly appearing. Particularly during late slavery, apparently whole plantation communities fell into a morass of interracial sexuality as men of the master class spawned one child after another with their female slaves, usually mulattoes and usually maids in the manor house. Perhaps pedestalizing the white mistress of the plantation was an attempt to salve the wound that had been done, and was being daily done deeper, to the Southern lady by husbands, sons, and fathers in liaisons with slave women.

Probably in no other area was the drive for a unitary society so effective as it was in wooing white women of the elite group into the system. Blacks might well have been reluctant to see themselves as Sambos, and nonslaveholding white men might have still somehow resented the imperious airs of the gentry; but it is perfectly understandable that people who were constantly told, night and day, day in and day out, that they were the most beautiful, the purest, the most divine thing ever wrought in human clay might have been tempted to believe it. The Southern woman did sometimes internalize the image of the plantation lady, and sometimes grew blind to the fact that the darkling boys and girls with whom her children played were their own brothers and sisters and a living insult to her integrity.

The Romanticism of the late Old South might have been formed, in part, by the retreat of the female gentry from painful reality. They were being hard pressed to accept a system inimical to their most vital interests; and if they did retreat into make-believe worlds, it is understandable. It is probably no accident that students of literature have come to characterize the decade when a rash of romance broke out in Southern writing as "the feminine fifties." It was a literature by women, about women, and for women's peace of mind.

The attempt to press women into the mold was aggressive. Historian Dorothy Ann Gay, after extensive research in the diaries and letters of Southern women between 1830 and 1861, concluded that they were, indeed, a threat to the continuation of slavery, especially in their reaction against the sexual abuse of black women by white masters. The frequency with which white mobs in the South attacked, beat, and demeaned white men suspected of antislavery sentiments was a warning, she argued, to white women to stay in their place and support the peculiar institution. In addition, "Southerners always stressed the physical threat black revolt posed for white women." Women must either support the system of slavery or find themselves ravished and their children slaughtered.[36] In the 1830s Professor Thomas R. Dew of the College of William and Mary urged women to keep their place in the home. Two decades later the Carolina fire-eater William Porcher Miles wanted them to participate more fully in the life of society. But what he wanted out of that increased association was a more perfect complement to maleness in the Victorian model. By their beauty, by their queenly grace and purity, they would elevate the society of men. That women should come out in the world seemed to be his message, but in doing so they should clearly keep their place.

BLACK CULTURE IN THE OLD SOUTH

The result of the push-pull tension operating in Southern society was to suspend Negroes between two worlds.[37] Of necessity, black people generated a culture that was certainly neither purely African in America nor simply a reflection of whiteness. For convenience of description, it is useful to divide black life in the Old South into four parts.

First, a large part of black culture in the antebellum South was slave culture, and much of that was defined by what it meant to be a slave—either by conformity to the system or rebellion against it. The slave system, for instance, might forcefully promote habits of hard work, sobriety, and temperate language because the master class insisted upon this sort of behavior and had the power to enforce it. At the same time, the slave system produced other indirect cultural effects among black people. Unlike the great majority of white people, slaves in the mass simply did not have clocks or watches, or even calendars. Their sense of time must have differed from that of the whites. They lived by the sun and by the season. The South was vastly rural and agrarian, but Negroes as a people lived closer to the soil than anyone in America save, perhaps, the Indians. As a people they worked harder than white people, and they had different attitudes about their work. Slavery produced effects that white people did not want. There was always an undercurrent of rebellion among slaves, whether it took the form of a sullen manner, running away, dropping a rock among the fine teeth of the cotton gin, or outright and murderous rebellion. As slaves, black people generated attitudes about property that varied from those of whites. Northerners who came South to teach the freedmen during and after the Civil War were delighted at the temperate nature of their black protégés, but they were astounded and dismayed by their tendency to take things of small value found lying about. One Northerner might have had her curiosity satisfied by being told the old joke that from the slave's point of view no breach of morality was involved when he simply "put massa's chicken into massa's nigger." These whites had never been property themselves, of course, and the logic of property as seen by slaves and freedmen largely escaped them. Further, slaves might answer the demands of slavery but still, internally and beyond the eye of the master, evolve a life-style quite independent of it. Their religion, their entertainment, their diet, and their sense of family, justice, and self might all have dimensions well beyond the slave system as conceived by the white mind.

Second, black culture included free blacks as well as slave blacks. On the eve of the Civil War there were about half a million free blacks in America, half of whom lived in the South. As with slaves, most but not all of their culture was circumscribed by the world the whites made. To some extent, black culture resulted from black people's perception and imitation of the white way. Another part of it was made up of resentment and rebellion against the white world—much of this because white people would not accept the full humanity of black people in their world. Thus, for instance, in the years around 1800 the Negro Methodists in Philadelphia, Baltimore, and New York withdrew from white-dominated churches to establish their own institutions, the African Methodist Episcopal Church and the African Methodist Episcopal Church Zion. In the first third of the century, these churches gradually spread into the free Negro communities in the South, in the second third they were largely forced out, and again in the last third of the century they returned to become, along with the Baptists, the largest Negro denominations in America. These churches were undeniably Methodist, but they were also undeniably black and different by dint of their blackness.

It has been profitable to think of white culture in America as evolving in terms of a "frontier thesis," that is, as European culture altered by the physical and social environment of a new land. It is also useful to think of black culture in America as evolving, in part, in the same vein. Imagine, for example, that some pre-Columbian African adventurers had built a raft, some "kon tiki," and drifted with the currents across the Atlantic into the American South and established a colony there. That culture soon would not be African simply because the geography, the climate, the flora and fauna of the South were not African. In reality each locale in the South—the sea islands, the river basins, the swamps—had its own natural logic, and the Africans in America, no less than the English people in America, came to terms with a new physical universe. A third part of black culture came out of those physical conditions and did not depend upon slavery or blackness or even whiteness for its existence. On the large plantations and in the black belts where blacks were numerous and white people least often seen, black people met the land and created life-styles that had least to do with color of skin. Over the years the love of the land, the fondness for the place of their birth and breeding, marked American Negroes as it does all peoples. It was they who delved in that earth, and planted and reaped its harvests. It was they who trod its paths by day and by night. With their hands and feet they minutely mapped its topography and with their bodies measured its heat and cold. White Southerners, so specially possessive of the land themselves and so idolatrous of the legalities of ownership, could hardly contemplate, much less understand, and still less sympathize with, the feelings of Negroes about their mutually natal soil. Some whites later assumed that the hatred of slavery among blacks, which did exist, extended to the place of slavery. Quite the contrary was true. Blacks, like whites, tended to love the land upon which they were born and spent their lives.

A fourth part of black culture in the American South was African in its origins. The question here is not whether the African legacy has survived into modern times. Certainly it has, and not merely in the form of physical characteristics. Nor even is it a matter of how much of the legacy has survived. The real historical problem is how the African heritage was transmuted in the American circumstance: how it was changed by slavery, by the African's blackness in a white world, and by the novel physical setting. That problem is, at least, every bit as difficult as defining European survivals in white culture. And it is probably more difficult because the black experience was refracted through slavery and through a moral code reigning in the white world in which black quite literally often meant "bad" and therefore was to be suppressed. There is a peculiar and distressing insensitivity in the persisting argument that blacks have to "make it" in America just as the Irish, the Italians, and other more recent immigrant groups have done. Would that it were so simple. To dismiss the distinctive black experience in this facile way, one has to ignore a history profoundly shaped by white Americans' special perception of blackness in humans and their reaction to that perception. If in fact blacks have sometimes rotted at the doorstep, it is not because they take a perverse pleasure in giving their lives to offend white nostrils.

The problem of identifying African survivals is raised still one more level in difficulty by the truth that as whites invaded black life with a new intensity in the middle of the nineteenth century, they not only changed blacks; they were changed by blacks. Then and later whites would have been vastly resentful at the suggestion that blacks had educated them, so proudfully intent were they on unilaterally educating blacks. But without attempting to catalogue the entire range, it seems fairly clear that whites learned much from blacks in language, literature, and religion, in music and manners, and in cuisine and conjuring. It is probably not too much to say that a significant amount of the African heritage that survived in the slave South survived outside the black world in the white. Southern whites would have passed beyond resentment and into outrage at the idea

of themselves being Africanized, but the idea is not without an element
of reality.

A FUSION OF CULTURES AND COLORS

White people not only adopted and adapted African survivals from
Negroes, they also drew more broadly from the well of post-African
black culture to fill their own lives. For instance, Southern white religion
owed something to black religion. Southern whites did attend the sermons of black ministers, and sometimes they did so eagerly. "There was
a Negro meeting down at church and we hurried dinner to go," Ella
Thomas, the young wife of a Georgia planter, wrote in her diary in 1855.
At church she found a large crowd, overflowing the building and seated
on benches outside. "I procured a seat in church and heard an exhortation
from the Baptist minister Peter Johnson," she wrote. "A very fine looking
mulatto man, dressed very nice, with a gold watch and fob chain." Afterward Thomas was led to make a generalization about black ministers. "In
their exhortations they very often do much good," she concluded. "They
appeal to the heart more than the understanding." Johnson was impressive, but Thomas thought him "not so polished nor by no means so talented" as another black minister, Sam Drayton. In the following month,
she and several white friends went to hear Drayton. "I find it very delight-
ful to do down and hear Sam Drayton preach to the servants," she
asserted after that event. "He is a negro of extraordinary talent and cultivation and well repays one for listening to his sermon." Drayton earned
her admiration, so too did his wife. Thomas judged Mrs. Drayton to be
"one of the most ladylike persons I have ever seen."[38]

No one has yet described in detail the manner in which Southern
white children in the slave period were reared, or the effects the process
might have had upon the adult. But we do know that upon the large plantations typically the older slave women oversaw the young slave children
and that often white children shared some of the life of black children
until puberty, when a more careful separation began. Many whites later
claimed a close childhood association with some adult who was a slave.
Usually they claimed a "mammy," but now and again a white son of the
master class found his mentor in a sable hero, some black and accomplished Nimrod who tutored the boy in riding, hunting, and woods lore.
Possibly, the planter class learned its famous manners from its close association with blacks and especially, perhaps, with black mammies. Blacks,
being subject to sudden, violent, and often arbitrary punishments from
whites, developed a super-sensitivity to the thoughts and moods of others,

an interest and a capacity that they conveyed to the white children in their charge.

Ultimately, the process was probably much more intricate than one race simply teaching the other. What we have in the South are two cultures in symbiosis, each constantly taking from the other, but each filtering what it takes and absorbing it relative to its special perspectives. White culture feeds off of black and grows and changes, and black culture feeds from white and grows and changes. Finally, it is possible to speak of two cultures, one white and the other black, but it is also proper to speak of a fusion of cultures. This fusion, which occurred in the last three decades of slavery, forms the substratum that joins black and white today—it is the substantial beginning of the oneness of modern Southern life. It is why black people and white people in similar situations perform very much alike. It is why they share many of the same values. It is why they can, if need be, sometimes relate to one another with great intensity and understanding.

A fusion of colors in the South paralleled the fusion of cultures. Many contemporaries thought that the number of people of mixed blood was rapidly growing. Quantitatively, most of the mixing of black and white in the last generation of slavery probably resulted from what social scientists later called "internal miscegenation," that is, the marriage of Negroes of purely African ancestry to Negroes whose ancestry was partially European. The marriage of blacks to mulattoes was most pronounced on the frontiers of the cotton kingdom of the lower South where slaves of lighter color were being imported in unusually large numbers from the upper South.[39] Qualitatively, the most important mixing was by the planter elite itself. It seems that in almost every community in the slave South there existed at least one slave woman whose distinctly lighter-colored children testified to a falling from racial grace by one or more white men. Typically, the woman worked as a domestic in the house of a planter and was herself very light in color. Now and again, it appears that whole plantations were lost in the social void of interracial sex and a mixed progeny. The signs were that all too often for the integrity of an idealized Southern society, whole settlements were losing the color line in a welter of browns, yellows, and reds. In the last years of slavery, thoughtful whites in the South and in the nation came to fix upon race mixing as a clear and present problem. In 1850 the United States Census, for the first time, counted people in whom mixed ancestry was visible and labeled them "mulatto." By the end of the Civil War whites had invented the term "miscegenation" to cover the whole phenomenon of mixing black and white, and it was a term that carried dire implications.[40]

Like the geological fault line that exposes the layers underlying the earth's crust, the disparity between what mulattoes actually were and what whites insisted that they were revealed much about the composition of the racial world of the South. The public myth was that the mulatto population grew out of the midnight marauding of lower-class white males. The fathers of mulattoes were said to be poor whites, itinerant Irish laborers, and Yankee overseers who simply seized upon occasional targets of sexual opportunity and passed on. Doubtless some mulattoes did come from such casual connections. But significantly often these children were the sons and daughters of relatively well-to-do slave owners. However lightly or brutally the liaison might have begun, it sometimes ended with white fathers taking care about the upbringing, education, and economic security of their darker offspring. Related to the myth that socially sanitized the conception of the mulatto population was a publicly professed ignorance of the fatherhood of specific mulatto children. Yet, in every community it seems that whites privately knew well enough who fathered each light child.

Mary Boykin Chesnut, a highly observant and superbly intelligent plantation woman, recalled the "magnate who runs a hideous black harem with its consequences under the same roof with his lovely white wife, and his beautiful and accomplished daughters. . . ." One of her friends marked another awful example. "He was high and mighty," the friend averred, "but the kindest creature to his slaves—and the unfortunate results of his bad ways were not sold, had not to jump over ice blocks. They were kept in full view, and were provided for, handsomely, in his will." In the situation, the women in his family perfected their membership in the cult of true womanhood. "His wife and daughters, in their purity and innocence, are supposed never to dream of what is as plain before their eyes as the sunlight, and they play their parts of unsuspecting angels to the letter. They prefer to adore their father as the model of all earthly goodness."[41]

The increasing mulatto population was a profound indictment of the biracial Southern system. In the South's ideal world, all slaves were black and all blacks were slaves. Further, the black as slave was locked into place as the perfect complement to the white as free. A rising rage for identity among whites left increasingly little room for a blurring of the color line, and a civilization on the make took great pains to blind itself to the whiteness of its mulatto children. The white world tried to ignore mulattoes, but mulattoes repaid that attempted neglect with an intense scrutiny of the white world and, generally, with that best form of flattery—imitation. Mulattoes usually knew who were their white fathers and mothers, and they were led by their society often to value their lighter color and to relish the culture that it represented.

On the eve of the Civil War, the problem of the mulatto in Southern society took on a new and, had it continued, an unbearable strain. Some eminent white men were having not only one child by a Negro woman but several children. Further and worse, far from having the decency to apologize for their transgressions and to go and sin no more, they compounded racial outrage with social confusion. Rather than casting aside this strange fruit of the Southern racial tree, they tended to acknowledge the relationship and to honor it by bequests of property. Tensions were rising—tensions between masters and slaves, between plain folk and patricians, between free Negroes and whites, and between slaveholders and their wives, daughters, and mothers. But probably nowhere was the social order more visibly fractured and loyalty to the system more severely taxed than by the presence of increasing numbers of mulattoes in the homes of leading Southerners. It raised doubts as to the moral capacities of the men of the planter elite themselves.

By way of illustration, witness the experience of one deep South plantation family. In 1856 Samuel Townsend of Madison County, Alabama, died, freeing by his will some forty of his slaves and leaving to them an estate valued at over $200,000, including other slaves. Shortly before, another man in the family, perhaps his father, had died leaving a will in which he bequeathed an estate worth some $500,000 to his two mulatto children. The earlier will was successfully contested by white heirs, but Samuel Townsend's testament was honored and executed with great fidelity by his friend and neighbor, S. D. Cabaniss. Cabaniss sent agents north and west to search out homes and possible schools for the Townsend people. Shortly he had resettled some of the Townsends in Leavenworth, Kansas, and others in Xenia, Ohio. Over the next twenty years, in war and in peace, in slavery and in freedom, Cabaniss continued to manage the estate. He sent some of the children to Wilberforce University, a vigorously antislavery black school in Ohio. Indeed, on the eve of the war, the estate owed the university the considerable amount of $593.08 for the education of these children.[42]

It is almost certain that this peculiar Alabama story occurred because the master family, perhaps for two generations or more, became inextricably mixed with several of its own slave families. These were set aside and freed. Their separateness and freedom were underscored by the facts that other slaves labored for their prosperity and that the very capable administrator of the estate actually bought and sold other blacks for their benefit. Because they were men of large affairs and because they took care to state their intentions in wills, the Townsends left a clear trace of their mulatto progeny. More and more, available evidence suggests that the Townsends were hardly unique. Rather was it that in almost every community there were mulattoes of recognized and respectable white parentage. In certain communities, perhaps, white society was losing the landmarks afforded by a distinctly biracial human geography. If white was right, was half-white half-right? On dark seas and in high hot winds some men—and women too—were running wild, dashing their culture to pieces upon the rocks of miscegenation. When the culture crumbled and sank in 1865, it left a flotsam and jetsam of human fragments adrift upon the social sea, united only retrospectively in the great ship of slavery that had gone down.

Thus, in 1861, at one level white life was driving hard toward realizing an idealized, unitary, organic society in which there was a place for everything and everything was being put in its place. At another level, the South as such an entity could not last because things were not staying in their places. Not only was the master class, seemingly, too often losing control of itself emotionally and sexually, but Sambos, women, and even the lower orders of whites were all beginning to stir and dissent.[43] Inevitably the system, as a system, would have collapsed before it reached maturity. It fell, however, before its own weaknesses became manifest. Perhaps unfortunately for the future tranquility of the South and the nation, it fell not because it was a society based upon unreal assumptions about the basic natures of blacks and whites, men and women, and not because it was a society committed to a hierarchical ordering of people, a concomitant inequality in the administration of justice, and a crudely color-coded split-level view of humanity. It fell, finally, by the raw physical power of a North that flatly would not tolerate first disunion and then slavery. The great moral defection of the North, the great sin of the North against the South, was to destroy slavery and yet not destroy the culture that slavery had generated. The result was to doom a whole people to the fate of the Flying Dutchman, to abandon them to pursue a culture whose primal base, whose very reason for existence, had been forever lost, to ride a social ship that could never find haven or harbor.

WHITE RECONSTRUCTION, 1865–1889

For a full generation after slavery, the dominant effort of Southern whites was to restore race relations, in so far as conditions allowed, to some semblance of what they had been—or, more accurately, what controlling whites assumed they had been— in the years before the Civil War. During Reconstruction that antebellum mode of thought, which we might aptly call the Conservative mentality, was embattled. In some places and during some times it seemed as if the old order would be lost beyond recall. However, Reconstruction was not deep enough, nor did it last long enough to give firm root to dissident styles. With the recapture of political control of their states by the Southern elite came a Conservative Restoration. That restoration was political and racial, but it was also broadly social. During the 1880s the Restoration regime was solidly established, and, while it was often vigorously challenged from within by native whites, it proved to have lasting strength.

"Place" was the key word in the vocabulary of Conservatism, and place applied not only to blacks, but to all people and to all things. One Southern white perception of Radical Reconstruction was that it seemed to be precisely a concerted attempt to put things out of place. It was a horrendous effort, not simply to destroy the Conservative world but to make of the social order in the South a monstrosity. In the reduction of the planter elite and in the liberation of the slave and his elevation in civil life, it was as if the conquerors had lopped off a head and sewn on a foot in its place. Hearts had been removed and put where hands should be. The resulting creature was not unlike those Old World sixteenth-century depictions of New World people as misshapen monsters. It is ironic and revealing of the essential disjunction between Southern white and Radical Republican perceptions of blackness that the latter frequently boasted that "the bottom rail is on top." Bottom rails have no business being on top. Some rails are better than others. In Southern minds there was an appalling imagery associated with the charge that the Radical Reconstructionists were filling the legislative halls of the South with common field "hands." Hands, simply, could not be heads. No more could heads or hearts become hands. Southern ladies and gentlemen could not become laborers and servants and remain ladies and gentlemen. From the Southern point of view, Radical Reconstruction's ultimate horror was that it mocked the Southern genius for social order by distorting it. Something of the resentment of an outraged people was shown in the seemingly endless bitterness that Southerners poured like vitriol upon the heads of Radical legislatures, even after they ceased to exist. Racially mixed Republican assemblies were called "ring-streaked and striped," like some mongrel and unlovely cat. Black legislators were described as eating "goobers" (peanuts) during sessions and making a mockery of parliamentary order by their misunderstanding of terms and procedures. The democratic faith implicit in Radical Reconstruction was almost unthinkable to Southern minds; it sat crosswise over the molds of what ought to be racially and socially. In Southern eyes, Reconstruction was, in its essence, an ordinance against nature and a denial of God.

Reconstruction was the "nadir of the Southern white" just as the turn-of-the-century years were the "nadir of the Negro." For white people, life in Reconstruction became very much a physical matter; it was a struggle for survival. The disengagement, alienation, and disintegration that marked black life after Reconstruction also marked white life during Reconstruction. The mark was especially deep in the lower South, and particularly so in those states where the proportion of blacks to whites was greatest.

In South Carolina where the ratio of blacks to whites, at 58 percent, was higher than in any other state, the contrast between the tone of white life before emancipation and after was most striking. In that state, by the early 1870s, white people were clearly suffering from a rising confusion of identity. Increasingly powerless as the war drew to a close and Reconstruction progressed, relieved of command of their collective destiny by losing their grasp upon the formal and compulsory agency of the state government, in the racial minority as they were, Carolina character began to fall away from the highly advertised, cocksure, dead-game, self-propelling personality that had reduced Fort Sumter to rubble in 1861. During Reconstruction, Carolinians saw clearly the specter of a perpetual reign of blackness and a prostrate state that would never rise in the same body again. With the dark abyss before them, white society began to disintegrate very much as black society under white domination was to do a generation later. Factionalism in white politics (nearly all Democratic, as black politics after Reconstruction was nearly all Republican) rose and ran the gamut from stubborn reactionaries who refused to recognize an end of slavery to native white men who became black Republicans. Scalawags were, after all, often merely Uncle Toms of a different color, and Klansmen were nothing less than white militants, some of whom were willing to die with their guns in their hands, as they saw it, in the defense of their manhood, homes, and families. As white society disintegrated institutionally, so too did white values and character. Gray zone morality touched business and especially business that touched government. Probably, the first black legislator who was bribed in South Carolina took money raised for the purpose by leading and socially respectable Charleston businessmen who sought, and got, exclusive access to phosphate beds (fertilizer) owned by the state.

As Carolina whites lost their sense of self and ideals became blurred, the cement that had held their society together seemed to melt. They tended to fall away from one another, to turn their loyalties to local and sometimes isolated institutions— to the local church, the lodge, the family—and ofttimes to pull loyalties downward from ideals and institutions to individuals. It was, in brief, a sort of feudalization, a settling for less in order to have anything at all. This fragmentation in life that came to the South during Reconstruction probably had much to do with the generation of a modern Southern culture that remains distinctly different from that of the nation. It might have to do, for instance, with why the South eventually came to be characterized as the "Bible belt," possessing some extra-ordinary quality of spirituality, some richness in the goods of the next world to match its material poverty in this one. It might also have to do with why the South is a region where family identity remains remarkably strong. The clannishness as well as the Klannishness of Reconstruction ought to be understood in the context of this vast societal disintegration. It might relate, too, to the rise of a new model in Southern politics. It might be that Wade Hampton operated in the style of a latter-day liege lord for South Carolina whites during Reconstruction and Redemption very much as Booker T. Washington did for blacks a generation later. Both men seemed to function as overlords who gave lesser, more local nobles a modicum of common orientation and a formula for survival. Moreover, both men practiced the same sort of ever-ready accommodationist tactics. Each would try for the best for his people, and settle for what he could get. Each would be very patient and wait for opportunities. Finally, just as Washington's aides referred to him reverentially as the "Wizard," Hampton's lieutenants labeled him the "Chief."

In other states in the South were other Hamptons, and sooner or later they were all successful. And while there was never a single white leader to organize tightly all Southern whites as Booker T. Washington organized blacks, there was a beginning of "white soul." In the end, the essence of the old order, the sense of Southernness and whiteness as qualities uniquely valuable, was saved. An identity that had been sorely burned in the Civil War and very nearly drowned in the swirling currents of Black Reconstruction was regained, and a positive image of Southern self took root and life again. As Southerners looked back upon Reconstruction, they felt that they had been all but lost in a world that was all but lost, but then they were found. For a time they paused and contemplated the abyss that yawned at their feet, panting like victims snatched from the jaws of destruction. The term that they applied to regaining control of their states was as fully laden with meaning as the Christian view of the rebirth of the spirit. They called it "Redemption." It was indeed a secular salvation, a new infancy that began a higher and truer life. When they had caught their breath, they turned and moved on, "born-again" Southerners.

The Conservative mentality in the South was not totally unprogressive. Indeed, it seemed to possess a slow, strong, and subtle intelligence that allowed it to recognize and absorb, albeit reluctantly, new realities.

Conservatism did change, and it had an uncanny ability to change just enough to survive. That carefully measured flexibility was—and is—its genius. For example, within months of Appomattox, the great mass of thoughtful Southerners accepted the death of slavery, the very foundation upon which their prewar culture had been built, and they moved out to reconstitute Southern society without the benefit of the peculiar institution.

As a part of that transition, feelings about paternalism made a most amazing travel between 1865 and the 1880s. In 1865 and 1866 many whites who had been closest to large numbers of Negroes as slaves and who previously had been most paternalistic in their expressions of sentiment about black people now evinced a bitter hatred of the freedmen. Particularly was this true among whites who had owned large numbers of slaves and who as a class had been among the most earnest in pleading paternalism as a justification of slavery before the war. It was almost as if they blamed the Negro, rather than the North or themselves, for the war that had freed him and the ruin that followed. The passage of the first Reconstruction Act in March 1867 in effect established universal male suffrage among Southern Negroes. Thereafter, some Conservatives made a brief ploy in the direction of attempting to persuade the freedmen that those who had lately been large slaveholders were their best friends, tried and true, and that blacks should vote for them rather than the new-coming Yankees and defecting scalawags who were then so sweetly wooing them. In this first blush of Radical Reconstruction in 1867 and 1868, Wade Hampton in South Carolina and others who clung to the paternal ideal indicated that they had advocated giving the ballot to educated and propertied blacks in the fall of 1865, well before there was pressure from the North for them to do so. Blacks, with a unanimity that was distressing and humiliating to their late masters, rejected such overtures. After that abortive attempt, ex-slaveholders generally turned and precipitantly fled from the concept of paternalism. As Radical Reconstruction deepened and the prospect of Redemption seemed more remote, paternalism seemed to turn to pouting and petulance. For a time, "ungrateful child" was the salient tone of white attitudes about black people.

In the 1870s paternalism was revived as a device to promote the process of Redemption. A part of the rhetoric of those campaigns asserted that aliens, foreign and domestic, had misled the Negro and brought both blacks and whites to the current sad state. Now that the Negro had learned the error of his ways, he would turn again to support his old friends, his true friends, his recent masters. In South Carolina, at least, a large part of that rhetoric was uttered in calculated bad faith. In that state, in 1876, the Redeemers copied very carefully the plan that had been used in Mississippi in 1875. A part of the Mississippi Plan was to claim during the election campaign that the vast majority of Negroes were going to vote Conservative and to insist after the election that blacks, had, indeed, cast their ballots for the Democracy. "The negro was not with us, did not vote with us, and still has an idea that he did not," a Mississippian explained to a prospective Carolina Redeemer in January 1876, "but he had no one on the spot to show him how the thing was done, but he sees that it was done, hurras for the winning side, and now, it is a hard matter to find a negro *who did not vote the people's ticket*. All that is necessary is to obtain the result, no matter how, and Mister Nigger accepts it as satisfactory, and claims that he helped to work out the problem."[44]

In South Carolina, in the campaign of 1876, the Redeemers pointedly preached the paternalistic line, organized pet clubs of Negro Democrats, gave them conspicuous places in parades, barbecues, and rallies, and moved the few black speakers they had from county to county to heighten the illusion of a credit-worthy black leadership within the Democratic camp. The paternalistic gambit in the Redemption campaign was made possible and highly plausible by Hampton's acting as the gubernatorial candidate and the white spokesman. There was no blot on his escutcheon either as a master of slaves or as an aristocrat among freedmen. He was the impeccable paternalist. His campaign slogan addressed to blacks was "free men, free schools and free ballots." Hampton himself was an honorable man, beyond suspicion of the deceit that his managers assiduously practiced. Even so, Hampton's paternalism was severely limited. There were no blacks on his ticket, and what he meant by free ballots was that Negroes would be free to cast their ballots for whomever among their late masters they chose. Before the election, Hampton's campaign manager Alexander C. Haskell claimed that 7,000 blacks would vote for the Democrats. After the election, he insisted that 9,000 had done so. Democrats, counting the votes to their own advantage, dared claim a total majority of only slightly over 1000. To have claimed more would have made the fraud too blatant. Nevertheless, it was a stolen election, and the rhetoric of paternalism covered the theft.[45]

Hampton, himself, meant what he said. As governor, he even made some well-advertised appointments of blacks to lowly offices. But most of the Democratic leadership regarded the rhetoric simply as a means to the all-important end of regaining power. Shortly Hampton, as Redemption leaders so often did, moved on to join the club of genteel gentlemen then sitting in the United States Senate. At home in South Carolina in the ensuing years, blacks were progressively squeezed down in their freedom—in politics, in education, in economics, and as individuals. It is probable that Hampton and many of the better sort never really recognized that fact.

If less money were spent on black schools than white, it was because the educational needs of blacks were less than those of whites. If fewer blacks voted than whites, it was because fewer were qualified or really cared to do so. All of this was merely a part of solving the Negro problem. Life was getting right again in the Southern world and, if the cream was rising to the top, the baser elements were floating properly and evenly to the bottom. Men of Hampton's class steadily reiterated their paternalism, past and present, and it was a very convincing pose. In the end, probably not a few Redeemers fell victim to their own rhetoric. They really came to believe their own campaign verbiage about Negro loyalty and white noblesse oblige, in both slavery and freedom. As the actual experience of Redemption became more remote, the myth grew more comfortable. But in the decade of the 1880s, paternalism remained form without content, a sentiment without broadly effective action as black and white worlds drifted apart.

After the war, when whites saw the seemingly ceaseless motion among blacks, the apparent idleness and aimless wandering, the flocking to the cities, and the rise in violence and disease, they concluded that blacks were indeed destined to die away. When the census of 1870 failed to document the anticipated event, when instead it indicated that the Negro population had actually increased slightly over the decade, many whites insisted that the count was in error. The census throughout the South had, after all, been taken by ignorant blacks and their Radical carpetbag and scalawag masters who saw political advantage in swelling black numbers. In South Carolina, the charge actually produced a recount in several counties with the result that the initial figures were judged to be essentially correct. And yet, even today, there lingers about the census of 1870 an air of special distrust. Probably that census was not significantly less accurate in counting people than those of neighboring decades. What we have inherited in the suspicion surrounding the census of 1870 is probably a remnant of the disparity between what Southern whites assumed to be true about black people and what actually was true.

During the decade of the 1870s, various surveys made by states, including the school censuses, indicated what the federal census of 1880 confirmed—that blacks were here to stay. Increasingly, as Conservatism faced the new realities, the "Negro problem" shifted in meaning. It was no longer a phrase that meant rebellious blacks. The Negro problem became a very mild issue, centering on the question of how far beneath white people black people were to be. The problem was very much a matter of defining and adjusting society to the limited abilities of black people. Thus, the Conservative mentality changed from an accepting, sometimes almost a gleeful (because self-vindicating) anticipation of the disappearance of blacks in the first years of freedom, to alarm and rejection during Reconstruction, and, finally, to a calm acceptance of the black presence in the future South during the decade after Reconstruction. If the attempt to put a new bottom on the boat of race relations in the South between 1865 and 1877 could be called Black Reconstruction, the same effort in the 1880s could well be called White Reconstruction.

CHAPTER II

Black Life in the South, 1865–1915

In the hard-soft life of the last days of slavery black people identified with white ideals as they never had before. Slavery and other devices of race control not only provided the white community with instruments to promote·that education, they also gave them the means to dam up black behavior and to prevent blacks from living the very life they were taught to idealize. Emancipation and the disordered times that followed broke that barrier, and black behavior tended to flow quickly, easily, and smoothly into channels already pre-set in black minds. It should occasion no surprise that while white politicians in Washington were still trying to decide what black people ought to be, black people in the South were already becoming what they would be. Further, it should occasion no embarrassment that they aspired to be what generations of example and one generation of intensive indoctrination had taught them that everyone—white and black—ought to be. In the first flush of freedom, black people in the South wanted families; they wanted farms; they wanted schools; and they wanted full citizenship and a recognition of their equal humanity, not only in their governments, but in their churches and in their society.[1]

BLACK RECONSTRUCTION

Black people were in motion all over the South during the summer and fall of 1865. White observers looked at the seething mass of black atoms and interpreted the movement as a simple minded, child-like jubilee. Blacks were indeed jubilant at the end of slavery, but their motion was highly purposeful and calculated to give very solid substance to their freedom. Usually black travelers were simply going home, having fled during the war when Union armies drew near or having been taken away by their masters to prevent flight. Frequently, they moved to rejoin families broken by slavery. Much of this movement was only local as a husband or a wife used freeedom to join his or her mate on a neighboring plantation, or a son or a daughter who had been hired out as a slave came home as a free person. Now and again, a freedman who had been sold away to the southwest in the flush times of the 1830s crossed half a continent and half a lifetime to come again to the people and the land that had given him birth. Increasingly, the evidence seems to indicate that, once together again, fathers and mothers; aunts, uncles, and cousins; brothers, sisters, and children, all slipped familiarly and comfortably into roles already well defined in their minds. Those roles would prove to be deeply and persistently Victorian.

The typically quiet and certain way of family re-making, often in spite of the wishes of either their late owners, or of the occupation officials who urged blacks to stay where they were until the harvest was completed, was caught by R. B. Anderson on his father's plantation in piedmont North Carolina. Anderson was a Princeton graduate and a Presbyterian minister. He had married the daughter of James H. Thornwell, recently the president of South Carolina College and one of the foremost of the proslavery protagonists. "A few changes have taken place, since you left, amongst the negroes," Anderson wrote to his wife in September 1865. "Carolina & Sally with their families moved the next morning after my return. C. was greatly distressed & couldn't help weeping aloud. Father gave her a cow to begin housekeeping with. A few days before I got back Henry left; & Franky had gone to live with her husband. This morning a boy nearly grown—Strephon—whom father hired to a man in the neighborhood [at the] beginning of this year, came home & wanted to work: he is in the field. Ellen's daddy went after her & first thing father knew she was here on the place. He gave out nothing but a quart of meal for her & told Minerva that she, that is E., must leave; but I believe she is lurking about still."[2]

Black men in agriculture, like white men in agriculture, visualized an ideal in which each man worked his own farm. The ideal had been given substance in the nation at large in the various land laws before the war. During the war, the concept was further promoted by the Homestead Act that allowed heads of families to claim 160 acres of public lands essentially by using them. The same spirit showed itself briefly during the war in sporadic attempts to divide up the plantations of the conquered South into forty-acre plots for the settlement of the freedmen. Ultimately, the sanctity of private property—even the property of rebels—overruled such a division of the land.

However, even as Congress and the national executive faltered and failed in programs of land redistribution, individual blacks in the South were acquiring farms for themselves precisely as the white ideal had long and rather ostentatiously espoused as a proper American goal. Further, they were doing it without violating current concepts of the rights of property. In some cases they bought land with savings put together during the war, but in the mass they did it by renting farms for a share of the anticipated crop. Sometimes the farms were carved out of the very plantations upon which they had labored as slaves, almost always out of plantations within a few miles of the home place. In securing farms, either by purchase or by renting as tenants, blacks moved against the explicit desires of white landowners. Whites wanted neither to sell their lands nor even to break them up into individual farms for renting. The plantation system had not arrived at its relatively high state of efficiency by accident, and planters were not eager to sacrifice that efficiency by dividing their land into so many small parcels and, in a large measure, losing control over its management. The great majority of planters would have much preferred to keep their estates intact, to work the available labor day by day as they saw fit, and thus to maintain the closest control. But the freedmen themselves simply would not have it that way. They much preferred to rent their forty acres for a share of the crop, to borrow—as it were—their mules, and to live upon their own small farms, tenanted if necessary rather than owned, and to do so even if it was less economic than the plantation system. The Negroes were, as one planter phrased it, "rent crazy."

Thus, the breakup of the plantation system in the South was caused in a major way, not by whites, but by black people refusing to work in gangs under white supervision as they had in slavery. Shortly the slave quarters were well nigh deserted as ex-slave families moved onto the lands they either bought or rented. Sometimes new tenants agreed to build a cabin on their plot of ground in lieu of the first year's rent. Occasionally the cabins of recent slaves were hitched to teams of animals and pulled away from the plantation village to the new farm. One could hardly imagine a more graphic declaration of independence by the freedman than his literally dragging his home away from the home of the late master.

Quite clearly, the freedman wanted to work his own farm under his own supervision, and he also wanted his family on that farm. Once made, the division of the plantation into family farms tended to perpetuate itself. The family needed a farm; and, hardly less, the farm needed a family—

not a man alone, nor a woman with children, but a family in which each played his role. The black family patterned itself on the Victorian model. The father ruled in worldly matters, the mother in things spiritual. Fathers were the breadwinners, mothers were the conservators of morality. Men generally went into the broad world, women stayed home. Negro men ran the farm. They did the heavy, muscular labor, and they removed their women from the fields whenever they could. Ideally, women did the housekeeping, the cooking, washing, and sewing, and very often they managed a garden for vegetables and flowers. As with the whites, it was the women, primarily, who reared the chilren. Much of the decline in agricultural productivity that came to the South immediately after emancipation resulted, first, because, black people simply refused to work in the fields as they had in slavery and, secondly, because the men strove to keep their women at home with the children and out of the fields. Much of the return to productivity had to do with the lavish use of commercial fertilizers beginning in the late 1860s.

The family on the farm was the massively usual pattern of black life in postwar America, a pattern that lasted well into the twentieth century. Until World War I, when the need for labor brought a flood of blacks into the North and West, roughly 90 percent of the black population lived in the South, and the vast majority of those lived in rural settings as did a large proportion of those who lived in the North and West. The evolution of the black yeomanry was not, then, simply a process in which whites in freedom developed a mastery of the land and credit as tools of social control to replace a mastery of people exercised in slavery. Black people themselves created the black yeomanry. Outside of racial considerations, there was nothing at all revolutionary in the move. The family farm was, after all, the realization of an ideal that was as respectable as Thomas Jefferson and greatly valued, at least rhetorically, by this nation of farmers, North and South, black and white.

Blacks also used their freedom to refine their Christianity. In none of the white churches were they accepted as fully equal members, and from each the withdrawal began with emancipation and proceeded rapidly. Most freedmen went into denominations that were totally black. Still the black church strived to be what the white church ought, ideally, to have been. In structural terms, the congruity was high. Just as there had been white churches named Trinity and St. Mark's, Mt. Zion, and St. John's, so too would black churches have the same names, and in them congregations ostensibly would practice the same ritual and profess the same theology. Precisely as there were bishops, presiding elders, ministers, and probationers in the white church, so too would there be blacks with the same titles in its sable sister. And yet the black church was not white . . .

nor was its God. The division between the white church and the black, between white Christianity and black, that existed in slavery persisted in freedom. Impressionistic accounts then and later asserted that the black church was more spiritual and less formal, more emotional and spontaneous and less philosophical and structured than its white counterpart.

In three vital areas of their lives, then—in their families, on the farms, and in their churches—blacks were moving physically away from whites. Ironically, even as they moved away in the physical sense, they gained the freedom they needed to be more like whites. These things they did almost coincidentally with freedom, beginning even in the war years when their freedom was uncertain. In a large measure, this exodus to whiteness was a playing out of an impetus that had been pressed upon them in the last years of slavery. The freedman was the black man that the slave South wittingly and unwittingly had made, and in freedom he seemed to be getting whiter every year. But even as blacks were first moving to realize this special vision of the promise of American life as taught by Southerners, a relief team of Northern teachers was moving southward to expand black expectations and to elaborate details in a multitude of ways.

Black Southerners did not wait for the arrival of Northern teachers to commence their efforts in education and politics, but those teachers obviously added important new dimensions to black efforts in these and other areas. Through the army of occupation which penetrated every community in the South, through the Freedmen's Bureau which was nearly as pervasive, and through the host of educational, religious, and political missionaries who flooded in after the war, the instruction of black people went on. It was an instruction marked by high intensity and sharp focus. Northern white ministers preached to Southern Negro ministers and congregations. Northern educators taught Negro teachers and students, and they taught behavior and values as well as academics from the homely homilies of Guffey's readers, Webster's *Blueback Speller,* and Morse's *Geography.* Carpetbaggers instructed Negro politicians and voters; Northern lawyers indirectly taught Negro lawyers, jurymen, and witnesses. Northern businessmen sometimes established connections with Negro merchants. And the great mass of blacks, being farmers of one sort or another, immediately entered the same hard school of colonial economics in which their white neighbors were already establishing records for perfect attendance and poor grades. Thus the Northern message of whiteness was carried to the Southern Negro in massive, pointed, "professional," person-to-person encounters that rivaled in intensity the black-white bonds of late slavery and has not yet been matched—even in the Second Reconstruction. Finally, there were in the new wave of tutors a highly significant few who taught that Negroes were, after all, only white men with black skins. These whites held up a very special mirror in which the Negro might see himself, a revolutionary mirror that tended to filter out black as a meaningful part of his self-image.

If Negroes in the South during Reconstruction were not in fact white people with black skins, the thrust of the times—at least briefly and upon many levels—was to make them so. This is not to say that Northern whites were not conscious of the darkness of Negroes. Only a few of the missionaries were nearly aracial in their thought and behavior. Most Northerners were, in fact, racists who equated dark skin with inferior capacity. But the racism of Northerners in the South during Reconstruction usually wore the benevolent clothes of paternalism. It was seldom spoken and almost never—if we can exclude the soldiery of the occupation forces—violent. They dwelt upon, and they were obsessed with the current lacks of the Negro. Indeed, that was at the heart and soul of their profession. But they seldom ventured to predict any natural limits to his elevation. In the cultural sense, for black people Northern Reconstruction in the South was an invitation to whiteness—even though Northerners seldom forgot the color of the freedman's skin.

In Reconstruction, Negroes, too, were sensitive to their blackness. There was a positive pride in blackness, a pride that sprang in part from having survived great tribulations together. Further, there was a distinct and impressive racial solidarity. At the very least, black people were joined together in their opposition to white prejudice and the unwillingness of whites to afford them full citizenship. A black legislator in Reconstruction South Carolina, chided by a white member about black members all voting together on issues, answered that blacks voted together because whites voted together to deny them full citizenship. He predicted that when blacks were treated as citizens equally with whites, they would divide their votes as did whites. Often it seemed that the force of the bond between blacks was equal and opposite to the force that oppressed them and excluded them from the culture espoused by whites. Indeed, in the Reconstruction South there was very little that could be called Black Nationalism, if one means to suggest by that term an exclusive black culture, fully self-conscious, and determined to carve for itself a permanent and separate place in the cultural federation in America. On the contrary, black leaders in the South saw themselves as pioneers in a progressive age in which color in people would rapidly lose significance. Further, there was very little concern among Southern blacks to recover their African heritage. Such interest as existed was designed, it seems, not to separate themselves from their white neighbors. Rather was it directed toward building an admirable trans-Atlantic past, a laudable antiquity much as white Americans claimed.

It is not too much to say that blacks in the South during Reconstruction were becoming the most American of Americans. In those areas, like South Carolina, where Negroes were in the majority and the promise of true democracy did hold up a reasonable prospect of effective black power, that power was turned—not to black exclusiveness or the cultivation of a black mystique—but toward pressing the whole society up to its own best ideals. Black power worked for public education for all children, full civic equality for all peoples, and the humane treatment of the insane, the sick, and the criminal. The system of public schools in existence in South Carolina today, for example, was begun by a predominantly black legislature. Before the war, public school systems were nearly universal north of slavery. In the South, only North Carolina had made real progress on that front. After the war, black legislators in every state participated in making the American ideal of public education a reality. So, too, of American ideals in almost every area of life. It is a true, and intriguing, and a revealing paradox that if every Southern white person had deserted the South after the war, if the whites had left the task of rebuilding on that land entirely and exclusively to Negroes, that a perfectly Black Reconstruction would have been, in cultural terms, very white.

DISENGAGEMENT AND ALIENATION

In Reconstruction black people came to be relatively deeply engaged in the mainstream of American culture. That engagement, in itself, lent a structure to black life that was marked initially by very great disparities. Some blacks, for instance, had just been freed from the darkest and most brutal slavery on the southwestern frontier. Others had been slaveholders and planters themselves, often possessed of large estates. In New Orleans and Charleston and in parts of Louisiana the mulatto elite approached the white elite in culture and wealth. When emancipation came, however, the mulatto elite joined missionaries from the North—white, mulatto, and black—in moving into the hinterland to raise up the freedman in the scale of Western civilization as they understood it. Close engagement in the economy as free individuals, in national patterns of education, family, and society, and in politics and civic affairs—along with a lingering engagement in white Christianity and with white denominational orders—plugged black people into a ready-made cultural system and gave them a valuable degree of unity. Pre-schooled even in slavery, black people were prepared to flow with striking rapidity into the molds ready-made by the white world. Emancipation broke the dam, Northern tutors replaced Southern, and a gold team trotted onto the field to work in tandem, push-pull, with the blue. It was during Reconstruction, this complex time of national transition, that modern black America had its signal beginning. For a time the prefabricated structure of white culture afforded black people a framework within which they might shape their lives in a meaningful and satisfying way. The end of Reconstruction, however, brought a rising disengagement and alienation of black people from the white world, and with that phenomenon a loosening of the threads in the fabric of black life. When the weave was made tight again, the cloth would be unique, and the uniqueness would be distinctly black. But that end, the crystallization of modern black culture in America, was not achieved without much searching and a great struggle.

The disengagement of black people from the white way began, paradoxically, even during Reconstruction when black life was rushing into the white mainstream with unprecedented mass and strength. The very separation of the races in the physical sense, for example on the land and in the churches, reduced interracial contacts and inevitably made it impossible for blacks to maintain a high level of awareness of the ever-changing white world. Moreover, while black people were moving more deeply into the white world in some areas such as politics and family and civil life, they were moving out in others such as religion.

Even Northern educational efforts, which did so much of the labor in holding up white models for emulation by blacks, did not follow the smoothly progressive path that a reading of the general record would imply. In 1868 the Freedmen's Bureau had hardly completed the organization of a widespread and increasingly effective system of schools in the population centers of the South when it began drastically to curtail its efforts in that area. Officials explained their withdrawal on the grounds that state governments, installed in nearly all the South in that year by Congressional action, were traditionally and constitutionally responsible for public education. Also, Northern benevolent associations, anticipating the resumption of educational activities by the reconstructed state governments, having sent hundreds of Yankee teachers into the South during and immediately after the war, began to redeploy their forces by withdrawing from elementary education and moving into trade and normal schools, and into secondary and college level education. Lamentably, both the federal government and the associations acted prematurely. It was two years and more before the Reconstruction state governments got their educational programs under way, and even then those programs were modest enough in the face of the gigantic task to be done. Taken all together, the beginning of public education by the Bureau and the benevolent associations, the stopping after 1868, and the beginning again by the Reconstruction state governments was a crippling blow to the quick integration of blacks into the main current of American life through education.

If a firm plan for educational reconstruction had been implemented at the war's end (including, for example, integrated public schools), a great deal of suffering might have been prevented. Given even that failure, if the reconstructed state governments had continued in power for a generation, previous interruptions might have been rendered insignificant. But with Redemption came not only another stoppage of the scholastic heart, but the beginning of an erosion. It was not so much an absolute decline as it was a relative one. Generally speaking, the statistics of enrollment, attendance, length of school year, and adult literacy recovered and progressed nicely. This in spite of the fact that after Redemption the per capita amount spent on black school children declined steadily compared with that spent on white children. Rather was it most essentially an erosion of vision, a loss of clarity among young black people in perceiving the goals of white American life and how those goals were to be achieved. Indicative of the broad trend was the fact that white teachers were disappearing from Negro schools. The visible example of whiteness was evaporating, as well as the substance of what they taught. Increasingly, Negro students were taught by Negro teachers, and later by Negro teachers who had been taught by Negro teachers. The number of Northern whites working closely and helpfully with blacks dropped drastically with the end of Reconstruction. Further, by the turn of the century, Southern whites who had sometimes taken jobs teaching in black schools in the hard times of Reconstruction had almost disappeared. Individual white models became less visible as Negro schools became thoroughly black, a consummation not much resisted by black teachers and administrators. With all of this came a rising loss of capacity among black people to perceive clearly the white ideals and an evaporation at the mass level of the resources necessary to pursue those ideals.

What began as day by day disengagement ended as lasting alienation. As the black world moved away from the white world and solidified, disengagement became institutionalized. Schools and churches, for instance, became all black as black people filled the places that had once been filled by whites. The growing alienation of the black world from the white that was evident in education proceeded also at various rates and in various forms in religion, civic affairs, and politics, on the farms, in commerce, industry, the professions, transportation, libraries, music, drama, the opera, the arts, restaurants, bars, ice cream parlors, and even in the rites of death. It seems that even the language of the whites was increasingly foreign to blacks as they lost access to white culture.

THE FEUDALIZATION OF BLACK LIFE

It is indeed an irony that focus upon the white world of Reconstruction and early post-Reconstruction times gave the black experience a basic centrality. The pursuit of white cultural forms gave black life what some social scientists call "integrity." A society with total integrity has fully developed economic, political, religious, familial, and other systems, all rationally inter-related and supportive of individual personalities. In Reconstruction and for some years afterward, a firm focus upon white ideals lent integration, in this sense, to black life. It might well be that whiteness afforded a highly convenient point of communion among black people during this critical time of transition. Perhaps a rather clear focus on white values and the use of white language provided the necessary bridges upon which blacks of very disparate backgrounds might quickly cross to relate to each other, to establish, for instance, the meaning of blackness itself, to articulate goals, and to define programs of action. However, with black people increasingly separated both physically and mentally from whites, the aims and energies of the Negro community lost a measure of integration, lost clarity, and became diffused.

Possibly, in this time of rising frustration and disorientation, individual Negroes sought islands of certainty in local and highly tangible institutions such as churches, schools, and businesses. It may be that even as the total picture disintegrated, parts of the picture gained autonomous definition and strength, and that these, to some extent, commanded attention and obscured the widening loss of unity in the total round of black life. For the great mass of black people, probably the local church—the Mount Zions, the Bethels, and Ebenezers—began to support a life that included satisfying styles of politics, social structure, and entertainment as well as religion. Black educational institutions may have performed the same functions for the more fortunate and ambitious. Atlanta, Fisk, and Straight Universities, Hampton and Tuskegee Institutes, Penn School, and Mt. Holly perhaps became not only the source of employment and education for administrators, faculty, students, and alumni, but also a satisfying source of politics, religion, economics, social structure, and entertainment as well. It could be that as the messages of denial from the whites continued to crash in upon the black world, loyalties and energies that had once reached up toward nation and state were pulled down to local, more palpable and responsive institutions. It seems that many black people of talent increasingly found their lives rather completely absorbed—not with national or state politics and not with large and national concerns, but rather with local activities, as they became leading ministers, educators, or businessmen. Conversely, those who continued to concern themselves with national matters in the mid-nineteenth-century style, as did Frederick Douglass, lost relevance, audience, and influence.

In sum, energies that were encountering rejection in the broad white world were now being vested in local and very tangible enclaves. The turndown was less than obvious. In fact, it was masked by some signal successes by individuals and by an "up from slavery" rhetoric that insisted to the world that Negroes were getting better and better every day in every way. It was true that Negro churches increased in numbers, church property rose in value, and the roll of members swelled during these decades, while black education at it best was indeed impressively progressive. But it was also a fact that as the 1890s gave way to the twentieth century, the quality of life for blacks who were not privileged to be members of these enclaves degenerated to its modern low. There were great numbers of black people who fell away from farms and families and who by-passed entirely the churches and academic institutions to live on the nether side of life, usually in the cities and towns of the South.

It is not too much to say that a species of feudalization occurred in black life in these turn-of-the-century decades. The centrifugal forces in black life were losing power as the minds and motives of black people tended to fall away from the single center that a common focus upon the white ideals had previously afforded and to transfer their loyalties to more proximate and palpable institutions. The faithful pursuit of abstract ideas of democracy, freedom, and equality had proved less than fully rewarding. Tuskegee Institute, Mount Bethel AME Church, Atlanta University, and North Carolina Mutual Insurance Company, or other such concrete and serviceable institutions offered much more satisfying engagements. These enclaves became the storehouses in which black people deposited their loyalty. They drew out, in return, some measure of security and satisfaction in a life that was hazardous at best.

Out of this fragmentation, this feudalization of black life emerged what amounted to a new black "nobility." The new noble was, perhaps, a minister or a bishop, the principal of a school, the president of an insurance company, or a political boss. Like the feudal lord, he offered his followers protection and maintenance, and he demanded loyalty and labor in return. He was invariably the self-conscious strong man who brooked no opposition within his domain. He was capable of using his people and his institution as a warrior would his sword to cope with an extravagantly hostile environment. A part of his method was to impose what might seem to whites to be a harsh and arbitrary discipline upon his followers, not entirely for the inflation of his own ego as some might judge, but for the salvation of the group. He was a leader like Toussaint

L'Ouverture who, in the black revolution in Santo Domingo about 1800, was alleged to have marched some of his men over a cliff to their death as an exhibit to the French general Le Clerc of the determination of the rebels to fight to the bitter end. The black feudatory in the South was hardly less determined, and he was willing to sacrifice some to save the remainder. Ralph Ellison caught the awful side of that reality perfectly in his novel, *Invisible Man.* In that story he depicted a tyrannical college president, Bledsoe, who expelled the student who became Invisible Man for a careless mistake involving a white benefactor. The expulsion consigned Invisible Man to the living death of attempting to survive alone in the white-dominated world outside the enclave, a world that seemed unable to recognize his essential humanity and was bent on his destruction.[3]

Whether avowed or not, the black feudatory was steadily at war with everyone outside the enclave. There were powerful whites sitting on his borders, often quiescent but always potentially hateful and terrifically destructive. And there were always the other black barons all around eager to grab a larger share of the limited resources available for survival. Vitually never did the black baron openly defy the local whites, but there were ways to carry on the combat covertly. In dealing with the outside world, he exhibited a Machiavellian flexibility. In so desperate a struggle, strong enemies were to be appeased and weak ones brought to their knees or destroyed. Shrewd and often secret diplomacy would be linked with the select and sometimes brutal use of power. The black feudatory might use local whites against local blacks he considered inimical to the welfare of his people. He might try to turn the local whites most favorable to blacks against those whites least favorable; and he might, while avowing all love and obedience to the Southern white neighbor, secretly and diligently woo some super-powerful Northern white force to crush him. Whites were often appeased by the syrupy accommodationism of the black feudatory, but they were appalled by what they thought was their almost mystical power over their vassals. They soon concluded that a deeply personal, almost a slavish vassalage to a black tyrant—such as Booker T. Washington, Marcus Garvey, Daddy Grace, or Father Divine—was a natural and unfortunate portion of the life of the average Negro. In some degree white perceptions of the case were true; and in a large measure they were true because a relentless hostility on the part of whites to black equality made them so.

Black life was feudalized and, inevitably, there was constant warfare between the feudatories. Independent and all-black African Methodists warred against the independent and all-black Zion Methodists. Both coldly scorned the Colored Methodists as the fawning constituency of the

child church organized by the white Southern Methodists. Blacks who
remained in the white-controlled Episcopal Church often assumed un-
Christian airs of superiority and were repaid with disdain. "Among the
people of my race, we who belong to The Church [the Episcopal Church]
are regarded almost heretics and have to suffer something of a spiritual
isolation at times," complained a black who had been born into the
church as a slave.[4] William H. Councill in his state school at Normal
struggled against Washington at Tuskegee for educational leadership in
Alabama, and Washington and Tuskegee Institute, themselves, steadily
resisted the ever-threatening encroachment of the denominational impe-
rialists, such as those, for instance, who sortied out from that Congre-
gational fortress, Atlanta University.

It may be that such rivalries were only the common lot in American
life. After all, whites often opted to tie their lives closely to a profession
or to a single institution, and bitter rivalries were not unknown in the
white world. Even so, there seemed to be a quality of ferocity and quiet
desperation among black warriors that was not usual among their white
contemporaries. It was as if life were a card game in which the white man
could make error after error and yet play again. But a black man who
overplayed his hand lost his life at the table, instantly, violently, with
table upturning, cards and chips scattering, and a body crashing to the
floor. Thus black leaders were compelled to watch the game too closely,
study their cards too carefully, and spend tremendous energies calculating
minor and sometimes imaginary chances. A trivial error in play might
become a devastating blow to a black leader. Booker T. Washington was
probably the ultimate master in this intense, back-to-the-wall, super-cau-
tious style of play. It was fully appropriate that his people should call him
the "Wizard of Tuskegee." He rarely lost a hand, seeming almost to put
mathematical odds in suspension, and he often finessed hands that he
should by great odds have lost.

In this view of black leadership at the turn of the century, Booker T.
Washington becomes the most effective feudal lord of them all. Because
he managed his own domain so superbly, he came in time to possess an
hegemony over those who were less effective. Eventually, he evolved into
a sort of overlord, a feudal monarch. Like the Capetians in tenth-century
France, he began with a self-supporting, superbly administered, and
totally disciplined home base. Washington's Paris was Tuskegee. This
tight bastion gave him the resources and the strength to expand his influence, to prepare elaborate outworks, to undermine the power of his
immediate enemies, to win allies abroad, and to wait and choose his time.
Also, like the Capetians, Washington wisely settled for a manageable
kingdom rather than spending himself futilely in search of an improbable

empire. He pulled back from the more ambitious and exposed frontiers of earlier efforts. He retreated from an overt and exciting claim to perfect equality, and, whatever his goals were in his own mind, he seemed to white people to settle for substantially less. Thus leadership in the white world, North and South, felt safe with Washington, and they applauded the expansion and consolidation of his power in the black world. Even so, the sage of Tuskegee shrewdly pressed for possession of a realizable and very defensible territory. He claimed for his people the family farm and areas of skilled labor. His "divine right" to rule came through his discovery of the almost providentially available "Tuskegee idea," the idea that black people by "industrial education" would achieve both productivity and moral character in learning to work with their hands and their heads on the farms and in the trades. He espoused for Negroes the great virtues—simplicity, practicality, patience, and industry. Tuskegee Institute was the model for the plan, and by 1915, when he died, the South was full of Tuskegees, each run by a carefully selected Tuskegee disciple who spread the gospel with the same jealous thoroughness exemplified by his master. If the black South in the early twentieth century was a late medieval France, Booker T. Washington was its king.

NOBODY'S NEGRO

Separation and alienation from the white world loosened the threads of black life for a generation or more. For each individual black person, taken all together and totaled up, there was a measure of disorientation, an anarchy, a chaos and loneliness compared both with what their white contemporaries then knew and with what black individuals had known before and would know subsequently. The poor and the young, as usual, suffered the most.

As the black community lost integration with the white world, individual blacks tended to fall away, not only from the sun-center afforded by white ideals, but from all centers. Some black individuals seem to have shot like meteors through the gravitational fields of the lesser satellites of church and school and spun off into space, losing the power to relate to an accepted human universe. Their world became their person and their person became very much physical. Black men peculiarly suffered this fate. Out of place and out of law, they were sometimes lynched, they were sometimes quietly murdered, and they were sometimes slaughtered in murderous riots. More often they wore the stripes and chains of convict labor. In most Southern states convict labor was leased out to private entrepreneurs who used it hard and ate up black lives like some monstrous ogre. In Texas, for example, about one-quarter of the population of the state was black but more than half of the convicts were Negroes. In the United States, the normal annual mortality rate for prisoners was about 25 per 1000. Yet in the Lone Star State it was 49 for those who were leased out on the plantations, 54 for those in the iron works, 74 in railroad construction, and 250 for those so unfortunate as to be rented out to the isolated timber camps in the swamps of eastern Texas.[5]

Awful as were the quick deaths in lynchings, murders, and riots and the slower deaths of the convict lease system, these probably accounted for only a few of the vast number of victims. The great truth is that most blacks died by black hands. Walled away from the dominant white society, denied the order afforded by living in that relatively stable universe, and missing the protection of a black enclave, some black people were left to isolation, to self-denigration, and ultimately to self-hatred. At its worst, black life was cheapened in the estimation of blacks themselves, and too often individual Negroes destroyed one another or themselves in a churning, nearly formless black rage. Such, seemingly, is the lot of oppressed peoples everywhere, of colonialized and powerless peoples, of, as Franz Fanon has called them, "the wretched of the earth."[6]

Here and there individual Negroes fell entirely out of all society, white or black, and took to a roaming, reckless, and often enough violent existence. It was these that the whites most feared—the strange "nigra," as whites of the more fortunate class would have called him. As in the time of slavery, they might say, it was not my Negroes that I fear nearly so much as it is yours, and not yours nearly so much as nobody's. The "nigger loose"—without place, without the restraining, taming, legitimizing white-man link to the white man's world—was the worst of all social crises in Southern communities. The strange black man, the "nigger in the woods," only glimpsed and seldom totally seen, like Edgar Allan Poe's "Raven" or William Faulkner's Joe Christmas, menaced whites in awful ways that only a mind that did not know him could create. It was especially bad in the rural communities where whites were few and policemen fewer.

The black menace, the "nigger loose," was born in the country and moved to the city. The black family might well have been at home on the land, but the deepening agricultural depression of the late 1880s and on through the 1890s drove large numbers off the land. A tenant farm on moderately productive soil might have supported a black family in relative comfort when cotton was selling at twelve cents a pound; but it could not be worked at all at seven, six, and five because landlords and creditors would not invest in advances for food and supplies. The result was that less productive farmers on less productive soils were squeezed off the land.

By the Victorian model the young men would leave first, looking for work. The search might prove endless and lead them to a perpetually marginal existence, hovering on the fringes of organized life. Ultimately, they might come to New Orleans, Memphis, or Atlanta, or one of the lesser cities. Loosened males tended to congregate in the cities, and Negro families in the urban situation tended to lose the forms of family that farm life had supported. Ironically, it would be the women—rather than the men—who succeeded best in finding work in the cities—typically as domestics in the kitchens of the whites. Urban middle-class white women had to have Negro maids even as they actually needed them less and in spite of depressions. Negro men and their labor, in contrast, were tangential to and increasingly expendable in the commercial and risingly industrial society. Trapped in the city, young black men might sometimes take to a street-corner, pool-hall hustling, and petty criminal way of life. Of necessity, they generated a set of values to justify their lives, values that directly countered those of the Victorians. If the black male could find no decent job, it was because he was too smart to work. If he seemed to travel from one woman to another, sleeping in the bed of the white folks' maid, and eating the "take-homes" from the white folks' table, and if his children did not all live under the same roof, it was simply because he was too much man for one woman to handle. The street-corner, counter-value, male-worshiping society that became so very evident in black life in the nation later actually emerged in the urban South in the turn-of-the-century decades. Along with it, and complementary to it, was spawned the "black matriarchy," also later evident and usually imputed to slavery. In reality, both were new, and they were the unfortunate children of the marriage of the industrial revolution to white racism. Together they constituted a model diametrically opposed to the Victorian order.

Inevitably, social denigration at the hands of the dominant whites in the post-Reconstruction decades laid its special tax upon each black personality, including those highly placed as well as low. To some extent the black reaction to alienation was an aggressive one. The black psyche became suspicious, not only of whites, but of other blacks. Negro leaders were inordinately jealous of other leaders in the community, and too often they would, in effect, rather see a black project fail than a black man succeed. James A. Whitted, a school principal who was soon to be highly successful as president of North Carolina College, tried very hard in 1890 to get the black portion of federal land grant funds for his school in Durham. He experienced extreme difficulty organizing the local black leadership into a united front. "I am afraid that petty jealousies among our big men will cause them to fall out by the way," he confessed to a fellow principal. "Some men want to be sure that they are carrying all the honors, especially in the estimation of 'God's flaming chariots.'"[7] Below the top ranks of leadership, blacks with some degree of authority sometimes used that authority in picayune ways, attempting to grab back some of the self-esteem taken away in the broader social world. Blacks bent on getting things done often saw the elaborate routines invented and presided over by black petticrats as pure obstructionism. An agent trying to get exhibits from the Negro fair in Washington in 1886 to include in the North Carolina fair later in that year vented his irritation in a letter to a friend. "There is so much 'pomposity' [,] Sham dignity and red tape about everything done here of a business character, it is trying to the Soul of a man who means business to deal with these people."[8]

If some Negroes reacted to their alienation more or less aggressively, others responded passively. A black woman in Wilmington secured pledges of articles for exhibits at the fair, but placed small faith in the promises. "You know that we Wilmingtonians have but little, if any, energy, enthusiasm, race-pride, or any of those grand qualities which go so far toward the making of a people," she asserted.[9] Apathy at the mass level was distressingly apparent at voting time. George Washington Murray, the last black member of Congress from South Carolina, complained after the election of 1898 that, while many whites in Charleston voted for him, "many Negroes, who were qualified[,] abstained from voting."[10] Black leaders were appalled by the failure of Georgia Negroes to react against a disfranchising move there in 1899. Booker T. Washington, as usual playing the black man's hand as best he could, found the situation difficult and exasperating. "It is a question how far I can go and how far I ought to go in fighting these measures in other states when colored people themselves sit down and will do nothing to help themselves," he complained. "They will not even answer my letters." Shortly, he journeyed to Atlanta where he found the conservative Democratic organ in the state, *The Constitution,* the most effective force for the benefit of blacks. "If we do not win," he asserted, "we have certainly shown them that we were not cowards sleeping over our rights."[11]

The process of disintegration in black life was, as I have said, less than obvious. It never became total chaos, complete anarchy, or absolute disorientation. It was a relative matter, but it was nonetheless real. Also it was a process that has been awkward for historians to treat because it was a phenomenon that does not relate directly to statistics or the palpable things of this world, or even with thoughts that are coolly rational and logically explicable. Rather was it a matter of individual psychologies, of emotions and moods, of vague sentiments and feelings, that scholars in the past have usually preferred not to discuss.

The masses of black men who were thus cast out probably had little comprehension of what was happening to them; but the truly tragic people were those more thoughtful blacks who sensed the meaning and depth of their denial. If the ideals of the total culture were white and the most talented Negroes were denied access to the ultimate satisfactions in the pursuit of those ideals, then there must have been a certain vacuity in the lives of gifted Negroes, and that emptiness must have existed in the life of the mind, the most vital and, potentially, the most satisfying portion of their being. The missing portion—the part denied—was sometimes lesser, sometimes greater. In Reconstruction it was less than it became after the turn of the century. But until the times of our own lives very few Negroes in America have had a chance to be totally whole, totally complete in the way that some few favored white people have been, and every white person has had at least an opportunity to be. Until very recently, black life in America began with a closed door.

DEFINITION: WASHINGTON AND DuBOIS

By the late 1890s, black intellectuals and leaders in the South were turning their energies away from a relatively single-minded pursuit of whiteness from within their various enclaves and were falling back, in one sense or another, upon the black masses. There was always, of course, a distance between the vanguard and the rank and file, a lapse in time between the definition of a new course and its pursuit by the mass of black people. Black society moved much like some loosely organized army. Often scouts and leaders found themselves out upon new ground, in effect, without followers, alone and wasted. Some, who had previously enjoyed the followship of the masses, found themselves unaccountably deserted and irrelevant. Frederick Douglass—black abolitionist, assimilationist, and the most famous black man in America before his death in 1895—was one of the latter. With the end of Reconstruction his power steadily dwindled. With his marriage to a white woman in 1884, it practically evaporated altogether. Still others in the vanguard beat a path forward and looked back, eventually, to find—perhaps with a measure of surprise—that the masses had moved in behind them and were following. Booker T. Washington was one of these. He did not at first so much offer himself as he was chosen. His successor, W. E. B. DuBois, was at first not so much chosen as he offered himself.[12]

In the deep South blackness was most massive, chaos most frightening, and the drive for a viable structure most imperative. Out of the struggle came two grand and conflicting schemes for organizing black life in

America. Booker T. Washington offered one alternative, a relatively accommodative one in which blacks would strive to be superbly white but only in areas carefully selected to appear nonaggressive to whites. Washington's appeal to both blacks and whites was almost overwhelming in the turn-of-the-century years. What he would preserve for black people were precisely those things, religion aside, they held most dear: the farm, the family, and education. What he gave up were claims to things that blacks in a large measure had already lost in fact if not in law: physical integration and full political participation. Moreover, by giving up demands for integration in public places and universal male suffrage, he seemed also to surrender any claim to the "social equality" that so thoroughly frightened whites.

Washington and his program came to stage center on the speaker's platform of the Atlanta Cotton States Exposition in 1895, the very year Frederick Douglass died. In an address given as a part of the opening ceremonies, he called upon both whites and blacks to "put down their buckets" where they were, to come to terms with one another, and to draw upon the rich resources that each afforded the other. Black people had been loyal to their masters during the war, they had labored faithfully, and they would be loyal to white employers now and work "without strikes and labour wars." The white South after emancipation had given black people "a man's chance in the commercial world." For future progress, black and white had only to band together again, to deal with one another in a spirit of trust as they had in the past. Implicit in his words was the program he had followed at Tuskegee with signal success for more than a dozen years, a program that he had evolved out of his experience at Hampton Institute. In the exchange as offered in 1895, black people would accept some things and expect others. Washington symbolized his idea with a dramatic gesture. He held up his right hand, fingers spread. "In all things that are purely social we can be as separate as the fingers," he declared. Closing his fingers into a fist, he concluded, "yet one as the hand in all things essential to mutual progress." This "Atlanta Compromise," as it came to be called, was Washington's offering to the white people as the basis for an interracial peace. The audience accepted it with thunderous applause, with, indeed, a standing ovation.[13] It was not, it must be noted, a representative audience. In fact, the stage was filled with Georgia Republicans, a Reconstruction Republican governor had introduced Washington, and a Republican federal judge followed him as speaker. Finally, the whole Exposition was gotten up by business interests as a commercial device to combat the great depression of the 1890s.

Even so, the event served to thrust the baton of black leadership into Washington's not unwilling hand. During the next several years he was, in effect, the undisputed leader of the great mass of black people in the South. Some 90 percent of the Negro population was in that region, and Washington thus became the spokesman for the great mass of black people in America. In those years, very few black leaders in the South refused to applaud Washington's stance in race relations, if not Washington himself. White leadership in the nation at large moved to take advantage of the convenience of having a single black leader, someone who could not only speak for his people, but make commitments and deliver as promised. In the fall of 1901, Theodore Roosevelt, then President by dint of the assassination of William McKinley, invited Washington to the White House to discuss political appointments in the South. Soon Washington was generally understood to be Roosevelt's principal adviser on Southern appointments. His power, even over the political affairs of Southern whites, became highly impressive. For instance, in Alabama in 1901 it was probably his endorsement that effected the appointment of a conservative white Democrat, Thomas G. Jones, to the federal bench against the wishes of the senior Alabama Senator, a Democrat.[14] Washington's power in the field of black education was even greater than in politics. Southern white leaders soon come to request Tuskegee men to manage black education in their states and communities. Finally, Northern philanthropists, eager to pour money into Southern education, called upon him to point out the deserving. Washington had no difficulty in identifying his friends.

Ironically, even as Washington's power grew, the inadequacy of his accommodationism in the face of a rapidly deteriorating state of race relations became increasingly apparent. What changed was not Washington or his racial philosophy, or even his tactics, but rather the racial posture of the white world with which he had to deal. Washington, in essence, had offered an arrangement to whites who were racially conservative, to men who thought of blacks as a people created for a subordinate and serving place in a world dominated by benevolent whites. As the years clicked over the end of the century, however, these people lost control of their communities and, in the deep South, they lost whole states to racial extremists who regarded black people as hardly more than dangerous beasts. Washington had negotiated a compromise with benevolent establishments only to find many of those establishments dissolved and replaced by ones that were positively malevolent.

The racial world changed; so also did the material one, and that change compounded racial difficulties. Washington's program was designed for the agrarian order of the nineteenth century. But even as Washington gained power, the United States and the South were moving into an industrial order that would dominate the lives of the great mass of working America in the twentieth century as agrarian orders had dominated their lives in the nineteenth century. There had been a place made for black people in the old order. In the new order, powerful elements would press for their exclusion.

The message of denial from whites was manifested in many ways— by legal segregation and disfranchisement, by a broad social proscription that went far beyond specific discriminatory laws, by an imbalance in educational resources, by a progressive squeeze upon black tenant farmers, and by a drumfire of horrendous lynchings that left the landscape dotted with hanging bodies and charred remains. Especially did it come crashing in with a wave of violence at the turn of the century. In this time of riots, beginning signally with the outburst in Wilmington, North Carolina, in 1898 and ending with a massacre in Atlanta in 1906, upper-class blacks learned that in the South there were no citadels—nor even any refuges—in which any black person could find certain security. In September 1906, at last, the black businessmen along Auburn Avenue in Atlanta, who had taken Washington's advice and put down their buckets where they were with exemplary success, found themselves pursued, beaten, and their shops demolished by white mobs. Even the black professors of the elite circle of institutions clustered around Atlanta University found that their high culture, which certainly matched that of their white neighbors, afforded them no sanctuary. Their blackness alone was license enough to line them up against walls, to menace them with guns, to search them roughly, beat them, and rob them of every vestige of dignity.

With the Atlanta riot, in particular, it became apparent to thoughtful and objective blacks that even the most yielding of postures was not working in the South. In the North where there were few blacks, and where white assimilationists were persons of unusual power, black people could assert themselves and maintain their dignity. Occasionally in the South a Negro might aspire to the special kind of manhood projected in the image of Booker T. Washington and enjoy the carefully limited respect received by that sort of personality in the white world. But by the end of 1906, it was clear enough to those who would see that in the South Washington no longer had a contract that white men in the mass were bound to respect, and black claims to parity in any sphere would be met with terrible violence. If Negroes in the South were to regain their rights and dignity, it would not be by the further pursuit of accommodation.

Awareness of the racial realities over the next several decades not only fueled anti-Washingtonian attitudes of resistance among Negroes, it also lent strength to the idea that, after all, the Negro was not a white man with a black skin, and, moreover, that he could never be free within the given organization of Southern society. If Negroes in the South were to have ideals unstunted by limitations imposed by an insistent and omnipotent white society, those ideals would have to be distinctly black and quite apart from the ideals of the white world. If Negroes in the mass were to have ideals, values, and culture, these would have to be, in some significant measure and for some time to come, separated ideals, values, and culture.

The germ of the idea that proved to be the great alternative to the Washingtonian approach appeared a scant two years after the Atlanta speech. It was offered by W. E. B. DuBois, who came to the lower South in 1897 to take a teaching post at Atlanta University. DuBois, then twenty-nine, was a brilliant young man with degrees from Fisk and Harvard. He had studied at the University of Berlin under some of the foremost German scholars in that dawning age of social science, and he was completing a study of Philadelphia Negroes when he came to Atlanta. In 1897 in two little-noticed articles he introduced the revolutionary idea that the black experience in America was not only essentially different from that of the whites, but that it was necessarily and beautifully so. In DuBois's interpretation, every people was imbued by God at creation with a distinct genius. Throughout its life each people struggled, often in confusion and seeming contradiction with itself, to realize its special nature. Different peoples came to new and higher plateaus of self-realization at different times. Black people in America, so recently out of slavery, were a child race, only then coming to the threshold of self-understanding. There had been painful struggle, and there would be further struggle in which the true nature of black soul would become increasingly evident. But even then, he argued, even in 1897 it was clear that blacks were a specially spiritual people, living in the midst of an increasingly materialistic America. They were also an artistic people given specially to music, to colors, and language. In time, by virtue of their own striving, the genius of black people would manifest itself, and they would find themselves in close harmony with the prime being, and, presumably, through Him, with all else. Thus the path of progress, the way to harmony and a perfect assimilation lay in the pursuit of blackness not whiteness, in black people seeking communion with black people. Self-realization would not be achieved one by one, but all together or not at all. Consequently, a certain amount of black exclusiveness, a certain amount of voluntary separation from whites and confederation in all-black enclaves was essential to salvation.[15]

DuBois's racial philosophy was fundamentally different from that of Booker Washington, but the difference was not at first apparent. Indeed, the two men could come together readily and easily upon the ground of the necessity of concert among black people. Washington's program featured race pride, solidarity, and self-help. Du Bois, of course, could easily endorse these. Also, Du Bois was very much in favor of the economic improvement of black people, endorsed industrial education as legitimate, and applauded the rise of black businesses able to stand upon the patronage of black people. Most of all, Washington and Du Bois agreed on the necessity of black people organizing to pursue their interests. Finally, the principal and the professor both wanted full political and civil rights for black people, though they might differ as to how to achieve those goals. For a time, Du Bois could even be contented with a degree of gradualism. During the last years of the nineteenth century, he, along with nearly every other influential black leader in the South, applauded Washington's stance and followed his lead. Washington recognized Du Bois's talents and support. On three occasions he offered the young professor appointments at Tuskegee. On each occasion Du Bois turned down the offer with reluctance.

The primary cause of the break between Washington and Du Bois was the change in the interracial environment in which they labored. In effect, the white people with whom Washington had negotiated a modus vivendi in 1895 were, by 1900, rapidly losing control to people who had radically different ideas about the proper state of relations between the races. In the black belts of the South white attitudes of accommodation rapidly melted into universal rejection, and burning and bloody aggression. Whereas Conservative whites would have blacks stand in a subordinate place, Radical racists would reduce black people to supersubordination. As Radical racists gained power, they moved to effect that end. Washington, nevertheless, steadfastly maintained an overt posture of accommodation; indeed, he seemed psychologically incapable of altering that stance. Persistently he would try for the best, but he would take what he could get. Ironically even as his posture became less appropriate to the circumstances, his power to hold it and enforce it upon other blacks increased. By 1902 his command of the Southern black response to the white world was nearly complete, and even though he used that power to resist white encroachments strenuously, he did so secretly, deviously, and with only sporadic success. Under Washington and with accommodation, black resistance began from a kneeling position to face an onrushing, powerful, and fanatical foe bent upon nothing less than rendering black people prostrate.

Du Bois was the first black person to attack Washington's leadership with lasting effect. He did so initially in 1903 in his book, *The Souls of Black Folk,* the opening gun in a long and sometimes vicious battle for the leadership of black America. In 1905 Du Bois broadened the fight by organizing the so-called Niagara Falls Conference. The Conference included twenty-nine black leaders, only five of whom were from the South. Already black people in the South had been so reduced as to be practically powerless. There, overt resistance was met by galloping violence, rope and faggot, and expatriation. Any explicit contest for equality, clearly, would have to be waged, as it were, from exile. The Niagara Conference was candid in its intention to enter the fray fully erect and armed. It resolved that black people should protest vigorously against political, civil, and economic inequality. In a direct assault upon accommodationism, it denied that "the Negro-American assents to inferiority," or "is submissive under oppression and apologetic before insult." For itself, it declared that "we do not hesitate to complain and to complain loudly and insistently."[16] The Niagara Movement convened yearly thereafter. It was, indeed, very active in protest, and its impact was felt. At its peak it mustered some four hundred activists, and it sufficiently frightened Booker T. Washington that he resorted to his usual tactics of spying upon the organization, denying funds to some of its members while suborning others, and attacking the movement through the mouths of his agents. The militants responded in kind. Between 1907 and 1910 they sponsored a newspaper in the District of Columbia that attacked "King Booker" and his self-assumed absolutism, charged him with acquiescing in segregation, remaining "dumb as an oyster as to peonage," and discovering "that colored people can better afford to be lynched than the white people can afford to lynch them."[17]

In 1909 the members of the Niagara Movement began to merge with Northern white racial liberals to form a permanent organization, the National Association for the Advancement of Colored People. Washington again attempted futilely to undermine the organization. The alliance of black and white leaders proved highly effective. By 1914 the NAACP, headquartered in New York and with a permanent full-time staff, boasted 6,000 members, mostly black and Northern. However, it was very strong in Washington, D.C., and had some hard core representation in almost every large Southern city. Its journal, *Crisis* (founded in 1910 and edited by Du Bois, who moved from Atlanta to New York for the purpose), had a circulation of 31,540.[18] The success of the NAACP sprang from many causes, of course, but the key factor was that it met the burning issue— it moved head-on against the unequal treatment of black people in American society. In doing so it traveled squarely in the path of the ideas of American republicanism as announced in the Declaration of Independence and the Constitution as amended. The program of the NAACP was strikingly old-line, nineteenth-century, patrician liberal. Its first president was, appropriately, Oswald Garrison Villard, the grandson of the great abolitionist William Lloyd Garrison. In 1831 Garrison had simply stood for the recognizedly American ideal that all men are and by right ought to be free. The objectives of the NAACP represented a continuation and updating precisely in that channel. It moved directly toward the immediate assimilation of black people as equal citizens in the Republic.[19] Like that early movement, it had little direct economic consciousness, and such as it had was laissez-faire and conservative. Stressing assimilation, it frowned upon black exclusivism and the drawing of race lines generally. What was radical about the NAACP was not its philosophy or even its method. It was, as with those earlier abolitionists, that it insisted upon "freedom now." That stance made it anathema to the gradualist Bookerites and compellingly attractive to W. E. B. DuBois.

Scholars have long noted that DuBois was, himself, often at bitter variance with the parent organization of his magazine. The root of that variance ·was philosophical and lay in the fact that DuBois was not an assimilationist in the traditional sense. The NAACP searched longingly for the key to the integration of blacks into the mainstream of American life. For it, an ideal society would be one in which color had no practical significance. DuBois, on the other hand, thought of color as the key to salvation. Far from eradicating color consciousness, he thought it essential that it be promoted, developed, and refined. In insisting that blacks were innately and perpetually different from whites, DuBois took a position that was virtually opposite from the integrative, assimilationist stance of the NAACP. Inevitably, in later times the difference would cause a breach. It came in the 1930s when DuBois came out for black people voluntarily segregating themselves from whites in certain areas. Every other black leader, including his friends in the NAACP, vigorously opposed that program. Ultimately, DuBois went his own way. He became a Marxist and settled himself in Africa, where he lived his last years.

DuBois was the black radical in race relations in America; he was the revolutionary. Before his time, no broadly influential black leader, nor any white leader who was sympathetic to blacks, held that black people were God-givenly and essentially different from white people, and perpetually and beautifully so. Indeed, placed along the scale of assimilation versus nonassimilation, the NAACP and the Bookerites fell upon one side and DuBois on the other. The NAACP was spread along the far end of the assimilation side and the Bookerites were arrayed on the same side but inward and closer to center, while DuBois would stand close to the end on the other side. In the interest of black people winning a greater share in the good things of American life, both Washington and DuBois would move closer to assimilation. But where Washington would aspire to achieve a perfect assimilation, Du Bois would stringently resist that end. For him, blackness was to be preserved and perfected, never totally lost. Du Boisian assimilation would be of a transcendental nature. Black people had contributed and would continue to contribute to a total American culture that was both black and white, each pursuing its own identity and thereby to know itself and to know God, and through Him to achieve harmony.

Du Bois's plan was more comprehensive, more cosmopolitan than any other. It is highly significant that he stood in sharp contrast to Washington and the NAACP in his attitude toward Africa. Before Du Bois, black American leaders as a group exhibited little interest in Africa, and most of the interest shown was in Africa as a missionary field for the spread of "American" culture, not as the homeland of soul brothers from whom one might learn as well as teach. Washington's interest in Africa was practically nil, and the NAACP did not feature an African relations department. Probably most educated blacks would have agreed with the black writer Charles Chesnutt, who confessed that he was "not greatly concerned about Africa except as an interesting foreign country."[20] But Du Bois, as early as 1899, initiated the first Pan African conference. He was ecumenical in his blackness where his cohorts were provincial or, at most, national. Washington allowed black people to join his club if they were "good" blacks and industrious. The NAACP allowed them to join their club if they were "good" Americans. Du Bois allowed them to join the club if they were, quite simply, black. Washington's tenure as the spokesman for the black mass was actually relatively brief. He enjoyed great strength from about 1895 to about 1907, and considerable strength until his death in 1915. The NAACP would have a very successful life for over half a century. Ultimately, however, it would find that it could go only so far in making white people out of black people in America. In the 1960s, Du Boisian soul would prove to be the most powerful organizing idea of all. It would pick up all black people, the lowly more easily than the high, and practically none would escape the pull of its gravity. Bookerism and the NAACP, after all, were for the qualified few, while Black Soul was for the masses . . . wherever they were.[21]

CHAPTER III

Black Images
in Southern White Minds

The essence of what happened in the South in race relations during the last century and a half can be largely explained by a description of the evolution and interplay of three Southern white "mentalities." These mentalities could be aptly labeled "Liberal," "Conservative," and "Radical."

By mentality I mean to suggest something less perfectly formed than a philosophy. Like a philosophy, a mentality will have certain discrete ideas, but those ideas are not tightly knit into a smoothly finished and comprehensive web such as might be the case, for instance, with "Platonic" philosophy or "Christian" philosophy. On the other side, I use mentality to indicate something that includes but is more than "notions," "opinions," and "attitudes," all of which suggest vagueness, impermanence, individual thought rather than social thought, and thinking that does not compel action and is very often at variance with behavior. By mentality I want to suggest an intellectual atmosphere of a distinctive, clearly identifiable quality. It is derived from the broad society, touches a large number of individual minds, and flows and changes over time, influencing behavior and being influenced by behavior, and by the physical world. It is in part emotional, and it does compel action. Like a prevailing wind, it does not prevail perfectly in all times and places, but in the wide sweep of human history and total flow is virtually uniform and prevalent.

I can identify in the mind of the white South since the 1830s three rather clear and distinct "matched sets" of thought about Negroes as Americans. All three mentalities made a judgment, among many other judgments, as to the future of Negroes in America. In this relation, the three can be easily ranged on a scale running from optimistic to pessimistic.

At the top of the array was a mentality that I will style as "Liberal." Liberalism said, in brief, that it did not yet know the potential of the Negro. Racial Liberalism was strongest in the 1880s, and it was deeply impressed with the progress that black people had made under Northern leadership during Reconstruction, progress that antebellum whites would have declared impossible. Liberals rued the desertion of Negroes by Northern tutors after Reconstruction and the subsequent failure of Southern whites to pick up again the cross of missionary labor to blacks that they had, in their own eyes, carried before the war. In the 1880s Liberalism felt that the capacity of Negroes to absorb white culture in America had not yet been fairly tested, and it refused to close them out brusquely and across the board somewhere far below the white man. It was relatively open-ended in its view of the future of the Negro in the nation; and, most essentially, it possessed a sanguine faith, an optimistic adventurousness, a willingness to experiment in a search for progress that other mentalities lacked. Liberals were very few, but those few were articulate, highly energetic, and conspicuous.

Second, there was a "Conservative" mentality on race. Conservatism always began, proceeded, and ended upon the assumption of Negro inferiority. The Negro problem for Conservatives was simply a matter of defining the nature and the degree of Negro inferiority and of accommodating society thereto. It looked quite literally to the conservation of the Negro. It sought to save him by defining and fixing his place in American society. *Place* was the vital word in the vocabulary of Conservatism, and it applied to whites as well as to blacks. Conservatism probably had its effective beginning in the 1830s. It is the long-running and mass mode of thought on race in the white South, and, stubborn at its core and subtly pliant on its surface, it persists strong and essentially unchanged even today. Indeed, the other two mentalities, the Liberal and the Radical, are only the legitimate children of Conservatism. Each in novel circumstances ran elements of orthodox Conservative thought out to extremes, each acted aggressively upon its new racial lights, and each eventually lost its patricidal struggle.

At the bottom of the scale, most significant for race relations in the twentieth-century South, and most pessimistic, was "Radicalism." The Radical mentality emerged vigorously about 1889 and ran until 1915. Between 1897 and 1907 it possessed terrific power. Radicalism envisioned a "new" Negro, freed from the necessarily very tight bonds of slavery and retrogressing rapidly toward his natural state of savagery and bestiality. Liberalism may have been, in essence, merely an improved version of Conservatism, but Radicalism differed sharply from Conservatism in that it anticipated the ultimate demise of the Negro in America. Radicals insisted that there was *no place* for the Negro in the future American society, and, moreover, that his disappearance was imminent.

THE LIBERAL REVOLT

In the 1880s in the South, the Conservative mentality ruled in race relations. After the hard push for Redemption, it had, as it were, relaxed and drifted. Conservatism by its very nature tended to regard any peace as a good peace. It much preferred to let well enough alone. It was not aggressively anti-Negro, unless the Negro deserted his assigned place, and that place was always assumed to be somewhere safely below the place of white people. Conservatism was securely the mass mode of thought about race in the South in the 1880s, and it tolerated a wide range of varieties, the variety depending essentially upon various views of the innate character of Negroes. At the bottom of the scale, some Conservatives thought that the potential of black people was very poor, and they tended to regard a low level of Negro existence as his proper place, or a point on the path to finding that place. Other Conservatives were optimistic about the potential of black people for absorbing white civilization and attaining a relatively high place in the future society. Those who were most optimistic about black potentiality tended to be highly active in labor within the Negro community—in religion, in education, and much more delicately and carefully in matters economic, political, and societal.

In the early 1880s, a few thoughtful and highly perceptive Southern Conservatives became convinced that Negro life was losing sight of the ideals that whites cherished. They felt that black life, thus bereft, was in danger of disintegrating. In the crisis there was a reaction in the white community that might be called the Liberal revolt. It was a revolt against the apathy of the vast majority of whites in regard to black people, an apathy that, as Liberals saw it, sometimes bred ignorance and carelessness in interracial matters. It began as a call for a return to the paternalism of late slavery when the best masters had cared for and raised up the best blacks. But often it ended, as intensified interracial contact sometimes does, in a much less biased racial posture by some whites.

Racial Liberalism took a new view of race relations in the South by arguing that the Negro's capacity was as yet untried. It was distinguished by a faith that black people, properly nurtured, had the capacity to rise well up in the range of white culture. That nurture inevitably involved close instruction by whites and thereby a renewal of the physical propinquity between Negroes and at least some whites that had marked slavery. Indeed, the Liberal faith in Negro progress rested most heavily upon a rather roseate view of how greatly the Negro had been elevated in those last years of slavery in which whites had moved into black communities to Christianize and civilize the benighted. Liberalism was also influenced, though to a lesser degree, by an appreciation of how rapidly and how far Negroes had advanced under the aggressive tutelege of Reconstruction regimes. For instance, in 1860 Southern whites who presumed to know Negroes well were convinced that the black mind, while capable of managing simple arithmetic, would never be able to rise to the heights of abstraction necessary to master algebra, trigonometry, or calculus. Yet in Reconstruction, when the experiment was actually made on a large scale, often in schools sponsored by Northerners, that myth was dealt a crippling blow. Some blacks, obviously, were capable of taking giant steps into what had been previously regarded as an exclusive province of the white man.

Liberalism in the 1880s, then, was optimistic about the capacities of the Negro, and it called upon the best of Southern whites to pick up again the cross of labor among their darker brothers. Appropriately, Liberalism was open-ended in its view of the Negro's future place in Southern society. It could contemplate with relative equanimity, if not outright pleasure, an eventual parity of Negroes with whites in the enjoyment of many—but never all—white cultural ideals. Liberalism was also marked by adventurousness. Liberals were willing to gamble that improved circumstances and broader exposures would better the Negro, and they exhibited a disposition to be flexible and experimental in the pursuit of that end. There were limits, of course, to how liberal Southern Liberals would be. There were some Northern liberals, for instance Bishop Gilbert Haven of the Methodist Episcopal Church, who warmly espoused miscegenation as the solution to the race problem. Virtually no white Southerner expressed sympathy with that approach. The integration of black and white that Liberals envisioned was restricted very much to the mental and spiritual realm. Physical integration was licensed only to promote that end.

There was a lamentable paucity of racial Liberalism in the South even during its high time in the 1880s. But it did exist, and the current probably flowed most strongly among churchmen disturbed by what they regarded as a loss of religious values among Negro clergymen and a rise of dangerous emotionalism among the masses.

Atticus Greene Haygood was one of the first and probably the greatest of the Southern churchmen to revolt against the abandonment of black Christians. Haygood was the son of a country lawyer who had moved to Atlanta before the Civil War and had become a public spirited leader in that booming city. Reared in a devotedly Methodist family, Atticus was educated in staunchly Methodist Emory College. Resisting a strong temptation to enlist as a missionary to China, he became a minister, married into one of the leading ministerial dynasties in Southern Methodism, and very soon became the protégé of the foremost Southern Methodist bishop, George F. Pierce. During the war, he was a Confederate chaplain and did hard service among the troops in the field and in the hospitals, especially during the Atlanta campaign. After the war, Haygood rose rapidly to eminence in the church, not on the front lines of parish labor, but rather, one might say, by way of staff work at the rear. For a time, he was an editor in the Methodist publication complex in Nashville, quietly gaining recognition of his superior talents from the inmost hierarchy of the church. In the midst of the depression of the 1870s, he became the president of his alma mater, Emory College, and worked brilliantly to save the school from financial failure and dissolution. Finally, while still president of Emory, he took the editorship of *The Wesleyan Christian Advocate,* probably the most influential Methodist journal in the southeastern United States.[1]

Rather suddenly, in 1881, while he was president of Emory and editor of the *Advocate,* Haygood moved vigorously into the field of race relations when he published *Our Brother in Black.* He began that book by illustrating the childlike nature of Negro character through some two score anecdotes. Then he went on to criticize the necessity of Northern educational activity among Negroes in the South and to apologize for the lack of such activity by Southerners. The South had not produced slavery, but inherited it, he argued. Providence had not allowed abolitionism to become strong until white American civilization had reached a point where it could successfully resist amalgamation with the freedmen. Negroes were not white people, the two peoples would always remain racially separated, and white people could therefore relax in the black presence. But humanity was a single race, and whites might now safely reach down from their heights and teach Negroes to abandon their habits of thoughtlessness, drinking, fornication, and "debasement of 'worship' services." It was the duty of the white South to educate the Negro, and to include in that education a practical training that would allow him to win a stake in society and an appreciation of literacy in politics. Education, guided by whites, was the key to achieving a brotherhood of black and white. Finally, Haygood turned both to praise the Northern churches for their educational work in the South in the past and to discharge them from further responsibility.[2]

Our Brother in Black won high praise in the North. Within a year, Haygood was appointed the executive agent of the newly created Slater

Fund at the insistence of ex-President Rutherford B. Hayes, one of its organizers. The Fund was dedicated largely to the industrial education of Negroes and spent some $40,000 annually in the South. As agent, Haygood decided how and by which schools the funds were to be used. The indications are that Haygood wielded this power effectively. One of the largest beneficiaries was Booker T. Washington's rapidly rising school at Tuskegee. In the early 1880s Haygood was also the moving spirit in establishing Paine College in Augusta, Georgia. Paine was begun by the Southern Methodists to train Negro teachers and ministers for the Colored Methodist Church, but it soon became a key institution of black education in that area and a symbol of Southern, as opposed to Northern, white missionary efforts among the blacks. In the early 1880s, Haygood himself became the symbol of a willingness among Southern whites to pick up again their commitments to the Negro. At a meeting in Chautauqua, New York, in 1883, he increased his popularity among racial liberals everywhere by emphasizing his conviction that all races were one in humanity.[3]

Every major Southern church shared in some degree the concern for the Negro that Haygood represented in the MEC South. Each tried in some way to train a Negro ministry to work across the race line, and each attempted, at least spasmodically, to transmit the evangel directly through white ministers.

Probably Haygood was led to take his stand by a persisting paternalism that made him not only aware of the duty of favored whites toward blacks, but of the more fortunate whites to people not so favored everywhere—to whites, browns, and yellows as well as to blacks, and of Christians to heathen peoples all over the world. Haygood as a paternalist was a perfect example of the type, and he personified clearly the bridge between the old paternalism and what was soon to became the new. His father had been one of the kindest of slaveholders, and Haygood's own youth was spent in closest intimacy with Negroes. In particular, he was for a time given over almost totally to tutelege by a male slave, a man highly knowledgeable in hunting, fishing, and woods' lore. Atticus the boy had lived a Huck Finn–Nigger Jim relationship such as Mark Twain later depicted, and it marked his life.

Within the church, Haygood's mentor was Bishop George F. Pierce, himself a representative of the paternalistic side of Southern slavery. When a Southern bishop in the antebellem Methodist church, James O. Andrew, acquired slaves through a bequest to his wife, the Northern bishops demanded that he surrender either his bondsmen or his office. Pierce vigorously supported Andrew's refusal to do either and was a leader in the secession of the Southern Methodists from the national church in 1844. Pierce soon emerged as the leading Southern bishop. But he was most widely known and admired, not for his role in creating the Methodist Episcopal Church South, but for his sermons that called upon masters to be good to their slaves.[4] Pierce was himself an excellent example of how the "travail of slavery" might produce a selfless paternalism, and Haygood was the legitimate child both of his slaveholding father and his episcopal mentor. Paternalism was his heritage, and he reclaimed that heritage in the 1880s when he picked up the cross of service beyond the color bar. By 1881, the seeming sinfulness of Negro life, the chaos, the disorder, and the wickedness of the black ministry made action imperative to one who had been born and bred to bear a sense of responsibility for his brothers in black. Haygood's work in establishing Paine College, his labor for the Slater fund, his exhortatory speaking and writing were all movements in a grand symphony of Christian endeavor in race relations, of getting back, as he saw it, to the vital relationship Southern Methodists had achieved with blacks in the last years of slavery.

Haygood continued his labors throughout the decade of the 1880s. In 1882, he refused to accept election as a bishop of the church, probably because acceptance would have entailed, as it customarily did, removal to another diocese. Finally, in 1890, he did accept and became the Bishop of California, a post that included service as the missionary Bishop of Mexico. In 1891 he moved his family to California. Shortly thereafter, during a visitation in Mexico, an apparently already weakened Haygood contracted a fever that was to prove fatal. In 1893, when the family returned to Georgia, the fragile momentum of the revived mission to blacks that Haygood had achieved in the 1880s had been lost, and the current was running swiftly in the opposite direction. In 1895, several months before his death, Haygood wrote his final, and perhaps his most poignant, words on the race question for *The Methodist Review,* words that were perfectly prophetic for another crusade for racial justice a century after emancipation. "One chief trouble with us in the Negro problem," he said, "as in all things, is this: we are in a great hurry about everything. But God is not in haste about anything." Time, faith, and labor, he urged, were the tools of progress, but progress would be slow. "It will be a problem not to be solved offhand, as schoolboys show off on black boards how they have learned to 'do their sums'," he warned. "Those who are seeking the Negro's good," Haygood concluded, "deal with at least three generations—the people set free, their children, and their grandchildren. Our great-grandchildren, comparing 1865 and 1965, will rejoice, and glorify the Lord God and Father of us all. They will also help to build monuments to the heroic men and women whom their grandparents ostracised.

Among and by those monuments half a dozen of our people and time will be remembered. Would God there were more!"[5]

Haygood carried the banner of Liberalism into the clerical world, George Washington Cable, the New Orleans writer who became famous for his interpretation of Creole culture, carried it into the secular. Born in 1844 to a father who, at first, prospered as a merchant and then failed, Cable knew both affluence and need as a child. When his father died in 1859, George, to support his mother and sisters, left school to take the job in the customshouse his father had held. As a teenager he slipped away from New Orleans to join the Confederate cavalry and was dangerously wounded, but recovered and fought the war to the bitter end. After the war he began to work as a journalist and soon began to publish fiction in national magazines. In 1879, he published *Old Creole Days* and thereafter became one of the most celebrated of American authors.

Cable, apparently, was at first totally orthodox on the race question. He had been shocked during Reconstruction when Republican officials had failed to segregate strictly the public schools of New Orleans. However, when a mob of white men invaded the Girls' High School in 1874 and forcibly expelled every girl suspected of African descent, some of whom were visibly indistinguishable from other students who were undeniably white, Cable was outraged. He simply could not accept a racial system in which people who were perfectly white in appearance were designated black. For several years his fiction carried a very strong but usually subtle running indictment of the Southern racial order, and then, in 1885, he published "The Freedman's Case in Equity" in *The Century,* a leading national magazine. That article was an open attack on discrimination against blacks by white Southerners, and it brought the furies down upon his head. By year's end, Cable had moved his residence to Northampton, Massachusetts, where it remained until his death.

Cable insisted, in and after 1885, that there was a "silent South" consisting of thoughtful, leading men who, if they could be made to speak and act, would deliver to the Negro the full measure of justice to which he was entitled. In 1888 and 1889, in conjunction with William M. Baskervill, a young professor of literature at Vanderbilt University, he organized the Open Letter Club to bring forth those men. Hundreds of leaders in communities all over the South were solicited for their opinions on the race question, and hundreds responded. Their letters reveal that there was no such silent South as Cable had imagined. Evidently, the great truth was that the vast majority of thinking Southerners felt that the Negro was at, or very close to, his proper level in the scale of white civilization.

If he were not so, a gentle evolution would soon bring him to that point. Precisely because they were so sure of the innate inferiority of the Negro and his ultimate subordination, white Southerners in the 1880s were largely inactive and not greatly concerned about race relations.[6]

Haygood and Cable were the two conspicuous Liberals in race in the South in these post-Reconstruction years. Haygood, who certainly had good cause to keep count, said that there were half a dozen heroes in race relations in 1895. He wished that there were more; and we could very well wish that he had named those because it is now difficult to identify even six spirits of Haygood's caliber among his contemporaries. Ultimately, it can only be said that the Liberals were a small and embattled band, a corporal's guard thinly arrayed against a hostile frontier.

THE RISE OF THE RADICALS

It is, indeed, one of the great ironies of American history that when the nation freed the slaves, it also freed racism. After Nat Turner's insurrection, the marriage of slavery to race that had begun in America more than a century before was completed. In that union, race seemed, at first, to rise to domination. For a time, slavery was everybody's business, and race ruled slavery. By the decade of the 1850s, however, slavery clearly ruled race. White people in the South were no longer free to think what they pleased about black people. They could not, for extreme examples, think that any Negro could be totally white in the cultural sense or envision a South in which blacks did not exist. Sambo, the perpetually perfect servant to white masters, was a fair image of the black person that slavery sought and, in the white mind, found.

After the war, Southern racial Conservatives were not eager to let Sambo go in spite of his unseemly behavior and, with Redemption, he was regained. In the 1880s, Conservatives resisted strenuously and successfully the Liberal effort to raise blacks higher in the scale of white civilization. During the next generation, however, they turned to face a new and much more powerful foe in the opposite quarter. The new enemy was Radical racism.

Radicalism appeared in strength in 1889 and spread rapidly through the South. The core of the Radical mentality was the concept that Negroes, freed from the restraining influences of slavery, were rapidly "retrogressing" toward their natural state of bestiality. Older Negroes were susceptible to fall, but, more importantly, in the mid-eighties young Negroes were coming into manhood who had been born free and had never felt the civilizing effects of slavery. By 1889 the "New Negro," as white contemporaries labeled him, might be twenty-four years old. Indeed, he *was* a new man, and his potential *was* unknown. By the end of that year, very clearly, many Southerners were concluding that the essential nature of the newly matured black was bestial, and that, unsupported by the enforced moral behavior of slavery, the New Negro was reverting to a native savagery. The reversion, they concluded, came to its most conspicuous crisis in attempts by black men to rape white women. Ultimately, Radicals believed, there would be no place for blacks in the South or in America. The end might come in a kind of race war, not always physical, that the superior whites would win, or blacks might be transported to some foreign parts, but the two races together would not last. As one Georgia woman expressed it: "Since our old-time friends, the negro, who as a slave, was trustworthy and gentle, seems to have retrograded through freedom into a dangerous beast, it is surely necessary that he be removed from among us."[7]

Precisely why Radicalism appeared with such dramatic suddenness in 1889 and swept so powerfully through the South in the years that followed is beyond easy explanation. Quite clearly, the seeds of Radicalism lay deep in Southern race relations. The proslavery argument itself contained the prediction that outside of slavery blacks could not exist. However, during Reconstruction that belief died away, and after Reconstruction Southerners assumed that Negroes would have a lasting presence in their midst. Further, and happily for the white South, a wave of evidence indicated that the nation at large was again surrendering black people to the control of their late masters. In 1877 President Rutherford B. Hayes withdrew the federal troops from the state capitals of the South and, after he retired as President, greatly interested himself in race relations there. As the head of the Slater Fund, in and after 1881, he labored for black education, not with the rude and heavy hand of the outsider, but sympathetically and through the instrumentality of Atticus Greene Haygood. In 1883 the United States Supreme Court struck down a large part of the Civil Rights Act of 1875 and thereby took the federal government out of the business of enforcing the integration of public accommodations. Moreover, in 1884 the nation elected a Democratic President, Grover Cleveland, marking an end to the twenty-four-year reign of Republicans. Southerners assumed that Cleveland would be especially generous to the South. Some Southern Congressmen felt so secure that they began to jest in Washington restaurants about the prospective return of slavery and loudly claimed this or that individual Negro waiter as their future property. In the early years of the 1880s, Southern whites were gladly accepting a renewed responsibility for the management of black people, and they believed that the burden would not be inordinately onerous.

There were countercurrents, however, to disturb the tranquility of Southern white minds on matters of race, and the late 1880s saw them rise menacingly to the surface. Far from proscribing the Negro further, President Cleveland in office in 1885 actually initiated the practice of appointing leading black Democrats to six certain federal offices, each of which paid a good salary and carried with it a significant measure of power and dignity. This was a step strikingly beyond those of Reconstruction, during which more than a score of blacks were elected to Congress but not a single black person was appointed to an important federal office. The Republican victory in the national elections in November 1888 jarred the South even more profoundly than Cleveland's apostasy. "The Negro question is a live one just now," wrote William Baskervill to George W. Cable from Nashville in December. "There is great uneasiness about the President elect's plans and purposes."[8] Southerners had good cause for anxiety. In the campaign, the forces of Benjamin Harrison had made a superbly well organized play for the black vote under the leadership of James S. Clarkson, co-owner with his brother of the Des Moines (Iowa) *Register*. As a teenager Clarkson had helped guide Radical abolitionist John Brown across the plains at a critical juncture in his tumultuous career, and afterward he proved himself a steady ally of the Negro. As a reward for his efforts, Harrison made Clarkson his Postmaster General in 1889, and in that capacity, Clarkson later asserted, he caused some 16,000 blacks to be appointed to federal jobs.[9] In the higher offices, Republicans could hardly do less than the Democrats had done before them, and the Harrison administration appointed six black Republicans to the places that six black Democrats had previously held. Those six offices continued to be held by Negroes until the Democrats came into power in 1913.

In the elections of 1888 the Republican party gained control of the national executive, and it also won a majority of the seats in each house of Congress. Republicans could pass any measure they could agree upon. A long-running agitation for the enactment of the so-called Blair bill providing federal aid to education, including black children as well as white, now emerged as a very real danger. The Blair bill had never come to the floor of the House, but it had passed the Senate handily in 1884, in 1886, and again in 1888. If it succeeded and black people in the South were to be educated equally with white, their capacity for challenging white supremacy would be vastly improved.[10]

The South also had good reason to fear a resumption of Reconstruction in politics. Southern elections since Redemption had been uniquely and notoriously violent and fraudulent. In December 1889 President Harrison asked Congress for an elections law. The House responded with the

"Force bill," a measure introduced by Representative Henry Cabot Lodge of Massachusetts to ensure fairness in federal elections by the use of federal supervisors. Honest federal elections would have made illegal exclusion of black voters more difficult in state and local elections, especially those that occurred at the same time, and, hence, would have jeopardized an all-white Democratic supremacy at home. The Force bill actually passed the House and was halted temporarily in the Senate only by a Southern filibuster. It seemed for a time in 1889 and 1890 fully possible that both it and the Blair bill would sweep through the newly elected Republican Congress and pass on to enforcement by a fully receptive administration.[11] If these measures had passed it would have signified the beginning of another Reconstruction, and Southern white civilization would have been again sorely threatened. The danger was real, as Southern white leadership well knew, and it was present.

The South was deeply disturbed, too, by economic and political disintegration at home, an erosion that had profound effects in race relations. Farmers in the South in the decade of the 1880s moved from prosperity to deepening recession. As the recession deteriorated into a depression in 1892 and 1893, agricultural prices fell dramatically. Farms that had supported a family comfortably with cotton selling at twelve cents a pound became marginal at eight cents a pound, and failed totally at seven, six, and five—a point reached in 1894. The richest lands, such as those in broad river bottoms that refertilized themselves with every flood, came to be much prized because out of sheer productivity they might still show a living and even a profit at comparatively low prices. Those lands were the very lands that slavery had possessed to form the "black belts" of the South. After slavery they were most often tenanted by the freedmen and their descendants, usually, of course, as renters. In the early 1890s white farmers desperate to provide for their families resorted to violence in attempts to displace black tenants from those more desirable lands. In 1892 and 1893, for instance, in soil-rich Amite, Franklin, and Lincoln counties in southwestern Mississippi, organizations of farmers known as "Whitecaps" operated much like the Ku Klux Klan of Reconstruction years to terrorize Negroes off farms rented from landlords and country merchants. White landlords who controlled Negro labor soon took alarm, and authorities moved to squelch the terrorists. When a band of Whitecaps attacked the Lincoln County jail in the spring of 1893 in an effort to free ten of their friends who had been arrested, the governor of the state joined local officials in firmly crushing that particular movement.[12] In some areas, however, whitecapping seemed to become a habit, and even after the return of prosperity white farmers continued into the twentieth century attempts to drive blacks away so that they might themselves take up the best lands as renters.[13]

Plain white farmers probably had good reason to fear competition from black farmers. Many white landlords and merchants much preferred black tenants and creditors to white for reasons both real and imagined. Moreover, there are suggestions in agricultural statistics that black farmers, so recently out of slavery and beginning almost literally only with the clothes on their backs, farmed their lands—whether rich or poor—more intensively than their white contemporaries and that their level of indebtedness tended to be lower. In 1910, for instance, the census indicated that black farmers in the South had improved 66 percent of their land whereas white farmers had improved only 39 percent. In the North the proportions at 71 percent for blacks and 70 percent for whites were essentially equal.[14]

As the economic plight of the farmers became more extreme in the late 1880s, they began to organize themselves into the Farmers' Alliance. The repeated failure of the Democratic party to respond to their needs, capped by the nomination of conservative Grover Cleveland for the presidency, led many Southerners to join with Westerners in 1892 to form the People's, or Populist, party. The division that became official in 1892 was already profoundly present in the late 1880s. By 1889 incipient populism was visibly under way among men who still called themselves Democrats. The old order was under attack, not only economically but politically, and anxiety levels rose accordingly.

The recession of the late 1880s and the depression of the 1890s also produced profound psychological effects. Southern whites had been very much taken by sex and family roles prescribed in the Victorian era. Men saw themselves as the providers and protectors in their families. As the economic world constricted, men found themselves less and less able to provide for their women in the accustomed style, and there seemed to be no promise of an end to the decline. For those men at the lower end of the economic scale fulfillment of the provider portion of the role became nearly impossible. But even those at the top generally suffered a relative reduction in their capacity to give satisfaction in the role, and with that loss, doubtlessly, came feelings of inadequacy. It seems fully possible that the rage against the black beast rapist was a kind of psychic compensation. If white men could not provide for their women materially as they had done before, they could certainly protect them from a much more awful threat—the outrage of their purity, and hence their piety, by black men. What white men might have lost on one side in affirming their sense of self, they might more than compensate for on the other. Bread for their women was important, but it was as nothing alongside their purity. Of what earthly good was the body if the soul be lost?

The particular conjunction of sex and race that seized the South in 1889, and has not yet let go, probably had its immediate origins in Southern acceptance of the Victorian model of sex roles and familyhood by both blacks and whites in the last generation of slavery. Ironically, the same Victorianism that cut black men loose from hearth and home in the 1890s to roam the roads of the South in search of work generated in white minds a perception of them that would lead to the most awful display of interracial violence the South has yet experienced. The way in which the white South chose to react to the great depression of the 1890s is, indeed, curious. White Southerners might have responded economically with great cooperative combinations, or politically by radical new organizations. Instead they seemed to respond radically only in race, moderately in politics, and hardly at all in the sphere of direct economic action.

Whatever political, economic, and psychological realities underlay the Radical upsurge, Radicals themselves did not relate their special thinking to those causes. On the contrary, Radicals believed that their views rose solely from racial realities, easily observable. Ironically, Radicals were much like such Liberals as Atticus Haygood in that they were obsessed with what they perceived to be an alarming deterioration in black life. But Radicals differed, radically, from Liberals in that they sustained no hope, ultimately, for the salvation of black people in America, and they espoused programs designed to put black people down and out rather than up.

In the Radical eye, there were many signs of black retrogression. One of the most telling was an appalling rise in Negro criminality. Whether or not Negroes were actually becoming more criminal in their behavior we shall never know. Many whites who were most sympathetic with blacks thought so, as did indeed many well-informed blacks. Economic hard times, after all, do generate higher crime rates regardless of race. Nevertheless, Radicals could imagine no cure for the criminal propensities that they saw spreading like a plague among Negroes. In the crisis, some turned against any formal education at all for blacks. They began to argue that the New Negro was innately bad and any increase in his talents or capacities by education only heightened his potential for evil. Even the kind of industrial education that Booker T. Washington offered was dangerous. But most pernicious of all, because it held up false hopes, was the kind of liberal learning advanced by such Northern benevolent organizations as the American Missionary Association and institutionalized in such schools as Atlanta, Fisk, and Straight (now Dillard) Universities.

In the Radical mind, the single most significant and awful manifestation of black retrogression was an increasing frequency of sexual assaults on white women and girl children by black men. Above all else, it was this threat that thrust deeply into the psychic core of the South, searing the white soul, marking the character of the Southern mind radically and leaving it crippled and hobbled in matters of race long after the mark itself was lost from sight.

The assault upon idealized Southern womanhood by the "nigger beast" was the keen cutting edge of Radicalism. Let Benjamin Ryan Tillman of South Carolina catch the scene for us, as he did for his colleagues on the floor of the United States Senate in 1907. As he drew the picture, white women in the rural South were virtually besieged by Negro brutes who roamed almost without restraint, their "breasts pulsating with the desire to sate their passions upon white maidens and wives." Every Southerner returning home was fearful of finding his wife or daughter ravished. Forty to a hundred maidens, he said, were sacrificed annually to the Minotaur, and there was no Theseus in sight.[15]

Rapes and the lynchings that followed became the special studies of the Radicals, and provided the most vital of their statistics. It is vastly significant that the lynching of black men for the rape of white women was not the subject of intense observation and comment in the South before 1889. There had been a great fear of blacks certainly, but the older fear was that they would rise massively and kill whites, or do them bodily injury, or destroy their property—not that they would rise individually and sporadically and rape white women. In and after 1889, however, that crime and its punishment commanded a new and tremendously magnified attention.[16] Of course, lynching had long existed in the United States, and it had been common enough in the South. It derived its name, in fact, from a famous practitioner of the method upon Tories in Virginia during the American Revolution. But, generally speaking, during the 1880s lynching was a Western and all-white phenomenon, often having to do with bands of cattle rustlers. In the 1890s lynching became a special Southern occurrence in which black men were the special victims. In the decade of the 1890s, 82 percent of the nation's lynchings took place in fourteen Southern states. In the three decades from 1889 to 1918, that proportion increased to 88 percent. Beginning in the year 1889, in the South and in the nation at large, the lynching of Negroes increased markedly and within a few years reached its height. In 1892 the number peaked at 156. The sudden and dramatic rise in the lynching of black men in and after 1889 stands out like some giant volcanic eruption on the landscape of Southern race relations. There was, indeed, something new and horribly palpable on the earth. It was signalized by the mob, the rushing, swelling fury of a mass of struggling men, the bloody and mangled bodies, and the smell of burning flesh. It would be some years before anyone would earnestly contend that actually only about one-third of the lynchings were committed for the "the new crime" (the rape of white women by black men), and many more years before Southerners at large would acknowledge that lynching was itself a crime.[17]

That the number of lynchings decreased after 1892 might be attributed primarily to a rising caution among black men that led them to avoid occasions that could possibly be twisted into a semblance of rape or an attempt at rape. Almost certainly, black men came generally to avoid being alone with white women, were careful not to meet feminine eyes with a level gaze, and guarded the tone of their voices in the presence of white females. Much more were they not inviting white women to join them in adventures in interracial sex. For this and for other reasons, from decade to decade after the 1890s the number of lynchings decreased. In the nation, at large, from 1889 to 1899, on the average, one person was lynched every other day, and two out of three were black. In the first decade of the twentieth century, a person was lynched approximately every fourth day, and nine out of ten were black, a ratio of black over white that held into the 1930s. In the second decade, one person was lynched every five days, and in the third, one every nine days.[18] In the 1930s lynching declined significantly. Still, between 1889 and 1946, a year widely accepted as marking the end of the era of lynching, almost 4,000 black men, women, and children had been mobbed to their deaths.

In the 1890s, when lynching was most prevalent, no one really knew how many rapes or attempted rapes there had been, or how many lynchings, or that the whole distressing process would end this side of disaster. Furthermore, contemporaries were keenly aware that they did not know. Looking backward from the present, it seems likely that all kinds of criminal activity, including the rape of white women by black men, was on the rise in that depression-plagued decade. Whatever the realities, it is clear that contemporaries vastly exaggerated the problem. Even heads so cool and minds so fair as that of Bishop Atticus G. Haygood, in 1893 freshly home to Georgia from California, were turned and made feverish by the seeming prevalence of such outrages. Writing for a national magazine, he declared that he personally could recall but a single case of a Negro assaulting a white female before the war. That man had been burned. Now, he recognized "the unmistakable increase of this crime," and observed that "it has become so common that it no longer surprises." Haygood cited the belief of a leading Southern Methodist editor that "three hundred white women had been raped by negroes within the preceding three months," and the Bishop thought that the editor's estimate

was low.[19] Black leaders too were perplexed. Some were driven to con-
clude that where there was so much smoke, there must be at least some
fire. They gave birth to the idea that many of the rapes had actually been
perpetrated by white men who disguised themselves with burnt cork to
sate their sexual appetites and blame black men. In 1904, George Harvey,
a leading Northern journalist, published an article on the subject in *Harper's Weekly* that by its very title, "The New Negro Crime," conceded
that rape was on the rise.[20]

Radicals were generally less philosophical and less well integrated in
their thinking about the race problem than were Conservatives. Also
unlike Conservatives, Radicals were not given to writing out elaborate
verbalizations of their ideas. They much preferred the more evanescent
performance: the impromptu talk, the lecture from the platform, the
speech on the stump, the newspaper interview, the editorial, and, later,
the oration in the halls of Congress. It seems that each vociferous Radical
soon developed a standard inventory of arguments and proofs that he
ticked off eloquently and passionately, with obvious satisfaction to himself and to the decided interest of his audience. Also, Radicals did not
have the relatively high degree of communication with one another that
Conservatives had. The result was that virtually every Radical spokesman
evinced a somewhat unique mosaic of ideas and evidences, and each
offered his case with a flourish distinctly his own. It is hardly surprising
then, that there were relatively few full and carefully written presenta-
tions of the Radical cause. On the other hand, Conservatives often seemed
driven to pour out in ink their views on the race problem, and many of
them wrote entire books on the subject.[21]

LEADERS IN THOUGHT AND ACTION

Generally speaking, leaders in Radical thought could be divided into two
groups. Some were primarily intellectuals who provided the ideas, the scientific and scholarly apparatus, and rationales for Radicalism. Often these
people were academicians in leading universities. Others led the troops,
one might say, in front-line combat.

Probably the first significant person to promote the theory of
retrogression in a scientific way was Nathaniel Southgate Shaler, a professor at Harvard University, and after 1891 the Dean of the Lawrence
School of Science. Shaler was a natural scientist, trained by the world
famous Louis Agassiz, whose chair at Harvard he assumed upon the death
of his mentor. A Kentucky gentleman and the son of slaveholders, he had
graduated from Harvard in 1862. Shaler was a man of many parts. He

was a Union officer of artillery during the Civil War, but near the end of
Reconstruction he published a series of widely read and very unflattering
articles on Radical Republican rule in the Southern states. Afterward,
hardly a year's issues of any national magazine appeared without some
contribution from his pen. He wrote about the earth and the universe,
and about the influence of the earth upon man. He wrote fiction, history,
and travelogues, and he established himself as a national adviser on higher
education. He was a tremendously popular lecturer at Harvard. His general course in geology had to be moved to a large auditorium to accommodate an admiring throng of students. Shaler had a broad and already
interested audience for whatever he might choose to say about the race
question. And he chose, again and again, to talk about it.

As early as 1884, Professor Shaler stated the retrogression theory in
an article in *The Atlantic Monthly,* one of the leading national journals.
His article wove the American race problem smoothly into the new science. Nineteenth-century science had expanded the history of the earth
and of man on the earth from a few thousand to several hundred thousand years. Shaler postulated that human behavior was not something
that was formed within the memory of man. It had, rather, evolved over
the eons. The different races, occupying different lands, had developed
different traits, and those traits were deeply rooted in time. They were, in
practical effect, fixed. White people were marked as great organizers and
builders. Black people were imitative. The restraints of slavery had kept
black people close to whites, and the imitative trait had served to make
black people sufficiently white-like to survive. With the black man freed
from slavery, Shaler predicted that "there will naturally be a strong tendency, for many generations to come, for them to revert to their ancestral
conditions." Those conditions were, of course, savage.[22] Repeatedly, during the next two decades he sounded the same theme. In 1890 he warned
whites to take care "lest the old savage weeds overcame the tender shoots
of the new and unnatural culture," and he urged scholars to undertake
studies of the black man in Africa in order to understand the true nature
of the African when he reappeared in the freedman in America.[23]

Shaler's contributions to early Radicalism were highly significant. He
gave the theory legitimacy by his position at Harvard, by his clearly superior credentials as a scientist and an intellectual, and by his perfectly
paternalistic and gentlemanly attitude toward Negroes. In 1904, two
years before his death, he fired his last important shot at the race problem
in a widely noticed book, *The Neighbor: The Natural History of Human
Contacts.* In this rather strange mixture of science and sympathy he postulated that the "currents of our fears, loves, hatred, and other streams of
instinct flow in the ancient deeply carved channels which the ages of life

of our pre-human ancestors have worn." Various peoples had cultivated various instincts, and those could not be immediately changed. Negroes, he repeated, possessed a "remarkable imitative faculty." In America they had used that talent so well that some whites had come to think that Negroes were, after all, simply white men with black skins. But it was becoming clear that such was not the case. "Here, as in the Old World, the Negroes have not only failed to exhibit a capacity for indigenous development, but when uplifted from without have shown an obvious tendency to fall back into their primitive estate as soon as the internal support was withdrawn." Slavery had offered such support. Personally, he had never heard of a case of rape in slavery, but he thought that the fact that "assaults of Negroes on white women in the South have increased since the emancipation appears to be clear." It was a common belief, he found, "that the Negro is sexually a very brutal creature who cannot be trusted in contact with white women."[24]

In 1884, Phillip Alexander Bruce, a young southside Virginia aristocrat, a graduate of the University of Virginia, and, later, editor of the state's most prestigious journal of history, published an article in the New York *Evening Post* in which he expressed the fear that Negroes were falling away from their prewar level of civilization. He used the term "regression" to describe the savage tendencies of blacks and called on Southern whites to labor to save the Negro and to supplant the Northerner as his tutor. In 1889, in a book entitled *The Plantation Negro as Freeman,* Bruce elaborated upon the regression theme. He found that young Negroes then coming to maturity approximated "more closely to the original African type than the character of their fathers who were once slaves." In the end, he thought, there would be no place for these two distinct peoples, and there would come "a sharp contest." The whites, of course, would win that contest. There were many evidences of black retrogression, but the most striking was the increasing frequency of crimes of impulse, especially that "most frightful crime," the rape of white women by black men. Bruce offered a detailed explanation of why black men were so driven. "There is something strangely alluring and seductive to them in the appearance of a white woman; they are aroused and stimulated by its foreignness to their experience of sexual pleasure, and it moves them to gratify their lust at any cost and in spite of every obstacle. This proneness of the negro is so well understood that the white women of every class, from the highest to the lowest are afraid to venture to any distance alone, or even to wander unprotected in the immediate vicinity of their homes; their appreciation of the danger being keen, and their apprehension of corporal injury as vivid, as if the country were in arms." When the attack occurred, whites were outraged, "and not unnaturally, for rape, indescribably beastly and loathesome always, is marked, in the instance of its perpetration by a negro, by a diabolical persistence and a malignant atrocity of detail that have no reflection in the whole extent of the natural history of the most bestial and ferocious animals. He is not content merely with the consummation of his purpose, but takes that fiendish delight in the degradation of his victim which he always shows when he can reek his vengeance upon one whom he has hitherto been compelled to fear; and, here, the white woman in his power is, for the time being, the representative of that race which has always over-awed him."[25]

Still another expert often quoted by Radicals was Frederick L. Hoffman, a statistician for the Prudential Insurance Company of America. In 1896 the superbly respectable American Economic Association published his study, *Race Traits and Tendencies of the American Negro*. Hoffman thought that the deterioration of the black race in the United States had been in process "ever since 1810, but less intense before emancipation than during the past thirty years." The census of 1890 admittedly counted more blacks than ever before, but, Hoffman contended, it also indicated a rapidly rising mortality among Negroes, especially among the young, "for the root of evil lies in the fact of an immense amount of immorality, which is a race trait, and of which scrofula, syphilis, and even consumption are the inevitable consequences."[26] During slavery "the negro committed fewer crimes than the white man, and only on rare occasions was he guilty of the more atrocious crimes, such as rape and murder of white females." In the 1890s that crime was increasing at an alarming rate, he thought, and "the rate of increase in lynching may be accepted as representing fairly the increasing tendency of colored men to commit this most frightful of all crimes."[27] Hoffman concluded: "All the facts brought together in this work prove that the colored population is gradually parting with the virtues and the moderate degree of economic efficiency developed under the regime of slavery. All the facts prove that a low standard of sexual morality is the main and underlying cause of the low and anti-social condition of the race at the present time." There was no relief, he decided, either in religion, education, or economic improvement, and he predicted the "gradual extinction of the race."[28]

There were a number of other scholarly contributors to Radical theory. Walter Francis Willcox, a professor at Cornell University, Chief Statistician of the United States Census, 1899–1901, and a significant influence upon the kind of statistics gathered by the Census Bureau in and after 1900, did a special study of Negro criminality. Using the census figures of 1890, he described a massive and disastrous increase in crimes committed by blacks. He presented his conclusions, which were widely quoted, at the 1899 meeting of the American Social Science Association in Saratoga, New York. At the Montgomery Conference on Southern race problems during the next year, he went on to predict the ultimate extinction of the Negro in America.[29]

Edward Drinker Cope, scion of a wealthy Philadelphia Quaker family and Professor of Zoology and Comparative Anatomy in the University of Pennsylvania, spent most of his life winning fame for his research in vertebrate paleontology. However, in the 1890s he digressed to apply his great learning to prove the inferiority of Negroes and to warn against the danger of miscegenation in the South, an event that would destroy "a large portion of the finest race upon the earth, the Whites of the South." His specific solution was the total deportation of the black population regardless of cost.[30] According to Hilary A. Herbert, a leading student of the race problem who presided over the Race Conference in Montgomery in 1900, "Professor Cope tells us that the sutures of the skull which promote growth and expansion, usually grow up, as they do not in the white man's at about the age of 14 years." Thus blacks were perpetually arrested in early adolescence.[31]

REBECCA LATIMER FELTON

Scholars such as these lent sophistication, credibility, and intellectual integrity to Radical thought, but most important was the thinking and action of those Radicals who were engaged in the front lines, in the trenches as it were, of interracial combat. As previously noted, Radicalism was an uneven and complex terrain that can only be imperfectly mapped. But let us attempt to survey that ground and, additionally, get some bearing upon how and why people were Radicalized by looking closely at the lives and works of three leading activists in the Radical movement. Rebecca Latimer Felton illustrates well the case of a woman who became a Radical. Benjamin Ryan Tillman offers the example of a Radical in politics. And Thomas Dixon, Jr., illustrates a mass leader as Radical.

Rebecca Latimer Felton (1835–1930), journalist, politician, feminist, prohibitionist, lay leader among Southern Methodists, and the first woman to become a United States Senator (in 1922 by appointment upon the death of incumbent Tom Watson), was one of the most interesting women the South ever produced. Her father, Charles Latimer, had been brought to central Georgia as a child. In Maryland, his family had been eminent planters on lands just across the Potomac River from Mount Vernon. They were, in fact, related to the Washingtons and the Fairfaxes. In Georgia, Charles married into a locally prominent family of planters.

He "married" slaves, he inherited slaves, and he bought slaves and land. In addition, he opened a store and tavern near what was to become Atlanta. Charles Latimer was a very successful businessman and by the time Rebecca was five, he could afford to organize a local school, taught, interestingly, by the uncle of Atticus Haygood. When Rebecca's education had progressed sufficiently, Charles bought a house in Decatur and established a household there for the purpose of allowing his daughter to continue her studies at "an academy of high grade." At fifteen, Rebecca enrolled in the Methodist Female College in Madison, and there she acquired one of the best educations available to a Georgia girl at that time. She completed her studies in 1852 at "sharp seventeen," married the commencement speaker, Dr. William H. Felton, at eighteen, and gave birth to her first child at nineteen. Dr. Felton settled with his bride on a plantation near Cartersville, a village on the rail line between Atlanta and Chattanooga. Working closely with his widowed father, he prospered as a planter. In 1860, between them, they owned fifty slaves, twenty-eight of whom were "prime hands," that is, they were extraordinarily productive and very valuable. Because of ill health, Dr. Felton had given up the practice of medicine, but he did devote much of his time to service as a Methodist minister.[32]

In the secession crisis the Feltons were not fire-eaters, but during the war they were loyal Confederates. At Cartersville their plantation lay alongside the railroad that supplied the Confederate Army facing the Union forces in Chattanooga. After the extremely bloody battle of Chickamauga in September 1863, Rebecca Felton did hard service tending the wounded and dying as they streamed back toward Atlanta on the trains. Young men who had gone whooping off to war, now returned, packed into car after car, lying on the floor—bloody, bleeding, and dying. When the trains paused at Cartersville to take on water and fuel, she and other women went among the men, cleaning them, swabbing feverish throats, ministering and comforting as best they could. In one car she found a young Texan, shot through the body. She wanted to take him home and care for him. He shook his head and would not go. He began to call for his mother, and Rebecca Felton felt his hand grasp hers. He was dying. She wept bitterly—and never forgave the men who made the war.[33]

Anticipating Sherman's assault upon Atlanta, the Feltons took refuge on a farm near Macon in the spring of 1864. Atlanta fell in September, and Sherman turned his army toward Savannah. In Macon, the Feltons experienced the effects of Sherman's "March to the Sea." Rebecca Felton herself soon had dramatic evidence that not all who suffered horribly were Southerners. During one cold and rainy night in December 1864, while she was trying to escape by train from Sherman's advancing forces, she passed a line of flatcars on a siding. The open platforms were loaded with prisoners of war being transferred from infamous Andersonville to some prison more remote from Sherman's line of march. She saw the skeletal bodies and haggard faces of the Union soldiers. She later recalled that by the flickering light of torches she "could look into their faces within a few feet of the train." She noted their Confederate Army guards, posted at intervals, muskets ready. On the station platform, she saw the body of a Negro shot minutes before by one of the guards for alleged impudence; "the quivers of dying flesh had hardly subsided." "I became an eyewitness," she said in regard to the Union soliders, "to their enforced degradation, filth, and utter destitution and the sight never could be forgotten." Rebecca Felton feared throughout the war the death of her only brother, nineteen and a captain at the end of the struggle, and she did suffer the death from disease of two of her children during her enforced exile. She came to appreciate the lesson Sherman had set out to teach the South—war was hell . . . hell on both sides and both sexes, and it was death to young men. She came to despise the men who had so eagerly made a war in which other men died.[34]

After the war, back on their plantation near Cartersville, the Feltons began again, almost literally, from scratch. Within a few years, they were safely beyond poverty. But by 1873, Rebecca at age thirty-eight had lost four of her five children. She bore no more, and she turned to enter public life with a verve unique among Southern women of her day. Before 1919 women in America did not vote except in scattered and special instances; but women were nevertheless in politics, sometimes through their husbands, sometimes as suffragettes and crusaders for women's rights. Rebecca Felton began politics with her husband, but she soon became herself a politician. Almost certainly she was able to perform as she did because of the unusual qualities of the men in her life. Her father had obviously taken great pains to educate his girls in a time when Southern girls were not often very well educated. At eighteen she had married a man of thirty-five. In an age in which women were to be seen and not much heard outside of the home, in a state where husbands might legally whip their wives and sell their property, each of these men was uniquely sympathetic toward Rebecca Felton's rise in public life.

In 1874, Dr. Felton, always a reformer, ran as an independent for Congress and won. During the next six years while he was a Congressman, Rebecca was always at his side, spurring on his campaigns, and writing for the press in his behalf. She lived with him in a Washington hotel filled with Congressmen, including Alexander Stephens, lately the vice president of the Confederacy. Stephens was another older man whose protégé she became. She mixed with people easily and freely, and she learned the ropes of national power. At various times, the Feltons were out-of-party Democrats, Greenbackers, proto-Populists, para-Populists, and friends and allies of Tom Watson. Rebecca actively promoted her husband's political career, and as he came to be better known, so too did she. Soon, she began to construct a public life of her own. She published often in the Georgia press, eventually generating an ardent following and her own regular column in Hoke Smith's Atlanta *Journal*. First and foremost, she fought for women's rights. But often that transcendent passion led her into other reform movements—prohibition; improved treatment of convicts, including women; the industrial education of young white women, particularly in the mountainous region of Georgia; and access for women to the pulpit of the Southern Methodist Church. In a sense, she was also a New Southite; she supported industrialization in northeastern Georgia, and herself bought successfully into mining interests there.[35]

By 1890 Rebecca Felton was well known in national circles, in part because of her close association with the political work of her husband. In that year she was appointed one of the Southern representatives on the board of "Lady Managers" of the Chicago World's Fair, to be held in 1893. Her intelligence, seemingly endless energy, and extraordinarily high organizational abilities soon earned her a significant influence in the selection and arrangement of exhibits. As a Southerner she was offended by a display in honor of Harriet Beecher Stowe, including a bust of the woman and pictures of Uncle Tom. To counter such Yankee propaganda, Mrs. Felton arranged an exhibit from the South featuring "real colored folks," doing real things like weaving mats and baskets, spinning and carding cotton, and playing the banjo, showing, as Mrs. Felton said, "the actual life of the slave—not the Uncle Tom sort." The editor of the Atlanta *Constitution,* Clark Howell, agreed to raise the money necessary to finance the exhibit, and Mrs. Felton proceeded to recruit two elderly "sober and well behaved" Negroes she knew, Aunt Jinny and Uncle Jack, to serve as the living antidote to Uncle Tom. The whole purpose, as Mrs. Felton explained to her husband, was "to show the *ignorant* contented darkey—as distinguished from Mrs. Stowe's monstrosities—to illustrate the slave days of the republic."[36]

After her return to Georgia, Felton became increasingly concerned with blacks and especially with the rising threat of the black savage to white womanhood. Her interest attracted correspondence from others of like mind. "I have Kept Steadily up with the Negro procession," wrote Leonidas F. Scott from Conyers, Georgia, in 1894, "and it will alarm any thoughtful mind to notice the awful extent of these most awful of all crimes, and notice that they excite only a 'news special' from the community where the crime is committed. If the brute is caught, if the Victim has many friends, he is lynched, if a poor white woman or girl, the law is allowed in some instances 'to take its course,' and the Sheriff complimented by the reigning governor for maintaining 'law and order' when the land is full of murder, outrage, and arson and all sorts of crime." Freed from the restraints of slavery, Scott continued, the Negro had become a curse aggravated by idleness, by "free schools with the Boston social equality attachment," and by a religion that "only affects the head." Deeply appalling was the fact, as it appeared to Scott, that "white people appear to be reasonably well satisfied to have these brutes around, leaving every home in the South, with mother, wife, sister and daughters subject every hour in the day to these brutal outrages, and this crime is alarmingly on the increase whereever [sic] the negro lives." In his own home county of Rockdale, the Negroes seemed a peaceable "Set," but, Scott cautioned, every day "they are inching towards the danger line and the teachers and preachers and negro women are so immoral that they exert no good influence over the more uneducated." The South must be alerted to the danger. "The white people seem to have forgotten that all the Old Uncles and Aunties are gone, and do not know how to figure the possibilities of the new issue. I thought that possibly you might get a chance to hit the subject a lick at some opportune time. The people of the South had better become emancipated from the negro, and practice and not preach White Supremacy."[37]

One might be tempted to think that Leonidas Scott was a lonely man living some harmless and colorful fantasy off in the piney woods by himself. Actually, he was highly active as a Baptist layman who, in 1904, became the secretary of the Home Missionary Board. In that office, he succeeded William J. Northen, the "reigning governor" who had excited his ire in 1894 by vigorously opposing lynching. The Board represented the entire Southern Baptist Church and had been headquartered in Atlanta since 1882. Thus, after 1904, the very man who was most responsible for coordinating the labors of the church among blacks thought that blacks were rapidly and inevitably deteriorating into savagery.

In the summer of 1897, Rebecca Felton was given an excellent opportunity to "hit the subject a lick," and she struck a devastating blow. She had been invited by the State Agricultural Society of Georgia (the largest, wealthiest, and most influential organization of farmers in the state) to address its annual meeting on Tybee Island, a resort near the mouth of the Savannah River. She chose to speak on ways to improve farm life and one suggestion was that farmers ought to afford more security for their women. "I warned those representative men," she recalled a year later, "of the terrible effects that were already seen in the corruption of the negro vote, their venality, the use of whiskey, the debasement of the ignorant and incitement of evil passion in the vicious. That week there were seven lynchings in Georgia from the fearful crime of rape. I told them that these crimes had grown and increased by reason of the corruption and debasement of the right of suffrage; that it would grow and increase with every election where white men equalized themselves at the polls with an inferior race and controlled their votes by bribery and whiskey. A crime nearly unknown before and during the war had become an almost daily occurrence and mob law had also become omnipotent. . . ." She called upon good men to do their duty. " . . . if it takes lynching to protect woman's dearest possession from drunken, ravening human beasts," she cried, "then I say lynch a thousand a week if it becomes necessary."[38]

To our minds, educated away from this peculiar mode of licensed law-lessness, Felton's words are shocking. But to many Southern minds, besieged by the great fear of those times, they seemed the gospel truth. In part because her words were picked up by the Northern press and she answered their attacks with her usual headlong, full-throated vigor, Felton's speech received national publicity. With wonted extravagance she concluded an exchange with the editor of the Boston *Transcript* with the charge that people such as he were inciting the "new Negro" to rape, and "that the black fiend who lays unholy and lustful hands on a white woman in the state of Georgia shall surely die!"[39] Rebecca Felton knew whereof she spoke. She, herself, had already heard the rush of a lynch mob as it swept past her country home near Cartersville.

It is ironic that Rebecca Felton had thus sown the wind in an almost incidental fashion. Actually, she had dealt with the black threat only as a part of the larger effort to improve the quality of life for farm people. But that seed, cast upon a soil fertile and already well prepared to give it nour-ishment, grew rapidly and prodigiously. Georgia was already moving into a Radical revolution in race, and Felton served eagerly to give it focus and effect. On Tybee Island, she recalled in an interview a year later, hundreds of "good, true men cheered me to the echo. . . ."[40]

Rebecca Felton was in the vanguard of a Radical element that revo-lutionized popular white thought in the South about black people during the turn of the century decades. For her the fact that black men could outrage white women at such a high rate was primarily but another evi-dence of the abuse of white women by white men. Felton was keenly alert to the violations of her sex, and she, like many other thoughtful Southern women, came to lay the blame on the heads of the leading men of the South. Her blows hit Southern men at their very roots, in their sense of themselves. The protected charged their self-styled protectors with failure at the crucial juncture.

BENJAMIN RYAN TILLMAN

In the early 1890s Benjamin Ryan Tillman (1847–1918), the governor of South Carolina, also joined the Radical vanguard. For Tillman in the 1890s the translation from thoughts to acts was nearly perfect. In South Carolina in that decade, if Tillman was not the glory, he was most decidedly the power, and his thoughts had weight. From 1890 to 1894 he was the governor, and afterward he took Wade Hampton's seat in the United States Senate, where he continued to be a highly effective political force until his death in 1918. Ben Tillman is worthy of close attention. For students of race relations, he exhibits both the making of a racial Radical and what a Radical might do with political power. For historians of politics, and particularly of politics in a populist style, he is a prime example of a much neglected type—the agrarian rebel who captured the Democratic party in his state instead of leaving it to begin another.[41]

The Tillman movement in South Carolina was, essentially, a rebellion in the usual Southern style. It was a division among the leadership rather than a surge up from the lower levels of society. Tillman and most of his lieutenants were not plain farmers and had never been such, even though in the 1880s and 1890s it was expedient to assume that guise. Like the leaders they opposed, they had participated in the "Redshirt" campaign of 1876 and 1877 that redeemed the state for home rule and founded the new establishment. However, in the 1880s they awoke with intense resentment to the fact that a clique among the Redeemer leadership had seized control of South Carolina and of the Democratic party. The ruling clique, they felt, had stolen the fruits of the victory won by them all and sold out to the business interests in the state and nation. Sometimes called "Bourbons," more often called "conservatives," the ruling ring was dominated by ex-Confederate generals Wade Hampton and Mathew C. Butler. The conservatives were, in truth, very much under the influence of commercial, banking, and industrial interests and the lawyer servants, local and national, of those interests. In South Carolina, this meant that the conservatives were deeply entrenched in Charleston and Columbia and intimately associated with cotton, railroads, and banks, and with the fertilizer and textile industries.

As the 1880s wore on, Southern agrarians of all classes found themselves trapped and relentlessly squeezed in a contracting economy. Distressed and at first unfocused, farm elements in South Carolina soon discovered a strong voice in Ben Tillman and effective organization under his leadership. The Tillman movement was, in part, a revolt of the "red necks," that is of the renters and small farmers who bore the brunt of a vast agricultural depression. But the overwhelming majority of white men in South Carolina were farmers in that style, and any political movement that succeeded—including that of the Bourbons—required their votes.

Like every other Radical leader, Ben Tillman began life as a racial Conservative. The portion of Tillman's inaugural that dealt with race relations was political, almost blandly Conservative, and could have been written by Wade Hampton himself.[42] But sometime between December 1890 and the summer of 1892 Tillman turned into the channel of Radical thinking. One evidence of his conversion to Radicalism lay in his attitude toward lynching for the crime of rape. As late as September 1891, he congratulated a sheriff who had saved a Negro prisoner from a mob and declared that "lynch law will not be tolerated."[43] However, during the gubernatorial campaign in the summer of 1892, he evinced a distinct reversal in his attitude. "There is only one crime that warrants lynching," he declared to an Aiken audience, "and Governor as I am, I would lead a mob to lynch the negro who ravishes a white woman."[44] By the spring of 1893, Tillman was quietly encouraging lynching.[45]

Ben Tillman was undoubtedly the prime mover in organizing the South Carolina Constitutional Convention of 1895 in which the chief work was the disfranchisement of black men in the state. Clearly Tillman had political reasons for his actions in this case. He relished the practical termination of Negro registration and voting by legal devices. In addition he was happy to save white men from the necessity of committing fraud and violence in stealing elections. But there were also other reasons for his behavior, and primary among these was his desire to impress firmly upon the black man his inequality with the white man. The lesson of inequality applied immediately at the polls, but its application was also general, and especially did it apply to the embrace of white women. When Tillman took the lead in disfranchising black men, he probably did so more for racial than political reasons. He was driven by the conviction that Negro retrogression was under way, manifested most awfully in the outrage of white women by the black beast rapist. Like Rebecca Felton in Georgia, he did not invent the idea. Rather he moved with a climate of opinion that swept over the state like a storm. The number of lynchings in South Carolina rose from one in 1891, to five in 1892, and to eleven in 1893.[46] Nor was Tillman the only intelligent and responsible person to succumb to the hysteria. In the convention itself Tillman was much aided by his erstwhile enemies, the conservatives. John Pendleton Kennedy Bryan, a prominent Charleston lawyer, did more than any other man to perfect the legal language of the disfranchising provisions. In the end, only two out of the some thirty conservatives in the convention voted against the new constitution.[47]

When Tillman, the agrarian rebel, went to the United States Senate in 1895, he carried the Radical brief with him. He urged Congress to do its duty by lowering the expectations of blacks. He himself struggled toward that end and, on a personal level, in his own relations with blacks, he was dramatically successful.

Tillman clearly linked the black man's expectations of political parity with his hopes for social elevation. Consequently, he urged the political reduction of the Negro at every opportunity. He opposed the appointment of Negroes to the most minor of Federal offices because in the South "we realize what it means to us to allow ever so little a trickle of race equality to break through the dam."[48] He was brutally candid in relating what South Carolina had done to Negroes in Redemption, and, by implication, what they would do again if necessary. "We took the government away," he boasted. "We stuffed ballot boxes. We shot them. We are not ashamed of it."[49] Speaking in Baltimore, in a state that had failed to disfranchise its blacks by legal means, he openly recommended a disfranchising device, the understanding clause, as "the most charming piece of mechanism ever invented." By this clause, white judges could qualify an otherwise ineligible voter by an oral examination to test his understanding. Negroes were simply asked difficult questions, he explained, and whites easy ones.[50] He repeatedly warned his colleagues in the Senate that the black peril was fully upon the nation. If encouraged only slightly, the rash young Negroes would drive for full power in regions where blacks were in the majority. Young whites would rise to face them. The inevitable result would be a war of races and, inexorably, the virtual end of the blacks. The South, he said, teetered "on the edge of a volcano."[51] In 1912, two decades after he himself had awakened to the threat of the "black brute," Tillman was still urging whites to stand to their arms.[52]

TOM DIXON AND *THE LEOPARD'S SPOTS*

As suggested above, there was no collective *Summa Theologica* of either the Conservative or the Radical mentality. It is probably significant that the one work nearest to a codification of the Radical dogma came not at all in a scholarly form, but in a novel. That book was *The Leopard's Spots,* written by Thomas Dixon, Jr., in 1902.[53] Immediately it was a best seller, and Dixon soon produced another, *The Clansman,* in the same vein. In 1905, he fused the two into a dramatic production, *The Clansman,* also a popular and lasting success. The novel *The Clansman,* finally, supplied the basic story for the film, *The Birth of a Nation* (1915). Plots, scenes, and characters changed superficially, but the racial message remained the same in all Dixon's works. Somehow the Negro had caused the Civil War, and the failure of the North during Reconstruction to recognize the rising reversion of free blacks to bestiality had continued to divide the nation. But Southern Anglo-Saxon blood had mustered its will to dominance and had redeemed itself from Reconstruction. Further by 1900 it was rapidly educating the North to the true nature of the Negro in freedom. Thus tested and tempered by the awful fires of Civil War and Reconstruction, North and South were reuniting, joining together the material genius of the North and the spiritual genius of the South to realize the promise that God had given his chosen people, white Americans, for all mankind. "The future of the world depends on the future of this Republic," one of Dixon's characters declares in an echo of Lincoln's Gettysburg Address.[54]

During the early years of the twentieth century, Dixon reached millions of people through his novels, plays, and the film *The Birth of a Nation.* He was so very effective because his work said in a total way what his audience had been thinking in fragments. His grand themes educed precisely what a vast number of people were instinctively and passionately certain was true. In Dixon's work they saw their own genius ratified, and further, glorified. Moreover, it was done and redone in forms that were forceful and exciting. Whatever the form, all of Dixon's later work on race relations merely recapitulated the statement made initially in *The Leopard's Spots.* That book, so worthy of historical notice, is virtually an encyclopedia of Radicalism, catching the movement during its apogee and weaving together into a single and simple piece nearly all of the various and complex strains of the Radical mentality.

There are two grand themes in *The Leopard's Spots:* national unity and the retrogression of the American Negro. The two are deeply interwoven. American national unity, ultimately, depended upon a full recognition of the rising bestiality of the Negro, first by the South and especially the young men of the South, and then by the North. The novel is useful in the study of black-white relations in the South because it so thoroughly captures the key elements of the Radical mentality. Dixon himself is worthy of study because he offers some understanding of how the deeply personal and largely secret psychic needs of an individual might impel that person to extreme racism.

Tom Dixon had very deep psychic needs of which he seemed unaware. He needed devils, and he needed gods. Or, rather, in his case, he needed goddesses. He found both of these outside of himself, devils in black people, goddesses in white women. He used the great power that he had as a highly talented, well placed, and superbly energetic white male in attempts to impose those roles upon those persons. In his fantasy world, he enjoyed a striking success in that effort. As students of racism in America, we are fortunate to have in Dixon a person who was exceedingly influential in the Radical movement. We also have a person who left a clear array of evidences of the psychic plight that made him a racial Radical, and that condition is representative of the psychic plight of several million contemporary white Southerners.

Thomas Dixon was conceived and born in very unusual circumstances, circumstances that were indeed linked to the death of the Confederacy and the birth of a nation. That fact, as he later asserted, deeply influenced his life. In the fall and winter of 1863, even while George Cable was riding and fighting in northern Mississippi and Alabama, while Atticus Haygood and Rebecca Felton were ministering to the stricken soldiers who had fallen defending Atlanta, and while young Ben Tillman and his mother waited anxiously on the plantation in Edgefield for news of the fate of Captain James Tillman on the front, Thomas Dixon was nearby, but still unborn. During those very bloody months, Tom, as a child in his mother's womb, crossed that same torn and worried ground upon which the two armies struggled. He was carried by an extremely anxious mother. Amanda Dixon at twenty-nine was understandably concerned about her pregnancy. She had been married at thirteen and gave birth to her only surviving child at twenty. Before the war, she and her preacher husband had taken their slaves, adventurously, to join relatives on new land in central Arkansas. Soon came the war with all its troubles, and, then, the conception of still another child. Amanda grew afraid, so far from home. The Dixons packed their things into a single wagon, took their animals and their thirty-two slaves, and began the trek homeward toward Shelby, high in the foothills of North Carolina. "This covered wagon passed between the line of Sherman & Hood's armies & was 3 months in the journey," Dixon wrote in 1927 to the widow of his elder brother Clarence. "Clarence was 9 years old. They brought their slaves with them & my Father Told me he always slept with his hand on his gun expecting to be killed by bandits or deserters every night he lay down. I was their only child born during the Civil War & it has always exercised a profound influence on my character."[55]

Tom was born early in 1864 in a farmhouse near Shelby, a village in Cleveland County, North Carolina. In that community he spent his first years, a child of prominent families through both parents. His mother's people were large planters and slaveholders in neighboring York County in South Carolina. One of his mother's brothers was LeRoy McAfee, who won first honors in his graduating class at the University of North Carolina in 1859, rose to a colonelcy in the Confederate Army at twenty-five, and died of tuberculosis during Reconstruction. After the war McAfee was a lawyer in Shelby, a prime leader in the Ku Klux Klan in Cleveland County, and young Tom's idol. Tom's parents had met in the "social life" of York County, and they had married in 1848. His father was a descendant of the first white settlers in western Carolina and the grandson of one of the leaders of the patriot forces in the battle of King's Mountain. Tom's father, Thomas Dixon, Sr., through his marriage to Amanda McAfee added substantial wealth to an excellent, if only local, reputation as a Baptist minister. At the end of the war, "Elder" Dixon freed his slaves, retaining in the household only one aged "mammy." Afterward, he managed to make a living by combining farming and the ministry. A significant part of Tom's early life was spent in tiresome and, as he saw it, dulling farm labor.[56]

During Reconstruction, the Dixons like so many others in the South were poor in the goods of this world, but they were very rich in spirit. They claimed much of the intensely immediate and personal communion with God that was the great coin of status in that very Baptist realm in western North Carolina. Most of all, the Dixons had grit, and with grit, all things were possible. Tom's father vowed that his children would have the education of which his own father's drinking and early death had deprived him. At great sacrifice, the family sent Clarence first to Wake Forest College, where he finished at the head of his class, then through the Southern Baptist Theological Seminary, which was then in Greenville, South Carolina. Clarence next filled a succession of prestigious pulpits. One of his first was that of the Baptist church in Chapel Hill, where he baptized, among others, two young students in the university, Charles B. Aycock and Locke Craig, each of whom was to become governor of the state in the early years of the twentiety century. In June 1883, when Tom graduated from Wake Forest with the most honors ever earned by any student there, including his brother Clarence, he could feel proud and secure in his own reputation and that of his family.[57]

Dixon's brilliant record at Wake Forest earned him a graduate scholarship at the Johns Hopkins University in Baltimore. In the 1880s Johns Hopkins was deliberately structured to be a congenial environment for Southern scholars, and it was to be expected that Dixon would be happy there. He chose to work with Herbert Baxter Adams, whose seminar in history and political science was patterned on the German model. The teaching methods were Germanic, and so too were the assumptions of what lay at the roots of the subjects they studied. One assumption, often called "germ theory," was that each people had a genius, some God-given seed that in time would mature and flower to enrich the world. For instance, the genius of Teutonic peoples was a capacity for cultivating self-government.

In going to Johns Hopkins, Dixon was traveling a path that many other young Southerners, soon to find national and international fame, followed after the university opened in 1876. Walter Hines Page, later publisher and diplomat, had already come and gone; John Spencer Bassett, the historian, would soon arrive. On his right hand in the very first seminar that Dixon attended, as he later recalled, sat a student only freshly arrived from Asheville, North Carolina, a young man who would become the next Southern-born President of the United States—Woodrow Wilson. Wilson was a very mature twenty-seven, Dixon only nineteen, but the two became friends. They shared a passion for the theater, and Wilson helped his youthful friend win a place writing reviews of theatrical performances for a Baltimore newspaper.[58]

Within four months, Dixon withdrew from the university and hastened to New York to study acting. Mollie Faison Dixon, Clarence's first wife, deplored her brother-in-law's fall. She had rather see Tom in the poor house, she declared, than associated "with such wicked men and women."[59] Tom soon bought his way into a traveling company that a trade paper labeled worse than a burlesque, and took to the road. While Dixon's troupe was touring through upstate New York doing Shakespeare and doing it badly, the manager absconded with the company funds. On borrowed money, Tom returned to New York and attempted still again to penetrate the world of the theater. Standing six feet three inches tall and weighing 150 pounds, so obviously youthful, it was inevitable that he would have difficulty becoming the serious actor that he wanted to be. Finally, a director whom Dixon respected convinced him that he could not then succeed as an actor, and he came home to Shelby.[60]

Warmly welcomed, the prodigal son soon redeemed himself. Dixon began to read law and, following his father's advice, sought election to the legislature even before he was old enough to vote. The forensic skills he had developed at Wake Forest, plus his tendency toward the theatrical enthralled Cleveland County voters and won him the seat over two veteran contestants. Before the assembly met, Dixon was already running for the office of speaker of the house. Only at the last moment did the older members of the legislature awaken to the danger and combine to defeat the startlingly aggressive young man. In the legislature in 1885, Dixon took an active part in pressing for progressive legislation for education and won credit for promoting the first state law for the pensioning of Confederate veterans. However, by the end of the session he was disgusted with the venality of politicians and what he considered to be the failure of his colleagues as leaders. He returned home, vowing never to partake of politics again, and continued the study of law.[61]

In 1885 Dixon went to New Orleans for Mardi Gras. There he met Harriet Bussey of Columbus, Georgia. At first accepted as a gentleman by Harriet's father and then rejected by him as a prospective son-in-law, Dixon returned to Shelby. For a time he concentrated upon his law practice. Still he could not forget the attractive Georgian. Finally he could stand it no longer. In a fever he rushed to Harriet's side, defying her father's wishes. He proposed "late one afternoon at the falls of the Chattahooche River," was accepted, "and we drove home in the twilight." The couple eloped, married, and settled in Shelby.[62]

Even as he flourished as a lawyer, Dixon grew disillusioned with the legal profession. He won the cases he should have lost, he felt, and he lost those he should have won. Decisions, he concluded, depended too much upon the lawyer and too little upon justice. The end of that career came when he worked very hard to send a man to prison for twenty years for arson, only to become convinced soon afterward of the man's innocence. Within a few weeks, he had persuaded the governor to pardon the victim of his earlier zeal. Frustrated, depressed, he journeyed to Wrightsville Beach, near Wilmington, to meditate. For more than an hour he stood high on the dunes looking out over the ocean where a storm was brewing, fixed by the beauty and power of giant waves rolling in to crash against the shore. In such a glorious display of nature he saw God and felt himself at "one with it all." Dixon then knew that he was called to the ministry. He stumbled down from the dunes a changed man. "I breathed deeply," he later wrote, "and took a new hold on life."[63]

After a brief period of study, Dixon was ordained in 1886 and took his first church in Goldsboro. Then, in April 1887 he was called to the Second Baptist Church in Raleigh. In the capital city Dixon joined a remarkable coterie of young Carolinians, including the lawyer Charles Brantly Aycock who was elected governor in 1900; Walter Hines Page the publisher; and Josephus Daniels, soon to become the state's most influential editor and publisher and later Woodrow Wilson's Secretary of the Navy. Within another six months Dixon had left the South and was in the pulpit of the Dudley Street Church in Boston. Soon after his arrival, he attended a lecture on the "southern problem" at Tremont Temple. When the speaker depicted the South as a continuing menace to the nation, Dixon sprang to his feet, denounced the accusation and its source, and very nearly caused a riot. From that time forward, he later asserted, he studied the Civil War and its aftermath with the view, someday, of telling the true story of the South. Far from casting him out for this public display of temper, Dixon's Yankee congregation relished their fiery young minister. When a call came from the Twenty-third Street Baptist

Church in New York in the summer of 1888, they offered to double his salary if he would remain.[64]

In New York, Dixon worked hard in his ministry and on his sermons. Thinking his audiences overly populated with women, he strove to make his messages intellectual and relevant to the special concerns of young men of the time. Soon his sermons came to bear directly upon the problems of the new urban environment. In this way Dixon became a pioneer in preaching the social gospel, in bringing Christianity to the new economic and social order of America. He was a highly effective evangelist. Tall, "weirdly gaunt," closely shaven, with "plentiful coal-black hair," a "strong, almost cadaverous jaw," and "black, deepset, and scintillant eyes," Dixon was impressive in the pulpit. His carefully rehearsed, controlled delivery had "an almost hypnotic effect" upon his audiences. Within a few weeks, he became tremendously popular and had to move his meetings to the auditorium of a nearby YMCA to accommodate the multitudes who came. Among those who attended was fellow Baptist John D. Rockefeller. Rockefeller began by inviting the twenty-four-year-old minister to dinner, and he ended by offering to pay for half of a one-million-dollar "temple" in the middle of Manhattan. Dixon found he was unable to raise the other half, and the project failed. Still, the imperious young Carolinian continued to preach freely and vigorously on all issues—and he prospered.[65]

Increasingly, however, Dixon chafed at the restraints of a denominational ministry. In 1895, amid a storm of criticism, he resigned from his church to create one that, he claimed, rose above the sectarian. "I believe," he announced, "it is more important to lift many men out of the ditch than to spend my time making a few men Baptists."[66] In spite of his desire to include men in his audiences, Dixon was always sympathetic to the recognition of women and he ruled that half of the Board of Deacons of his new church would be women. The "Church of the People" actually had no building, but met in the auditorium of a music academy.[67]

Sunday after Sunday, Dixon sermonized to overflow crowds upon every social issue that crossed his sights. It was as if the restlessness that had marked his life before had now found focused release. He denounced Tammany Hall. He thought that free silver and Bryan were a "bunko-steering business." He supported the vigorous and youthful reformer Theodore Roosevelt for the governorship. Soon, his new church became an American headquarters for Cuban liberation from Spain.[68] Typical of his activism was his appeal to Populist Senator Marion Butler to use his power in Congress to secure recognition of Cuban independence and to end Spanish attempts to crush the rebels in "this war on the white flag of a hospital. . . ." To delay, he warned, was "to cover our history with ignominy and hand down to our children the legacy of Cowardice, stupidity & infamy." Dixon, now thirty-two, pointed the way. "Why don't you younger men who represent the new nation get together [and] answer this cry of Humanity?" he urged.[69] His church also became a forum for social justice oratory. He brought the Populist Mary Ellen Lease, the "Kansas Pythoness," to speak; and he heaped encouragement upon Butler, a young Southerner with ambitions equal to Dixon's own and already the chairman of the national executive committee of the People's party.[70]

Before the Spanish-American War, Dixon had been ardent for Cuban liberation from Spain. But in 1898, he was an eager imperialist for the United States. He urged Butler to shift his position in the Senate to endorse the annexation of Hawaii. "Hawaii will be annexed," he predicted, "every inch of soil over which the flag is lifted as conquered territory will be held." He hoped that Butler would rise to the challenge and grasp the opportunity. "I write this to you simply from my deep regard & admiration for your talents as a Young Southerner," he confessed. "I had dreamed of the day your opportunity might come to try your fortunes for the White House."[71]

Meanwhile Dixon himself had returned to the South in a significant way. Late in 1893 on the eve of his thirtieth birthday, he developed a serious but ill-defined malady. For weeks he could not stand noises or light and lay in his bed fearing insanity and death. His physician advised a move away from the city, and the Dixons soon found a retreat in Virginia. In 1897 Dixon bought and grandly restored Elmington Manor, a fine old plantation house in Gloucester County, Virginia. At one time the estate had belonged to the aristocratic Dabneys. Dixon's lands bordered on Cape Charles, and he pursued his developing interest in boating. Finally he himself supervised the construction of one of the prides of his life, an ocean-going yacht that he named "Dixie." All of this was financed, not primarily by his New York church, but by his growing reputation after 1894 as a star on the lecture circuits. Dixon was a master orator, and he perfected a series of lectures on topics with such titles as "Backbone," "The New Woman," and "Fools." These appealed unerringly to his audiences. By the turn of the century he was much in demand and earning a thousand dollars for a night's performance. He developed a pattern of preaching in New York on Sunday, retreating to Elmington Manor until mid-week, then lecturing at night and traveling by day until he needed to return to New York for his Sunday service.[72] The fact that he could range far out into the Midwest in his circuit was a comment on the rising efficiency of the American railroad passenger system of the day. Finally, in 1899, he gave up his New York church and never took another.[73] Popular, affluent, connected with important persons, with a beautiful wife, three children, and an elegant Virginia estate, Thomas Dixon, Jr., was living, it would seem, an idyllic life.

Early in 1901, while he was on a lecture tour, Dixon happened to attend a stage production of *Uncle Tom's Cabin,* the 1852 antislavery story that won such an amazingly long life in America. Incensed at the libel against the South (as he had been by the lecture at Tremont Temple in Boston more than a decade before), he resolved at once to write a reply in the form of a novel. All during that year, while he continued to tour the lecture circuits, he put together a thousand or so pages of notes he had gathered on Reconstruction and planned out the novel. Then, in sixty days of intensive writing, he produced *The Leopard's Spots.* Without revision, he mailed it off to an old friend from his Raleigh days, Walter Hines Page. Page had recently joined in the formation of Doubleday, Page, and Company and was rapidly becoming one of the most creative, influential, and successful American publishers of his time. Page began to read Dixon's manuscript at breakfast one morning. He was so fascinated by the story that he continued to read as he walked down Fifth Avenue toward his office. Absorbed, he was knocked down at an intersection by a passing cab. Retrieving the crumpled and soiled manuscript, he continued to read as he walked to his office. When he finished, he sent an enthusiastic telegram to Dixon, inviting him to come to New York to sign the contract. Dixon did so, and in March 1902, the book appeared. Within a few months, it had sold over 100,000 copies. Eventually, nearly a million copies were printed—roughly one copy for every eighty Americans.[74]

THOMAS DIXON'S COMPLAINT

Dixon became a Radical and wrote *The Leopard's Spots* because he had a very deep emotional problem. Rightly or wrongly, Dixon's complaint was that his mother had been sexually violated as a child, and he was not able to cope with that thought. This is evident in a letter he wrote to his sister-in-law, Helen C. Dixon, in 1927 when he was sixty-three years old. Helen was the second wife of his older brother, Clarence. She was gathering information on the family history for a biography of Clarence, who had died in 1925. Arguing mildly with Helen over his mother's age, Dixon pled a case for a specially intimate relationship between himself and his mother. In Dixon's mind, that intimacy was closely associated with a certain period in his life. "I know I am right about mother's age," he insisted. "She and I were perhaps more intimate *friends* than any other group in the family. When her nervous system collapsed during her change of life, the burden of the house fell on my boy shoulders. Clarence was at College. During this period of tragic Shadow *I* Kept the house, made the beds, swept & Kept it clean & my father & I sat up all night with her for many pitiful months—he sat up till 1 o'clock and I from 1 till dawn. I was a very little boy but 8 years old at first and the most vivid & terrible memories of my life are the black hours outstretched by her bedside. When in her delirium she would say terrible things I would put my hand on her mouth, cry & beg her to not talk. She would often awake into calmness—herself quite—& tell me to go to bed—which of course, I couldn't do. In one of those vivid times of mental upheaval she repeated a scene with her own mother (long since dead) which could only have been from memory in which she bitterly upbraided grandmother for marrying her—taking her out of school & forcing her into marriage before her *mensus* had appeared—and She repeated again & again the fact that she was barely 13 years old. I have always been sure that this premature marriage was the underlying physical cause of her pitiful collapse in her menopause." Dixon went on to explain that his mother's failure came "after 4 months of menstrual flooding which the doctor was unable to stop." In the same letter, he described the trying times that his mother and the family had endured in the months before his birth, their trip in the winter of 1863–64, across the dark and bloody ground between Arkansas and North Carolina, and the imminent danger of violence from brigands and deserters. The circumstances of his birth, he was certain, had "always exercised a profound influence on my character."[75]

Helen Dixon soon discovered that Tom had not been "a very little boy but 8 years old" at the time of his mother's collapse. He had been twelve. She challenged him on that fact. He conceded but went on to make the point that his mother's illness followed closely after the birth of his youngest sister, Addie. "She was 52 years old when Addie was born & eighteen when the first baby came—which she told me was *five* years after her marriage."[76] After further research, Helen found Tom once more in error. His mother was in fact forty-one at the time of the birth of her last child and subsequent breakdown. Challenged again, Tom replied defensively. Frustrated, seemingly exasperated, he stressed what he obviously thought were the essential truths in the matter. "My mother was married 10 years before her first children [were] born & three children died, I think before Clarence was born." He admitted that he might have been mistaken about his mother's age at the time of her collapse, and closed the correspondence with a very revealing spurt of words. "Of one thing I am absolutely sure—She married my father in her 13th year," he declared. He heavily penciled over the "3" again and again. "She told me this so many times—and reported it so often in her delirious hours I couldnt be mistaken. Why not leave out the attempt to fixed calendar dates? It never seemed to me of any importance. . . . Frankly I think they cumber a Story & make it less interesting. If I were you, I would omit the dates & get the Spirit of the story in your own mind into the *heart* of the reader.[77]

Clearly, in Dixon's mind there was the conviction that his mother had been ill-used by a premature marriage and early attempts at childbearing. Dixon's impressions are supported by the facts evident in the family history. In 1847, Amanda at thirteen was married to Thomas, Sr., at twenty-seven. She then suffered a succession of miscarriages or infant deaths, perhaps three, before Clarence survived in 1854. It was usual in that time for healthy women of childbearing capacity to deliver a child every two years. Some nine years after the birth of Clarence, in the very eye of the storm of war, Tom was conceived and born to a highly apprehensive mother. He was delivered on January 11, 1864. Two years later on February 9, 1866, his brother Frank was born, followed by sister Delia in 1872, sister Addie in 1876, and a collapse. Indeed, it does seem that his mother had been married prematurely, and subsequently had suffered an unusually painful history in the birth of her children. This impression is strengthened by other facts. According to Helen in her biography of Clarence, the aunt of the child-bride lived with the couple "for some years at the beginning of their life together" and managed the household. Further, young Mrs. Dixon spent so much of her time by herself devouring romantic novels that her husband was forced to express his disapproval. Nevertheless, so thoroughly romantic was she, that she named her first surviving child Clarence, not after her husband or some respected kin, but after one of her fictional heroes. It remained for the second son to inherit the name of his father. Helen Dixon, in her book, did not give Amanda's age at the date of the marriage. "Girls of the sunny South are apt to mature early," she said brightly, rushing past the fact of Amanda's youth. As if in extenuation of the still unconfessed truth, she described Amanda as "tall," "handsome," "much overgrown for her age," and "brimming over with the spirit of romance" while "in her teens."[78] It was true that women in the antebellum South did often marry young. It was not uncommon for girls of seventeen and sixteen to marry. But fifteen-year-old brides were rare, fourteen remarkable, and thirteen even then, as now, a curiosity.

Tom Dixon seemed unable to suppress in his own mind the knowledge that the youthful innocence of his mother had been violated. Nor was he able to forget what appeared to be the awful consequences of that violation. But who was the violator? Who was the guilty party in the assault upon his mother? Was it the mother who pulled the girl unwilling and unready out of school and pressed her into the embrace of a man fully matured before she had become a woman? In his letter to Helen, Tom quickly dismissed the grandmother as "long since dead" at the time of Amanda's collapse. Was it Tom's father, the man who over those first years had inspired perhaps as many as three dangerous and painful disasters in his child-bride before an infant finally survived? Clearly, Tom Dixon was a child of the Victorian age when society and religion combined to insist that fathers knew best and must be honored by their offspring. In Tom there was no sign of remarkable hostility toward his father. There was a rather ordinary resentment that, on one occasion, his father had whipped him too severely for procuring whiskey for his paternal grandmother against the explicit orders of his father. And there was a show of independence made in Tom's scandalous infatuation with the stage. Far from attacking his father, Tom overtly revered the man. On the other side, it appears that he never quite won the kind of approval from his father that he wanted. By entering the ministry, he finally did precisely what his father had done, what his older brother had done, what his younger brother did later, and what his father had wanted him to do. With that step, he recalled, "I breathed deeply and took a new hold on life."[79]

On the other hand, Tom was distinctly hostile to his brother Clarence. That hostility exceeded the usual sibling rivalry and stood in contrast to his highly protective attitude toward his younger brother and two sisters. Possibly Tom made a scapegoat of his older brother because, first, Clarence was the only living child born before himself and hence a convenient physical symbol of the abuse of his mother in her early marriage, and, second, because Clarence was away when he was most needed both by his mother and by Tom during her collapse. If Clarence, then twenty-one, had come home, the keeping of the house and the night watch over his mother might not have fallen so heavily upon his "boy shoulders." Later in life, Tom apparently competed with Clarence, embarrassed him sorely, and outrightly assaulted him verbally. At Wake Forest, the college that his father had wanted to attend but could not because his own father drank to excess, Clarence had won the highest honors in his class. Tom followed Clarence to Wake Forest and won more honors than anyone else up to that time. Signally, he won the Orator's Medal while still a freshman, whereas Clarence had won it only as a senior.[80] When Tom went off to Johns Hopkins in the fall of 1883, it happened that Clarence had just moved to Baltimore to take his first metropolitan pulpit. Clarence was already a striking success in life. He was well on his way to a progression of celebrated pulpits and a national reputation as a staunch defender of religious conservatism. Indeed, he would become the founding editor of *The Fundamentals,* a series of publications from which the twentieth-century fundamentalist movement gets its name. Tom not only went to Baltimore, he also moved into the house with Clarence and his wife Mollie. Almost immediately he began to embarrass them by attending the theater and writing about it in the newspapers. Then he deserted not only Southern Baptist orthodoxy but respectability and morality as well by quitting school and striking out for New York and the sinful stage. In the 1890s, in New York as a minister of the social gospel preaching that the church must go to the people where they are, he finally descended to attacking his brother in the public press for his theological and social conservatism. It was, perhaps, not entirely coincidental that at that time Clarence was minister to a prestigious congregation in nearby Brooklyn.

Tom's attacks on Clarence were unfair and vicious. In his own mind, Tom excluded Clarence entirely from caring for their mother while she was passing through those very dangerous straits of the change of life. He and his father each alone, were the nurses, he insisted. Actually, according to Helen Dixon, it was decided that Amanda's illness was not serious enough for Clarence, a seminary student in Greenville, South Carolina, at the time, to make the short trip home. Further, Tom exaggerated the time span of the illness and, by implication, the seriousness of Clarence's defection. Tom said it lasted "many painful months," whereas Helen found that it lasted only a few weeks.[81] Somehow, he failed to mention that there were three younger children in the house at this point, as if he were her only child. In later life he was usually highly supportive of and deeply paternal toward his junior siblings. He tried very hard to find Frank a good pulpit, and he encouraged him to final success on the lecture circuits. He was very helpful to Delia in her long and ultimately successful struggle to become a physician, the first woman in North Carolina to do so. As late in life as 1927, Dixon was still unwilling to give his older brother much credit with his mother in a biography to be penned by a fond and intelligent widow. Instead, her inquiries brought forth a rush of bitter and rather sanguinary thoughts—fantasies—lives that were never lived.

Ironically, it seems that Dixon ultimately blamed himself more than anyone else for his mother's plight. At one level it was almost as if his guilt derived simply from being born, of having jeopardized his mother's life merely to possess his own. More speculatively, perhaps it sprang from some minor fact and some major fantasy in the child's mind related to his mother's collapse. Perhaps he blamed himself for some failing in his mother's sickroom in the midst of night when she raged in fever and delirium and he was a child of twelve, frightened, frustrated by his inadequacy in the emergency, and alone. Perhaps, the child simply could not cope with the specific nature of his mother's illness. He associated her physical condition with her delirious raving about being married too early in life. He sought thereafter to protect her, not only in the present and in the future, but in retrospect as well. At another level, perhaps he even went so far as to project himself into his father's place as his mother's lover because if he were his mother's lover he would have saved her from all that. In his mind, eventually, his mother became all white womanhood, and to protect her from attack was to protect all women from attack upon their sex. If defenses failed, and there were violators, then the violators must be punished —including even himself.

As an event in the life of Thomas Dixon, *The Leopard's Spots* was an attempt by him to achieve a psychic cure. As an event in race relations in the South, the book represented a great leap forward in the popular promotion of Radicalism. The conjunction was fortuitous. Dixon was a person who needed a devil, and Radicalism gave him that devil ready made. It remained only for him to turn the instrument to the special purpose of his own salvation.

In 1902 when Dixon sat down in his log cabin study behind Elmington Manor to write out his novel, Radicalism was gaining popularity and power. Indeed, at the very time that Dixon began writing, a constitutional convention was meeting in Richmond to decide whether or not to disfranchise the Negro. The delegates from the east, where Dixon lived, were vigorously, almost violently, in favor of the total disfranchisement of blacks, and that position reflected the racial feelings of their white constituents. Eastern Virginia in 1902 had fallen into the Radical hysteria.

By 1902 Dixon himself had come to something of an impasse in his life. He was thirty-eight, and he had not yet found himself. Outwardly, he was a highly successful man, but so were many others. His chance of making his special mark on the world, of doing something truly and historically grand was slipping away. He had searched in vain for a key to greatness. He had played at national and international politics, but had found no place to stand in order to move the world. Now his life was closing down to the comparatively little worlds of a shadow ministry, the lecture circuit, and the lord of Elmington Manor. Others might have relished life in those realms, but Tom Dixon was a driven man. Becoming a novelist was a way of breaking out yet again, of not closing down his chances for greatness in life, of keeping the game going, and of keeping what was probably a truly Napoleonic ambition alive.

The Leopard's Spots is Thomas Dixon. It is his life as seen by himself looking backward from the high ground of Radicalism in 1902. It is an impressionistic story, quickly and loosely drawn, very imperfect in historical detail, a mixture of fact and fancy, told very much like a patient on the psychiatric couch, trying for the first time to put his life into a single frame. The author was strangely ambivalent about his finished manuscript. He vacillated a few days and then impulsively mailed it to his friend Walter Hines Page in New York. He was obviously anxious about it, elated by its acceptance for publication, and deeply distressed by the first cover, which he saw only after publication. Rather than the tobacco plant he had wanted, it featured a hangman's noose. Dixon reacted instantly. He telegraphed his publishers to withdraw all copies at his expense. They dissuaded him, changed the cover, and Dixon, elated, entered his new career.

For Thomas Dixon, writing *The Leopard's Spots* was a sort of attenuated ink blot test. The image held up was the South in the nation after the Civil War. Into his interpretation of that image, Dixon poured a lifetime of emotion, and at least a dozen years of travel, observation, and brooding about himself and his society. Through it all, the characters are rearranged and moved to suit Dixon's own psychic needs. It was his fantasy life, his dream life, the life he felt he should have been living all along. The actual writing was a way of reliving his life as in retrospect he would have it.

Central to this psycho-play was the setting of himself aright in relation to his mother. Simultaneously, however, he set himself aright with the South. Under the circumstances, it is perfectly understandable that Dixon should have been disturbed by the unfortunate sex and child-bearing life of his mother and frustrated because social convention prevented his expressing his feelings against his father and grandmother as the persons most responsible. *The Leopard's Spots* functioned as a vehicle by which Dixon discharged a great store of aggressive potential, partially resolved his feelings of guilt, and repaid in some measure an imagined debt to his mother. As an attempt at psychic self-cure, it was a brilliant, disingenuous performance in which, in brief, Southern white maidenhood substituted for his mother, the black beast rapist was a surrogate for her never named violator, and the violator in the person of the black beast was horribly punished.

Dixon was programmed for Radicalism. He was pre-set to see and eagerly to use the black beast rapist for his own salvation, to make himself whole and well-placed in the moral universe. He might have found other scapegoats, other devils, He might have become violent against the new immigrants, Catholics, drink, or goldbugs. In later times he might have seen the devil in anti-Semitism, or in Fascism or Communism. In still later times, he might even have seen the beast in white racism and become, ironically, a liberal idolizing blacks and damning Southern whites as devils incarnate. In emotional terms, Tom Dixon was a loaded gun, cocked, and ready to fire in any direction. But popular Radicalism offered him precisely the devil he needed when he needed it, the black satyr, the beast with cloven hoof, a scape*goat,* and Dixon quickly embraced the idea and made it his own.

The Clansman, his second novel on Reconstruction, replayed the same grand themes exhibited in the *The Leopard's Spots.* He wrote the manuscript in thirty days in 1905 after sifting through more than five thousand books and pamphlets. Within a few months *The Clansman* sold more than a million copies.[82] Dixon reworked *The Clansman* into a play in the same year, 1905, in which it was published. The play had its premiere in Norfolk, Virginia. Dixon joined the first road tour of the play to offer, from the stage at the conclusion of each performance, a talk explaining his work. In Norfolk, in the heart of black belt Virginia, the play and the speech were enthusiastically received. At the next performance, in Richmond, it was also loudly applauded, but conservative newspapers were critical of its extreme racism. The company performed throughout Southern and Midwestern America and, while it drew conservative fire rather steadily, it was clearly a popular success. Toward the end of the year Dixon returned to New York to organize another company to play *The Clansman.* Early in 1906 he brought his play home to Shelby, where, of course, it received a tremendous ovation. However, there was at least one dissenter. His father thought that "once or twice you bore down a little too hard on the Negro. He wasn't to blame for the Reconstruction." Tom answered that he had tried to make that point, but the elder Dixon responded, "I wish you had made it a little plainer. You couldn't make it too strong."[83] That probably was the cruelest cut of all. When Clarence had written very critically of the inflammatory quality of *The Leopard's Spots* four years before, Tom had answered with verve and heavy sarcasm. "I assure you I cherish no hard feelings toward you," he began, "I've quite made up my mind always to love you as my 'big brother' in spite of your hideous theology." However, he admitted that he was a bit hurt by Clarence's accusation that he wrote the thing for money. He did do it for money, he said, but only in the sense that Clarence preached for money. To a charge from his brother that he had been neglecting family prayers, he replied that "I don't have family prayers." "I confess," he continued, "that as I grow older, those things bore me more and more—all *formalism* does."[84]

Both companies of *The Clansman* continued to circulate through America during the next several years, and Dixon came to the idea that he might after all succeed in the world of the theater, one of his first great passions. In 1907 he turned *The One Woman* into a successful play, as he did two of his later books, *The Traitor* (1907) and *The Sins of the Father.*

The last opened in Wilmington, North Carolina, in 1910. After the performance, the cast decided to go bathing at Wrightsville Beach, the scene of Tom's earlier enlightenment, with the result that a passing shark chanced to eat the leading man. Who then was to play the part of the hero suddenly vacated by the collision of the unfortunate actor and a hungry fish? Tom Dixon, of course. Thus it was that Dixon's great ambition to be an actor was fulfilled. During the next forty weeks he traveled and acted the hero in his own play, and then, tiring of the provinces, he returned to New York for more ambitious roles.[85]

Meanwhile, in 1905 Dixon had moved his home from Elmington Manor back to New York to a mansion on Riverside Drive. Over the next several years he worked as a novelist, producer, playwright, director, sometimes actor, and financier. He lost a fortune speculating in cotton futures and in the stock market crash of 1907. However, he quickly amassed another fortune through a steady large stream of productivity.[86]

In 1912 Dixon attempted to translate *The Clansman* into a motion picture but failed. In 1913 he sold the film rights to a company in which David W. Griffith proved to be the cinematic genius. The price was 25 percent of whatever profits the company might make. In a few weeks of intensive labor, Dixon helped produce a script that Griffith took, with other materials, to Los Angeles to make the film. The story in the movie was basically that of the novel, with touches added from other pieces of his fiction. The magnificent artistry of the film is clearly Griffith's but, no less clearly the story is essentially Thomas Dixon's.

In February 1915, Dixon went to a theater in New York to preview the film version of *The Clansman*. Before that production, moving pictures in America had been short and rarely rose above the burlesque. Griffith not only made the first lengthy film developing a full story line, he was also the first to use the montage, the iris (circular) frame, the dissolve, and the close-up. He also made full and imaginative use of music. Performed by an orchestra in each theater where the production was shown, some of the music for the motion picture was adapted from black folksongs, but much of it was Wagnerian, taken from *Die Walküre* and *Rienzi,* as well as Bellini's *Norma.* In one dramatic sequence, the Klan rode to the super-masculine pounding of "In the Hall of Mountain King."

The experts had predicted failure for the film, and the showing in New York was a desperate attempt to enlist the support of the few score influential theater people invited. Dixon, fearing the worst, retreated to the balcony with the intention of slipping quietly away afterward.

After the showing, with grave misgivings as to the reactions of the others, Dixon came cautiously down the stairs. In the lobby, he found an excited, bubbling enthusiastic crowd. Suddenly elated, he saw Griffith across the room. "This is bigger than *The Clansman*," he shouted to the director. It deserved a better name! The better name was *The Birth of a Nation*.[87] It was not merely superb showmanship that led to that better name. In Dixon's mind, birth, sex, and blood, life, soul, and nation were all intimately and intricately linked, and that rather sanguinary net held the core of being. The birth of a nation was the very heart of what Dixon had been talking about since 1902, and, more, it was his life. Up in the balcony, he had again just saved a larger than life American white woman from the monstrous black beast. He had saved a whole nation of people from division and racial damnation and given them life. With all of that, he had redeemed himself anew. He was transported, ecstatic. It is ironic that *The Birth of a Nation,* a film that did make history, was, in its origin, simply the birth of Tom Dixon.

Using his personal friendship with Woodrow Wilson, Dixon arranged, early in 1915, for *The Birth of a Nation* to be viewed by the President, his cabinet and their families in the East Room of the White House. Afterward, President Wilson made the totally apt remark that the film "was like writing history with lightning." Unfortunately, he added his opinion that "it is all so terribly true."[88] On the very next evening, Dixon set up a special showing for the justices of the Supreme Court and invited members of Congress, Chief Justice Edward Douglass White having been a Klansman in his youth. The film had been under heavy fire for its racist content, but with these seeming endorsements arranged by Dixon it entered a very vigorous early life.

Dixon died in 1946, but *The Birth of a Nation* lived on, a monument without inscription. Never without opposition, it was nevertheless tremendously popular. In attendance, it was not surpassed until the film *Gone with the Wind* appeared in 1939. In recent times, very few Americans recognize the name of Thomas Dixon. On the other hand, very few would not recognize at least vaguely the title *The Birth of a Nation,* and many would know something of its racial meaning. Moreover, the film has experienced recurrent revivals, lamentably in part because those revivals mirror the fact that Dixon's world is not yet dead in America. It seems apparent that whatever Dixon did for himself in creating the story in the film, he gave a significant portion of white America precisely what it wanted. Unwittingly, he told a story deeper than he ever imagined, a story about sex and race.

Even today it remains difficult to imagine that a vast part of the leadership in the turn-of-the-century South could actually have embraced the Radical mentality. Contemporary Conservatives tried to ignore Radicalism, hoping that with time it would go away. Later, Southern liberals and historians tried to dismiss manifestations of Radicalism as aberrations, extravagances incidental to economic and political machinations and unworthy in themselves of serious attention. Along with the studied neglect of Radicalism and its effects there went a studied neglect of those who espoused the doctrine. For years the tendency has been to dismiss Radicalism as the work of a scattering of mavericks, maniacs, and demagogues of lowly origins and to recognize the Radical ideas of some otherwise admirable leading men and women with the apology that they were odd in that single way, or that years of frustration in the good causes finally drove them forgivably mad. But the truly surprising thing is that Radicals and Radicalism can be found in every Southern state, and that, far from being mavericks, madmen, and malefactors drawn from the dregs of society, the leaders of the Radical movement were the ordinary leaders in their communities and, as such, largely representative of the hearts and minds of their people.

CHAPTER IV

In Violence Veritas

Thus far we have talked about Radicalism in terms of leadership. Now let us begin to consider Radicalism at the popular level. There were an infinite number of ways in which Radicalism manifested its presence among the white masses, but easily the most visible was the syndrome of violence. In these encounters whites revealed their racial feelings with a fullness and a veracity that they did not always exhibit otherwise. Often in life the Latin phrase "in vino veritas" is apt; in race relations in the South "in violence veritas" is more than apt.

POPULAR RADICALISM

Radicalism was, of course, politics, economics, religion, and everything else, but it was in a major way a phenomenon in social psychology. For instance, it was not primarily for political, economic, religious, class, geographic, or philosophical reasons that Thomas Dixon became a Radical and wrote the deeply racist diatribe that is *The Leopard's Spots*. It was rather because his own personal psychology required that act—or some such act. The array of human qualities that drove Dixon so forcibly toward Radicalism doubtlessly thrust thousands of other white Southerners with similar psychological needs into the same path. Many of these men and women had been children during the Civil War when great numbers of fathers left home for the war and many never returned, when starvation became a real possibility, and powerlessness in the face of a despicable enemy was risingly the rule. Moreover, these people, like Tom Dixon, were the children of a Reconstruction in which all of these things persisted in some degree, and to which was added the menace of the freed slave, presumably ready for a vengeance that matched the cruelty suffered in slavery. In retrospect, it seems not so strange that the adult of later life should be forced to pay some tax for the sad plight of himself as a child, and that these children as adults should seek and find around 1900 a long-needed fulfillment in imagining a North that no longer threatened from abroad and in the discovery of a formidable enemy at home who, by an exercise of will, could be lynched and killed. In 1900 Southern whites of the middle generation might well feel that they had regained, at last a power over their lives and persons that their fathers and mothers had lost.

At the mass level, it was as if Radicalism were a current of thinking joining with currents of Conservatism and Liberalism to form a large stream of racial thinking flowing like a river through time in the composite mind of the white South. With a great rush and turbulence, Radicalism, after 1889, pressed down into the mainstream, swelling its volume and speeding its flow. During its high time, between 1897 and 1907, Radicalism was a very broad current in the whole of white racial thought in the South, and it stood out in sharp distinction from the remainder of that stream. If one could quantify popular thinking, if one could somehow weigh for duration and intensity every thought about blacks that passed through every white mind in the South between 1897 and 1907, most of those thoughts would have reflected the Radical mentality, and hence Radicalism would have outweighed Conservatism. Possibly those dates might be extended backward into 1889 and forward into 1915 without tipping the scales in the opposite direction. After 1907, however, the current of Radicalism began to lose its distinctive color as it mixed and flowed with the whole stream. By the end of 1915 it was lost from sight. It ceased to be a separate current, and Radicalism as a mentality, as a thought-set, died. The river was now again essentially Conservative, flowing smooth and wide, the father of Southern racial waters. Subsequently, Radicalism was all but forgotten. Still, its parts had mixed thoroughly with the whole stream, giving it a new complexion and a different constitution from any that had gone before. Radicalism changed the nature of race relations in the South in a physical way. But even more important it changed them in a ideational way. Finally, it was, as we shall see, a vital part of a drastic change in the whole broad course of Southern culture.

As popular thought, Radicalism was distinctly a black belt phenomenon. Its major geographical outlines can be described accurately enough in terms of racial ratios. Whites in areas one-third or more black tended to be Radicalized. When the proportion of blacks rose above the two-thirds mark, Radicalism continued to prevail as thought, and perhaps even became more intense, but it seemed in these areas to be slightly less vociferous, less physical, and less overtly violent in its manifestations.

Radicalism was also marked by the way in which state boundaries fell across the black belts. In 1890 in South Carolina, Georgia, Alabama, Mississippi, and Louisiana, blacks outnumbered whites 3,528,000 to 3,377,000. In these five contiguous lower South states, where the proportion of Negroes to whites ran highest, Radicalism tended to dominate white thinking throughout each state. Radicalism, then, prevailed in the hill counties where whites might outnumber blacks ten to one, and it also ruled racial matters in the lower, "piney woods," swampy, and "wiregrass" counties where blacks were not numerous. Official and unofficial institutions in these states—educational, judicial, penal, political, economic, and religious—came to be informed by the Radical persuasion. To be a Mississippian or a South Carolinian was ipso facto to be a Radical or else to be alone in one's racial views. In the deep South, where the power lines of traditional statehood encompassed the great mass of black Americans, lay the heartland of Radicalism.

There were also Radical areas in what might be called the "whitebelt" states, those lying generally north and west of the deep South. These areas contained a high proportion of blacks in the population. As might be expected, it was in these areas that slaves had been most numerous in the antebellum period. These included eastern Texas, eastern Arkansas, western Tennessee, and, in Kentucky, regions centering on Louisville and Lexington (the bluegrass country). In the east, Radicalism also prevailed in northern Florida, in the eastern portions of North Carolina, Virginia, and Maryland, and up into southern Delaware. Oklahoma, with its mixture of Indians, Negroes, Kansas Yankees, and deep South Southerners, was a special case. But there too Radicalism was rampant in the "little Dixie" section in the southeastern part of the state.

The habitats of racial mentalities coincided with racial ratios, but one might also think of race relations in this time in ecological terms. In the 1880s there was a relative stability in the interracial environment, both in the actual physical relationships between blacks and whites and in the thoughts that persons of each color had about the other. The balance was only slightly disturbed by the Liberal revolt. In and after 1889, a new organism, Radicalism, appeared. Whenever white encountered black, in body or in mind, Radicalism strove to dominate that contact, to feed upon it. As Radicalism grew rapidly stronger it engrossed the available food supply. Every thought, every act in race relations tended to become Radical. Other organisms, other patterns of interracial thought, Conservative or Liberal, deprived of food, withered and wasted away. Once Radicalism won dominance in the social ecosphere, it jealously denied the breath of life to any alternative. Thus, the racial ecologies of the black belts of the South were profoundly altered. Where Radicalism lived, it throve; and it ruled with force and fire. But it did need a special kind of food to survive—the vision of the menacing black male. When that image was lost to white minds, Radicalism perished.

For Radicals, the "Negro problem" was how to control the blacks as they passed through bestiality and into extinction. Radicals often saw the solution as a two-sided effort in education. Negroes must be thoroughly educated to the rule of white supremacy, and the great mass of whites must be brought to an active understanding of the true nature of racial affairs. All too often blacks could only learn by force. That, after all, was the nature of the beast. The ultimate test of racial intelligence among the mass of whites, then, was their readiness to do violence upon black men—to do with deliberate speed the swift and certain violence of rushing the black monsters to their awful end whenever needed. In the Radical years, white violence assumed two essentially new and highly significant styles: lynching and rioting.

LYNCHING

The lynching of Negroes by whites in the South has indeed had a strange career. During slavery, Negroes had been lynched, especially after about 1830. But, even then, it was not at all common, and lynching was by no means reserved for blacks. In Reconstruction there were assaults by gangs of whites upon Negroes as individuals, but the pattern differed from what came later. These early attacks were often in response to trivial abuses— an alleged breach of contract, a verbal insult, a push on the sidewalk, or the display of weapons—and rape or the threat of rape played no extraordinary role. Further, white vengeance, even at the height of Ku Klux activities, was often satisfied with whippings that were graded in severity more or less to match the seriousness of the alleged offense. Atrocious as such punishments were, they stopped short of murder. Negroes were killed by whites in Reconstruction, but when this happened, they were usually shot to death instantly, without torture, without ceremony, and because they happened to be black, not because of some alleged individual transgression. It is interesting that the ubiquitous punishment of slavery, whipping, persisted through Reconstruction. It was almost as if white men reared under the peculiar institution were incapable of innovation in doing physical harm to blacks. The ultimate in studied violence against black people, death by lynching, had to wait for a new generation of young whites to grow to adulthood. Like the "new Negro," perhaps the "new whites" had not enjoyed the "civilizing" effects of slavery. Radicals did not feature blacks as children, of course, and certainly not as their children. In Radical eyes, whipping for blacks was not the ultimate punishment.

For a generation after the Civil War, Southern whites seemed to have no greater fear of black men as rapists than they had of white men committing the same crime. What they did fear, and feared immensely during the first few years after emancipation, was black insurrection, a massive and horrendous upheaval in which vast numbers of whites—men, women, and children—would suffer and die from the black rage.[1] With the rise of Radicalism came the new fear, the fear of the Negro as rapist. With both came interracial violence in a distinctly different mode from any that had gone before. Whites began the practice of lynching as a reaction against the presumed threat of the black beast to white womanhood, but it soon became an appalling habit, applicable to a wide range of offenses, real or imagined.

One of the most striking aspects about the lynching phenomenon was, as we have seen, the suddenness of its appearance in and after 1889 as a distinctly interracial happening in the South. In 1888 there was little indication that in the following year the hysteria would be sweeping through the black belts of the South. Witness, for example, the personal transformation of Marion Butler. Butler, as mentioned before, became the chairman of the national executive committee of the Populist party in the 1890s. In 1889 he was a recent graduate of the University of North Carolina and had become the editor of the Clinton (Sampson County) *Caucasian*. Sampson County was significantly black, with more than one-third of its population Negro. The *Caucasian* itself, as its name suggested and its banner line candidly declared, was devoted to the cause of white supremacy. But the white supremacy to which it referred was that special style that ended Reconstruction. By 1889 that style of racism was rapidly becoming antique, like the Bourbons who represented it in the nation's capital. However, in Sampson County in that crucial year, Butler's own editorials began to add a sharp new cutting edge to the traditional racial sword. In September, he recommended to his readers Nathaniel S. Shaler's thinking on the Negro. "Prof. Shaler (of 'Cambridge')," he said, "considered that the negro was elevated under the conditions of slavery and he [is] losing that elevation under the experiment of citizenship—sinking back to the conditions of barbaric Africa. Prof. Shaler is the author of the new and probably correct theory for explaining the unprogressivism of the negro, namely that his animal nature so preponderates over his intellectual and moral natures, that in the age of puberty, when the animal nature developes, that the moral and intellectual qualities are clouded by the animal instinct and not only cease to develop but really retrograde."[2] A month later Butler was still able to respond to a lynching in a piedmont county by asking for action "to prevent further taking of human life in the barbarous manner in our State. . . ."³ But two years afterward, an alleged rape by a Negro man of a fifty-five-year-old white woman in his own county brought on what was by then the all too usual lynching and a radically different response from Butler. "This is the first lynching that has occurred in Sampson County within our remembrance," declared the thirty-one-year-old editor, "and though a dangerous precedent, is justified by public sentiment, if not by law. A more fiendish deed has not been attempted in our community in many years."⁴

It is astounding how quickly respectable, intelligent, educated, and leading Southerners turned to support lynching on the basis of the Radical rationale. Butler, whose origins and education would seem to predict an orthodox, conservative view of blacks, executed a perfect about-face within two years. Governor Tillman, as we have seen, turned from a pronouncement in September 1891 that lynching would not be tolerated to a promise in the summer of 1892 that he would himself lead a mob to lynch a rapist.

As Radicalism seized the leaders, so, too, did it seize the masses. In the 1890s in fourteen Southern states, an average of 138 persons was lynched each year and roughly 75 percent of the victims were black. From 1900 to 1909, the number of lynchings declined by half, but Negroes were 90 percent of those lynched and the lower South remained its special scene. Between 1885 and 1907 there were more persons lynched in the United States than were legally executed, and in the year 1892 twice as many.

Awful as they were, published statistics in the period undercounted the number of lynchings. Frederick Hoffman's account (1896) of the wave of lynching was one of the first that presumed to thoroughness and scholarly objectivity. His work was widely cited, but, as he candidly admitted, it was drawn from popular sources and was not nearly all inclusive.⁵

Whatever the numbers, the cold statistics hardly begin to capture the emotional heat generated by the crisis of sex and race in the South in the early 1890s. If rapes had risen in the last few years from practically none to some fearsome number over a hundred each month, as some well-informed contemporaries thought, what was to be expected in the future? If intelligent and informed persons could believe these things, what could minds less sophisticated believe? Clearly, something drastic would have to be done, and done soon.

It is small wonder, then, that lynching increased in the South and very shortly became a regional ritual. By 1893 lynch mobs were already performing much as if their members had attended formal schools on procedures. Witness the ritual in the burning of Henry Smith in February of that year in Paris, Texas, a small town in the richly agricultural north-eastern portion of the state. Smith had been accused of having raped, "with demonical cruelty," little Myrtle Vance, aged three years, eight months, and a day. By Bishop Haygood's account, after the sexual assault, the monster took the child by the heels and literally tore her asunder "in the wantonness of gorilla ferocity."[6]

Horrible was the crime, and horrible would be the punishment. For four days 2,000 men combed the countryside in search of the alleged murderer. Finally, law officers apprehended Smith in a neighboring county, and he was brought back to Paris by train. As he stepped down from the cars, thousands of waiting people cheered. By prearrangement, a "cotton float," a huge platform wagon used for hauling cotton, was brought up. Upon it was a large box, and upon the box was fixed a chair. Smith was tied to the chair. The wagon was driven to Paris, where it circled the square in the center of town so that a great crowd of people could observe the monster. Then it moved out into the open country to a place where a platform had been erected some ten feet above the ground. There, about 10,000 people had gathered. Special trains had brought in hundreds of spectators and, according to one informant, "Fathers, men of social and business standing, took their children to teach them how to dispose of negro criminals. Mothers were there too, even women whose culture entitles them to be among the social and intellectual leaders of the town."

[The father of the murdered child mounted the platform and asked for quiet while he took his revenge. He promised that when he had finished he would surrender the fiend to any who cared to punish him further. The wagon arrived and Smith was hoisted to the platform. He was bound securely to a stake that ran from the ground, through the platform, and head-high above. "A tinner's furnace was brought on filled with irons heated white. Taking one, Vance thrust it under first one then the other side of the victim's feet, who helpless, writhed, and the flesh seared and peeled from the bones. . . . By turns Smith screamed, prayed, begged, and cursed his torturer. When his face was reached, his tongue was silenced by fire, and henceforth he only moaned, or gave a cry that echoed over the prairie like the wail of a wild animal. Then his eyes were put out, and not a finger's breadth of his body being unscathed, his executioners gave way." From time to time, Vance had been relieved from his grisly labors by his brothers-in-law and his fifteen-year-old son. Now they stepped down and "combustibles" were piled around the entire platform. Smith was soaked with oil, as were his clothes and the entire platform. Then the whole was fired.]The Paris lynching not only provided a spectacle, it also provided lasting mementoes of the event. An enterprising photographer took a series of pictures of the occurrence, and it was said that a "graphophone record" of the whole proceeding—including the cries of the victim—was made. On the day after the burning, the ashes were raked as people took out buttons, bones, and teeth for relics.[8]

In the early 1890s there emerged a pattern of lynching. There were definite seasons for the act—July being the most favored month. There were also favored places. Lynching tended to reoccur in the areas where a lynching had happened before. Also they tended to occur in areas undergoing rapid economic changes or in counties where murders had been frequent and murderers rarely punished. There was a general distrust in the latter of the surety of justice in the courts and the integrity of lawyers, particularly when the offended parties were poor. It was a common attitude, with more than a grain of truth at its base. But even if the courts had been perfect, a public trial in cases of rape was seen to be more of an ordeal for the woman than for the criminal—since she must testify and, in that sense, relive the assault (a fate worse than death). Usually the mobs worked up a degree of enthusiasm before the lynching, often running through days of conversations, impromptu meetings, and rhetoric. Typically, too, the crime was seen to be part of a larger interracial conflict. White society was endangered. Negroes were becoming "uppity," presumptuous, bumptious. Strangely, whites seem to have recurrent manias about blacks' "bumping" whites, especially white women, off the sidewalks. Sometimes the whites suspected some monstrous secret organization among the blacks and feared a grand uprising. Thus, symbolically, the lynching was often seen as an act against the whole black community and not merely the execution of one or more criminals. In 1908 Albert Bushnell Hart, Harvard University historian, captured the feeling neatly in an interview with a young Mississippian. "You don't understand how we feel down here," the young man explained bluntly; "when there is a row, we feel like killing a nigger whether he has done anything or not."[9]

The physical process in the ritual of lynching was carried out by an active core, perhaps several score men, moving with considerable discipline under the direction of one or a few leaders. Often they took the victim (or, in some cases, victims) quietly. If he had been arrested and the officers resisted, the officers were usually outmaneuvered and overpowered without harm. Occasionally officers saved their prisoner, sometimes they saved him only to lose him later. Ordinarily, there were hundreds and sometimes thousands of spectators. It was not uncommon for railroads to run special "excursion" trains to the site. The mass of whites not only signified their assent to the proceedings by their presence, but also exhibited an active sympathy with the execution. To be sure, some of the interest arose from ghoulish curiosity, but apparently much more of it sprang from an eagerness to see the black fiend get his just deserts. Lynchers saw lynching as "justice." The platform upon which Henry Smith was tortured bore that single word conspicuously displayed in large printed letters. A usual part of the process was the private identification of the assailant by the offended woman, if possible. Later, when lynching had come to be applied to a wide range of offenses, the offended party or, in cases of murder, a relative would confront the accused in some way with the charge. Occasionally, the lynchers would decide that some associate of the accused was not guilty enough for execution in that style and be turned over to the care of the local jailer. Usually there was some effort to elicit a public confession from the accused, and before his death the executioners were almost always satisfied that they had found their man (or, in a few instances, their woman).

The way of death in a lynching generally bore a direct relation to the crime. Often the punishment came within sight of the scene of the crime, or, if convenience permitted, on the very spot. Torture was reserved for the most heinous of offenses. Sometimes the victims were hung without having their necks broken by a fall so that they slowly strangled to death. Usually in such cases, after the bodies had hung for several minutes they would be riddled with bullets. In that process, sometimes, armed men would be organized like soldiers into a firing order—some in front on the ground, another rank kneeling behind, and a third tier standing. The way would be cleared, and at the command hundreds would fire into the body or bodies. Now and again the lynchers would halt their proceedings and pose with their victim so that photographs could be taken or, sometimes, stand aside so that the victim could be photographed alone. Such discipline suggested recognized leadership, understood procedures, and concerted purpose. Lynchers knew what they were doing. Hanging with a quick breaking of the neck, hanging with strangulation, shooting, hanging and shooting, burning, slow burning, dragging, and cutting were all used to kill. Increasingly, simple hanging was thought to be too noble an end for such a wretch. Rumor had it that blacks regarded the hanging of one of their race by lynchers as a martyrdom. Burning, riddling with bullets, mutilation, and exhibition were used both before and after death to demean the victims. Rapists ordinarily suffered the loss of sexual organs. Bodies were always left in plain sight for some time after death, a deterrent to those who might be deterred. Fingers, toes, ears, teeth, and bones were common souvenirs. A pro-lynching governor of South Carolina, Cole Blease, received the finger of a lynched black in the mail and planted it in the gubernatorial garden. A staunchly anti-lynching governor of Georgia in the early 1890s, William J. Northern, frequently received pictures and fragments of victims to remind him of where the power of life and death in that state ultimately lay. In 1906, in Salisbury, North Carolina, several Negroes were hanged and their bodies riddled with bullets, allegedly for committing a set of horribly brutal ax murders. There is a story that the next day, a thoughtful friend brought a female relative, the person of the "little old lady" image, in his car to see the remains and, doubtless, to relish the sweets of revenge. The woman descended from the vehicle, gazed up for a time at the still swinging bodies, opened her purse, took out a knife and cut a finger from the hand of one of the victims. She put the knife and the finger in her purse, closed, it, climbed into the car again and was driven away.

After a lynching, anti-black lawlessness usually worked itself out in sporadic beatings and whippings until the white community as a whole grew irritated by such disturbances. Then the assaults would stop. The tendency was for the white community to ascribe the actual lynching to boys and men of the lower class, but also to say that the victim fully deserved his fate. It seems strange that the active executioners were seen clearly enough to establish that they did not represent the quality of the community, being merely large boys and barroom toughs, but they were seldom seen clearly enough to be convicted in the courts of murder or any other serious charge. Indeed, probably the first lynchers ever to be sent to jail for murdering blacks were two of the leaders in the Salisbury case, a railroad engineer and his fireman. The lynching, most often, was accomplished by "persons unknown." Even though some of the local intelligentsia might well deplore a lynching some distance away in another county or another state, one in their own community was almost always excused if not applauded. When the crime of the lynched person was acknowledged to be anything other than rape, the argument was offered that this lynching could not be condemned for fear of rendering this ultimate tool of justice unavailable when the awful crime did occur. Not only was the person executed guilty in the opinion of the white public, he was often also somehow seen as an alien in that society. He was a drifter or an incorrigible criminal; he was feeble-minded, or he was insane. And, always, he got what he deserved; he reaped as he had sown. During the 1890s numerous leading Southerners were caught up in the Radical mentality and turned not only to excuse lynching but, as with Rebecca Felton and Ben Tillman, actually to crusade for it. At the end of the decade they were receiving the ghastly tokens of their success in a parade of horrific lynchings that made the Paris lynching of 1893 seem ordinary fare. Finally, in the close detail in which lynchings were reported and in the wide dissemination that the reports received, Radicals everywhere shared the effect of each event. In the Radical era, a little lynching went a long way.

RIOTING

With the Wilmington riot in November 1898, the South entered yet another phase of heightened violence, a phase that reached its tragic climax in Atlanta in September 1906. Like lynching, the riot in the South in this era was essentially a new tool for the control of blacks in a Radical racial environment. However, unlike lynching, which singled out individual Negroes for punishment, in the riots white marauders broadened their sights to include any and all blacks. Further, the riots of the Radical era differed significantly from those of Reconstruction and before. During Reconstruction, Negroes in the black belts typically won such fights in the sense that they inflicted more pain upon the whites than they themselves suffered. In those affrays, the side that had the most men and the best weapons was the side that won. In the Radical period, on the other hand, the whites seemed to have the capacity to punish the blacks almost at will, in any area, and as severely as they wanted—indeed, until they exhausted themselves in the effort if they so chose. Riots in Reconstruction seemed to happen more spontaneously, with less preliminary agitation, and yet both whites and blacks seemed not greatly surprised when the fighting began. Typically both sides had their arms ready at hand, people shot and were shot at. In the Radical era, the riot was usually preceded by a long period of agitation on the white side. Radical rhetoric rang to the skies, and blacks did not respond in any effective way. Indeed, blacks appear to have been caught practically unawares in these bursts of violence. They were at first unready and unarmed, even though tensions on the white side had been building for weeks and months before the event and were clearly evident.

Essentially, riots and near-riots, which were much more numerous, were simply symptoms of the prevalence of the Radical disease. However, several of the early outbreaks and threatened outbreaks were triggered by the elevation of Negroes to relatively important political offices. Particularly, many of these were associated with the appointment in the South in and after 1897 by the Republican administration of Negroes to certain federal offices, especially to positions as postmasters, particularly in the black belts. The confluence of these events—the rise of Radicalism and the development by the Republican party of a new Southern strategy dependent in part upon the appointment of blacks to important federal offices—opened a gaping wound in the social body of the South.

The first of these eruptions, the Lake City riot of 1898, occurred after the McKinley administration saw fit to appoint a young politician named Frazier B. Baker postmaster in that South Carolina village. Whites in the area objected that Baker was a Negro and, further, had not previously been a resident of the county. Soon they petitioned the Postmaster-General to remove him. Before the petition was acted upon, on the night of February 21, several hundred persons surrounded Baker's home. The house was set afire. Three of his children were wounded, shot down as they fled from the burning building. While his wife was running out of the house and away from the flames, she was shot through the arm. The same bullet killed the year-old baby she was carrying. Baker himself was killed by bullets fired into the house. A local newspaperman who witnessed the scene wrote that "the postoffice authorities in Washington are largely responsible for the death of Frazier B. Baker."[10] A startling pronouncement. Yet, in the Radical mind, an obvious truth in that officials had not responded to clear warnings of impending crisis.

The appointment of Baker to the Lake City post office was only one of a large number of such acts in and after 1897. The dust had hardly settled from the hustings of 1896 before the McKinley administration began to tender temporary appointments to hundreds of Negroes in the black belts of the South, primarily postmasterships. Probably these were simply the "spoils of office" promised in 1895 and 1896 for black support for McKinley in securing the Republican nomination for the presidency. Black Republicans in North Carolina were especially prominent in the process because blacks functioning through the Republican party had fused with Populists in 1896 and seized control of the state. Recognition of that power came in the form of scores of blacks being named to postmasterships in the eastern counties where Negroes were numerous, most conspicuously in what was called the "Black Second," a Congressional district in the northeastern part of the state where the Negro population was solidly in the majority. In 1888 it had elected a black Congressman, and then in 1896 it again did so in the person of George H. White. White was not only very intelligent and superbly well organized, he was also militant. He made it his special business to press aggressively for the appointment of blacks to postmasterships in his district, patronage traditionally attached to his office, and to concern himself with the appointment of blacks to federal offices generally in North Carolina. Thus it was that in the hamlets, villages, and towns of eastern North Carolina, an extraordinarily large number of such commissions were given, and the blacks were, indeed, "rising." These appointments, made on a temporary basis by the President in the spring of 1897 while Congress was recessed, had to be confirmed by the Senate in order to become permanent. Immediately incumbents began to press for confirmation, and native whites began to respond.

What bothered the whites, of course, was the fact that their womenfolk were forced to do business with black postmasters and clerks, often enough with their political cronies hanging about inside the post office. It was in the nature of politics that some of the same blacks who were most influential in the elections ran saloons, bars, or dives of various sorts, that some of these had reputations for living with women to whom they were not married, and, occasionally, of having scars and sores suggestive of venereal disease. Black officeholding at any and all levels, harmless as it might later seem, was viewed by Radicals with distress. Physical contact through the mutual handling of mails and monies was bad enough, but even more awful was the prospect that black men in office would make all black men assume themselves more powerful and be led to approach white women sexually. When rejected, some black men would naturally fall over the edge of civilization and into a *furor sexualis.* The local post office, then, was becoming an institution in which a heedless and heartless federal government was casting white women into the very den of the Minotaur. The objections sent by citizens in eastern North Carolina to post office authorities in Washington became increasingly strident, and eventually they appealed to Populist Senator Marion Butler, who happened to be on the Senate Post Office Committee, to block the appointments. Ironically, most leaders in these towns were staunchly Democratic, and Butler was their bitter enemy, but he was also their last desperate hope in a struggle that was beginning to transcend politics.

The experience of eastern North Carolina was repeated throughout the black belts of the South wherever the Republican administration appointed blacks as postmasters. In 1903, Senator Ben Tillman even objected to naming a Negro *woman* to head the post office in Indianola, Mississippi. There the office was of such small consequence that it was housed in "Cohen's Brooklyn Bridge Store." In Sunflower County, where Indianola was located and where 6,000 whites faced 18,000 blacks, Radicals were sure that even this token exhibition of black power had dangerously aroused the black beast. Already, as Tillman told the Senate, the presence of the black postmistress had caused an "insulting, infamous proposition and insult from a negro man to a white woman, a poor Jewess who was clerking in the same store."[11] That incident and the continued incumbency of the black woman had brought the white people of Indianola to the brink of riotous violence.

Negro leaders seemed unaware of the real virulence behind white opposition to black postmasters. There was good reason for them not to be aware. They were, after all, simply pursuing and achieving the American dream of personal progress, and they could hardly take seriously white assertions that retrogression to a bestial state was their destiny. Radicalism, of course, was a white disease, and it raged on the white side of the line—not the black. The color line itself was like a firewall, allowing some heat but no light to escape to the other side. Occasionally, however, the wall might crumble locally and blacks who happened to be nearby would suddenly feel the searing flames. Blacks might also be caught unawares because they would remember that only recently the Harrison administration (1889–93) had appointed thousands of blacks to federal positions, not a few of them to postmasterships in eastern North Carolina. The second Cleveland administration (1893–97) had only gradually removed these postmasters. What could be more natural with the advent of another Republican administration than that the black postmasters should return to their places?

As the campaign of 1898 began, black leaders in eastern North Carolina, looking at their recent political victories, had good reason not to be fearful of whites and to feel confident about an increase in their own power. In 1896 the Republican-dominated fusion with the Populists had already floated a host of blacks into state and local offices. In Rocky Mount, for instance, the Harrison postmaster had been a black man named William Lee Pearson. During his tenure as a postmaster Radicalism had not yet acquired the power it was soon to achieve, and Pearson enjoyed his office in relative peace. Moreover in 1898 he had moved up to the state senate and the world must have seemed to him a very fair place indeed. All over eastern North Carolina the prospect was the same, blacks were rising at last to ordinary stations in political life. In the euphoria of immediate victories, black leaders failed to see the awful force that was to bring them so suddenly low.

However, it was precisely in eastern North Carolina that the intense racial heat generated in the "white supremacy" campaign of 1898 first raised white tempers massively to the rioting point. In that area, Republicans had joined Populists in 1896 to win a highly significant number of offices for blacks. As the election of 1898 approached, the signs were that the blacks, who made up the overwhelming majority of the Republican electorate, were going to demand and get offices in proportion closer to their numbers. In brief, blacks were rising and whites were horrified. Beginning early in 1898, elements of the Democratic leadership recognized that danger and moved to translate it into a political issue. At precisely the same time, elements of Populist leadership saw the same danger and the same political potential. However, the undisputed leader of the Populists was Marion Butler, and he refused to substitute racial goals for the economic goals he had long espoused.

The case of James Hunter Young illustrates well how the Democrats responded by placing the race issue—and the sex issue—at the center of their campaign. Young was a middle-aged mulatto legislator from Wake

County (Raleigh). In 1897 he was named one of the directors of the state's Deaf, Dumb, and Blind Institutions. Probably no legislator in the 1890s had been more effective in improving these important and theretofore depleted facilities and more deserved the appointment. Nevertheless, in the campaign of 1898, white supremacists cartooned Young inspecting the separated living quarters of the blind white girls, and the Democratic party's handbook of that year concluded the matter by asking "How do you like such white slavery to a negro master in Raleigh? . . . Jim Young is a hard man to satisfy."[12] Whether the Democratic leaders really believed the pictures they drew, or whether they were merely creating campaign propaganda, the effect was the same. Whites in eastern North Carolina had been thoroughly Radicalized. They were bound to hear, to believe, and to act violently upon such thoughts. In the summer and fall of 1898 very respectable young Democratic politicians such as Charles Brantley Aycock, Locke Craig, and Robert Glenn, all to be governors of the state early in the twentieth century, went there to fan the flames and beat the Radical drum.

Even so, it was not a world they ever made. If white supremacy politicians in some shape had not existed in North Carolina in 1898, they would have been created by the Radical hysteria. And they would have been molded from any clay—Democratic, Populist, or even Republican. Each of these parties had a very large and important lily-white faction, and each was poised for a flight into Radicalism. In North Carolina, the Democrats took flight first. For a time they grounded the rest, in part simply because whatever a Democrat was, a Populist or a Republican ought not be. The young Democrats who opted for Radicalism chose to ride the wave of the future. They thus assured themselves of possessing high power in their state in the formative decades of the twentieth century, and, incidentally, of gubernatorial, senatorial, and congressional seats as well.

THE WILMINGTON RIOT

The Wilmington riot of November 10, 1898, was the first in a series of outbreaks in which large numbers of blacks were killed, still larger numbers hurt, and hundreds of Negro families driven forever from their homes. Wilmington, in southeastern North Carolina, was the great port city for the state and the commercial center for a vast agricultural hinterland in and about the Cape Fear River basin. The city itself was more black than white, and the county in which it was located, New Hanover, had 14,000 blacks in a total population of 24,000.

The primary cause of the riot was Radicalism. Its rise to feverish intensity in the 1898 campaign had the effect in Wilmington, and in eastern North Carolina generally, of breaking down political lines and erecting in their stead a single line—the race line. Increasingly, white people were forced to choose not between parties but between colors. "The situation here," reported a Wilmington Populist to Marion Butler in October, "derived from the pronounced negro office-holding and their consequent insolence, has produced an issue rather of race assertiveness than of questions of political economy. So ominous is this condition that partisan affiliation is divided and but one question irresistible possesses the attention of our citizens—that of race supremacy."[13] Equivocation brought threats of horrendous violence. As the summer wore on into fall, individual white Populists and Republicans published advertisements in the newspapers announcing their withdrawal as candidates for office. In addition, they often proclaimed their endorsement of the white supremacy crusade. "I have always been and still am for anglo Saxon [*sic*] Supremacy in all things pertaining to State as well as national affairs," declared one retired Populist candidate in Wilmington. "I have always tried to make this plain to fair minded people."[14] In the heat of racial conflict, Populist and Republican leaders lost control of their parties, and so, too, did the Democrats. Democrats chose the right issue upon which to ride back into power. But they did not create the Radical hysteria, nor did they control it. It would be much more accurate to say that in North Carolina Radicalism, for a time, seized and shaped a willing Democracy.

Given the extravagance of the white supremacy campaign, it is remarkable that the Wilmington riot occurred two days after the election rather than during the turbulent weeks that preceded the balloting. Yet, race not politics ruled, and it seems inevitable that interracial violence would have erupted somewhere. The riot that happened in Wilmington could have happened in a score of eastern North Carolina towns, and it very nearly did. For instance, it almost occurred in Wilson where, again, the McKinley administration had appointed another Negro postmaster. In Wilson, on the day after the election, it was rumored that some two hundred Negroes had gathered at a baseball field nearby and were marching on the town. The white population, in a frenzy, armed itself (primarily with Winchester repeating rifles) and hastily organized for the onslaught, which, of course, never came.[15] Once the riot had actually occurred in Wilmington, there was no need for it to happen elsewhere.

There were, of course, a multiplicity of local and immediate causes of the riot. There were Democratic politicians who had been displaced—largely by black and white Republicans—in the fusionist upsurge and who did, in fact, return to offices by dint of racial fears and violence—

fears they shared with their white neighbors generally, and a violence they promoted but did not create. In the economic realm, laboring class whites did sometimes find themselves in competition with black labor. This was particularly true of those more recently arrived from abroad and, more particularly still, of the late-coming Irish. Further, established white artisans were embattled by blacks moving into their trades. Lower-class whites generally had been gerrymandered into voting districts with blacks so as to be overwhelmed by the blacks and thus rendered powerless politically. Land and business values were depressed and falling because of Republican dominance in city and county governments and prolonged political unrest. Thus, better-to-do Wilmingtonians grew more desperate. Finally, the fusionist legislature had altered the charter of Wilmington, as it did with a number of black belt towns, to throw the city into the hands of blacks and Republicans by extending its borders. Still the evidence is great that, ultimately, the effective ingredient in the riot came from that unnamed hysteria that swept through the white communities in the black belts of the South in the 1890s. Whites in the port city saw a rapidly rising rate of crime among blacks. Black presumptuousness approached aggressiveness, and often whites feared that blacks were arming themselves and secretly organizing for a general insurrection. Overall, Wilmington whites assumed that there was a widespread lusting among black men for white women.

THE ROBERT CHARLES RIOT IN NEW ORLEANS

Two years later, in 1900 in New Orleans one of the most serious outbreaks of racial violence since Reconstruction occurred. At the center of the conflict was a remarkable man, until recently perhaps one of the most neglected historical figures in American race relations.[16] His name was Robert Charles, and possibly he was the first fully self-conscious black militant in the United States. Not only was Charles, apparently, a black nationalist in the intellectual and rhetorical sense, he was also an activist, and, as he soon proved, unique in that he maintained his militancy until death.

Charles came to New Orleans in 1894 after experiencing some difficulty with the authorities in Copiah County, Mississippi, involving the illicit sale of whiskey. In terms of age, he was precisely the most adult issue possible of the "new Negro" of Radical myth, having just barely escaped the "benefits" of slavery. In fact, Robert Charles was conceived in slavery and born in freedom in late 1865 or early 1866. His father and

mother were sharecroppers in Copiah County, some thirty miles southeast of Vicksburg, and Robert was the fourth in a line of ten brothers and
sisters. He was like many young black folks, who left the tenant farms to
seek more lucrative jobs in the modernizing South. In his case, he became
first a day laborer on the railroads. Some time in the 1890s, probably in
1894, in the midst of the great depression, Robert Charles came to New
Orleans. In New Orleans and elsewhere, he valued his family and his
friends from Copiah, and maintained his connection with them until the
very end of his life. In the year of the riot, Robert was thirty-four and
unmarried, a sturdy dark brown man some six feet in height and weighing about 185 pounds. He was literate and, indeed, rather studious over
the newspapers and textbooks he saved. In addition, he kept notebooks
in which he wrote from time to time. There was no indication that he
was a church member, belonged to any fraternal order, or was an intimate
in any other enclave in black life. He drank moderately, affected a droopy
mustache, and dressed well, rather stylishly, favoring a brown derby.
Charles worked as a laborer in a succession of jobs, finally in June 1900
losing his job stacking lumber at the Pelican Sawmill Company. He
moved frequently, living in perhaps a dozen places after his arrival in the
city before he came to share a room on Fourth Street with nineteen-year-
old Lenard Pierce, another black man out of work. Charles had different
jobs and addresses, he also had different names. Sometimes he was Curtis
Robertson, and sometimes he was Robert Charles. Having two names
was a way of dealing with the white world and the white man's law, but
Charles saw to it that each name had integrity. Indeed, when Curtis Robertson got arrested and convicted for selling whiskey in Copiah County,
fled, and somehow avoided serving his sentence, he managed some two
years later to return and set the matter straight. Finally, Robert Charles
liked women. At the time of the riot he had been special friends for some
three years with Virginia Banks, "a young brown-skinned woman . . .
possessed of more than average intelligence" and probably employed in
the city as a domestic servant. The New Orleans riot began on Monday,
July 23, 1900, while Robert was waiting for Virginia.

That afternoon about sunset Lenard had come home from a day of
searching for work to find Charles writing at a small desk in their room.
He was dressed to go out—dark striped trousers, white shirt, black coat,
and brown derby. Lenard knew that the bulge in Charles's coat was the
.38 Colt revolver he usually carried. Charles asked Lenard if he would
like to go with him to meet two women. Lenard asked if there was "anything in it." Charles assured him there was, and Lenard washed and
dressed, thrusting his own .38 Colt into his waistband before they went
out. Charles was going to see Virginia, and he probably invited Lenard

along to meet her roommate, Ernestine Goldstein. Charles understood that Virginia and Ernestine had taken an excursion trip to Baton Rouge that day and would not return until later in the evening. Meanwhile, he took Lenard to visit another young woman. Almost certainly the young woman was his married sister, Alice. Leaving Alice's residence, the two men approached the house in which Virginia and Ernestine lived about 10:00 p.m. They waited for a half-hour at a streetcorner nearby, perhaps assuming that the women had not yet returned home, or, perhaps, waiting for Virginia to fetch them when her landlady had gone to sleep. Pierce grew nervous about the police, and about 10:30 they moved closer to the house, seating themselves on a step in front of the house of a white neighbor. Once or twice they walked down to check Virginia's house and returned to sit on the step.

About 11:00 police Sergeant Jules C. Aucoin, in charge of the night shift in the precinct, encountered a black man who told him that "two suspicious looking negroes" were sitting on the doorstep of a house nearby. The sergeant gathered two of his patrolmen and confronted the two men, demanding to know what they were doing there. The men responded vaguely about having been in town only three days and working for someone. One of them added that "they were waiting for a friend." Charles rose, and one of the policemen, taking the move as a threat, grabbed him. They scuffled. The policeman began to beat Charles with his billy club, then drew his pistol. Charles did the same, and both opened fire. The policeman was struck in the thigh, and so too was Charles, who nevertheless escaped, running zigzag down the street as two of the officers fired at him. Meanwhile, Sergeant Aucoin was holding a gun at Lenard Pierce's head. The policemen took Pierce to the station house where he was questioned by Captain John T. Day. Captain Day was one of the real heroes of the New Orleans Police Department, in 1894 having rescued fourteen people from a fire in the St. Charles Hotel. Large and handsome in the portly style of the time, John Day at thirty-seven was the pride of the NOPD. By 2:30 a.m. he had "sweated out" of the unfortunate Pierce the name Curtis Robertson and the Fourth Street address. He emerged from the station to join a squad of policemen saying, "I know where I can get the nigger now." Warned to be careful, Day replied casually, "Oh pshaw, I'll go and take that nigger myself."

Meanwhile, Charles had returned to his room on Fourth Street, probably to get his Winchester, a lever-action, rapid-firing rifle. It happened that Captain Day arrived with his men just as Charles was about to leave his room. The room had a single door, opening onto an alleyway running perpendicular to the street. The Captain stationed three of his men on the street while he led Sergeant Aucoin, Corporal Trenchard, and Patrolman

Lamb down the alley toward Charles's room. With them was a citizen volunteer named Schmidt, who carried a lantern. As they approached the door Trenchard ordered in a loud voice, "Open up there!" Charles suddenly flung open the door and fired a bullet straight through the Captain's heart. Day wheeled, made "an awful cry," and fell dead. Schmidt dropped the lantern and ran. The policemen were frozen in disbelief. "My God, Corporal," said Sergeant Aucoin, "our Captain has been killed. Look at what that negro has done." As if in answer, Charles then fired several more shots into the fallen body. Two of the policemen were now up against the wall of the house by the door. As they began to talk to one another, Charles shouted at them, "You _____ I will give you all some!" Thereupon he fired from the doorway, sending a bullet through Patrolman Lamb's right eye and out the back of his skull. An elderly black woman living down the alley then called to the two remaining officers to slip into her room. They did, and hid there in the darkness for two hours. Charles stalked about in the alley looking for the policemen, cursing them, and daring them to come out. The three policemen on the street declined to enter the dark alley. Finally, about 4:30, Charles came to the street and fired at one of the policemen. At seventy-five yards, in the semi-darkness, he grazed the officer's cap with his bullet. Finally, then, the officers called for assistance, which arrived at 5:00 only to find that Charles had fled.

What drove Robert Charles to defy the police, knowing that the odds of his survival in such an affray were virtually nil? Distinctly, at least three things moved him. Since 1896 he had been an active and earnest advocate of the emigration of American blacks to Liberia. In that year he joined the International Migration Society, an organization that promised transportation to Liberia and three months' supplies to members who would pay the society a dollar a month for forty months. In 1899 Charles had also become, at his own request, a subscription agent for the *Voice of Missions,* a paper published by Bishop Henry M. Turner of the AMEC. Turner was then unrivaled among black leaders in urging Negroes to return to Africa. Among Charles's effects, police later found a great amount of literature advocating emigration to Africa.

Charles was also moved by one of the most horrible lynchings that had yet occurred in the South. In 1899, near Newnan, Georgia, Sam Hose, a black man, reputedly killed a farmer and raped the farmer's wife on the bloody kitchen floor next to the still warm body. Hose was tortured, burned, and then his body reclaimed from the fire and slices taken from his heart and liver. One of the lynchers journeyed to Atlanta in an attempt to deliver a slice of Hose's heart to the governor. News of the Hose lynching threw Charles into a rage. His acquaintances said they had never seen him so totally angry. As one observed, Charles was "beside himself with fury." Shortly thereafter, he asked to become one of Turner's agents.

Finally, Louisiana had just moved in 1898 to disfranchise black men, and the election of 1900 was approaching. Some Democratic leaders had indicated their willingness to count out the Republicans and their Populist allies even if they were fortunate enough to win the now rigged elections. An opposition spokesman voiced a very hot reply to this threat, suggesting that his partisans "*oil up their Winchesters* and prepare to fight," if need be, to seat their candidates. Later police discovered that Charles was carrying a two-column newspaper account of that speech with him when he died.

Clearly, Robert Charles was giving up on America. When the policeman began to hit him with the billy club and drew his pistol, Charles was ready for war.

Early Tuesday morning the police realized that Charles had again escaped and they mounted a vast search. As the hunt proceeded, the mobs rose. Just as Manly had been an excuse for riot in Wilmington, Charles became an excuse for riot in New Orleans. As in Wilmington there were many causes of the riot, underneath which Radicalism beat like a steady pulse. Black people had been crowding working-class whites for jobs during the depression-ridden 1890s. Further, there had been a move in the state legislature to segregate more strictly the streetcars in New Orleans, a move that was popular in the state at large and was defeated by interested parties only by quietly burying the measure in the state senate. Finally, each of the four major newspapers in the city moved toward radical extremism, and two of these attained that end. Both the press and the police in June and July noticed that young blacks were misbehaving in the city's parks. These young men, it was reported, would "lie in the grass, evidently waiting for the young maidens to pass them," and they would make "questionable if not indecent remarks." In the same months a New Orleans physician, Gustav Keitz, published a series of articles in the *Times-Democrat* in which he claimed that his medical friends were "agreed that the number of negroes should be reduced, and have discussed asexualization, a measure which should be practiced at the earliest possible period of life." Finally, many blacks, especially young men, did not hide their approval of Charles's actions. White people claimed to have heard remarks praising Charles and his "war on the whites."

On Tuesday, groups of white men, almost totally unchecked by police, began to range through the city, attacking blacks. Indeed, the mobs, allegedly made up exclusively of young men, boys and habitual hoodlums, apparently thought of themselves as the allies of the police. While the police did not share that view, they handled the situation by

arresting blacks who seemed too assertive and too approving of Charles.
On the third day, Wednesday, the mobs became stronger and increasingly
unruly, and it seemed as if the city might plunge into anarchy. The acting
mayor issued a proclamation calling for law and order. On the other side,
all four newspapers clamored for Charles's apprehension, two of these
indirectly urging mob action. A rally was held at the site of Robert E.
Lee's monument on Wednesday evening, and it was decided that Pierce
would be lynched. A mob of 3,000 marched to the parish prison, only to
find it too strongly defended. They then moved on to Storyville, the vice
district, intending to attack the black establishments there. Again they
were thwarted. Black Storyville was locked up tight and deserted. The
mob was reduced to attacking the few as yet unaware and hapless blacks
caught on the darkened streets. During the night three black people were
killed, and six were seriously injured. Fifty blacks were beaten badly
enough to be treated for injuries at the city hospital. Additionally, the
mob accidentally shot two white people and beat three streetcar employees who fought to keep the mobs off their cars. On Thursday, the mayor
of New Orleans, who had been ill and out of town, returned. He enlisted
a volunteer police force of 1500 men, and the governor sent him militia.
These were stationed at strategic places, and officials began to gain control of the city again. Even so, three more black people were killed on
Thursday, and fifteen were shot or severely beaten. Then, on Friday, the
fifth day, a black man informed the police that Charles was hidden in a
house on Saratoga Street, only fourteen blocks from his room on Fourth.

Precisely as the press and the populace had charged, Charles had been
hidden by his own people. The black "criminal" was given refuge in the
New Orleans home of friends from Copiah County. It fell to one of the
most respected men on the force, Sergeant Gabriel Porteous, to check out
this latest report on Charles's whereabouts. He took with him a corporal
and two officers. Arriving at the address a bit after 3:00 p.m., Porteous
stationed the two patrolmen on the street while he and the corporal
entered the house. Charles had established his retreat, perhaps for the
whole three days he had been missing, in the closet under the stairs in the
two-story dwelling. He had spent some of his time making bullets out of
lead pipe and reloading cartridges with tools that he had brought with
him. He knew that the officers were coming. As Porteous approached the
closet, Charles stuck his Winchester through the slightly opened door
and fired, killing Porteous instantly with a bullet through the heart. Rapidly working the lever of his Winchester, he then shot the corporal
through the stomach. The corporal collapsed, and Charles ran upstairs.

Hearing the shots, one of the officers from the street came in. He sent
for a priest who came and administered last rites to the dying corporal.

No one guessed that Charles was upstairs. A crowd was gathering in the yard when Charles leaned out a window and opened fire. He shot a young man, apparently chosen at random, first in the hip and then quickly, as the man tried to escape, through the heart. By this time a melange of police, volunteers, and militia were arriving and returned the fire. By 4:00 there were a thousand men with guns around the building, and within an hour some ten to twenty thousand men had rushed into the area. This small army sprayed the flimsy structure with bullets. Later, the curious would estimate that some five thousand bullets struck the building during the hour-long siege. Every minute or so Charles would create a distraction at one window, then suddenly pop up at another and fire. Observers estimated that Charles fired about fifty times during the fight. With those shots, he killed two more men, a jailer and a visiting Mississippian, and wounded nineteen others, seven of them seriously. None of the other shots failed to stir the air disturbingly close to their targets. Robert Charles was an uncanny marksman.

Finally, the whites attempted to smoke Charles out by igniting a mattress on the stairs. The mattress, however, set fire to the house. Charles, who must have been hit several times by then, came down the stairs and out the door. He still wore his derby hat, set low over his eyes, and he carried his rifle raised to fire, elbows poised. He dashed across twenty feet of yard toward the entrance of a facing house. He was hit, at last, by a rifle bullet from the room he was about to enter. He paused, his arms weakened and sagged. Then he gathered himself again, pulled up the rifle, and crashed into the room. There were eight men in the room, three of them police detectives. But it was a young medical student from Tulane University, a volunteer policeman, who fired the first shot, the bullet that brought Robert Charles down. The black man fell within two feet of his executioner, Charles A. Noiret. Charles tried to move, and Noiret shot him three more times.

Then everybody in the room began shooting into the body, some cursing, some howling. More men rushed into the room and did the same. They dragged the body into the street and fired into it again and again. Corporal Trenchard, who was later dismissed from the force for cowardice in the first confrontation, pointed a double-barreled shotgun at the body. "Now who says I am a coward," he cried and fired both barrels. The mob allowed the son of one of the slain policemen to stomp on the face of the corpse. Finally, officers brought up a police wagon. They flung Charles's body onto the floor between the seats, leaving his head hanging over the end. As the wagon rattled down the street toward the morgue, the battered head, flattened, almost unrecognizable now, jerked crazily about.

On the same day, after Charles's death, the mobs broke loose again, burning down a large school building for blacks, killing three more black people, and beating many others. Finally on the next day, Saturday, the violence subsided, and hundreds of people filed past Charles's body on view at the morgue. The mobs had killed at least a dozen black people and injured scores of others. On the other side, Charles had killed seven white people, four of them officers of the law; seriously wounded eight others, three of them officers; and marked for life with his bullets twelve more.

New Orleans hardly knew how to cope with the memory of Robert Charles. Many people believed that he drew his courage and his coolness from cocaine. Journalists claimed that evidences of that substance had been found in his room. The Republican paper explained him away as a man driven to desperation, presumably by the Democrats, but it, too, hinted that cocaine had been involved. The conservative Democratic press blamed the affair upon incitement by the liberal North and pronounced Charles the worst and last example of that rare type—the "bad nigger," as if in killing him the danger had passed forever. Paradoxically, one of the most virulent racists in the city, the owner and editor of the *States,* Henry J. Hearsey, the very man who had been most rabid in advocating the quick destruction of Robert Charles and scornful of the cowardice of the police, was the one public person who gave him the most respect. He could not, he declared, "help feeling for him a sort of admiration prompted by his wild and ferocious courage." Never had one man stood off so many for so long. It was, he said, "the courage of the brute[,] the lion or the tiger." Just as Thomas Dixon in fiction had a strange affinity for the bestial black, so too did Hearsey respond to Robert Charles.

On Sunday, the seventh day, the authorities took Charles's body to the city's potter's field—under military guard, secretly, and before dawn. The final earth was shovelled onto his grave just as the eastern sky began to brighten. The plain cross marker bore no name, and New Orleans hastened to erase his memory as they erased his grave. *L'Abeille (The Bee),* the French language newspaper of New Orleans, probably summed up accurately enough the sentiment both of its neighbors and itself when it closed the Robert Charles story with the declaration that he was a black fanatic, in revolt against society.[17] He was crazy, and hence dismissable. Charles and the riot were soon all but lost to the memory of New Orleans, gaining less than three pages in the two thousand-page history of the city that appeared in 1922. He was also lost to history at large, neither he nor the riot gaining more than a few lines in histories before the "Soul Movement" got well under way in the late 1960s.

Black people, especially some black people, had more difficulty forgetting Robert Charles. A black man in Chicago became mentally unhinged when he heard about the New Orleans affair and began to pray in the streets for protection. Questioned about his behavior, he answered that he was "afraid of snakes and white folks." In southwestern Louisiana, a Negro man riding a train, suffered illusions about himself being lynched, grabbing over his head at an imaginary rope. When the conductor approached, the man shot him. At the next station, he was taken off the train and lynched. In Battle Creek, Michigan, a black man walked into the police station and fired a pistol at the chief of police as an act of sympathy for Charles. In New Orleans, five Sundays after the burial of Charles, Lewis Forstall, a black man living on South Rampart Street, walked across the street to where his neighbor, Fred Clark, also black, was seated in a chair reading. Forstall was known to be an admirer of Robert Charles and had brooded about his death. He pulled out a revolver, put it to Clark's head, and pulled the trigger. The gun misfired. He pulled the trigger again. This time the gun fired, killing Clark. Fred Clark was the man who had told the police where to find Charles on the day he died.[18]

THE CAUSES OF THE ATLANTA RIOT

The high tide of Radicalism came during the riot that raged through Atlanta for four days beginning on September 22, 1906.[19] The all-pervasive cause of the Atlanta riot was racial Radicalism. However, that violent eruption had its immediate cause in the confluence of Radicalism and several reform movements, each of which had been seeking, for a decade or more, to achieve its special goal in Georgia. Especially important were four varieties of reformers: prohibitionists, feminists, urban "progressives" and rural "progressives."

Georgia prohibitionists had long recognized their state, wet as it was, as a missionary field of magnificent possibilities. However, during the summer of 1906 the movement assumed a revivalistic fervor much as if the millennium were at hand. In the city of Atlanta, the dry finger of righteous reform pointed quite properly to Decatur Street. That street offered such a plenitude of saloons and other sinful diversions (some for whites only, others for "colored only") that "Decatur-Street-dive" had practically become a single word, and a bad one. In Atlanta, the prohibition effort was spearheaded by the ministry. Conspicuously in the advance was the Reverend "Sam" P. Jones, an evangelist of national renown. During the summer, the Reverend Jones preached sermon after sermon attacking the Decatur Street dives, depicting all manner of debaucheries there and rousing his audiences to frenzies. As the prohibition campaign approached a climax, it came to rest heavily upon the evils of drink among black men. Whites generally thought that black men were specially excited by alcohol, and that their excitement was most especially erotic. They came to believe that pictures of undraped white women were blatantly displayed in the dives frequented by black men. Further, the bottle in which a certain popular gin was dispensed supposedly bore the embossed image of a nude white woman. The idea of the fair figure under the scrutiny of black men and roughly caressed by the dark fingers even as its contents inflamed their passions was almost too much to bear for minds infused with Radicalism. Finally, many whites assumed that blacks liberally laced their drinks with cocaine, thus freeing themselves from whatever shreds of inhibition might have survived the alcohol. It was during these early years of the twentieth century, in fact, that Southern whites first experienced a great apprehension about the use of drugs. For decades, they had themselves freely used a wide variety of narcotics for relief from minor discomforts as well as major pains. Now there began to appear newspaper stories of black men here and there taking "dope," usually cocaine, and running murderously amuck. Southerners, inspired by the black menace, began to think fondly of laws, even federal laws, to regulate the use of drugs. Senator Ben Tillman, for instance, in 1913 was led to explain his position to a constituent who was a physician. Tillman asserted that the Congress did not want to tax doctors of medicine, but cocaine and opium, he said, "are causing so much trouble among the negroes." By way of immediate illustration, he added, "I suppose you saw in the papers some days ago where the two mulatto boys in Harriston, Mississippi, got crazed on cocaine and went on the war path with the result that eight people were killed and a large number wounded."[20]

In Atlanta, in 1906, whites thus thought that blacks were slipping away upon a flood of alcohol and drugs. As white Atlantans looked at Decatur Street, they saw hundreds of wandering vagrant black men daily steeping themselves in corruption, drowning in a carnal sea. The runaway black male of slave times, the "nigger in the woods," had come to town in the modern South. The immediate presence of the Negro beast gave instant urgency to the prohibitionist cause. Georgia drys reminded their more liquid neighbors that the federal government had found it necessary to deny "fire water" to the American Indian. Now they called upon their fellow Georgians to deny drink to themselves, not only for their own salvation, but for the preservation of the purity of their mothers, wives, and daughters, and to save the black man from a "relapse into animal-ism." Before 1906, Georgia prohibitionists had rejected active participation in the movement to disfranchise blacks, fearing that it would confuse the pursuit of their favored reform. In 1906, they reversed themselves and concluded that the disfranchisement of blacks was a necessary prelude to prohibition. The liquor interests would corrupt the black man and steal his vote to keep Georgia wet. Prohibition, the path of progress, lay directly across the prostrate form of the political Negro. Unhesitatingly, they put their foot upon that path.

Feminist reformers, too, saw black men as roadblocks on the way to reform and eagerly fanned the Radical flames. Rebecca Felton, after all, had long been saying that white men in equating themselves with black men at the polls were encouraging the latter to assert their equality elsewhere. More broadly, Georgia women could easily see their interest in prohibition. Women at large had always known who, ultimately, paid the bar bills. Clearly, the disfranchisement of black men was a move in the right direction.

The riot was also promoted by politicians shaped in the new urban progressive mold. In Georgia, pre-eminent among these was Hoke Smith. Smith had lived most of his young years in Chapel Hill, where his father was Professor of Modern Languages at the University of North Carolina. During Reconstruction, the family moved to Atlanta where Smith read law and was admitted to the bar at the age of seventeen. After years of assiduous application, he arrived, Horatio Alger fashion, at the pinnacle of his profession. In the 1880s he was reputed to be the most effective lawyer in Georgia for suits against corporations and especially suits against railroads. Quite literally, he capitalized upon an increasing popular irritation with the arrogance of railroad management that produced favorable juries, and an imperfect technology that produced a steady stream of accidents for which the railroads could be sued. Smith claimed that by the 1890s his practice paid at least $200 a day and often $500. It was accurately reflective of his character that he made such a statement. He soon bought controlling interest in the Atlanta *Journal,* and in 1892 he used that paper to campaign against the tariff and for Cleveland. As a reward, President Cleveland appointed him to his cabinet as Secretary of Interior. In Cleveland's service (1893–97) he showed himself to be an ardent goldbug and a stalwart enemy of the liberal, Bryanite, silver wing of the Democracy.[21] However, after the turn of the century, Smith emerged as a progressive Democrat in the urban style.

By 1905 Hoke Smith was ambitious to sit in the governor's chair in Georgia. In the pursuit of that end, he allied himself with the more liberal, agrarian Populistic forces dominated by his old enemy Tom Watson. The price of support of the Watson element was the disfranchisement of the Negro. Behind the scenes in arranging this odd marriage between gold and silver and all that each stood for was, first, James R. Gray, who had followed Smith as the dominant force on the Atlanta *Journal.* Subsequently, Congressman Thomas W. Hardwick, one of the most Radical of Southern politicians, took up the management of the alliance. Hardwick pled for a holiday from partisanship among white men for the necessary end of achieving the complete disfranchisement of the black. The alliance was made, and in one of the most strenuous and prolonged gubernatorial campaigns ever waged in the South, from mid-1905 through the summer of 1906, Smith sought the Democratic nomination for the governorship of Georgia. By this time, the Democratic party of the state nominated its candidate for governor in a primary election preceding the general election. Because the Democratic party was all white, the primary was all white. Because the Democratic party was overwhelmingly the majority party, winning the primary was tantamount to winning the election. Of necessity, then, the campaign was one for the minds of the white masses and newspapers were vitally important to success. Journalistic efforts in the campaign soon descended into the "yellow" style.[22]

On the campaign trail, Smith ripped like a fury unleashed into both the evils of the corporations and the race issue.[23] In Atlanta, where the racial fever centered and where the two candidates lived, he concentrated his rhetoric increasingly upon the black menace and the necessity of controlling the blacks. Reputedly, he announced his willingness to "imitate" the example of Wilmington if necessary. His principal opponent, Clark Howell, the editor of the usually calm Atlanta *Constitution,* strove only to prove that he was whiter than Smith. He did not support disfranchisement, he apologized, only because blacks were already disfranchised.[24] In Atlanta in 1906, as in Wilmington in 1898, the campaign came very close to transcending politics, party, and even personalities. It was a vast social movement in which all the whites were on one side and all the blacks—unaware, unwittingly, and not by their own efforts—were on the other. It was an intense bipolarization with, paradoxically, one pole missing.

All during the long, hot summer of 1906 both sides beat the war drums to the chant of Negro beast. Rival newspapers vied with one another in whipping the populace into a frenzy. Speaking for Smith, the Atlanta *Journal* indicted ruling politicians for having permitted any Negroes at all to vote, and it was furious in pointing out the results of such libertarianism. Allowing black men to participate equally with white men at the polls promoted black presumptuousness in the social realm, the *Journal* insisted.[25]

In addition to politics, there were many other elements contributing to the deterioration of race relations in Atlanta. As we have seen, young blacks, like young whites, were streaming into the city as the marginal farms of Georgia collapsed. Young whites could go into the cotton mills (which reached the crest of a building boom in 1906), into the factories, and into the stores and offices of the city. Black women could find places as domestics in the homes of the rapidly growing white bourgeoisie. But there were relatively few places that black men could go in the new economic order, and those few were typically the places of low-paid menials and roustabouts. The result was that many young black men who came to Atlanta in the turn-of-the-century years did not work steadily; they did in fact often become floaters. Many took their money wherever they could find it and often came to depend on black women working for whites and "toting," that is, bringing home food from the white family's table every evening.

In Atlanta and in cities all over the South, there grew up among urban black males a streetcorner society of pool halls, juke joints, and women. It was a counterculture in which Victorian values were up-ended, and in which the hero was too smart to work and too highly sexed to be satisfied by one woman. Young black men who had been born on the farm and reared to work a full day six days a week and go to church on Sunday came to the city to cultivate the hipster-trickster role, to have a succession of addresses, a number of names, no lasting job, no wife, and no child to call his own. Young black women reared to be wives and mothers on the farm and to stay at home found themselves working in white people's kitchens and minding white people's children. In this new economic order, black women became, per force, the wage earners, the providers for the family, supporting not only their children but, sporadically, the fathers of their children as well.

Thus black culture in Atlanta (and elsewhere in the industrializing, commercializing, progressive South) entered the twentieth century with something distinctly new added. The Victorian order of the peasant past might have sometimes seemed stultifying, but the new roles were not all that gratifying, neither for males nor females. Probably the secular music of these people, the plain black people, told their story best. If the "blues" was not born in the South in the few years around 1905, it should have been. It was then that young black men and women, people like Robert Charles and his woman friend Virginia Banks in New Orleans, found themselves in a world that would not allow them to sustain the values to which they had been born and reared. The early blues was the cry of the cast-out black, ultimately alone and lonely, after one world was lost and

before another was found. Small wonder that they bewailed their plight
. . . and cursed the people who had brought them to this low estate.

White Atlanta, of course, could not even begin to understand what
had happened. In their minds, black men willfully persisted in idleness at
the very time when there was a scarcity of labor. Seemingly black men
were dissipating their days in Decatur Street dives while the city hungered
for labor. There was bitter resentment in boomer Atlanta, and a great
amount of it, against black men who seemingly refused to work. Shortly
before the riot, concerned citizens counted hundreds of black men idling
away working hours in Decatur Street dives.

Closely related to white views of black idleness was a rising crime rate
and the convict lease system. Judged by the ratio of arrests to population,
Atlanta was the most criminal city in America. In 1905, out of about
80,000 whites and 50,000 blacks living in the city, Atlanta police made
17,000 arrests. Roughly 10,000 of those arrested were black men. Among
those arrested, convictions ran high. Many of the convicts were leased
out to the lumber companies, brickyards, and plantations around Atlanta,
all of which were contributing to the city's prosperity. Attrition by death
among the convicts was about 10 percent a year. Thus, in reality, black
men were serving Atlanta very well indeed.

The seeming idleness, criminality, physicality, and super-sexuality of
the young black male in the counterculture fitted snugly into Radical
imagery. When Tom Dixon brought his play *The Clansman* to Atlanta
in the fall of 1905, white audiences readily recognized its certain truth.
At the first performance, the audience responded with loud enthusiasm
and kept the author standing before the final curtain for several minutes
of applause.[26]

Ultimately, of course, at the very heart of the riot lay the Radical mentality. Fed by the prohibition and political campaigns, racial Radicalism
reached a new and dangerous plateau in Atlanta during the summer of
1906. Early in August, Graves and Charles Daniel, the editor of the
Atlanta *News*, discovered the existence of a veritable epidemic of rapes—
a "torrid wave of black lust and fiendishness" as one journalist soon
labeled it. The racial apocalypse, long predicted by the Radicals, had
arrived. Black men were spilling pell mell and massively over the rim of
civilization into "lust and animal insanity."

By mid-August white Atlanta felt trapped in an "intolerable epidemic
of rape." Ray Stannard Baker, a nationally famous journalist, came to the
city several weeks after the riot and hired investigators to search out the
truth in regard to the fifteen rapes or attempts at rape alleged to have
occurred in the six months before the day the riot began. He found that
three of these had actually been committed by white men. These three

received little notice in the press, even though one was a most awful and murderous affair. On the other hand, the twelve cases involving black men were played up in the press tremendously. Two of these attacks went beyond simple brutality, one of the women suffering an eye gouged out. Three other cases were "aggravated attempts" (probably meaning that some kind of assault did occur), and three more might have been attempts. Finally, three were definitely imagined and one was an attempted suicide that the woman tried to mask by making a false charge.[27]

Given the rough and rapid growth of Atlanta in the previous decade and the relative inefficiency of the city administration, it is not surprising that there should have been perhaps as many as eight cases of assault by blacks upon white females in six months. What is surprising (and revealing) is that the white community from top to bottom and across all spectrums had been so thoroughly Radicalized as to lose all perspective on the subject. Baker himself, a highly sensitive, close, and careful investigator of social happenings, perceived at once how greatly the fear of rape worked upon white minds. "I was astonished in travelling in the South to discover how widely prevalent this dread has become," he asserted. Still, the best precautions failed, and the white man's awful revenge spread a terror through the black community that whites rarely even saw—much less understood. "And yet every Negro I met voiced in some way that fear," Baker reported. "It is difficult here in the North for us to understand what such a condition means: a whole community namelessly afraid!"[28] Perhaps in any community fear can not go endlessly on. In Atlanta, they ended it with violence.

THE ATLANTA RIOT

Atlanta was ready for riot; and late in the afternoon of Saturday, September 22, it came. The wagonyards in the city were filled with farmers in from the country for a day of buying and, perhaps of drinking. It was sultry and hot. All day long the saloons on Decatur Street had been filled. About five o'clock newsboys ran through the streets selling papers reporting an attempted assault by a black man upon a white woman. Within four hours, three additional assaults were reported. Two might have been real, two more were obviously imagined.[29] Each crisis brought forth extras from the presses. Seemingly, no one thought of disbelieving the outrageous reports. The evidence was all too clear, the plague of black bestiality had struck and its victims were falling all around. As evening approached, Atlanta was distressed, distracted, quivering in a heat of anxiety.

Beginning about 6:00 p.m., groups of white men began to congregate at streetcorners to discuss the reported outrages. A massive "Negro uprising" was rumored. Blacks gathered in small groups to discuss the news and to wonder at the agitation of the whites. Blacks, of course, discounted the rumors of rape and rebellion. Some whites on the edge of the crowds began to break away temporarily to harass passing Negroes. By 8:30 stories were being circulated of fights between blacks and whites, probably arising from these streetcorner encounters. Near the intersection of Decatur and Marietta Streets, a man climbed on a platform and began to harangue the crowd. Holding up a copy of an extra advertising "THIRD ASSAULT," he shouted, "Are white men going to stand for this?" The response was loud and quick. "No! Save our Women!" cried the mob. "Kill the niggers!" Now and again, fragments of the crowd would break away to encircle and attack blacks who happened to be passing. Other crowds began to move and became roving mobs. Bands of whites surged through the streets, yelling "Nigger!" whenever they saw a black face and rushing after their prey.

On into the small hours of the night white mobs prowled Atlanta freely, dragging black people from streetcars, smashing black businesses on Auburn Avenue, and, in a telling gloss to Henry Grady's "New South" message, laying the bodies of three victims at the foot of his monument in front of the offices of the Atlanta *Constitution*. One of those bodies had someone's initials carved on its back. On Monday the riot flared again in Brownsville, the adjacent black community in which Atlanta University, other prestigious institutions, and the homes of a number of the most eminent black leaders were located. Finally, only after the mobs had spent their fury did the violence subside.

AFTERMATH

Atlanta has been described as "Janus-faced." Indeed, the two-masked symbol of the dramatic arts, one happy and smiling backed against the other sad and tragic, representing the universe of comedy and tragedy, does seem appropriate. The city has been at once radical and reactionary, forward and backward, progressive and regressive, sophisticated and savage, raw and refined, and urban-bodied while it has remained country-minded. So, too, in race relations has this paragon of New South cities been both Conservative and Radical. During the summer of 1906, as Radicalism seized the city, the smiling Conservative face was almost lost in race relations. Like a tightrope walker on a suddenly elastic line, Atlanta swung distressingly low and almost lost its balance. But when the riot was over, when the disaster had run nearly as far as physical and mental endurance would allow, and a black man of eminence and obvious merit said, in essence, to a meeting of the most influential Atlantans, "What, for God's sake, do you want us to do?", the rope grew taut again. There was, embarrassingly, no answer. The great mass of blacks in Atlanta had been doing precisely what the whites told them to do—working, churching, and quietly managing their own affairs. They had been doing what Booker T. Washington had advised all blacks to do in that much celebrated speech in the city more than a decade before. They had cast down their buckets where they were, and now the water came up salty, bitter, and foul.

After the riot, there was clearly a Thermidorian reaction among whites. The Radical face receded as the Conservative mask rotated to the fore. With strong, bold, deft strokes of the trowel, Conservative Atlanta quickly mortared over the large and unsightly cracks left by the racial earthquake. Almost a fourth of the police force was fired and its administration reorganized. Courts that had sent so many blacks to the chain gangs now sent to jail some of the white mobsters. Far from being praised, members of the mobs were frankly labeled murderers. The streetcar companies rearranged their vehicles for a clearer separation of the races and ordered better treatment of blacks by their employees. The fact that mob action and lynching did not deter the potential rapist was recognized and publicly advertised. The grand jury censured the newspapers, and the *News* in particular, for their indulgence in sensationalism before and during the riot. Most journals vowed to do better. A Civil League of leading whites and blacks was organized to promote interracial harmony. Many influential whites began again to beat the happy racial rhythm and sing out the sweet song of how the best whites take care of the best Negroes . . . their "nigras." When they paused to listen, they seemed to hear the black voices responding harmoniously from the other side, uniting with their own.

Two-faced? Precisely. But all of this was better than what had gone before. A white lie, even a very large one, is better than murder. Further, if the Conservative face did not speak the whole truth, it did speak its own truth. It was real. When Atlanta was playing the conservative role, it was Conservative. It was not dissembling to appease the North, and it certainly was not dissembling to appeal to the blacks. Radical Atlanta had, itself, scared Atlanta straight, and Conservatism came to the fore. The city had become Conservative because it could not see itself in its ideal image and continue in violence. Atlanta, in its own eye, was progressive, it was rational, generous, and genteel. Ray Stannard Baker arrived in the city as the Conservative face of Janus was rapidly turning the Radical face to the rear, and he took the Conservative face for the true face, which it then was. Had Baker come two months before, he would have seen another face, and one no less true. As violence came, white fear receded; as violence receded, so too did the desire for violence. Law and order became the great goal, and even the memory of violence faded rapidly away from white minds. Shortly after the riot, one close observer thought that forty blacks had perished in the fray, an estimate commonly accepted. Some weeks later Baker reported ten blacks and two whites dead and sixty blacks and ten whites wounded. A 1969 study counted twenty-five blacks and one white dead and one hundred and fifty persons seriously wounded. The very count of the black dead reflected public consciousness of Radicalism's existence. It moved down from forty to ten to nothing as the riot was forgotten, and rediscovery only occurred late in the Civil Rights movement. The Atlanta riot, like the Robert Charles riot in New Orleans, was practically erased from popular memory and was generally refound by historians only in the late 1960s.

After the riot, whites in Atlanta were more careful in race relations, and blacks became very quiet. Blacks acquired a new caution, both with whites and with each other. Blackness became a serious liability and promiscuous association with other blacks a dangerous matter. They had learned, from bitter experience, to distrust the ability of the friendly face of Janus to control the hate face. Violence could come again. Blacks searched for a modus vivendi in a traditionally cautious style, by withdrawing. Sometimes they left Atlanta, and often they left Georgia, often by the hundreds and sometimes by the thousands. But, mostly, the black world retreated into itself.

The risingly Conservative leadership of white Atlanta worked hard to blame the riot on the lower and ragged fringes of the city's population. It was, so the rhetoric ran, the vagrant and criminal Negro who committed the exciting acts that gave the kernel of truth to the great fear of rape. It was the "white trash" who made up the mobs that stupidly punished all blacks. This lower order consisted of white bodies existing beyond the reach of society and without class. They were pariahs, untouchables, soulless white flesh, "skins," in the language of the day. Worst of all, they punished the best of the blacks for the sins of the worthless few. White trash hated Negroes, while their late masters loved them—in their places,—and jealousy led the lower order to hate the best of the colored people with double strength. Behind it all lay the saloons, and lawless men of both colors. Upper-class whites bore the original sin of not being properly vigilant before the riot. But now, they were ready, and they were redeemed. They were engaged, as Baker so elegantly phrased it, in an "extraordinary reconstructive work" to abolish saloons, vagrancy, and ignorance. Drink had corrupted the flesh, both black and white. Prohibition would begin to effect the cure and compulsory public education would carry it forward. Baker caught the new mood perfectly and, indeed, shared it heartily. His apologia for upper-class white Atlanta was contained in his article "Following the Color Line," which appeared in *The American Magazine* in April 1907, and was read nation-wide.[30]

Within a decade the black beast rapist practically disappeared as an image in the mind's eye of white Atlanta. But so too did the Washingtonian image of the black as progressive—working, saving, building, proudly earning his way into the world. In their stead came a resurgence of the image of the black as child, as neo-Sambo, appealing and appalling again, but most of all needing the helping hand of patrician and paternal whites to hold a place in the society.

What was true in Atlanta was true in the South generally. Black people who did not fit the stereotype of neo-Sambo had no presence in the eyes of whites. Black man as a man became "Invisible Man." The bad image of the black as beast went underground and re-emerged to be applied not to blacks, but to aliens. In the Frank case in Atlanta in 1913, as we shall see later, the beast became a Northern Jew with a German name, a college bred, opera-going urbanite, a wealthy factory master who would grind our girls into dust for gold. Sometimes the beast would be the alien Jew, but often he would take on other guises: he would be alien and Catholic; in both World Wars he would be German; and after the Russian revolution in 1917, he was most often Communist and eager to disturb our otherwise good black people and use them as tools against us. By the 1930s, the black beast of Radicalism had come to be, most often, the Commie-Jew-labor-organizer. It was no mere coincidence that in the 1950s during the Cold War and the rage for McCarthyism that deep-South Southerners, the very sons of secession, became the most loyal of Americans, the foremost of America firsters, totally undeceived by, as FBI Director J. Edgar Hoover called the communists, the "Masters of deceit."

CHAPTER V

The Inner Civil War:
The Conservative Mind
Confronts Radicalism, 1889–1915

Violence and the great threat of violence was one way in which Radicals sought to lower the self-esteem of blacks and thus render them more controllable on the way to their demise. But there were other, more subtle means to effect that end. We could never catalogue and describe, nor even count all of these instruments of discrimination. Indeed, the process can not be caught in words that must follow one upon the other. White people talking to blacks in the Radical mood, for instance, was not only a matter of choosing specific words to fall in sequence; it was also a matter of speech inflections, pauses, rises and falls in pitch and volume, of body postures and relative positions, of movements of eyes and hands, all simultaneous and beyond words. It was also more. It was a matter of dress and costume, of naming and titles of address, of place and setting, money in the bank, and talking down from the porch to the yard. Two of the tools used to reduce and, hence, to manage blacks were disfranchisement and segregation. Radicalism had a special motive in its effort to pass laws to disfranchise black men and to separate the races in public places, one that was distinctly different from the special motive of Conservatism in the same process. The Radical motive was to depress the expectations of blacks, especially black men, to make them less secure and ultimately less aggressive, to lead them to follow with minimal resistance the inevitable path to racial extinction. Radicals readily recognized, as Clark Howell said about disfranchisement in Georgia, that blacks were already practically disfranchised and segregated, but to Radicals the laws were useful in showing explicitly and blatantly the power of whites. They were tokens of hard and present truths and signs of things to come—of the surety of white supremacy and the futility of black resistance. Robert

Charles read the signs perfectly in Louisiana in 1900, and his death seemed to confirm the truth of his understanding.

Conservatives did respond to aggressive Radical actions. They responded to lynching, rioting, and the push to enact severe measures of disfranchisement and segregation. But the response of the Conservatives was always muted by the special character of Conservatism. Conservatives were never spectacular. They were not gladiators who descended into the arena to do combat with the barbarian, to do and die. Rather, they were willing to make a test, and to make a true test. But if they did not win that test, they would retire and wait. Conservatism knows that in the end it will win, and it knows that winning is a matter of action, but Conservatism also understands that winning ultimately is a matter of waiting for the right time, the right place, and the right issue. God is in his Heaven always, and in the end all things will come right on earth. The response of Convervatism to the Radical upsurge, then, was a generally soft reaction. It was executed by people possessed of a terrific patience that renders them very nearly unbeatable.

DEPOLITICALIZATION

The movement to disfranchise blacks by legal and constitutional means that swept through the South in the generation after 1890 was only a part of a larger and longer process that might be called the depoliticalization of the Negro. To focus upon legal and formal disfranchisement is to run the risk of neglecting the broad and much more important occurrence. Substantially the depoliticalization of the Negro had been achieved with the close of Reconstruction, especially in the deep South where blacks were most numerous and where they had been most active in the politics of Reconstruction. There, indeed, the political reduction of black people—by persuasion if possible, by fraud and intimidation if necessary—was precisely the central process of Redemption. The effort had its practical side in relieving Negroes of offices and removing ballots from black hands, but it also had a psychological aspect. A major part of Redemption involved enforcing upon Negroes the conviction that significant political power would never be theirs again. Most blacks, it seems, learned that lesson well. They simply retired from practical political activity. During this great emotional recession after Reconstruction, blacks moved downward from a practical inability to vote, to an inability to register to vote, to an inability even to participate in Democratic party activities and the Democratic primary (which, in effect, soon became the real election), and, finally, to an inability to maintain their undisputed representation in national Republican conventions, and, hence, from that, by the 1920s, to a loss of federal patronage.

But when one has said that blacks had already been largely removed from politics by Redemption, one must also hasten to say, "but not quite." Indeed, never quite. Somewhere in the South, blacks always voted, and somewhere in the North there was always sentiment that it should be so. The struggle of black people in the South to maintain a political life for themselves after Reconstruction was most striking in three forms: a persisting activism in certain enclaves heavily populated by blacks where Redemption had not thoroughly penetrated, a rather curious phenomenon that might be labelled the "echo Reconstruction" that occurred in the states of the upper South in the 1880s and 1890s after Reconstruction had definitely died in the lower South in 1877, and various upsurges of blacks in politics as allies of white splinter movements. These forms were not mutually exclusive, and now and again all three combined in one movement.

Paradoxically, one area of the deepest, longest-running, and most powerful participation by blacks in politics in the South after Reconstruction came out of compromises made in the black belts by Redemption itself. In some states in the early years of Redemption, the process of expelling Negroes entirely from politics appeared so vast an undertaking as to seem impossible. Therefore, Redeemers frequently resorted to programs of "containment." They gerrymandered black strength into restricted areas and conceded certain offices to blacks in return for other offices for whites. The South Carolina Democracy, for instance, yielded some offices and functions in the counties around Beaufort and Georgetown where the black majorities were no less than massive. Black political dominance in those areas eroded only gradually as local whites pressed, with aid from a state government firmly in the hands of whites, for more and more control. The gerrymandered black belt Congressional district in South Carolina seated a black Congressman, George Washington Murray, as late as 1896 and a black state representative as late as 1900. All-black militia companies, unarmed, persisted until 1905, and a black man remained as the Collector of the Port of Beaufort until ousted by Ben Tillman early in the Wilson administration in 1913.[1] In North Carolina, the Redeemers created the "Black Second" Congressional District, previously mentioned, to absorb a great portion of the black votes in the state. In 1888 the Black Second elected the state's first Negro Congressman, Henry Cheatham. Beginning with the enclave of the Black Second and thriving under a fusion arrangement with the Populists, Negroes in eastern North Carolina in the mid-1890s generated a growing, strengthening, grass roots variety of black power that was killed ultimately only by the white power that it, itself, unwittingly engendered in a state that was 75 percent white.

There was a rather striking persistence of black activism in politics in the upper South generally. In fact, it is possible to contend that in the upper South in the 1880s and 1890s there was a second Reconstruction, followed by still another Redemption. It was, in a sense, an "echo Reconstruction" that has, as a whole thing, gone largely unnoticed. When we generalize about Reconstruction in the South, we are often referring to Reconstruction in the deep South where blacks were most numerous and where the process ran its course fully and deeply before the end of 1877. In the upper South, the first Reconstruction was not only much more short-lived, it was also milder. This was true, perhaps, because blacks were few enough and native white Republicans were numerous enough to reduce substantially the strength of race as an issue and to make the first Reconstruction a milder thing—more of a conflict between white men and less of a contest between white and black, and therefore relatively less heated.

Tennessee affords a good example of an early Reconstruction and Redemption and a later recurrence of the process. The first Reconstruction in Tennessee began under the leadership of native whites in 1864 and was so far accomplished by 1867 that the radical Congress exempted it from the military rule established in that year in the other ten ex-Confederate states. The ease with which Tennessee passed through that first phase had much to do with the fact that unionism was very high in the state before and during the war (especially in the mountainous eastern portions), and the Republican party was able to muster into its ranks after the war a solid phalanx of native whites. Soon, the Democrats reclaimed the state, but in 1880 they lost the governor's chair to a still vital Republican party. In the 1880s, the as yet unchastened blacks of Tennessee were encouraged to attempt to move more fully into political life, first as followers within the resurgent Republican party and then, more assertively, as leaders willing to cooperate with white Democratic reformers against their own erstwhile white Republican bosses. The rebellion entered a critical phase as black leaders, such as John C. Napier, George W. Cable's Nashville friend, moved to claim offices for themselves and urge legislation favorable to blacks. Soon, the rebellion came to an abrupt end, brought up sharply against a risingly popular and lethal lily-whiteism among Republicans in the state. Finally, Democrats used the racial division among Republicans to reduce black political participation in Tennessee to a minimum.

In 1888 Tennessee Democrats pushed through a law that required citizens to establish their eligibility to vote by registering during a specified interval well before elections and then closed the books to additional registrations for some time before elections were actually held. Drawing out the process and making it complicated had the effect of discouraging the less well informed and determined among potential electors. Most of all, registration allowed political managers to go far toward molding the electorate into the exact shape that they desired and to monitor its performance.

In the same year, the "Volunteer State" was the first in the South to introduce the Australian ballot. This ballot simply listed all of the candidates for each office on a single slip of paper, indicating the party of each candidate and providing some means for the voter to mark his preference in the secrecy of the voting booth. Previously separate ballots for each party had been supplied, usually by the party itself. The voter had only to appear at the polls, ask for the ballot of the party of his choice, and place it in the box. This system lent itself to frauds of many kinds. For instance, voters could "stuff" a ballot box by carrying in a number of counterfeit ballots and covertly casting them into the box along with their legitimate votes. Under the Australian system, widely hailed as a progressive reform, there was but a single ballot and the voter claimed his ballot from the election officials at the polls. He then went into a closed place, and there, in private, marked his choices before placing his ballot in the box. Under the old system, any watcher could learn how a man voted. Under the Australian system, the voter's preference was his secret, and political bosses were thus presumably foiled. Use of the Australian system obviously required more than bare literacy on the part of the voter. The Australian ballot doubtlessly did promote honesty in voting in the South, but it also effectually disfranchised vast numbers of illiterates and near illiterates, black and white. It was, in essence, a moderate literacy test and was sustained as such by the Supreme Court in 1893.

In 1890 Tennessee improved upon the already remarkable results of its registration and balloting laws by adding a poll tax requirement for voting. Thereafter, the state seemed substantially relieved of concern about black voting, even though the black population comprised a quarter of the total and western counties were heavily Negro. Tennessee did go Republican in 1910 and 1912, but it was not because of black votes. The state had long nurtured a very strong white Republican element in its eastern, mountainous portions. A Republican Tennessee, then and since, does not at all imply a black Tennessee.[2]

What happened in Tennessee happened in other states of the upper South as well, but with less clarity. Possibly, there was an "echo Reconstruction" in the upper South in part because the first had not sufficiently raised the race issue, and, consequently, Redemption had not sufficiently downed it. The first Redemption had not "taken," and another, stronger innoculation was required to immunize those states from the ambitions of Negroes in politics. Thus, blacks in the upper South were substantially removed from politics only after the deep South Redemption in 1877.

There was a third form in which blacks re-entered politics after Redemption, and this phenomenon occurred in both the lower South and the upper. White splinter movements rebelling against conservative Democratic domination sometimes turned to appeal to potential black voters. In Virginia, in 1879, ex-Confederate General William "Billy" Mahone used black votes in his successful bid to gain control of the state. For a time he elevated himself to the United States Senate, and, as a by-product of his revolt, he raised the specter of blacks in politics again and absolutely horrified many of his fellow white Virginians.[3] In South Carolina, the Greenbackers did much the same, as did various elements of the warring Democracy in Georgia (in which, ironically, the Feltons were leaders) and Louisiana. In the 1890s Populists all over the South appealed to blacks for their support. In North Carolina, as we have seen, Populists and Republicans made the most successful fusion arrangement, one that held control of the state for four years after 1894, a control powered essentially by black votes. Spectacular as they sometimes were, these threats from white splinters were all evanescent, fading especially quickly in the deep South where blacks existed in relatively great numbers and where black Reconstruction had been most real. There, the very gathering of black power quickly—almost automatically—generated a counter-gathering of white power that ultimately prevailed.

Thus, during the post-Reconstruction era and on into the early years of the twentieth century, when Southern whites undertook to disfranchise black men further by legal and constitutional means, there was a real object in view. In every Southern state some black men did vote in some elections, and always there was a possibility that others might do so.

And yet those threats were limited. In the South at large, the great mass of blacks had not voted since Reconstruction. After Reconstruction black voting never threatened white supremacy in the South as a whole, nor was it ever an active threat in a given state for very long. The threat of black voting was spotty, and it was sporadic. When it arose, white politicians dealt with it locally and relatively quickly.

Why then did Southern whites pass laws to accomplish what had, in substance, already been accomplished? They did so, it seems, for varying combinations of three basic reasons: reform, politics, and race.

Disfranchisers of all persuasions clearly felt that they were acting in the spirit of reform. The fact was that previous disfranchisement had been achieved and was maintained by corruption, fraud, and intimidation, conditions that steadily tested the tolerance of the North and strained morality at home. The laws passed in and after 1890 sought to obtain the same end by legal means. The laws would purify the process, they would also purify the electorate. As the disfranchisers thought, legal disfranchisement would permanently remove corruptible voters from participation in the body politic—be they real or potential, major or minor, black or white. To them, the disfranchised were precisely the morally infirm, the ignorant, those who could be bought by the selfish interests or duped by demagogues.

Disfranchisement was also motivated by raw political partisanship. Parties in power do tend to attempt to load the electoral dice to reduce the potential of their opponents. This was true of Republicans, Populists, and independents as well as Democrats, and it was true in the North and West as well as in the South. Politically, the motivation of Massachusetts Republicans in attempting to disfranchise the newly arrived Irish who became Democrats was not vastly different from that of the Southern Democrats who attempted to disfranchise the newly emancipated blacks who became Republicans. Republicans in Reconstruction had disfranchised Democrats, and the Populists in power in the legislature in North Carolina in the 1890s were not at all above attempting to rewrite the charters of towns and alter town limits to throw those usually Democratic strongholds into the hands of Populists.

It happened, of course, that the Democrats were generally in power in the South in and after 1877. They sought, therefore, to disfranchise Republicans, Populists, and independents. Democrats did, in fact, pass laws that took the vote from the hands of hundreds of thousands of Republicans. But it also happened that the great majority of Republicans were black. To disfranchise a Republican was most often to disfranchise a black person. This raises a problem in ascertaining by the results which, between politics and race, was the primary motive? On the other hand, it hardly seems very necessary to establish a primary motive—both motives operated, and both operated powerfully. White Democrats were much gratified at the reduction of a Republican whether white or black, and to hit both with one shot would be especially gratifying. When Ben Tillman disfranchised the black man in South Carolina in 1895, he did not discount the income that would accrue to his party.

Finally the disfranchisers were also motivated by racism. More accurately, disfranchisers were motivated by two forms of racism—Radicalism and Conservatism—and each form had its special set of motivations, its preferences as to ways and means, and its concept of objectives.

Radicals disfranchised black men because, as Mrs. Felton declared, white men equalizing themselves with black men at the polls had the effect of leading black men to think that they could equalize themselves with white men elsewhere—particularly with white women. To Radicals, disfranchisement was a device to promote political and social—even psychological and sexual—purity. It was a way of removing the black voter from the path of progress, and also it was a tool for turning down black self-esteem. Radicals did see themselves as reformers, of course, but when Radicals disfranchised, race was the prime motivation, with partisan politics playing a strong secondary role.

Conservatives, far from thinking of disfranchisement as a way of ruling Negroes out of society, thought of it as a way of keeping them in, of protecting them and preserving them in their place. By relieving the incompetent black man of his vote, one relieved him of the power of abusing himself and others—and, consequently, one relieved whites of the necessity of abusing blacks by fraud and violence before and at the ballot boxes. Partisanship was present in Conservative disfranchisement, of course, but it was probably the least of three motives. On the other side, reform placed a very strong second, if indeed with many Conservatives, it did not place first.

Often, both Radical and Conservative disfranchisement used combinations of the same devices to effect their distinctly different ends, and thus it has been easy to assume a unity of motives among the disfranchisers that did not, in fact, exist. There was a profound division between Radical and Conservative disfranchisement, and that division was reflected subtly in the means preferred, if not always used, by each.

Like a golden thread running through an often confused weave, Conservative disfranchisement was marked by a willingness to leave the best of the blacks enfranchised and, conversely, to disfranchise the worst of the whites. For instance, in Virginia, where the Conservative mentality ultimately prevailed, the disfranchisement provisions in the 1902 Constitution resulted in leaving some 30,000 black voters on the registration books and removing some 60,000 whites. Conservatives, then, would nod approvingly at an aracial application of legal disfranchisement. On the other side, Radicals drove to disfranchise all black men and enfranchise all white men. Moreover, Radicals would never give more than lip service to a racially impartial application of the disfranchising process, and that was given for the benefit of a justifiably suspicious North. Seldom would the Radical yield even that. Like Ben Tillman, he much preferred to advertise loudly that all Negroes, regardless of merit, were going to be disfranchised, blatantly and in the greatest possible numbers and that the South was a white man's country.

Radicals also soon came to distinguish themselves from Conservatives by their preference for the "understanding clause" as a loophole device for letting in white voters and excluding black, while the latter came to prefer the "grandfather clause." These devices grew up in the 1890s as states rewrote their constitutions to meet the new times.

In eight Southern states, disfranchisement was sought by either amending or rewriting the constitution of the state. It will occasion no surprise that all five states that formed the Radical heartland (South Carolina, Georgia, Alabama, Mississippi, and Louisiana) were among the eight that wrote their actions into their fundamental law. Additionally, Virginia, North Carolina, and Oklahoma did so. In those eight states, disfranchisers of both persuasions typically set up standard qualifications of property, education, and good citizenship for voters. The reforming fathers then added a clause allowing prospective voters to by-pass those strict requirements by meeting some other special test. Soon, two alternative tests came to be the most favored: the "understanding clause" and the "grandfather clause."

The understanding clause permitted a citizen who could not qualify as a voter under the ordinary standards to do so by explaining a section of the state constitution read to him by an election official. Usually, three election officials judged the performance. Ideally, the understanding clause was a test of civic intelligence. Ultimately, however, it reflected in its results the intentions of the officials managing the election. Originally, the understanding clause was introduced in Mississippi in 1890 as an attempt to purify the electorate by constitutional means. Mississippi later became one of the most Radical of Southern states, but in 1890 it was still decidedly Conservative, and disfranchisement there was first sought in a spirit of racial Conservatism. Constitutional disfranchisement, the leadership thought, would save whites from the necessity of corrupting themselves in the election process, and it would also allow blacks to find their proper place in the body social.

Conservative Mississippi invented the understanding clause, but Ben Tillman in South Carolina was the first to turn it to Radical ends. Endorsing its use to disfranchise Negroes in a flagrantly discriminatory way, Tillman argued that "some poisons in small doses are very salutary and valuable medicines." In 1895, in drafting a new constitution for his state, Tillman got what he wanted. Briefly, the new constitution established adult male suffrage based on residence and poll tax requirements, plus an absence of convictions for certain crimes. Until January 1, 1898, anyone who met these qualifications and could read a section of the constitution (a literary test) or explain it when read to him (the understanding clause) would be registered for life. After that time, in order to register, an applicant must be able to read and write a section of the Constitution (a more stringent literacy test), or pay taxes on property assessed at $300. The administration of the understanding clause in the "Palmetto State" produced exactly the kind of disfranchisement sought by Radicals. Virtually no white man who seriously wanted the vote was denied, and practically no Negroes were allowed the privilege. Indicative was the fact that there were six black delegates in the constitutional convention itself. They were without any power save that of speech and a minority vote, both of which they used adroitly. Nevertheless, within ten years, South Carolina, a state in which a majority of the adult males were black, had no blacks in the legislature or any other significant state or local office, a condition that would prevail for more than half a century.

The understanding clause appealed to Radicals by the very fact that it allowed election officials to enroll whomever they chose as voters and to exclude all others. Conservatives grew to dislike it for precisely the same fact. Shortly, Conservatives came to prefer the so-called "grandfather clause," first developed in the Louisiana Constitution in 1898, as a means of purifying the electorate. Grandfather clauses used a variety of specific techniques, but all rested upon the basic idea that the voter who failed to qualify by other means might do so if either he or one of his ancestors had performed some certain act. Thus, the voter or an ancestor might have voted in some previous year (1867 was a favored year because blacks were not then generally allowed by the states to vote in state elections), or had performed some significant military service for the state or nation (in the Civil War, for instance). The great appeal of the grandfather clause to Conservatives was that qualification relied upon proof of some prior fact rather than the personal impressions of registration officials. A prospective voter or one of his ancestors either had or had not voted in 1867, either he or one of his ancestors had or had not served in the military. Cases thus were lifted out of the realm of personal impression into the realm of legally establishable fact. Law and order prone Conservatives relished this approach to disfranchisement. Not only did it secure the ends they desired, it also re-established rule of law in the stead of rule of men. Without rule of law, they thought, a society could not long survive.

Conservative disfranchisement was also marked by a preference for a short time interval in which the "loophole" device, be it either the understanding clause or the grandfather clause, was to be operative. Initially, both instruments were designed to function only for a limited period during which a new registration would be effected. Thereafter, theoretically, everyone, white as well as black, would have to meet the much more stringent requirements of literacy, property holding, or tax payments. Both Conservatives and Radicals seemed to assume that the few years of grace for white supremacy thus ensured would see whites sufficiently educated and wealthy to perpetuate their predominance. Behind that was the further assumption that whites were innately superior to blacks and would dominate in these areas in a free society.

At first, legal minds among the disfranchisers thought that a short life was essential to standing the test in the courts. However, as Radical politicians gathered experience in disfranchisement, they also gathered the courage to press for allowing the loophole clauses to run for longer intervals. Ultimately, some Radicals would give them life everlasting as a symbol of their intention that theirs would forever be a white man's country. In 1898, when the grandfather clause was first used in Louisiana, its operation was limited to some three months. North Carolina Radicals ultimately compromised for a constitutional amendment, passed in 1900, that allowed registration under a grandfather clause up to December 1, 1908. Virginia, in the end dominated by racial Conservatives, followed with a new constitution in 1902 that allowed its white supremacy clause to run only about a year and a half. Georgia in 1908 adopted disfranchisement with escape devices that included both understanding and grandfather clauses. The life of the grandfather clause would terminate in 1915, but the understanding clause, under Radical pressure, was made a *permanent* feature. In Georgia the line was clearly drawn: white men would vote in perpetuity as long as other white men so chose, and black men would not. Radicalism could hardly have displayed its power more arrogantly.

At the state level, disfranchisement was the first issue upon which Conservatives organized themselves to face the Radical onslaught effectively. In the deep South, Conservatives were usually easily over-run. For example, in Alabama, in a constitutional convention called in 1901 explicitly to effect disfranchisement, ex-governor William C. Oates led the Conservatives unsuccessfully against such vigorous Radicals as young J. Thomas Heflin. On the floor of the convention, Heflin predicted the coming race war and announced his intention to disarm the Negro politically and educationally prior to the fray. "I do not believe it is incumbent upon us to lift him up and educate him and put him on an equal footing that he may be armed and equipped when the combat comes," declared Heflin.[4] In the upper South, however, Conservatism fought and won. In Virginia and North Carolina especially, the Conservative response to the Radical challenge was clearly present in the struggle over disfranchisement, and the process in each state revealed much about the nature of racial Conservatism there and elsewhere.

DISFRANCHISEMENT IN OKLAHOMA AND ELSEWHERE

The framework within which constitutional disfranchisement occurred was constantly changing. Not only was it different in different states and in different regions within different states, it also changed over time. What seemed bold in Mississippi in 1890, or in South Carolina in 1895, or even in Louisiana in 1898, had become quite ordinary within a decade. By the end of 1902, six Southern states had passed disfranchising amendments to their constitutions, and Georgia, in 1908, was encouraged to follow. Oklahoma, in 1910, was the last state to incorporate disfranchising provisions into its constitution.

Oklahoma is, in many ways, the most curious of Southern states in race relations. In some aspects of racial activities, it is also the most revealing precisely because of its peculiarities. One obvious cause of Oklahoma's difference has been the presence there of a highly significant number of original Americans, the Indians, who have added a complicating third dimension to the bi-racial pattern usual in other states in the South. In addition, the northern and western counties in Oklahoma were populated by Yankees of a distinctly antislavery tradition. Many of these people filtered down from what had been in the 1850s "bleeding Kansas," bringing with them, if not a pro-Negro attitude, all of the special sensitivity about national democratic values and blacks that had marked that state in its birth. Oklahoma was a Southern state with a large Yankee colony. Finally, Oklahoma was the last in time of the Southern states to join the union. It became a Southern state, however, only after having been administered for a number of years by federal agents in a notably Northern and often Republican style. Government in the Territory of Oklahoma was Northern and officially aracial even though most of its population was Southern and white, many of these having come from Mississippi, Arkansas, and Texas. Because Oklahoma was thus ruled by the federal power between 1889 when it was first opened for settlement and 1907 when it gained statehood, it could be said that, in a sense, Oklahoma was the last of the Southern states to be redeemed from Reconstruction. The lateness with which Oklahomans gained self-rule allowed them to make up an official position on race relations out of materials already formed, to utilize the ready-made fabric that painful experience had woven in states east and south of them. Oklahoma had only to cut and sew, and then slip smoothly into its racial garments. In 1907, white Oklahoma had simply to decide whether it would opt for the Conservative dress or the Radical. At successive times, it would wear each.

Negroes had come into Oklahoma first as slaves, brought there by their Indian masters during the great removal from the southeast in the

1830s. In a peculiar variant, slavery had thrived in the Indian territory. Indeed, in all of the United States, slavery lived longest in Oklahoma. In the Indian Territory of Oklahoma, the Constitution and laws of the United States did not prevail. Relations between the United States and the Indians (described legally as "domestic dependent Nations") were carried on through diplomacy. Thus, the Emancipation Proclamation of 1863 freed no slaves in Oklahoma, nor did the passage of the Thirteenth Amendment in 1865. Slavery in the Indian Territory was ended by treaty, and only in 1866, a full year after emancipation elsewhere. Nor was this the end of the peculiar treatment of the slaves and ex-slaves of Indians. In the 1880s, when the federal government decided to divide tribal lands among individuals, the administration ruled that this special class of freedmen should be treated as members of the tribe of their late masters. Thus belatedly the Oklahoma freedman in the Indian nations actually received a homestead of, not the forty acres promised in the earlier Reconstruction, but eighty-eight acres.

In the decades after 1865, a large number of blacks migrated into Oklahoma. In 1907, when the territory passed into statehood, the black population was 120,000 or roughly 10 percent of that of the whites. Some of these had moved down from Kansas, others had participated in the so-called "run of 1889." Before 1889 settlement in Oklahoma by ordinary citizens, white and black, was illegal. Nevertheless, many frontiersmen had pushed into land supposedly reserved for Indians. The "run" occurred when the government finally capitulated to pressure and opened the eastern portion of Oklahoma to settlement. At 12:00 noon on April 22, 1889, at a signal from a cannon, thousands of hopeful settlers raced from the boundary line to claim their homesteads.

Those who evaded the authorities and entered the territory before the firing of the cannon were called "Sooners." In smiling recognition of this ambitious chicanery, Oklahoma has since called itself the "Sooner State." Among the fleet-footed, would-be farmers, were a number of blacks. For example, De Leslain R. Dawes, who had been born a slave in Georgetown County, South Carolina in 1860, was one of two Negroes who joined the race for land in Canadian County on that remarkable day.[5]

During its reign in the Oklahoma Territory, the federal government was conscientious in protecting the rights of black citizens. Particularly was this true during the Harrison administration (1889–93), at the very time in which Radical anti-Negro sentiment and lynching was on the rise elsewhere in the South. During these years and afterward, thousands of Southern Negroes moved into the Territory, where soon there were some twenty-seven all-black towns and one rural colony. These included Langston, named in honor of John Mercer Langston, the first Negro

Congressman from Virginia and once the president of Virginia State College; McCabe, named for a leading black come-outer; and another town whose name was politicly changed to Taft in 1908. Existing into 1907 in a relatively free federal enclave, Oklahoma blacks seemed to have generated a strong sense of self-worth that they brought into statehood after 1908. When the racial push came, Sooner State blacks pushed back. They did not always win, but neither did they always lose, and race relations in Oklahoma were always a bit different and a bit better than in most of the South.

Even so, Oklahoma was no paradise for black people. Generally whites and Indians were not sympathetic to their darker neighbors. In some communities in the turn-of-the-century years, "Whitecappers" appeared, attempting by the use of white hoods, threats, and violence to drive blacks away. On the urban scene in Oklahoma in 1902, inter-racial warfare flared in Lawton and Shawnee as if in echo to that of Wilmington and New Orleans.

As statehood approached, the position of Negroes in Oklahoma became more precarious. In 1904–05, a lily-white faction emerged even within the Republican party in the state. Still, the official attitude of the party—influenced especially by the racially liberal Kansas wing in the north and west—was very much for equal rights. Under the Roosevelt governor, Frank Franz, a Montanan who had been a Rough Rider with Teddy in Cuba, the Territory was carefully prepared both for statehood and a Republican ascendancy. In 1907, on the eve of the meeting of a convention called to draft a constitution, the Republicans stoutly declared that they stood on a platform of "equal rights to all persons regardless of race, creed, color, or locality."[6]

It soon became obvious, however, that Southern Democrats were most numerous in the territory and would dominate the convention. The overall tendency of the meeting was decidedly anti-Negro and veered toward the Radical. A suffragette, on the scene lobbying assiduously for her cause, tried to enlist the prestige of Radical Ben Tillman under the banner of women's rights. Indulging in truthful flattery, she wrote to the South Carolina Senator that he was "personally greatly admired by the state, where one of the new counties had just been named Tillman."[7] In spite of its Radical proclivities, the convention produced a constitution that was only mildly anti-Negro. Charles N. Haskell, the floor leader of the Democrats, very shrewdly guessed that President Theodore Roosevelt would veto a constitution that was blatantly discriminatory against Negroes. He therefore overrode his chief rival in the party, Lee Cruce, one of several "die-hard segregationists," to write a constitution that was at least acceptable to the federal government. In November 1907, Roosevelt proclaimed the Territory of Oklahoma and its adjunct, the Indian Territory, a state.

In the gubernatorial contest that followed, Haskell for the Democrats faced Franz for the Republicans. Blacks, of course, supported Franz. The Democrats, who were most numerous in the southeastern portion of the state—an area that was Southern enough to earn the title "little Dixie"—strenuously opposed him. Haskell easily won the governor's chair, and the voters elected an inaugural legislature that was heavily Democratic and virulently anti-Negro. A wave of Jim Crow legislation came out of the very first session of the legislative assembly, immediately belying the moderation formerly exhibited in the constitution. Disfranchisement, however, had to wait until 1910 when Oklahoma had its own "white supremacy" campaign.

In the campaign of 1910, the question was not whether the black man was to be equal at the polls. It was, rather, what would be the form of discrimination against him. Lee Cruce, the Radical segregationist, ran against William H. ("Alfalfa Bill") Murray in the primary for the Democratic nomination for governor. Cruce's platform featured a white man's government and an end to "Negro domination"—in some minds, apparently, an imminent possibility in Oklahoma. Compared with Cruce, Murray was conservative. His wife was the daughter of an Indian chief, and he had come to control vast areas of land through his marriage. A progressive farmer, he was so ardent an advocate of alfalfa as a conservation crop that the sobriquet "Alfalfa Bill" remained with him throughout his life. Not only did Murray gain economically by his marriage to an Indian woman, he also gained politically. In some parts of Oklahoma, Indians had wealth, power, and status. In Oklahoma, rather obviously, the right kind of miscegenation was an asset, not a liability. "Alfalfa Bill" liked red, and also he was not consumed with hatred for black. He himself simply assumed that Negroes were innately inferior; hence he was not especially concerned about legislating their subordination. He had mildly supported the Jim Crow laws passed by the 1908 legislature, but he had at first opposed the addition of a grandfather clause to the constitution.[8] Cruce won the election, and the constitution was amended to include a literacy requirement for the suffrage with a grandfather device as a loophole.

Oklahoma was the last state to use the grandfather clause, but the Oklahoma provision was the first to be struck down by the courts. In June 1915 the United States Supreme Court ruled the Oklahoma clause unconstitutional. Governor Robert L. Williams began to sound out the party leadership on calling a special session of the legislature to offer substitute remedies. His respondents reflected well the sentiments of the Oklahoma

Democracy on the subject. Among those who answered the governor's inquiry was Oklahoma's blind Senator Thomas P. Gore. Gore was a Mississippian by birth, a Texas Populist by adoption, and finally a Democrat in the Sooner State. Gore thought that there should be an early meeting of the legislature to pass an amendment to the constitution that would give the legislature full and unspecified power in the matter of suffrage. However, one provision would deny any intention of evading the Fifteenth Amendment and another would rule out property qualifications— a sop to the numerous "home-grown" socialists whose presence added to Oklahoma's uniqueness. "My own judgment," said Gore, "is after looking over the field pretty well that Mississippi had devised the best solution of this problem." The understanding clause, he thought, could not be reviewed judicially.[9]

Most members of the legislature were in favor of vigorous action to take the vote out of black hands. A member from Idabel thought that "an election law to preserve white supremacy is the paramount question in southeast Oklahoma."[10] A representative from Washita County thought that the legislature had to save the ballot from "the ignorant and irrisponsible [*sic*] negro," while a member from Delaware County felt that "we must do something with these Niggers."[11] Shortly, the governor proceeded to call a special meeting of the legislature, which came to be known as "the Jim Crow session." It passed a law that opened up the registration books for a brief period during which whites were simply welcomed to the rolls and blacks discouraged. Apparently, the process was sufficiently effective until it was challenged in the courts in 1934.[12]

In Florida, Arkansas, Texas, and Kentucky, as in Tennessee, disfranchisement was achieved by means less drastic than constitutional amendment. In these states, many white leaders concluded that a poll tax requirement for registration and voting combined with the Australian ballot was the easy way to relieve themselves of black voters. In four of these states the black population was only a quarter of the total, and in Kentucky it was only a tenth. Hence, these people might well feel more in control of their situations than those in states where the potential black electorate exceeded or came near to the white.

In West Virginia, Maryland, and Delaware, the disfranchisement movement met its Waterloo. In those states, attempts to reduce the black electorate encountered stern opposition both from blacks and sympathetic whites. After sharp contests, the disfranchisers failed. Further North, in New York for instance, there was sentiment for the disfranchisement of blacks, and for the disfranchisement of the new immigrants as well. But, generally speaking, the sentiment produced no significant results in restricting the suffrage. In the North and in the border states, black men—and later women—did vote; and their votes worked to make them free. In 1912, some black leaders had sufficient strength to bargain with Woodrow Wilson before giving him their support for the presidency. It was no mere coincidence that the last black to come to Congress in the first black revolution came from the South, and that the first black to come to Congress in the second black revolution was Oscar de Priest, who came to Capitol Hill from black Chicago in 1929.

Southern Radical leadership never felt perfectly safe from Negro voting. Long after blacks had ceased to be an active threat to white political supremacy, they worked to hold tight the ranks against black intrusion. For instance, in 1914 Ben Tillman wrote an irate letter to a potential maverick in his home state. "To vote the Republican ticket, which you threaten to do, would carry with it your forgetting the great number of negroes in South Carolina who are watching and praying for a division among the white people," he admonished. "We have perhaps forty or fifty thousand who are eligible to register under our own laws, but they are now quiet and doing nothing in a political way. Do you want to wake them up and have a return of the years of 'good stealing'."[13]

Southern white leadership at large was also persistently fearful of Northern interference in Southern race relations. There were always some Northern white liberals who were not willing to let the Negro go, and these always had a measure of power within the Republican party. The result was that, not only did Northern Republicans continue to face the "Southern question," but Southern Democrats never lost sight of the "Northern question"—namely, the possibility of another Reconstruction of their homeland under the not-so-tender auspices of the federal government.

In these circumstances, it is hardly surprising that white leadership in the South began to gaze fondly toward the repeal of the Fifteenth Amendment. Conservatives saw in repeal a return to law and order and the safe restoration of power to the local, socially responsible leadership where it belonged. Alone and without distorting outside influences, the organic society would re-establish itself.

Radicals saw the repeal of the amendment as the *coup de grâce* to black political aspirations. It seems to have been a trend in those decades that reform efforts at the state level soon rose to the national. Even where Radical reformers won and enacted their programs much as they liked at the state level—as did Ben Tillman in South Carolina and James K. Vardaman in Mississippi—apparently their eyes soon lifted to the national arena. It was almost as if they had come to understand by experience the truth that in an industrializing, centralizing, nationalizing America, local problems were inextricably intertwined with national problems. Local and state solutions could only be piecemeal, and near satisfaction could only be achieved in the national arena. Interestingly, historians of Populism seem to have arrived at the same conclusion concerning the subjects of their study. Populists in power—as distinguished from Populists in rhetoric—were strangely slow and astoundingly moderate in the reforms they actually effected. It was as if their new power imposed upon them a realization of how powerless they actually were.

Many Radical leaders in politics did eventually find their way to Washington, and they carried in their luggage the fond dream of repealing the Fifteenth Amendment. Thomas W. Hardwick long represented that sentiment as a Congressman from Georgia. James K. Vardaman brought it to the Senate from Mississippi in 1913. Ben Tillman, of course, also relished the idea. But Tillman had been in Washington since 1895. He was wise to the delicacy of the task and sought to school his Radical colleagues. "It will take persistent and long agitation to educate the country and especially the politicians in it up to the point of openly and boldly advocating the repeal of the 15th Amendment," he warned his newly arrived and junior colleague from Mississippi. A step in the right direction, he thought, would have been the insertion of such a plank in the Democratic platform in 1912. He suspected that many Northern politicians were waiting for the day when they could vote for the repeal of the Fifteenth Amendment, and he prayed for the time when he could join in that effort. But, he cautioned, the time was not yet.[14]

Other Radicals arriving in Washington soon learned the lesson that Tillman taught. Several years after the Wilsonians had moved to Washington, Rebecca Felton rued the fact that "not a single Democratic Congressman" had offered a bill to disfranchise the black man nationally. "The South has long expected relief from the negro's ballot privilege if a Democratic Administration succeeded to the control of the Government," she declared. Still, she admitted that repeal would have been frosting on a very large cake already possessed by the Radicals. "It is a fact that the negro has no ballot privilege in the Solid South," she conceded. "Effectually hampered by registration laws, they are effectually disfranchised by white primary elections."[15]

Ultimately, it was not the myriad and ingenious legal stratagems of Southern white leadership that disfranchised and depoliticalized Negroes in the South after Reconstruction. This is true in spite of the fact that literally thousands of books, articles, pamphlets, theses, dissertations, treatises, and lectures have been expended upon those intricate cleverosities. Certainly laws were important to the process, but probably they were even more important as symbols than they were in positively denying the ballot to black hands. Shrewd old Ben Tillman's estimate was accurate: if white solidarity were broken, state election laws would provide only a poor defense. More vitally important than the laws were the economic, the physical, and especially the social and psychological sanctions imposed upon blacks to keep them from voting and participating in politics. In the end, it was white power and white solidarity in the desire to exclude the great mass of Negroes from political life that effected the political reduction of black people. Behind it all, in politics as well as in everything else, it was white unanimity against blackness, molded rigid in a white culture, monolithic, total, and tight, that put the black man either down or out. The exclusion of blacks from politics both drew upon and contributed to the exclusion of blacks everywhere. The Democratic party, the white primary, the numerous legal techniques, and the white men who monopolized the election machinery were but the cutting edge of a determination, deep and wide, already achieved.

Initially, whites had little faith in the permanency of black withdrawal. As the years slipped by, however, they began to take the nonparticipation of Negroes in politics as another sign of black acceptance of white superiority. What had begun as artifice ended as natural. There was much in the palpable world that seemed to certify white superiority and justify the political subordination of black people. By the 1930s, the white electorate, itself greatly reduced, was super-satisfied with its world. The exclusion of blacks from politics was not even thought about; it was accepted simply as the natural order of things.

The "American dilemma" between the ideal of democracy and the way Negroes were treated in the United States that Gunnar Myrdal discovered in the late 1930s and advertised in 1944 was purely academic. What was so very clear from the aracial heights of Sweden was all but invisible in the biracial bogs of the South. Ideally, neatly logically, there should have been a dilemma. In the real and conscious mind of the white South there was none. It did not even occur to the great mass of Southern whites in the 1930s that blacks ought to be in politics; Negroes had nothing to do with democracy. If idealized research could have looked into the hearts of its Southern white subjects in those years, it would have found them bleeding hardly one drop for the oppressed blacks. Instead, they would have seen hearts stoutly thumping with assurance that they beat in rhythm with heavenly drums. In fact, Southerners felt that blacks were in their appointed place, and that they, the Southern whites themselves, were the most democratic of Americans. In every primary election in the democratic, one-party South, every citizen could be a candidate for office, and the best man could win. It was an open game, and any number could play.

When white Southerners eventually discovered a dilemma in race relations, it was not in the realm of politics. Rather was it in the Kingdom of Christ. The evangelist in this Great Awakening was almost the opposite of the Scandinavian scholar in both philosophical and physical terms. He was a Christian spiritualist not a social scientist, he was black, and he was truly a native son, one of the deep South's own. He was, of course, Martin Luther King, Jr. In the end it was the power of their own idealized vision of themselves as Christians, transcended into blackness, personified in King and his seemingly loving and non-violent host, that shook them to the roots of self. King's power was, precisely, that he was so Southern. And when they smote him—as they inevitably must—they hurt themselves. Somewhere the whites had taught the blacks all too well, and the whites themselves had somehow learned to value blacks as a spiritual people too much. Through the blacks they became their own accusers, and their guilt was all too clear. Christ would not do what they had done. That knowledge—dim or clear—shook the Southern mind at its moral foundations; and it sent white souls, frayed and frightened, scurrying across the emotional landscape in search of a new peace.

THE SEPARATION OF THE RACES

It is fully appropriate that legal disfranchisement and legal segregation be linked. While legal disfranchisement generally ran its course between about 1890 and 1915, legal segregation generally ran its course between about 1889 and 1915. Also, just as disfranchisement was part of a much larger process that might be called the depoliticalization of the Negro, legal segregation was part of a larger process that might be called the separation of the races. The mental and physical separation of the races practically began, of course, with the beginning of British America. Black people were early distinguished from whites—if not simply by color, then surely by their being non-Christian and non-English—and the distinction soon came to be firmly institutionalized in slavery. Paradoxically, slavery enforced a profound mental separation of the races even as it compelled a physical proximity, a peculiar integration, between master and slave. Not all blacks in the American South were slaves, however, and in the last generation of slavery whites in power moved to bring the quarter-million free blacks under more stringent control. By the time of the Civil War, these people were, indeed, "slaves without masters," and one of the devices by which they were controlled was a more careful legal and physical separation.[16]

With emancipation came a great increase in the separation of the races. In quantitative terms, probably the most significant area was economics. Domestic servants in freedom fled the households of the white elite; but, more important, the demise of slavery meant the demise of the plantation as it had been both in fact and in mind. With certain crops and in certain areas, as with sugar in Louisiana and with rice in Carolina, plantations did remain intact as economic units, owned or leased and managed by one person with a work force of black people under his direct supervision. However, the vast majority of plantations, especially among those that had produced cotton or tobacco as their staple, broke down into so many farms. This occurred, as we have noticed above, because black people—not white people—would have it so. Blacks wanted their own farms, and they wanted their own family and no others on their farms. Whether by somehow buying land, renting for cash, or, as was massively the case, by share-cropping, this was their desire. It was a desire that went stubbornly against the strongly expressed wishes of the landed gentry. Landowners, with good reason, did not trust either the capacity or the willingness of tenants to take care of their lands under year-by-year· contracts. Moreover, in late slavery, plantations were thought to be relatively efficient economic units. There were, indeed, economies of scale in running a plantation under skilled managers that individual small farmers could never attain. Even so, because the freedmen simply refused to work in gangs as they had in slavery, their desire to break up the plantations into small farms was, for the most part, realized. Whereas black people in slavery had lived together in the very faces of the whites, they were now scattered over the countryside as separate families, relatively removed from the eyes of the whites. This was, in effect, a residential separation of a high order. The very place in which blacks had been proximate to whites before—in their work on the plantations—was now marked by a high level of separation, a separation upon which blacks themselves insisted.

Ordinarily, black people labored on their farms during the week, and on the seventh day they went to church. Here again the pattern went from whatever mixing there might have been in the churching of whites and slaves to a profound separation. Just as black people pulled away from white control on the plantations, so too did they move to pull out of white control in the churches. In the last generation of slavery, several hundred thousand slaves had been enrolled in white churches. Many hundreds of thousands more were supervised in one way or another by white churchmen in separated services. In emancipation, the white connection ended with amazing rapidity as black members withdrew from white churches and established their own. Black churches that had been physically separated but under white supervision also established their independence. In addition many blacks who had never been churched in slavery became so in freedom. Indeed, several hundred thousand black people joined the two great all-black churches, the African Methodist Episcopal Church and the African Methodist Episcopal Church Zion, both of which had often been excluded from the South in the previous generation. The whole process of withdrawal began with emancipation and by 1868 was practically completed. Certainly one could still find a black member in a white church hither and yon, even into the twentieth century, but a close look at those members would reveal that they were usually sextons, custodians, and servants in the parish parsonage. Even as it grew prodigiously in the first flush of freedom, the black church took on the separated character that would lead people a hundred years later to say with perfect accuracy that eleven o'clock Sunday morning is the most segregated hour in America.

In freedom, there were two areas in which the two races came physically together most often. The first was as domestics, and the second was in the towns and cities and in the public carriers that joined those towns and cities. In the first relation, mixing was very tolerable to whites because the relative condition of each race was clearly fixed. There could be no misunderstanding the fact that the servant was the servant of the master or mistress. Domestic service was tolerable to blacks as a way to earn a living, and they could always move on to another household if need be. Contact in the growing towns and cities where impersonal relations were on the rise was, indeed, a racial frontier. There were not many blacks in urban areas compared with those who remained on the land, but those city dwellers were riding the wave of the future. With federal guarantees of civil rights for all citizens embodied first in the Civil Rights Act of 1866 and then in the Fourteenth Amendment in 1868, urban blacks presumed themselves to have equal rights as citizens, including equal rights to public accommodations. The black codes enacted in the South by the Johnson state governments soon after the war were outlawed, as were a scattering of specifically segregative measures. Very generally, first the military governments and then the Republican governments in the various Southern states in and after 1868 made rules and laws that positively opened all public accommodations to all people. Finally, in the twilight of Reconstruction the federal government enacted the Civil Rights Act of 1875. These acts ruled that streetcars, trains, steam passenger boats, restaurants, theaters, hotels, and all such facilities were open to all persons regardless of race. Even so, the federal and state governments did not make violations of these laws criminal offenses; they were, rather, civil offenses for which the offended party might bring a civil suit and collect damages.

Numerous black leaders asserted their rights under these laws. Apparently, they were often denied in spite of the laws. When they pressed their cases to the end, they usually won. However, the litigation was long and costly, and often damages were awarded in such trivial amounts as to constitute an opinion of the lack of seriousness of these violations. In brief, even in Reconstruction, antisegregation laws were not well enforced, and after Reconstruction were effectually vitiated by the courts.[17]

During Reconstruction the great mass of blacks simply did not seek admission to white-dominated facilities. Even when they did so and won, some form of physical separation customarily prevailed. The fundamental fact was that during Reconstruction and for some years thereafter, the essential pattern of life of the great mass of black people precluded any significant mixing of the races. The vast majority of black people were rural and comparatively poor. They had neither access to nor money to afford public accommodations as did whites. Generally, they did not have the experience that would have led them to want to do what the whites wanted to do, and their way of life itself did not give them opportunity to try. In and for some time after Reconstruction, when one is talking about the mixing of the races in public places, one is talking about some of the most affluent blacks some of the time.

The one area in which integration in Reconstruction might have taken a great step forward was in the public schools. All over the South a mark of Republican Reconstruction regimes was to put in place legislation for compulsory education, and in every state some progress was made in the realization of that ideal. Yet, only in New Orleans were the schools integrated in some significant measure. Here and there elsewhere, black children and white children went to school under the same roof, but even in these circumstances some sort of separation usually prevailed. Even the integration that occurred in New Orleans was seriously impaired by mob action in 1874.[18]

The failure to integrate public schools in Reconstruction, potentially an area of recurrent and intimate association between blacks and whites, was a great loss to the nation. It was an opportunity to bring up a new generation—a New Negro and a New White—that had at least had contact with one another in formative situations in which the authorities were ostensibly committed to equality. The separation of the races in the schools not only perpetuated a separation of cultures, it promoted the cultivation, the enrichment of each to the exclusion of the other. The failure to integrate was based on a conviction among many black leaders and most influential whites in education that if they integrated the public schools, the whites would stay away and thus cripple the whole effort. Black leadership in South Carolina, for instance, argued the point carefully in a constitutional convention in 1868 and decided for allowing a voluntary separation on the understanding that in time white people in their own schools would be educated up to an acceptance of the civil equality of black people.[19] At the national level, ironically, some of the people who were most effective in promoting both white and black education—indeed, the real leaders in promoting public education in America—took the initiative in deliberately taking the schools out of the bill that was to become the Civil Rights Act of 1875.

Active in this connection was Barnas G. Sears, the primary agent of the Peabody Fund for disbursing educational money in the South. In the summer of 1870 he rued that "South Carolina, like Louisiana, is all afflicted with the curse of trying to have mixed schools."[20] Once that issue was cleared and the various states went for separation, the Peabody Fund moved ahead with alacrity to support separated systems. As the Civil Rights bill worked its tortured way through Congress, Sears took alarm that a provision calling for mixed schools would cause all of the white children to be withdrawn from the public schools and lobbied for its defeat.[21] Racially integrated education was not, of course, made a part of the act as finally passed.

The 1880s witnessed a rapid erosion in the legal claims of Negroes to equality of access to public accommodations. In 1883 the Supreme Court vitiated the Civil Rights Act of 1875 in all places except such federal enclaves as the territories, the District of Columbia, and aboard American vessels on the high seas. Beginning with Tennessee in 1882, the various states began to pass laws mandating segregation. In the famous case of *Plessy* v. *Ferguson* in 1896 the Supreme Court ruled constitutional a Louisiana law of 1890 separating the races on most railroads provided that equal accommodations were accorded to Negroes and whites. This "separate and equal rule" would guide the courts in such cases for the next sixty years.

The advent of Radicalism ushered in another era in the separation of the races. It was an era in which separation was legalized. Whereas in Reconstruction there had been laws against segregation, in and after 1889 there were waves of laws passed actually requiring segregation. This change represented no great revolution in physical arrangements because blacks had not been using these facilities in any large numbers anyway. It was a revolution, however, in declarations of intent by governments and the white constituencies they represented. These laws came in three waves: 1889–93, 1897–1907, and 1913–15; and they related to specific areas. The first two waves primarily affected public accommodations, especially common carriers, namely, trains, streetcars, and passenger boats. The third wave related to new industrial and urban situations. Specifically, it segregated facilities in factories, particularly toilets, and set up schemes designed to achieve block-by-block segregation in urban housing. That something new was happening in the separation of the races was indicated by the fact that a new word was required for such occasions. The word "segregation" apparently was not much used before 1899, and when it was used it had no special racial connotations. In and after that time, it was used frequently to refer to the separation of the races, and it seemed to carry with it the idea that the separation referred to was effected by law. The nationalization of the word seemed to occur in 1913 and 1914 with the attention that was focused on the attempt to segregate facilities in Washington, D.C.

Just as there were two essentially different kinds of disfranchisement, so too were there two different kinds of segregation. The laws in each set looked much alike, but they were applied to differing physical situations, they sprang from different motives, and they were designed to and did achieve different results.

Racial segregation as executed by Radicals was a deep South and a black belt phenomenon; the motivation there was to save the white people at the expense of blacks. Segregation was a walling out of black people to minimize the damage they might do to whites on their way to their demise. It was also a device for putting down feelings of self-esteem among black people, first by exclusion and then by relegation to inferior accommodations. Thus, while the Supreme Court had declared that separated facilities were to be equal, they were not so in fact. Often railroad companies argued that they used the very same cars on different runs for both races, but yet somehow black people kept getting the impression that their cars were older, dirtier, and more unsafe than those used by whites. In truth, Radicals wanted black people to have clearly inferior accommodations and to know that they were inferior. Like arbitrary disfranchisement, arbitrary relegation to always inferior facilities was a sign of where the power actually lay, and where it was likely to lie in the future. On trains, steamboats, and streetcars, an extra fillip was that segregation legislation made provision for the servants of white people to ride in the white cars if the white employers so chose. Obviously, the whites made the rules, and they could alter them at will to suit their convenience.

Segregation as executed by Conservatives was for a purpose quite different from that of the Radicals. Conservatives sought segregation in public accommodations to protect black people in their persons and in their dignity. For Conservatives, segregation meant giving the black person a very special place in which he would be protected. Far from putting down the self-esteem of black people, Conservative segregation was designed to preserve and encourage it. Conservatives also segregated for the purpose of saving whites from abusing themselves by abusing black people in public accommodations. White men lowered themselves by making suggestive remarks to black women in the second-class cars on the trains. Often black men resented those remarks, and fights broke out. If disorderly white men were removed from proximity to black people, then this kind of disturbance would cease.

Virginia offers a good example of Conservatism in segregation. There had been precisely such troubles on the trains in Virginia in the 1890s. When the reformers got firmly in control for a time after 1900, they passed a segregation law. It set aside facilities for black people, a place where black people could ride by themselves and have dignity as well as comfort. In true Virginia style, it also divided white facilities. Trains that made sufficiently long runs were required to provide not only a separate car for blacks, but also first- and second-class cars for whites. The second-class white car was for the less genteel sort, the people who wanted to do what they used to do in the second-class car, plus those who chose not to or could not afford to pay first-class fare. The first-class car, of course, was for ladies and gentlemen. Just as Virginia reformers were willing to leave some black men enfranchised and were not at all unwilling to disfranchise some white men, so too would they make a place for black people on the trains and segregate less worthy whites in second-class facilities. In segregation, as in disfranchisement, Conservatism moved in a mood distinctly different from that of Radicalism.[22]

By far the most vigorous acts of segregation came in the first two waves. The third wave, in 1913–15, was clearly feeble. Indeed, it was then that segregation was turned back at the borders of the South. Ordinances for effecting residential segregation block-by-block were reversed or failed to pass in Baltimore and Oklahoma City. In Wilmington, Delaware, a move to establish separate windows for black and white citizens to do business with the city was defeated. In the North, attempts to pass legislation based on Radical premises also failed. In 1907, for instance, a proposal by the future mayor of New York City, Jimmy Walker, to pass a law against miscegenation was defeated in the state legislature. Geographically, by 1915, Radicalism had reached its high water marks somewhere south of Wilmington and east of Oklahoma City.

After 1915 the era of legal separation expired. Obviously, segregation laws were passed in considerable numbers thereafter; but they were passed sporadically, spottily, and in a makeshift fashion. Often they came in response to new technology or new institutions. Thus, laws concerning elevators, airplanes, and buses appeared. Here and there laws required that textbooks that had been used in black schools could not be used in white, and separate Bibles were required in the courtrooms upon which to touch and swear.

Unlike laws disfranchising blacks, which at least were well-thought-out and internally consistent within each state, segregation laws within each state were passed over a long period of time, related to different areas, varied widely from state to state, and varied even more widely within each state as towns, cities, villages, and other local communities made their own laws. The results were rather chaotic, especially for a black person traveling. In 1892 a young black man from Raleigh, North Carolina, on his way to enroll in Meharry Medical School in Nashville, Tennessee, came to appreciate that fact. He had just been in railroad stations during his trip in which the drinking fountains were not segregated. Arriving in Chattanooga, he was bending down to drink at the fountain when he sensed some movement behind him. He turned just in time to see a policeman poised to bring his billy club down on his head. He was able to explain to the policeman that he did not know the local law or custom and escape beating and arrest.[23] Again the Radical point was vividly made. White people made the rules, and they could make them as arbitrarily as they pleased. If black people did not understand the rules, it was but another sign of their non-belonging in a white man's country.

THE SEPARATION OF CULTURES

The deep and peculiar separation of races that came to the South in the twentieth century was a matter of minds as well as bodies, and it had its roots in the separation of black and white cultures. There had always been separation, of course, but sometimes the distance between the races was greater than at others. Slavery bred its own curious brand of physical integration. Physically, of course, slavery required that blacks and whites be touching close day by day. Moreover, in its last generation the peculiar institution worked diligently to press a limited but smooth integration of the mass of black people into a culture ruled by whites. In Reconstruction, cultural integration continued, altered now to substitute Northern white ideals for Southern, as Northerners streamed into the South. However, even as Northerners in the South urged blacks, at least rhetorically, to join the mainstream of Northern white culture, Southern blacks were withdrawing physically—in religion, in education, and on the land. Paradoxically, even as black people were getting "whiter" in the cultural sense, they were retreating physically into enclaves that were increasingly black. With the exodus of Northerners after 1877, the process of disengagement accelerated rapidly, and the vision of white culture was practically lost to the immediate view of black folk.

The process of cultural separation was long in the making, but it was in full flux precisely as the passage of segregating legislation reached a crescendo between 1897 and 1907. In that decade, those multifarious black enclaves that emerged during and after Reconstruction were coming rapidly under the unifying aegis of Booker T. Washington, and in their many parts they carried within them the hard core of black culture for the twentieth-century South. Washington's leadership had many failings, but it did at least raise a flag under which the great mass of black people could rally as distinctly black. However arrived at, the South— and the nation—would soon have a black world on one side and a white world on the other.[24]

The growing separation of cultures in the postwar South was evident in many ways. One clear manifestation was in music. Blues was long considered "race" music; that is, for blacks only. As such, it was often denigrated by jazz musicians of both races. Unalloyed Bluesmen, such as B. B. King, found little audience for their talent outside of the "chitlin circuit," as the round of black clubs and theaters was called.

Cultural separation was also manifested in a separation of language. Black and white language evolved away from each other, and that process was succinctly illustrated, as mentioned before, in naming practices. In slavery, black people had typically taken names from four sources. In early slavery, African names, such as Sambo, meaning second son, persisted. As creolization occurred, and Africans in America began to generate a new world culture fitted to their lives on this side of the Atlantic, African names sometimes shifted into American variations. Negro children in America in the fifth, sixth, and seventh generations continued to receive African names or variants thereof, not in veneration of Africa, but rather in honor of some older American-born relatives who bore those names. In slavery blacks had also taken Biblical names such as Gabriel, Joshua, and Rachel, classical names such as Bacchus, Scipio, and Phoebe, and British names such as George, Charles, and Mary. In freedom, African-derived and classical names tended to disappear while Biblical and British names remained. Toward the end of the nineteenth century, however, black people began to invent given names that were not at all in the language of whites.[25] For examples, Robert Charles's youngest sister was named Floril, and a younger brother Aliac. Another brother, born in 1869, was named John Wesley, while three older brothers born in slavery were named George, Henry, and Charles.[26] In the twentieth century the tendency became even more pronounced, and one encounters Countee Cullen, Eartha Kitt, Wynonie Harris, and Leontyne Price. Beautiful, euphonious, and close-fitting names, but distinctly not white.

Given two cultures, the issue became not a matter of whether or not there would be separation. It was, rather, a matter of what would be the process and form of separation. There would be prejudice and discrimination on both sides, and there would be responses on both. There would be a white country and a black country, and the frontier would find itself wherever the balance between the needs and power of white people and the needs and power of black people was struck. How was the balance struck? Historically in the South it has been found in a process probably best described as the "etiquette" of race relations. That process has never been a matter primarily of either laws or no laws, and de facto separation is a rather clumsy term, hobbled specially by the fact that it has come to be reflexively juxtaposed to legal separation. Legal separation was embodied in the whole matrix and had no opposite.

In a very real sense, there was no single or unitary race line in the South either before, during, or after the era of segregative legislation. Probably, only a Northerner like the journalist Ray Stannard Baker, who wrote a book on the subject, could imagine that he was following a color line, and he, perhaps, was led to do so by his origins in a North that in 1908 was being flooded to overflowing by ghettoizing immigrants from Southern and Eastern Europe.[27] Just as the attempt to apply class lines derived from European culture does not work well in the homogeneous Old Settled South—indeed does more to confound understanding than it does to promote it—so too with race lines. Race relations in the South have been worked out very much like white relations have been worked out—each case, each event, each meeting between one and another as it occurred. When black met white, the nature of the exchange was negotiated according to the time, the place, and the individuals involved—with sensitivity to generally understood customs. There were guidelines to behavior, but what was to be done in a specific situation was what was most comfortable to the parties concerned. In a specific situation one could err in judgment and act beyond the tolerances of custom. But etiquette itself required forgiveness of the avowedly contrite transgressor. It was always a matter of individual responsibility. The two cultures evolved words to say, gestures to make—a language in which individuals might negotiate interracial encounters; but each situation was unique, and the solution in each situation personal and creative. There was a black country and a white country, and the frontier between them was not clearly marked and was ever-shifting as if in some undeclared and usually quiet war. The location and nature of the frontier were much more a function of mind than of matter, of white minds and black minds rather than white bodies and black bodies.

WHY SOME LEADERS BECAME RADICALS

A most revealing thing about white leadership in race relations during this generation is that they all—Liberals, Conservatives, and Radicals—shared certain characteristics. All these people were concerned about black people, and some were no less than obsessed by the subject. Not all white leaders in the South were so deeply concerned. One can read correspondence maintained by some whites while they lived in the midst of a sea of black people and find no mention of the other race. On the other hand, one encounters some diaries and chains of correspondence of whites that report minutely on the prosaic comings and going of blacks—preachers and politicians, workers, servants, and children. It is a fact that some whites have been very sensitive to the black presence, and others, relatively speaking, have not. The concern might manifest itself concretely in pro-black activities, as with Liberals or high Conservatives, or it might surface as Ku Klux terrorism. Some, clearly, are touched, and others are not.

Foremost among the traits common to all leaders in the three groups was that they were Southern "aristocrats," which is to say that they had been themselves or were the heirs of substantial slaveholders and relatively large landholders, were considered "well-to-do," at least in their home communities, and were well-educated, if only self-educated. From the beginning and on through the Radical era, no one who had any large influence on race relations was poor white, or came from a background that might be described as such. Moreover, none were even "plain folk," yeoman farmers, or urban middle class, or born of such parental stock. Of the many people who gained sufficient prominence to be mentioned as leaders, only one, Edgar Gardner Murphy, was not born to the patrician life. As we shall see, by the time he became an adult, he was himself a superb example of a Southern gentleman, and as such he would never have been so ungracious as to mention that anyone of proper manners and spirit had been born poor.

Poor boys—and poor girls too—have made it in the South, but they did not seem to make it in the age of Radicalism. Our cohort of Radical leaders all had a headstart in life by dint of being born to those certain parents. They were leaders at large at first, leaders in race relations later, and they all began as Conservatives. Exactly why some made the shift to Radicalism and others did not remains a difficult question to answer. At the mass level, I have suggested that it had much to do with psychological images of self, generated out of Victorian ideas and internalized in Southern culture in the years before the Civil War. In the agricultural depression in the late 1880s and through the 1890s, white men lost power in a new and frightening way. They found themselves disadvantaged and locked into a rapidly changing national and international economics that they were powerless to control. At the same time that the material pie was shrinking, blacks were becoming increasingly competitive with whites. Attempting to regain some measure of control through political action quickly proved abortive. The result was that Southern whites in the mass were unable to play the role of protector-as-breadwinner with the satisfaction to which they always aspired and had sometimes achieved. Embattled, white men picked up and emphasized another part of that role, the protector-as-defender of the purity of their women, in this instance against the imagined threat from the black beast rapist. Lynching and rioting, total disfranchisement, and blatant segregation formed satisfying displays of power in one area of their lives when they could no longer display power in another. Such displays were most gratifying in precisely the regions where they were most needed—in the black belts where the power of black men in Reconstruction had been most striking and their potential for displacing white men was now greatest.

One common thread that tied Radical leaders to followers and separated them from their Conservative neighbors lay in the realm not of economics or politics but of psychology. Some men and women among the Southern white elite seemed more susceptible to the Radical hysteria than others simply by dint of entering the era with psyches ready-made. Some needed devils, and Radicalism supplied the need with the full sanction of society and seeming truth. Thomas Dixon, for example, did not feel that he was being victimized materially. Indeed, he was rich and getting richer, but that was not enough. What he really needed was a victim to lay upon the altar of his mother's suffering, and the "black beast rapist" appeared as if by providence to supply that end. Ben Tillman was relatively rich, twice governor of his state, and a United States Senator when he led the disfranchising movement in South Carolina; yet he needed to see himself as the great protector of womanhood, and Radicalism allowed him to skip rather gloriously into that role. These two men were not only caught up in Radicalism, they moved to lead it as they moved to lead, if they could, whatever they were in. As leaders, they were tremendously effective in broadcasting its ideas and institutionalizing it in public life. In the whole of the white population of the South, they found millions of kindred spirits.

In that same Southern white population, there were people whose psyches sought angels, and they found these in such various places as in "woman," in churchly missions to their unspoiled Anglo-Saxon brothers and sisters at home, or the as yet untouched and un-Christian masses abroad. In the 1880s it was still possible for some whites to see blacks as innocents, as children of God. In the minds of the whites that image was never totally lost, and was most strongly held in the camp of the Conservatives. But even the most stringent Radicals were often rapt in their praise of the old-time Negro, the few long-lived Aunt Jennys and Uncle Neds whom they treasured. The slide from a Conservative to a Radical posture in race, from a need to see the Negro as angel to a need to see the Negro as devil, was deeply grooved and well lubricated. Atticus Haygood phrased it beautifully when he chided some fellow whites for having conceived of the black person as "an angel in ebony." When they found that black people could not live up to the expectations imposed upon them, he charged, the whites were sorely disappointed and reversed themselves. The Devil is, after all, a fallen angel, and, as Haygood suggested, the tendency of some of the disappointed was to race to the opposite extreme. Seeing the Negro as angelic child carried, built-in, the threat of seeing him as demonic adult. Moreover, as Radicalism carried the Negro down, it carried white women up, and it highlighted each at opposite extremes. Finally, Radical leadership was possessed of a curious tendency to externalize both good and evil, to see the source of each as emanating not from themselves, but from these visible bodies outside of themselves.

Rebecca Felton, too, had her special needs. What was she lacking that Radicalism provided? Woman's role was not that of breadwinner. As a "lady," she had only to stand upon the pedestal and offer images of piety, purity, domesticity, and submissiveness. Yet it seems that in 1873, at age thirty-eight, she decided to stop having children after four of her five children had died. Almost immediately thereafter she attempted to come down from the pedestal and to be something other than what the role prescribed—to enter active politics via her husband. No one would challenge Rebecca Felton's piety and purity, but, after 1873, her domesticity and submissiveness were seriously suspect. She later declared that for eight or ten years she hardly got outside her gate during that early period of child-bearing and rearing.[28] Any image of domesticity she might have previously sustained was severely damaged by her flagrant social agnosticism, and her submissiveness soon evaporated entirely. In the 1890s she was "no lady," but she was highly effective as a critic of her society. Like her fictive fellow Georgian Scarlett O'Hara and many other Southern women in and after Reconstruction, and especially in the seemingly never-ending depression of the 1890s, she had found herself in the difficult position of attempting to scrub the floor from the heights of the pedestal. Those women, perhaps, were conscious of the unfairness of being trapped between expectations and realities, and it would not have been unreasonable for them to assume that it was upper-class white men who had created that dissonant world. These men had indeed run Southern society through the Civil War, Reconstruction, and into the great depression of the 1890s, and they had made a mess of it—cumulatively. Felton's devils were men, not all men, but especially some men such as the *"poseur"* John B. Gordon on the white side and the black beast rapist on the other.

In the 1890s it was as if Rebecca Felton wanted to explode the world on the chance that when the pieces fell and came together again, the arrangement would be better. For her, Radicalism in 1897 was a splendidly clever bomb that she rolled boldly and squarely into the grand gathering on Tybee Island of the richest and most gentlemanly of Georgia farmers, and detonated. Rebecca Felton blew them away. She hoisted them by their own Victorian petards. Even if they did succeed as breadwinners, even if they lynched the thousand black men a week that she demanded, they could never save every single white woman in the South from violation by a black rapist. Given the retrogressing Negro male, white men could never be perfect in their role as white women could be in theirs, and, hence, they could never deliver as promised and never give satisfaction to the Rebecca Feltons of the South who called them repeatedly and firmly to their duty.

Radical leaders, like Radicals at large, seemed to be people specially affected by a sense of powerlessness, people who strove valiantly to develop power and exercise it to counter that feeling of vulnerability. Of course, managing black people in an arrogant and arbitrary manner was a satisfying exercise for such people, but there was another nemesis to be dealt with, and a very real one—the North. The North had crushed the South by raw force, and it was painfully evident to the postwar generations that the North was the victor. The North clearly had power over the South, and it could do with the South as it chose. In the 1880s and 1890s, it had chosen to do nothing in the South racially, nor to intervene politically, as long as the South in effect submitted to colonial status. The South obtained its first significant chance of redeeming itself in the nation by participating wholeheartedly in the Spanish-American War. Dixon, quite appropriately, made national reunion one of the two interwoven themes in *The Leopard's Spots,* (a pattern he repeated in *The Clansman* and carried into *The Birth of a Nation*), and he marked the beginning of success in that movement with the "splendid little war," as Theodore Roosevelt's Secretary of State, John Hay, called the Spanish conflict. At the same time, Ben Tillman was promoting the Great White Fleet, even if it meant doling out giant contracts to the much hated steel trust. By the end of World War I, the allegiance of the South to the nation had passed from the suspect to the assured. Southerners paid dearly in material terms for that confidence, but it seems that they paid willingly, and even eagerly.

The complexity of why some Southern leaders became Radicals while others did not is also related to the Janus-faced image I have raised before. It is in the nature of Western culture to see things in dichotomies—hot-cold, him-her, up-down, heaven-hell, angel-devil, love-hate, and so on *ad infinitum,* dividing every facet of life in two and stretching it out to either extreme. In that Southern world of human affairs there were many dichotomies and two faces for each. There was a face that looked politics, others, economics, religion, or race, and so on through a vast array of categories and sub-categories. Behind every face there was its opposite, and the opposites were joined in continuums. Every white Southerner, for instance, contained within himself a potential to see the black person either as child or as beast, joined together at the point at which the child becomes the beast. Each individual at a given time would come down on the scale at a given point, but he would show only a single face, or, briefly with the edge, none. In the same fashion, everyone carried within himself as a part of his culture a potential to go relatively Aristotelian or Platonic. If one got outside the South and outside Western Civilization, he might move out beyond the continuum and break it, but given the time and place the continuum contained the limits of possibility. In the South, then, every Conservative carried within himself the seed of Radicalism. Within the same universe in the white mind, the black child angel could shift across the scale to become the adult devil always there. With some Conservatives the shift occurred and the Radical potential took life in or after 1889. It grew and came to rule the person in racial matters. In others the shift never happened. In these, the Radical potential was arrested and held in check by the other, the Conservative self.

Radical leaders were people who came to stand high on the extreme end of certain scales, and who came together to agree upon a common perception of the nature of black people, and, hence, of the proper course of race relations. In the white leadership cadre of a black belt area there were people whose bias was already high as philosophical realists, who were willful, crisis-oriented, combative, simplex, prone to seek popularity, and who were always moved by basic feelings of insecurity that led them into hard drives for power, drives for a capability to rearrange and order the disjunctive world in which they lived. There were also among these people some who needed devils. In the late 1880s and afterward, as unrest—economic, political, and cultural—swept through the land, their previous attitude toward black people came unfixed and slipped across the mid-point to fill that need for devils. The child became the beast, and ideas about race began to fuse with ideas about other things—the nature of man, economics, politics—to form a world-view. As unrest continued and, indeed, raged in the 1890s, these people came to the fore and they fixed, from time to time, upon the retrograding black as the great evil. It was not, ultimately, that Radicalism was created in and after 1889, it was rather that a potential always latent had come into power in the black belts of the South.

Those among the elite who did not resonate to ideas of the retrogressing black lost out as leaders of the masses in racial matters. Racial Conservatives simply had no constituency if they happened to live in Radical areas, even though they might well retain great and even ruling influence in other realms. Leaders whose personal proclivities were idealistic, who saw a complex world and did not feel the need of adulation from the masses, who felt relatively well satisfied with themselves and did not need devils, and who held to the more tenable idea of Negro as child were simply by-passed in matters of race.

Thus many things combined at a particular time to give a tremendous thrust to Radicalism. Had there been no great world depression in and after 1893, had the material pie not been drastically reduced, people might have felt fulfilled in their images of themselves, and there would have been no Radical revolt. Had there been no industrial revolution, there would certainly have still been exploitation and there would have been racism, but it might never have achieved the vicious fillip that it attained in the turn-of-the-century years. Even more centrally, had there been no Victorian era in the South with exaggerated roles assigned by gender, had white men not seen themselves bound by God to the comfortable material support of their families and the domestication of their women, there probably would have been no Radical rage.

AN UNREAL WORLD:
RACE AND SEX IN THE MODERN SOUTH

But, of course, the industrial revolution did happen, and out of it spun Victorianism and, in the 1890s, a horrendous, seemingly unending depression. The special conjunction of two vastly powerful currents in the society, the one unreal (exaggerated sex roles) and the other all too real (the loss of material security as the economic depression lengthened), bore this strange, this peculiar and bitter fruit. Given the limits of its understanding of itself, given the acceptance of certain ideas of individualism, freedom, and laissez-faire economics, there was no way in which the society in the South could cope with the real problem. Unable ultimately to deal with the real world, Radical leadership opted to create in the life of the mind an unreal one. It was almost inevitable that they would use black people in this effort as they had used them before. Most signally, of course, they picked up on the idea of the retrogressing black. That idea finally expired of its own weighty untruth and fell by the wayside. But in the psychological realm the damage had already been done. Radicals had worked effectively to unplug the South from the real world at large by generating an unreal racial world. While they failed, finally, in bringing their racial image to earth in a new order, they nevertheless promoted a loss by Southerners of their grasp on reality. It is a great and terrible paradox that the Radicals, so realistic in every other way, should misperceive black people so grossly and thereby contribute to the generation of a twentieth-century set of race relations that was fundamentally unreal.

It was almost as if the Radical era were a rehearsal for the unreality that marked the South in the twentieth century. That rehearsal had as many aspects as did the play itself. But probably nowhere was the unreality so widely divorced from the reality as in the specific image of the black beast rapist. That mythical being, so totally the creature of the white male imagination, has labored for white people in and after the Radical era probably as no real black person has ever done. If we can understand how he came to be and how he functioned, we will understand much of the history of the Southern white male mind, and, indeed, of Southern culture. It is a case of unreality, *in extremis.*

By the time of the Radical era, Southern white men had painted themselves into a sexual corner. In the antebellum era they had pedestalized white women in their minds. In so doing they had violated the equal humanity of women and removed them, in some degree, from possibilities of real intimacy with themselves. The Victorian complex that they so eagerly embraced spun out the curious idea that men were more sexual than women and, more importantly, that women (in the South, white women only) did not enjoy sex, that sexual relations were painful to them and allowed only out of a sense of love and duty. In the circumstances, men who pressed their attentions upon their wives violated them. They were beasts who, brutish and totally physical, satiated themselves at the expense of the very persons whom they had sworn before God to protect.[29] It seems unlikely that white men, in fact, much denied themselves sexual pleasure with their wives or with white women in general. However, if they did deny themselves, they felt tension; but if they did not,

Victorian mores led them to feel tension of another sort, namely, guilt. Whatever they did, they were caught in a trap of their own making.

In the antebellum period, if men of the white elite denied themselves sex with their wives, they did have other resorts, and the signs are abundant that there were many who used those resorts. Indeed, in the Old South, if a man had money and was unfeeling enough, he could buy a woman for life and use her pretty much as he chose with no fear of the law and little fear of his neighbors. If he had enough money he could buy a very desirable woman. In slavery, slave owners had full access to slave women, at least mentally, whatever they might or might not have done with them in the body. The myth arose that Negro women were especially lusty creatures, perhaps precisely because white men needed to think of them in that way. With emancipation, however, white men's access to black women virtually ended. Miscegenation, contemporary observers agreed, practically stopped. Mulatto women and black went with their husbands, and dark Victoria was no longer easily available in either body or imagination to upper-class white men. Furthermore, black men, now free, denied white men access to the heretofore ultimately satisfying alternative, black women, while white men continued to see black women as superbly sexual creatures, uninhibited, unlimited in venereal appetites and potential satisfactions. Black men were now mates to the sexual earth mothers. In Radical eyes in the 1890s, black men came to be not at all the Sambo of antebellum myth, but rather the insatiable satyr, specially built both physically and mentally for the libidinal women they served. The satyr sought all women, and at his most outrageous he sought especially the white woman heretofore denied him. The white man in the black belts found himself alone and often lonely—his women angelic above him, the black male (fully supported by black women) below—and he strapped with the largely unrewarding task of holding the two apart. Of course, it was a task where success went unnoticed and unrewarded, and his inevitable failure from time to time was conspicuously marked and condemned. One careless moment and another black man crashed through the white lines, plunged into the interior and devoured another fair maiden. The black beast rapist was the only man on earth who had sex with Southern white women without inhibition, to the exhaustion of desire, and, *mirable dictu,* without guilt. Black men had achieved what white men, in the Victorian infatuation, had lost—"no-fault" sex. Simple death, clearly, was too good for them.

Black leaders who explained the alleged epidemic of rape in the South as the work of white men disguising themselves as Negroes with burnt cork in order to achieve sexual satisfaction and yet escape punishment were not, after all, very far wrong. There was a beast abroad in the land, but he lived in white minds rather than black. White men were projecting upon black men extravagant sexual behavior because they were, at varying levels, denying ordinary sexual behavior to themselves. Southern white men, and most especially Southern white men of the upper class, used Southern black men much as the fictional Dorian Gray used the canvas in his attic to draw the portrait of his ugliness even as he showed himself beautiful to the world. To paint the black man as ugly and then to destroy him was to destroy the evil within themselves. To punish the black was to punish themselves, without hurting themselves, a rare and pleasurable power. Excessive punishment of the sin constituted high penance and ensured re-entry into the communion. If black men were, in essence, having sex with angels while white men abstained, then the punishment of black men must be as awful as the white man's guilt in contemplating himself in the same act, compounded by his frustration in abstaining. Never before had white men in the South elevated white women so high on the pedestal as did this first generation of boys born to Victorian mothers, and never before had they punished any men, white or black, as horrendously as they punished some black men in those years. The lynching of Henry Smith in Texas in 1893 and of Sam Hose in Georgia in 1899 were and have remained unmatched in horror in the history of such events in the region. Something was indeed new on the Southern landscape.

Thus black men were lynched for having achieved, seemingly, a sexual liberation that white men wanted but could not achieve without great feelings of guilt. In their frustration white men projected their own worst thoughts upon black men, imagined them acted out in some specific incident, and symbolically killed those thoughts by lynching a hapless black man. Almost any vulnerable black man would do. In effect, the black man lynched was the worst part of themselves. A function of lynching, if not indeed the primary function, was to offer up a sacrificial lamb for the sins of white men. Only about a third of the lynchings had anything at all to do with rape. Yet for more than a decade Southern white men insisted that lynching was especially for that crime, and they became blindly furious when anyone charged otherwise. White men needed to count every lynching against the awful crime because they needed every such performance they could get to quiet the boiling seas of emotion within themselves. There could hardly be enough of lynching; and, to get the most out of each, lynchings should be reported widely and in the closest detail as to what the black man did to the victim and what the lynchers did to him. The lynchers, active and passive, needed constant assurance that the evil had been destroyed, precisely because it had not. Castration was an ordinary part of the lynching ritual as applied to alleged rapists, and genital dismemberment was not unheard of. That symbol worked to declare that the evil was abolished permanently from the earth. William Faulkner, with his usual unflagging instinct for truth about the South, caught the image perfectly in the lynching of Joe Christmas in his novel *Light in August* (1932). Percy Grimm, at twenty-five a bachelor, a totally sterile young man, and a captain in the Mississippi national guard who had missed his true calling by having been born too late to have fought in World War I, chases Joe down relentlessly and shoots him. Before Joe dies, Grimm grabs a butcher knife and cuts away Joe's genitals. Flinging away the bloody knife, he declares, "Now you'll let white women alone, even in hell."[30] Percy Grimm himself certainly let white women alone in the body all of his life, but God only knows at what cost or what he did with women in his mind.

It is small wonder that observers noted a generalized restlessness before the alleged crime that brought on the lynching; noted, too, the purposeful, judicial, and most of all, the weirdly silent proceeding of the mob; counted the hundreds and even thousands of onlookers, often including women and children and sometimes brought in by special trains; saw the feeling of satisfaction, of peace, that followed the event, and, finally, the fact that if a community had done it once they were likely to do it again.

In the myth of the black beast rapist, the Radicals joined race and sex together in a way that would be momentous for twentieth-century America. Within the South, particularly the black belt states of the deep South, the power of the whites over blacks locally was tremendous. With the further defection of the North in things racial, it grew even stronger. The people who held that power imputed, implicitly and explicitly, great sexual potency to black people, and especially to black men. Radicals came to be obsessed by the possibility of sexual relations between black men and white women. Radicalism died, but the institutions it bred, formal and informal (including the etiquette of race relations), spoke out the message with exceeding clarity—that black men were to be kept away from white women, precisely because black men were super sexual creatures. As time passed, many black men would hear that message from the dominant whites. Some of these came to divest it of bad connotations, to believe it, to weave it into a counter-cultural system of values, and to act upon it.

Radicalism was a rehearsal for unreality in the twentieth-century South. The black beast rapist did not exist and neither did retrogression. Southern whites had had a rehearsal for unreality even before the Civil War in the creation of the Negro as the stereotypical child. In the 1890s they again set out upon a Yellow Brick Road of race, seeking a Wizard of Oz who would supply their missing parts—courage, heart, a manageable universe—and make them whole. They were spurred forward in that quest by having almost totally lost control of their material and mental worlds. It was perfectly symbolic of their fall that most Presidents before the Civil War had been slaveholding Southern planters, while no dyed-in-the cotton Southerner was President for a century afterward. The loss of economic, political, and psychological power was simply the price of having gambled and lost, fair enough in the world of *Realpolitik*. But it was, nevertheless, a hard fate to go so suddenly from high to low. In the quick snap, Southerners tended to lose their grasp on this world, racial and otherwise, but, almost measure for measure, as they lost this world they tended to improve their grasp upon the next.

THE BIBLE BELT

There was a rhythm in the life of Radicalism that fits well with the psychological principle of cognitive dissonance. That principle holds that dissonance arises when people perceive a disjunction between their ideas of what ought to be and what is. Relief from dissonance is sought in new behavior. In the South, from 1887 into 1915, Southern white men passed through three cycles in their attempts to fulfill their assigned roles as the protectors of white women, both materially as providers and physically. In each cycle they attempted at first to deal with the real economic problems that had severely reduced their capacity to provide for the material support of their women and other dependents. In the first cycle they attempted to achieve economic reform by economic action. In the last two cycles they resorted to political action to achieve economic reform. However, each of these efforts failed, and they then sought and achieved some measure of relief by raising the idea of the black beast as a physical threat to their women and acting to deal with him. Ultimately, economic, racial, and political actions all failed to restore to Southern men a satisfactory sense of self. By the end of 1915 they had ceased their struggles to build new structures in these areas and turned their minds in a significant degree away from the things of this world in favor of contemplating the next.

The theory of cognitive dissonance also holds that when people have made a choice between two ideas, they tend to love the choice they made and hate the choice they rejected. This concept helps to explain the astonishing extremes in love and hate that appeared in race and politics in the South in those years, extremes that have deeply marked Southern culture in the twentieth century.

In the late 1880s the South was moving into an agricultural recession. Something was distressingly wrong in the economic realm, and Southerners who were most affected generated farmers' alliances, initially economic institutions, as an attempt to deal directly with the problem. By 1889 that movement was proving to be not very satisfying, and farmers were thinking in terms of political action to achieve economic ends. Still there was not much one could do politically in 1889. In fact, on March 4, 1889, the Republicans under Benjamin Harrison had taken office, having swept the nation the previous November on a platform more menacing than helpful to farming interests in the South. There would not be another election until 1890, and even that would not include a presidential choice. The result was that many people opted for race as the arena of activity. If the road lay not with economic or political action, perhaps it lay with race. Cognitive dissonance would say that they would love the choice they made, that they would embrace and promote their choice with extraordinary, indeed, with unreasonable fervor. Racial extremism matched in magnitude the extreme dissonance of their era. Race was hot precisely because Southern society was hot.

Rather clearly, Radicalism experienced three periods of heightened activity, and each followed a period of vigorous economic or political activity—the political activity in each case having a large economic input. Radicalism ran very hot from 1889 to about 1893, with a sudden swell of lynchings and a first wave of disfranchising and segregating legislation. Between 1893 and 1897 it cooled and was less active, as was evident in declining lynchings and the relative absence of new segregating and disfranchising legislation. It was as if racial extremism had not been very satisfying after all, and the political alternative resurged in attractiveness, especially among Democrats of a liberal persuasion but particularly with the appearance of a distinct body of dissidents in the form of the People's or Populist party in 1892. Populist rhetoric, contrary to what Populists actually thought and felt, was, indeed, famously and revealingly nonracist. Populists at first, like both Democrats and Republicans, would certainly have welcomed black votes for themselves and consequently did not often advertise their racism. The record of events suggests that if Populist leaders felt that they could win their rebellion with Negroes voting, they would smile; if they could win with no Negroes voting, they would smile still, and more broadly. Politics reached one of its hottest times in the whole of United States history between 1892 and 1897. This is, in fact, the only time since the 1850s when it has seemed likely that a third party might gain viability and replace one of the two dominant parties. However, that political thrust cooled rapidly after 1896. In the sequel, racism surged up again and ran with unprecedented fury from 1897 through

1906. This most torrid phase of Radicalism was marked by a racist rhetoric never equaled in virulence in America and a new high state of violence, rioting, distinguished from lynching by the fact that any black, not a specific black, sufficed as a target. It was also marked by the passage of a great wave of disfranchising and segregating legislation—again probably the greatest such yet seen in America. It was as if racial extremism offered the kind of satisfaction that extreme politics had proved incapable of affording.

By the early twentieth century a pattern had been established in which Radical leaders responded to the disorder in their lives in either one of two primary ways—either politically by attacking the great corporations as the authors of evil, or racially by attacking the retrogressing black. It is highly significant that Ben Tillman in those years concocted only two speeches for the lecture circuits upon which he so frequently and profitably appeared. One of his talks was "The Race Question," and the other was "Railroads, Trusts, Monopolies." Each of these, as one would guess, was extravagant and engaging. Tillman always allowed the audience to choose on the spot, and, as he later reported, his race lecture was by far the most popular. In Georgia, in 1906, Hoke Smith, too, soon found that on the hustings his race speech outran his "monopolies" speech in popularity. Even so, race faded after 1906. Preluded by the progressive politics of Republicans Roosevelt and Taft, from about 1911 through Wilson's election in November 1912, politics-as-economic-reform took stage center again. Between 1913 and 1915 Radical racism had a mild resurgence, especially in the nation's capital as Radical leaders moved to segregate further the federal service and in legislation in the South designed to effect a more perfect segregation in newly rising industrial and urban situations. Thereafter, with the exception of a brief flare-up in and after World War I, neither race nor politics ran very hot for more than a generation. Indeed, it seems that a little success and a great deal of frustration on both those fronts promoted the choice by the South, after 1915, of still a third way, religion, at the expense of both race and reform politics. (See p. 196.)

The South has been particularly, and accurately, marked in twentieth-century America as the distinctly religious region—"the Bible belt." By this, people seem to mean that the South is given to Biblical fundamentalism, a sustained religious enthusiasm, and a high level of active church membership. Tom Dixon, in *The Leopard's Spots*, probably caught the essence of the fundamentalist South in a description of the ministry of the Reverend Durham. The Reverend Durham, he said, had a profound mastery of the Bible and could "speak pages of discourse in its very lan-

guage." It was "a divine alphabet," from which all things could be
spelled. The minister and the Bible were one.

> As a preacher he spoke with authority. He was narrow and dogmatic in his
> interpretations of the Bible, but his very narrowness and dogmatism were of
> his flesh and blood, elements of his power. He never stooped to controversy.
> He simply announced the Truth. The wise received it. The fools rejected it
> and were damned. That was all there was to it.[31]

The idea of the South as "the Bible belt" was new. No one talked about
the South as a Bible belt before the Civil War. Indeed, when one thought
of red-hot religious fervor in those years, he thought of the "Burnt-over
district" in upstate New York, an area that had been so repeatedly swept
by the fires of Christian evangelism as to suggest a burned-over forest.
During the Civil War both the North and the South went through very
strong religious revivals; but the South, after the war, generally fell away
from religion. By the turn of the century, however, an all-white Protestantism was clearly on the rise, and it tended toward fundamentalism,
evangelism, and other-worldliness. Increasingly, the Southern church
absolved itself from responsibility for judging race, economics, politics,
or the social order.

Tom Dixon, again with his usual sensitivity to what was going on in
popular feelings, caught this withdrawal well in a passage in *The Leopard's Spots*. In the novel he paints his alter ego, the Reverend Durham,
as preaching in his church the purely spiritual message that transcends
events in the outside world:

> The Preacher never touched on politics, no matter what the event under
> whose world import his people gathered. War was declared, and fought for
> four terrible years. Lee surrendered, the slaves were freed, and society was
> torn from the foundations of centuries, but you would never have known it
> from the lips of the Rev. John Durham in his pulpit. These things were but
> passing events. He spoke of God, of Truth, of Righteousness, of Judgment,
> the same yesterday, to-day and forever.[32]

In this passage, of course, Dixon depicted his father's ministry and not
his own. He operated in precisely the opposite fashion and, accordingly,
soon found for himself no place in the Southern church. His father was
a fundamentalist, and Tom knew the style well. As a child he had probably gone with the senior Dixon to service country churches around
Shelby. His father was known as "Preaching Dixon," and tradition has it
that whenever he came to lead a meeting he always swung down from
his horse singing a hymn. As he marched into the church still singing the
congregation would take up the song with him, and from there on it was
pure gospel.[33] One of the hymns that the Reverend Dixon might have

sung was a Southern favorite that captured the mood perfectly. "This world is not my home," it declares, "I have no mansions here. . . ." After the turn of the century, the other-worldliness always latent in Christianity came powerfully to the fore in Southern Protestantism.

The transformation of the South into the Bible belt was not unlike the Roman reaction to the fifth-century invasions in which the city of Rome itself was sacked repeatedly, almost at will, by the barbarians. The final response of the Romans was encapsulated in St. Augustine's book *The City of God* (525 A.D.). The real city, he said, was not this earthly vanity called Rome. The real city was in heaven. The lesson is that when the earthly city becomes untenable, when we can no longer live in this world as we were wont to do, we retreat to the heavenly City of God. So, too, in the South.

The modern retreat of the South into the City of God might have had its beginnings on the bloody battlefields of the Civil War. That war brought Southerners from high to low very suddenly, so suddenly, perhaps, that they are as yet unable fully to absorb the fact of their defeat. Faulkner was probably right again when in his novels he went back to hang up Southern white youth upon that afternoon of July 3, 1863, just before Pickett's charge at Gettysburg. If one had to choose a specific point in time and a specific place when Southern white culture altered course, that was close enough.

The retreat of the South from reality might have been furthered by the seizure by the Yankee barbarians and the black defectors of the bodies of the Southern states during Reconstruction. The hard material realities of Reconstruction and the depression of the 1890s might have reinforced and exaggerated that alienation by unfreezing religion, as it unfroze race and politics, to produce a shift toward other-worldliness and Biblical fundamentalism.

When Southern life recrystallized again after 1915, religion was at stage center. By that time the experience both in politics and race had been, at once, satisfying enough and frustrating enough to open the way for the primacy of religion. Just as the South had previously sought relief from dissonance in extremes of politics and racism, it now sought—and found—relief in an extreme of religion. Southern white ideas and behavior, true to the model, changed profoundly. Both politics and race remained severe problems in the South, but Southerners developed and maintained in their retreat a capacity to see neither. Outsiders were more perceptive of the obvious. Even the Knickerbocker and thoroughly Northeastern President Franklin D. Roosevelt recognized in the 1930s that the South was the nation's number one economic problem. Ironically, Southern patricians were the least able among America's leaders to

PERIOD	IDEA	VS	IDEA	NEW BEHAVIOR	DISSONANCE, RELIEF
1887–89	True men protect women		Not doing so materially against economic monopolies	Farmer's Alliance	D
1889–93	"		Trying so physically against the black beast	Lynching, segregation, disfranchisement, proscription	R
1893–97	"		Not doing so materially against economic monopolies	Political action for economic reform, as in the People's party	D
1897–1907	"		Trying so physically against the black beast	Lynching, rioting, segregation, disfranchisement, proscription	R
1907–13	"		Not doing so materially against economic monopolies	Progressive politics with Republicans TR and Taft, Democrat Wilson	D
1913–15	"		Trying so physically against the black beast, but finally, 1915, with no great success	Segregation in urban and industrial situations, and in the federal service	R

1915–	Nothing to protect against in regard to women
	Nothing to protect in regard to women
	Piety and purity protected, in part, by ministers and evangelists
	Rise of otherworldly, spiritual emphasis in Southern thinking
				Acceptance of economic colonization
				  No farmer's alliance
				  No reform economics
				  No unions of workers
				  Paternalistic economics
				
				Acceptance of political colonization
				  Decline in meaningful political activity
				  No reform politics
				  Dixie demagogues
				
				Decline of race as an issue
				  Decline in lynching
				  Decline in riots
				  Decline in new segregation legislation
				  Decline in new disfranchising measures
				  Decline in new proscription practices
				
				Rise of the Bible Belt
					Consonance

recognize that fact. And, of course, in race, the Negro problem in the Radical vision was totally lost. Women were protected, or, more pointedly, there was nothing really to protect against. By the end of the 1920s there was *no* Negro problem at all in the South if outsiders would simply leave Southern blacks alone. The retreat, the withdrawal of Southern culture into other-worldliness was virtually measured—inch, foot, and mile—in the so-called "Monkey Trial" in Dayton, Tennessee, in 1924. In that trial, the court upheld a state statute banning the teaching of Darwin's theory of the origin of species in the public schools. The South held firmly to its cloud, and it would not come down to earth. Neither the whole subjects of science, economics, politics, or race would hold even half the charm for them as a whole people that several dozen evangelists would hold. Further, at least in regard to these men, piety and purity had become a male province, while domesticity and submissiveness was certainly left totally to women. Southerners had, in a sense, shuffled off this mortal coil, and they lived, really lived (and by their own lights thrived) in that other world. Southern strength in national councils in the twentieth century might, in part, be precisely a function of that talent. The Southerner is, in a sense, the other American distinguished from the real, body-built, getting-ahead-in-this-world American. The Southerner is the idealistic American as personified, for instance, in Billy Graham, Sam Ervin, and Jimmy Carter, men who perceive Truth as transcendental. When our armies are defeated on the frontiers, when the crops are burning in the fields, when the barbarians sit steaming, bloody, and furious at the gate, it is Southerners who sometimes seem to offer the ultimate haven, the world of the spirit where no hard and violent hand can touch.

THE CENTRAL THEME OF SOUTHERN HISTORY

The first lastingly famous scholar of Southern history was the Georgian Ulrich B. Phillips (1877–1934). In 1928 Phillips passed over political and economic explanations to declare that the "central theme of Southern history" was the resolve of white men that the South "shall be and remain a white man's country."[34] Phillips had come to maturity in that earlier Georgia, the Georgia of Rebecca Felton, John Temple Graves, Tom Watson, Thomas Hardwick, Hoke Smith, and the rage of lynching. He was himself a racial Conservative, but he knew the Radical mind and presence, and race to him was indeed wide, deep, and long-lived. But what he published in 1928 would have been much more comprehensible in his natal Georgia in 1906. Indeed, by 1928 the idea might not have been all that real in daily life and speech, and even in the facts of recent history it might not have been all that true. What is basically misleading about the idea as an interpretative device is that after Reconstruction white men *were* supreme by any general definition of the word, and the South *was* a white man's country. White supremacy was never thereafter successfully challenged for a long time or over a broad geography. While white men might have been resolved to maintain white supremacy, they were not often required to act upon that resolve. Thus the behavior of white men in the South after 1877 is not totally explicable in terms of race and the corollary of white male domination.

It might be well to amplify the Phillips thesis as an interpretation of Southern history for the half-century after Reconstruction by saying that white supremacy was central in that it touched everything, not in that it everywhere and always ruled everything. In some places for some times, for instance in eastern North Carolina from 1898 through 1900 and in Atlanta through the riot in 1906, race did rule everything, and the prime issue was indeed the resolve that this particular area would be a white man's country. It was these "runs" of Radicalism that gave form to the centrality of race in Southern life in the twentieth century. But in these runs, the question was not, ultimately, white domination versus black domination. The hard reality was that whites in America outnumbered blacks ten to one, in the South roughly two to one, and even in the blackest of belts the whites possessed the vast majority of material wealth and controlled practically all of the ruling local institutions—including the police, the courts, and the military. With hindsight, we feel safe in saying that, finally, white America at large stood behind the white South for white supremacy, and there was little chance that white supremacy would fail.

The real historical question was not whether whites would rule. It was how much it would cost them to maintain their ascendancy. And, further, what would be the nature of the costs? How much would they have to change their schools, their police, judicial and penal systems, their ideas about Christianity, their ideas about men and women, class, and so on infinitely in order to keep black people in their place? In brief, how much would white society have to change itself and white Southerners change themselves in order to keep black people down? When they were through with the Radical era, there was hardly a facet of life in the South in which the whites had failed to respond to the black presence, and the nature of that response gave Southern white culture in the twentieth century its basic shape.

I have argued here that the Negro was a scapegoat in the turn-of-the century South, that whites were having difficulty coping with a burgeoning industrial-commercial-political order as it impacted upon a social-psychological-sexual order earlier generated, and that in that crisis they used the Negro in constructing an illusion that they were indeed managing their lives in important ways. My argument assumes that race is, in fact, not a real problem, that any person of any race is not barred by any physical difference from belonging to any culture. Race, in brief, is a problem of the mind and not of the body. It also assumes that, overall, white people have the power to make scapegoats of black people, to manage them sufficiently to create the illusion that they want to see. Actually I have selected out only certain areas of scapegoating to explore. The uses to which white power put black people in this fashion were virtually limitless. Once the game started, the Negro could be made the scapegoat for any number of ills, either of the body or of the mind. Indeed, from the white point of view, one might say that the Negro-as-scapegoat has been one of the nation's most valuable renewable resources. He can be used again and again and yet again, and never wear out. Lynching soon developed sophisticated variations. One could lynch just as effectively by genteel means as crudely by rope and faggot. Negroes could be lynched by account books. And they could be lynched by written history. They could be blamed retroactively for the Civil War and for the alleged excesses of Reconstruction. The reduction of the Negro opened the way for an honorable reunion of North and South. The Negro had been wrong simply by being there, and North and South had both been right.

I have advanced a scapegoat thesis in which the controllers acted unconsciously. There is another scapegoat thesis that argues that in the turn-of-the-century South special interests of various sorts consciously used the racism always latent in the white masses for their selfish ends. A variant of the latter depicts the racial extremist as the reformer who has been counted out by the political Conservatives and, in his frustration, gone understandably mad.

There are elements of truth in each of these latter scenarios, but as generalizations with wide applicability, they do not hold. Conservative leaders could not simply wave the flag of white supremacy and drive reform issues away. The scapegoat thesis does not work at all well when applied to big business. The masses were not duped into attacking the Negro instead of the monopolies by the arrogant powers of big business working through its lawyers and political placemen. Big business was arrogant, and it did have legal and political minions that sought avidly to do its bidding. Further, they were certainly not above using race, the Confederate cause, or practically anything else to achieve their goals. But their efforts in this relation were not famously successful. Indeed, business in matters of race has been a paper tiger, seemingly all powerful and voracious, but actually following the dictates of its society, respectfully, often even meekly, and at a foot-dragging distance. Only when the *status quo* deteriorates beyond recall, and business sees the promise of peace, good order, and predictability on the other side, does it flex its rather strong muscles and move with seeming strength and self-assurance to cross over. The response is understandable. Business exists to make money. Segregated facilities were more expensive than unsegregated facilities so that businesses with unsegregated facilities resisted oncoming segregation. But disorder and violence destroy business altogether. If the violence was to be ended by segregation, business readily adapted and passed the cost along. Once segregation was in place, and the machine running smoothly again, business wanted the machine to continue to run without disruption. It supported segregation, and the racial establishment generally, until violence and disorder threatened again. In the 1960s when it saw order and predictability on the side of desegregation, it moved for that end. Business has never been a self-conscious prime mover in race relations in America; rather it has always responded to the obvious necessities of its own interests.

Largely arising out of the "grit thesis," there is also the idea that racism was a scapegoat used by unscrupulous politicians to secure offices and power for themselves. These people allegedly went about raising racial fevers where temperatures had been normal before. If demagoguery suggests a measure of deception, of leaders saying things they do not believe, this allegation is totally unfounded as applied to the Radical era. The Radical leaders that we have talked about thus far were not at all dishonest. Indeed, it is difficult to imagine anyone being more candid, almost brutally so, than Ben Tillman, Rebecca Felton, James K. Vardaman, and their cohorts. Radicals were, in fact, probably more candid than were the Conservatives, such as William J. Northen, who raised images of what ought to be as if they already existed. Radical leadership really believed that the Negro was retrogressing. They did not dissemble, and they moved, by their own lights, in a highly responsible way to meet the challenge. There have been a vast number of demagogues in the South, and race has been the favored vehicle upon which they rode, but they came later and basically only after Radicalism as a mentality ceased to be.

There is an elaboration of the scapegoat thesis that asserts that the racial demagogue in the early twentieth century was the honest reformer gone mad. He had fought the good fight and lost unfairly, by violence and fraud at the polls perpetrated by Conservative politicians. In his frustration the reformer lost his mind and turned aggressively upon the Negro. There is in the broad history of the Radical era a shifting between race and politics that gives verisimilitude to this theory. When politics was not working, race was. But yet, in the main, it seems that a given leader, such as Marion Butler, either was Radicalized or not early on, and circumstances sooner or later caused his Radicalism to manifest itself. Consequently, it was not that the given leader was racially Conservative, encountered frustration, and then became a Radical. It was rather that he was consistently Radical but found it politically expedient to closet his Radicalism for a time.

But once I have said that, yes, the whites unconsciously made the Negro a scapegoat for the unmanageable evils of the industrial Leviathan and for certain personal and social psychological difficulties, I must also say more. I must say that in certain places during certain times, white people in the main—high, low, and in between—saw the Negro in retrogression as the clearest and most present danger there was. In that sense, at the living level, the Negro was not a scapegoat at all. Regardless of the absolute reality that might seem clear to us in retrospect, the reality that they perceived was the one by which they moved and made history. There were no consciously bad motives in the rise of Radicalism, no dishonesty in seeing one thing and saying another. Radicals were horribly wrong, but they were not cheats. What they did is inexcusable, but it is comprehensible. These people took certain materials that were within themselves, they looked at the world about them, and, moved by a whole complex of motives, they brought themselves together again far over on the Radical side of the racial scale. The Radical possibility had long been there. In 1865 it was freed with the freeing of the slaves, and after 1889 it realized very nearly its worst potential.

During the Radical era, racial thought and act became as extreme as they ever became in the South or in America. Black people were murdered horribly and in great numbers, and the quality of black life was deliberately and cruelly reduced. For blacks, the promise of American life grew small and dim even as it grew bright and large for white Americans. The physical abuse was terrible, but the real revolution in the South in the 1890s was not one of the relative placement of bodies. It was a revolution of minds—first of white minds and then of black. Radicalism was at the very core of the process. It flashed a message to Robert Charles in New Orleans and to W. E. B. Du Bois at Atlanta University that there was no place for black people in white America. The response of each was that somehow black people were going to have to "come out" of white America and build for themselves a black life. Radicalism was extremely effective in throwing both white and black cultures into high flux, but, ironically, Radicalism as a mentality—as a system for thinking about black people—died after about 1915, and as a system it was virtually forgotten. Afterward, it was very easy, very convenient, and perhaps even seemingly necessary to lose sight of the depth of racism in those turn-of-the-century years, and to assume that racism in the South had always been steady, monolithic, and mild.

We found when we later rediscovered the Radical era that things had not always been the same. It was a highly valuable discovery. If racism in the South is and has been immutable, if it has always been unchanged and unchangeable, then there is little hope of betterment. If there were turn-times when race relations improved or grew worse, then, perhaps, turns can be managed. In the same vein, if there were varieties of racism, then some are likely to be more tolerant than others. One can favor the best and disfavor the rest. The 1890s was a turn-time in race relations, and the turn was toward the worst variety. We have tended to think of that turn-time and the racial extremism that occurred then as a "burst effect," a one-time aberration, built upon misunderstanding. And so it was. But, lamentably, the misunderstanding was not engineered by exterior devils. And the cure, hence, was not so easy as identifying the malefactors and erasing them. The mass of white people who became Radicals were not duped in any ordinary sense of the term. There were no barkers at car-nival side shows, though that certainly came later. The Radicals were mistaken in their perceptions as all people are liable to be mistaken in their perceptions, and to do horrible things in consequence. The rise of Radicalism attests to the fact that racism does evolve, but it also attests to the fact that it is deep and broad, more deep, more pervasive, perhaps, than we as a nation are yet willing to recognize. Radicalism also attests to the fact that there are different kinds of racism in America, and the differences are vital. But no kind of racism has ever been benevolent, and none are now. Racially speaking, every white person has a picture of Dorian Gray in the attic, and each would do well, very well, to put him in the parlor.

CONSEQUENCES

What came out of the combat between Conservatism and Radicalism in the generation after 1889 was that in the deep South, particularly in the five black belt states of the deep South (South Carolina, Georgia, Alabama, Mississippi, and Louisiana), Radicalism gained absolute ascendancy and ruled for a time. It had its special perception of the Negro, and, conse-quently, in power it moved strongly to build and to alter institutions and psychologies to conform to that perception. That process affected social structure, economics, politics, religion, education, medicine, and judicial, police, and penal systems, and both white minds and black. The result was that in whole states, indeed, in a solid block of five contiguous states, black people were deliberately and carefully reduced materially and spiritually. Moreover, there was a spill-over effect from the Radical heartland, so that adjoining black belt areas in the South tended to fellow-travel with the Radical core. Eastern North Carolina, Virginia, and Maryland, southern Delaware, northern Florida, western Tennessee, eastern Arkansas and Texas, and southeastern Oklahoma all shared strength with the Radical heartland. It was a vast, pervasive system, and it did have a devastating effect upon black people and upon race relations in America.

In the upper South, on the other hand, in North Carolina and Tennessee and states north and west of these, Conservatism eventually won the struggle. Radicalism had its impact in the upper South, especially in the black belts within the various states, but it did not rule those states, and it did not have a controlling hand in shaping public institutions. After 1915, even in the five black belt states, Radicalism as a mentality died of its own inadequacies. Nevertheless, it had prevailed for a time, and the material and mental reduction of the Negro continued as perpetuated by the institutions that Radicalism had set in motion. After about 1915 Conservatism did resurge in the black belts all over the South, but when it did so, it tended by its very nature to license what it found. If black people had been reduced because Radicalism had once ruled race relations in a given place, resurgent Conservatism worked to freeze them in that lowly place. The freeze would last approximately half a century, and it functioned to press black people down, not only in the black belts, but wherever they were.

Further north, black-white relations in the District of Columbia reflected the combat in process in the South. Ultimately, the Wilson administration brought the South to power in Washington and it also brought Southern solutions to the race problem to the nation's capital. The story of race relations in Washington during Wilson's two administrations was a replay on a small scale of the broad history of race relations in the South during the preceding generation. From Wilson's inauguration in 1913 into 1915, Southern Conservatives and Radicals in the government struggled with each other over race at the same time that they wrestled with others over the great social issues of tariffs, currency, and the regulation of national industries. Northern white liberals also entered the racial fray, as did black militants and accommodationists. Throughout the play there was much misunderstanding by each element of the motives and goals, the points of view of other elements, and of the real situation. Overall, the pattern was a nearly perfect repeat of a quarter-century of Southern interracial history. Initially a vigorous Radicalism attacked a rather complacent Conservatism; Conservatism withdrew until circumstances allowed its resurgence with strength; the counterattack regained some ground, but for the most part it fixed and legitimated the physical segregation that Radicals had achieved. Whatever was was right. As in the South, thereafter Conservatism drifted—with neither anchor nor direction, and in effect rudderless.

Finally in the North at large during the turn-of-the-century decades there was a steep decline in the commitment to blacks in the South. From the beginning, the liberality of the North to the Negro had been severely limited by its own racism. Led out by American ideals of equality, the North was always liable to be jerked back from its liberal posture by the shortened chain of its own prejudice. Tentatively and briefly committed to ideals of equal citizenship in Reconstruction, it soon tired and abandoned that effort. In the 1880s and 1890s, the North grew increasingly more concerned about problems at home, and as it did so it became less concerned about the Negro in the South. The rise of giant combinations of economic power and an influx of immigrants bringing "Rum and Romanism" threatened to drown the American image of the country as pure and Protestant. "Rebellion" now came to signify not only the past Southern penchant for rule or ruin, but also the future threat from the left, from organized and violent labor, and an array of frightening ideologies ranging through socialism and anarchism. In and after the panic of 1893, the anxieties of the preceding decade were heightened and reinforced. Rather clearly, the North began to think that it had problems at home more deserving of its attention than the racial situation in the South.

In the early years of the twentieth century the North had not only surrendered any serious idea of interfering with race relations as they were developing in the South; it was also coming to a rather open acceptance of its own racism vis à vis black Americans. "The plain fact is," Ray Stannard Baker told the Sagamore Sociological Conference in 1909 after extensive research on the problem, "most of us in the north do not believe in any real democracy as between white and colored men."[35] Southern blacks who went north had ample opportunity to test Northern attitudes on race as compared with Southern. An Atlanta University student who worked for a banker in Bridgeport, Connecticut, made it his business to study the difference during one summer. Prejudice in the North was milder, he observed, but the real result was the same. "I came to the conclusion," he wrote to his friends in Georgia, "that the luke-warm or mild race preduce [*sic*] in the large cities of the North works quite successfully against absolute *equality* of opportunity for all members of the Negro race with those of white people."[36]

In truth the Southern assault upon the North, first by the Conservatives and then by the Radicals, was an assault upon a hard thin shell. Once inside the walls, the invaders found little resistance. Still the prejudice of the North was more latent than manifest; its practical effects were scattered and relatively mild. Basically, the difference between the North and the South in racial attitudes was that the North had not yet discovered what its prejudices were. It had not done so because the number of blacks in the North was not yet great enough to force that region to a confrontation with its racial self. It was only in the latter third of the twentieth century, when half of the black people in America would live in the North and West, that the depth of the commitment of the North to racial equality at home would be hard tested—and found wanting. What the South got from the North by about 1915 was not so much an open and conscious acceptance of Southern racial attitudes (though the North had traveled far in that direction), as it was an acceptance of the South itself, including its racial attitudes, whatever they might be.

Race has happened all along and virtually everywhere in America, between whites, Indians, blacks, and Orientals. But specially it happened in the South in the turn-of-the-century generation. What happened there is the crucible of twentieth-century race relations in America. In that time and place the disengagement and alienation of black people from white people, signally begun in Reconstruction, was practically completed and the crystallization of a separated and viable black culture begun. In the 1890s, a distinct acceleration of the outmigration of blacks from the South set in. What began as a trickle became a flood between 1916 and 1930. In the decade before 1920 nearly a quarter of a million blacks left the five states of the Radical heartland for the North and West. In the next decade the number doubled.[37] In the diaspora, Southern blacks met Northern blacks, and, in the 1920s, in Harlem and elsewhere, black culture evolved into a phase of greater strength and conscious celebration. The outmigration ensued, in some measure, precisely because the North allowed the South greater freedom in ruling its own race relations, and those relations deteriorated. The North got at last what many Northerners had always feared would be the result of the death of slavery—an exodus of blacks to the North. The Southern race problem of the nineteenth century became the national race problem of the twentieth, in part precisely because of the abandonment by the North of the Negro in the South.

CHAPTER VI

White Soul

Race relations in America in the twentieth century took its essential form from both black and white reactions to developments during the Radical era. On the black side what emerged was an alternative to the Washingtonian program. Its prime spokesman was W. E. B. DuBois, and the concept was neatly encapsulated in the title of his book *The Souls of Black Folk,* published in 1903. On the white side there came an amendment to the Conservative mentality that profoundly influenced the nature of Conservatism from that time to the present. That variant amounted almost to another mentality, as we have defined the term, and we might aptly designate it "Volksgeistian Conservativism."

Ironically, both the black movement and the white were built up directly from the same philosophical foundation, and that foundation was a large current in the mainstream of Western civilization. Specifically, they were the direct offspring of the resurgent idealism that appeared in the West as a reaction against the extreme realism of the "Age of Enlightenment," dragooned, as it was, into disgrace by the excesses of the French Revolution and Napoleonic imperialism. In the vanguard of that grand and vigorous revival of idealism was G. W. Friedrich Hegel, a professor of philosophy in the University of Berlin after the Napoleonic era. Hegel's effectiveness as a thinker came to full maturity in the 1820s, and much of what he did found its way into the period that is often called "The Age of Romanticism," an age that cognates very closely with the beginning of what we have heretofore called the Victorian era.

DuBois left a great legacy to black people, but he also left something of value to white Americans. If one is white and American, appreciating the idea of black soul is a way of understanding one's white self more fully. Lamentably, white people in the South in the turn-of-the-century

206

decades had no DuBois to call forth so powerfully their better selves in ethnic terms. Their whiteness had focus, but the focus was all too often tragically directed against other races, specifically against blacks by Radicals. Yet, a few thoughtful whites in the early years of the twentieth century did borrow structures from Western idealism to build up a positive image for white Southerners just as DuBois drew materials from the same source to construct a positive image for blacks. These people respected the souls of black folk, and they generated a concept of White Soul, a Church White that paralleled Black Soul and the Church Black. They poured great energies into the effort to propagandize the gospel of whiteness and to realize its genius. The emergence among white people of popular education, popular religion, popular politics, and a warming interest in Appalachian and swampland folklore as deep-freeze depositories of Anglo-Saxon purity were all, in significant measure, conscious attempts to bring forth white soul. What might well be called "Volksgeistian Conservatism" was abroad in the land, and it left deep and lasting marks upon Southern white culture in the twentieth century.

The term Volksgeistian Conservatism describes this thought-set very well because, first, it presumed that God had implanted in Southern white folk a unique and valuable spirit—that is, a "Volksgeist"; second, it was a rather direct translation of Germanic, and particularly Hegelian, idealism into the Southern cultural and racial scene; and, third, it sprang from roots that were indeed squarely within the Southern Conservative tradition. It was no mere coincidence that those who led the Volksgeistians in the propagation of the gospel of whiteness were among those very persons who cared most for the souls of black folk. Often enough, individual Volksgeistians had initially launched efforts to raise the Negro. When those efforts failed, they turned their attention to the elevation of their white brothers and sisters.

Volksgeistian Conservatism, like Radicalism and Liberalism, was a splinter of racial Conservatism. Volksgeistians, like other white Southerners of their time, had all been born Conservatives. During the turn-of-the century years, however, they came to a new, more rarefied philosophical appreciation of the meaning of race. There were not many of them, but they were vastly influential upon people who had power, and, in that sense, Volksgeistian Conservatism was greater than the sum of its parts. It was as if it had a life of its own that transcended and outlived the few people who most clearly articulated it. It colored and moved everything that it touched, and it touched, in some way, everything. The institutions that ruled the South in the twentieth century were, essentially, the creatures of the early years of the century when the Volksgeistians waxed strong. Those institutions were deeply influenced in their inception by the

Volksgeistian mood, and they came to rule the modern Southern world, not only in race, but in economics, politics, education, religion, courts of law, prisons, medicine, public health, philanthropy, journalism, folklore, and literature. Ironically, by the 1920s Volksgeistian Conservatism was dead as a system of thought, but the assumptions of the Volksgeistians had marked and continued to mark virtually every aspect of Southern life.

EDGAR GARDNER MURPHY AS A PRIME SPOKESMAN FOR VOLKSGEISTIAN CONSERVATISM

A pioneer exponent of Volksgeistian Conservatism was Edgar Gardner Murphy (1869–1913). Professionally, Murphy was an Episcopal priest. He was born in Fort Smith, Arkansas, in 1869. When Edgar was only five, his father deserted the family, leaving his wife, Janie Gardner Murphy, with two young children and afflicted with tuberculosis. Janie, with the help of her sister, took her children and made the trip by rail, stagecoach, and army ambulance to San Antonio, Texas, where the dry air was considered the best palliative for her disease. In San Antonio, she opened a boarding house. Janie Murphy worked hard and not only recovered her health but also gained a mild prosperity. Her boarding house became something of a social center in the village. Among those attracted was the local Episcopal rector, Walter Richardson. The Reverend Mr. Richardson soon took Edgar into his choir, then into his church, and, finally, in 1885, persuaded the professors at the University of the South to take the young man on scholarship. At Sewanee, Edgar, already determined to enter the ministry, fell eagerly under the influence of William Porcher Du Bose, the Chaplain of that arch Episcopal institution and the founder of what soon became its School of Theology. From Du Bose, Murphy absorbed a commitment to "living Christianity," that is to a creed that linked the spiritual world with the real world and saw the Christian mission as one that pursued palpable earthly as well as heavenly ends.

Murphy worked diligently throughout his life to advance the cause of social Christianity, first as a lay assistant to the rector in San Antonio, next as an Episcopal priest in Laredo, then for six years as rector of a parish in Chillicothe, Ohio, and for another year at Kingston, New York. Murphy was "high Church," a phrase identifying those more aristocratically inclined Episcopalians who stressed the importance of ritual and hierarchy within the denomination. But he also believed that the Christian church had a duty to care for the bodies as well as the souls of all people—low as well as high. Consequently, wherever he went, he moved with what came to be called the "Social Gospel," establishing missions to the poorer classes, white and black, and clubs for the young. In 1898 he returned to the South to take the rectorship of Trinity Church in Montgomery, Alabama, probably the most influential Episcopal parish in the state.

As Murphy himself later declared, his initial public act concerned the race problem. Like many Conservatives, he was first activated by the monstrous evil of lynching. Early in 1893 he organized a petition in which a number of citizens of Laredo protested the torture-lynching of the "Negro Smith" in Paris, Texas. In the words of that document, written by the twenty-four-year-old priest, there was "no justification of a penalty which made an orgy of torture and a festival of agony." Even though the petition carefully stated that the signers complained only of the manner in which Smith was put to death and not his execution, Murphy was able to persuade barely a score of the men of Laredo to endorse the statement. Further, he suffered the direct opposition of many of the town's leading citizens, including members of his own parish.[1]

Undaunted, Murphy continued to labor for the salvation of blacks. In Laredo, Chillicothe, and Montgomery, he founded missionary churches in the black communities. During 1899, the first year of his renewed residence in the South, lynching seemed to reach a crescendo of horror, particularly in the neighboring state of Georgia. Deeply distressed, Murphy organized a "Southern Society" to study the race problem. Soon, the society planned a grand race conference to be held in Montgomery in May 1900. Presided over by the racially moderate and highly respected Hilary A. Herbert, recently Cleveland's Secretary of the Navy, twenty-one carefully selected persons addressed the Conference. Seventeen of these were racially Conservative, four were Radicals. Walter F. Willcox came from Cornell to give a social scientific prospectus for the evaporation of black people from America. Alfred Moore Waddell came fresh from the front lines of inter-racial combat in Wilmington to argue for the inevitable race war. John Temple Graves pled for racial separation, and Paul M. Barringer brought all of the prestige of the Chairman of the Faculty of the University of Virginia to preach, much to Murphy's distress, the gospel of black retrogression and dissolution.[2] After some discussion of the matter, it had been decided that no Negroes would be invited to speak, the leading candidate having been Booker T. Washington. However, on the night of the final session, several hundred blacks were admitted to the galleries.

Murphy's use of the conference was typical of the Conservative style of leadership. He immediately pronounced it a resounding victory for racial Conservatism and spoke as if the whole of the thoughtful South would fall into line. Somehow, he passed over the fact that he himself had loaded the dice and smoothly arranged the final score of seventeen to four.[3] Assuming that the world was ready for reform, Murphy immediately proposed the establishment of a national magazine to be called *Race Problems*. That journal, edited by himself, would serve as a clearing house for ideas on the subject. Further, he suggested the establishment of an advisory board on racial matters to operate at the national level and composed of men who thought along Conservative lines. The Montgomery Conference had been held with the idea that it would be repeated annually. For a time, meetings in other cities in successive years were suggested. After a few months, however, all this faded. No reason was given for the sudden collapse, only a muttering that time would be a better solvent to race problems than discussion.[4]

Murphy himself continued to think and to write on the subject of race relations in the South and in the nation at large. But his thinking and his writing on the matter turned into a new and highly important channel. This emerged most signally in two books: *Problems of the Present South*, which appeared in 1904, and *The Basis of Ascendancy,* which he published in 1910.[5] As an activist organizer, however, he all but deserted the black cause. Instead, he turned his energies into reform efforts for which the people were ripe and the response was—if not totally positive—ultimately gratifying. He turned initially to work on the problem of child labor, first in the textile mills of Montgomery and later in the South generally. Leaving that work in the care of a very able colleague, Andrew J. McKelway, he resigned from the priesthood in 1901 to become the Executive Secretary of the Southern Education Board. There he moved vigorously to meet the vast problem of public education in the South, especially the education of white children. In that effort he found his final and most rewarding call. For several years Murphy worked for the Board in New York and lived in New Haven with his wife and two sons. Soon he became one of the few most trusted brokers in the rapidly rising field of dealing out Northern philanthropy to Southern Education.[6]

From his academic training and out of his experience with the race problem, Edgar Murphy generated a relatively complete set of ideas on race in the South, a set that he shared with some of his more influential contemporaries. As a thought system that squared neatly with currently observable facts of life, it was a beautiful piece of work and it had, for that reason if no other, great power in its time. Quite clearly, it made a large contribution toward building the "mind of the South" that reached its zenith in the 1920s and 1930s.

At the core of Murphy's racial system and implicit in his life and work was the idea that each people, each racial folk, had a genius, a spirit, a "Volksgeist," that was God-given, distinct, and the key to progress. "The deepest thing about man—next to his humanity itself—is," he declared, "his race."[7] Each people had a moral duty to strive to realize its genius because therein lay the salvation of the race and individuals within the race. The soul was the part of God in every man. By introspection, by knowing thyself, one knew God best, and, thereby one knew his brothers. Ultimately, all things, the seemingly separate genius of each people, and the souls of everyone were joined in God. God was the source of all truth, of all reality, of life, of being, and in his mind all things were one. In God's mind there were no conflicts, no disjunctions, no disharmony. Life on earth seemed contradictory and conflict-ridden only because we were yet so far from God. Salvation lay in each person searching out the essential nature of his own soul, in stripping away the shadows, the unreal husk of appearances to uncover the kernel of truth within. One could hardly begin that quest without establishing a communion with his brothers of like spirit. Truth was collectively rather than individually perceived. Thus each people, black and white, must withdraw from the other in some significant measure, perfect a communion with its inner nature, and rise to a consciousness of its unique genius. One need not be overly concerned about a seeming hostility between blacks and whites in America because there would inevitably come a union in God's being for Americans of all races. Meanwhile, each race had its duty. In the South, there was white soul to be sought on the one side, and the rich earth of blackness to be cultivated on the other. When the white South was true to itself, it would be true to blacks, and to white America at large. Murphy, like DuBois, had full faith in "the unifying ideal of Race."[8]

By 1904 Murphy was arguing that "social segregation" was "the elementary working hypothesis of civilization in our Southern States." The separation of the black race was a necessary prelude to the raising up of black leadership and the cultivation of qualities of character among black people. Black folk, ultimately, could not be white, and it was a trespass against God's plan to attempt to make them so. There were, indeed, very narrow limits to what white people could do for black people. The real work was the definition and realization of black soul, and only blacks could perform that task. The primary obligation of the whites to the blacks was simply to give them the freedom, the isolation, the independence necessary for them to find themselves, to seek out their genius and to nourish it. White people must honor the efforts of black people. "If any race is to live it must have something to live for," Murphy insisted. "It will hardly cling with pride to its race integrity if its race world is a world wholly synonymous with degeneration, and if the world of the white man is the only generous and honorable world which it knows." America's best hope for progress, then, lay in a benevolent species of apartheid: "For the very reason that the race, in the apartness of its social life, is to work out its destiny as the separate member of a larger group, it must be accorded its own leaders and thinkers, its own scholars, activists, prophets; and while the development of the higher life may come slowly, even blunderingly, it is distinctly to be welcomed. . . ." Therein lies the real reason why America must license "race integrity."[9]

Murphy argued stoutly that segregation was not degradation. It answered the needs of both races. Of Negroes, he insisted, "every tendency of the present seems to be making not toward their disintegration but toward that social and domestic segregation demanded by their own interest as well as by the interest of the stronger race about them." In the Negro's behalf, the South had developed "customs which have protected him from hatred and have made possible his existence and his happiness." It was not at all a matter of separate and equal; it was a matter of separate and incomparable, of apples and oranges. Blacks were a child race and the white race was mature and strong, but neither race was inherently better or worse than the other. They were, simply, different. The desire of the South, he explained, "is not to condemn the negro forever to a lower place but to accord him another place." This was indeed something new in Southern white thought about blacks, and it was signalized in the phrase "another place." Potentially, it was revolutionary. In and after the last generation of slavery, Conservatism would have put the black man down in fixed subordination, and in the 1880s Liberalism would have put him up, in the 1890s Radicalism would have put him out, and, now, in the early twentieth century, Volksgeistian Conservatism would have put him, simply, aside. For Volksgeistians, the shoring up of the walls of segregation by legislation was acceptable because it decreased inter-racial friction, marked clearly the perimeters within which each race would find its identity, and promoted the growth of race consciousness. It was, as Murphy declared, but a wise extension of the rule that "good fences make good neighbors."[10] It behooved the white South to continue and to encourage the arrangement in order to allow black folk the freedom in which black soul could rise to self-consciousness unhampered by contact with whites. The alternative was to embrace the awful plight of the ancient mariner, to suffer marriage to a dead and dying thing, to tie the white South to soul-less flesh—the very negation of life.[11]

Race identity was a necessary stage in the advancement of world civilization, Murphy argued. For a time, whites must concentrate upon nurturing their whiteness as blacks must cultivate their darkness. In America, where whites were most numerous and where white soul was already well developed, white assertion would admittedly violate the ideal of democracy because blacks would in some degree be controlled by the stronger whites. But that was a temporary expense. "As a basis for democracy, the conscious unity of race is not wholly adequate," Murphy conceded, "but it is better as a basis of democratic reorganization than the distribution of wealth, or trade, or property, of family, of class."[12] Thus white racial democracy would save us from more egalitarian reorganizations such as socialism or communism. In one sense, antagonism between the races was lamentable. In another, it was natural because the races must hold themselves apart during this transitional stage. Particularly would race enmity be a trait among young persons because, more than their elders, they were empty vessels free to find and take their fill of the new race consciousness. Probably taking his thought from the current term "the new Negro," which was applied by whites to blacks born after 1865, Murphy suggested that Southern whites reared after slavery were also new men. "Between the new negro and the new white man, there is likely to be enmity and there is very sure to be suspicion," he declared.[13] But this seeming curse was actually a blessing. Among other things, it was reducing miscegenation to negligible proportions. The mulatto population, he surmised in an egregious and revealing error, was not the product of recent years, nor even of slavery ("for the old negroes are the black negroes"!). They sprang instead, he declared with astonishing sureness, from the loins of the marching armies at the close of the war when "the lower classes of the Northern army demoralized by idleness" and "the lower class of the Southern army demoralized by defeat" were "thrown into contact with the negro masses at the moment of their greatest helplessness."[14]

Like many white liberals in the late 1960s, Murphy concluded that, ultimately, only blacks could save blacks, and that the true labor of white leaders lay on the white side of the color line. " . . . the white race, in the interest of the efficiency and the happiness of the masses of its own life, must bring its culture still more closely into relation with social needs." The culture of the South, he declared, will find "its supreme and immediate interest" in "the undeveloped force of the stronger race."[15] Murphy's philosophy reflected the facile and graceful turn that he himself had made, swinging his primary effort within a few months from the white man's burden *vis à vis* blacks to one to save white children from the bone-crushing jaws of the industrial Leviathan, and then, within another few months, still again to a very satisfying crusade to bring all white children into the white communion by way of a compulsory public education. God's time may not have arrived to save whites from committing atrocious crimes against blacks. It did so only painfully and slowly for child labor reform. But clearly the *Zeitgeist* favored the public school movement, and Murphy spent the last dozen years of his life in that labor, joyfully and triumphantly.

Edgar Gardner Murphy could thus serenely leave blacks alone because he confidently expected that in the end American democracy would open its arms to embrace all colors. He could easily differ with Booker T. Washington on such issues as the repeal of the Fifteenth Amendment—which he favored, contending that the Amendment was an artificial construction not in harmony with the times—because, as he phrased it, he had faith in the eventual "realization" of ideals, in this case, in the ideal of democracy. One key idea that was bound to rule eventually was the Christian ideal of the brotherhood of man. In the last order, there would be a grand democracy in American life, and "its unity is truer and richer because not run in one color or expressed in monotony of form. Like all vital unities, it is composite."[16]

DEMOCRACY AND EDUCATION IN THE NEW SOUTH

Conservative thought did change from time to time. One of the ways it changed in the late nineteenth and early twentieth century was to come about to accept the arrival of an all-white "democracy." For instance, Walter Hines Page, in "The Forgotten Man," a famous speech given in Greensboro, North Carolina, in 1897, called for the elevation of the plain folk of the South. By 1902 he was hardly less than ecstatic in anticipating that event. The South, he thought, held the promise of evolving a more perfect democracy than any yet seen in America. Southerners, he concluded, "are the purest American stock we have," and it was their destiny to generate "a democratic order of society which will be a rich contribution to the republic that their ancestors took so large a part in establishing."[17] Page was not alone. In contrast to the horror with which some earlier Conservative spokesmen had viewed "levelling tendencies" in the 1880s, there was a curious happiness in the acceptance of the "new democracy" by Conservatives at large in the turn-of-the-century years. That shift was probably closely related to the abundant presence of blacks no longer under their control and to the rise of Radicalism, and it was definitely facilitated by the rationales of Volksgeistian Conservatism. If the matter of the race problem was getting out of hand, if blacks were acting independently and whites were outrageous, Volksgeistian thought offered a marvelous retreat that allowed one to say, after making an effort at racial reform and the restoration of social sanity, that there was presently nothing of substance to be done with black people. Furthermore, if a white Conservative found himself powerless to accomplish anything helpful on the black side of the race line, it was consoling to know that he could be highly effective on the white side—and this meant effective among white people of the lower elements. Whatever the reasons for their acceptance of the new political order, whatever the sources from which their rationale was taken, many Conservatives, especially those accustomed to working in intellectual circles, came easily to embrace the "new democracy" and place it firmly in an idealistic setting that was distinctly Germanic.

Implicitly, Murphy applied the Hegelian formula to the South as he saw it in the early twentieth century. The Old South had represented a new and higher stage of society. Most of all the institution of slavery had generated a patrician leadership, conscious of its place, its honors, and its responsibilities to the masses, white as well as black. Paternalistically cared for by the elite, but "outside the essential councils of the South," were two great classes of people, the "non-participants," as Murphy labeled these two classes. The non-participants were the Negroes and "the non-slaveholding white men." As the early twentieth century unfolded, it was evident to him that white society in the South was ready to rise another round on the scale of progress and achieve a flowering on a higher plane. Through the travail of slavery, through the test of fire in civil war, and through the hard moral tribulations of black Reconstruction, the lower elements of white people in the South had suffered and risen to a more refined level of purity, of spirituality, of self-consciousness. Even in the antebellum South while non-slaveholders were sometimes opposed to the thesis of slavery, they were nevertheless absorbing something of the manners, ideas, and values of the slaveholding elite. What followed the dialectical struggle between thesis and anti-thesis was the synthesis that had already occurred in the early twentieth century. The line of division between the old elite and the white mass was still visible, but total fusion was inevitably coming. Even then lower-class whites were being rapidly integrated into Southern life—politically, economically, and socially. Thus it was that "the expanding and enlarging life of democracy has included in the conscious movement of our civilization the most important of the non-participants of the older order." Murphy hailed the transition as a significant event in the progress of the world. "It is," he declared, "one of the far-reaching achievements of a democratic age." One should not be disturbed that it was the whites who rose first. "It was inevitable that the movement of democracy should have included the non-participants of the homogeneous population," he explained.[18] A later stage would embrace the blacks.

In this synthetic phase, the new democracy was not without its dangers, and Murphy hastened to warn the South against itself. Democracy could err, and when it did, there was grave danger that the error would be made to seem not an error but the opposite because in the new age mass sentiment tended to be accepted as morally correct. Thus, it was easily possible to introduce a wrong "into the national life and national spirit" that could not be easily removed. The preventive was a moral and intellectual leadership, a leadership that the masses might cultivate by according "trust and reverence everywhere to the policies of freedom," especially to freedom of thought and expression. Paradoxically, Murphy's concern to save the people from error almost brought him back to deny democracy by giving a license to the authorities to thwart the popular will. Sometimes, he pointed out, "those who have served democracy most truly are those who have saved the people from themselves."[19]

Predictably, Murphy thought that the universities of the South were key centers for the development of the moral and intellectual leadership desired. Here was where the masses must allow a maximum of freedom and tolerance. Here young men would hone themselves to a sharp perception of God's will in this world. In the universities would be generated the diversity of ideas from which would emerge the single ideas, one after another, that would bring the South up through successive stages of progress. A wide range of perceptions, bred in open and intensive inquiry, would prove the saving grace of Southern civilization. It was around this banner of freedom of thought, perhaps more easily than around any other, that racial Conservative leaders—both Volksgeistian and regular—in the New South could rally.

The masses must give latitude to their leaders, Murphy argued, but the leaders had obligations to the masses. The South was particularly fortunate in having an upper class that possessed a high sense of responsibility for the lower orders. Ironically, slavery itself had deepened that sense of *noblesse oblige*, of paternalism. This was, to quote Murphy, "the noble and fruitful gift of the old South to the new, a gift brought out of the conditions of an aristocracy, but responsive and operative under every challenge in the changing condition of the later order." Paternalism, an idea generated directly by a ripened slavery, tried, tested, and found true in the Civil War, was a central value of the old order that would be brought to the new. The idea was brilliantly "personified in Lee." Robert E. Lee was the perfect product of the idealism of the Old South. He had himself shouldered the blame for the defeat at Gettysburg, and when asked why he was so protective of his men, he answered: "Because they are under me." General Lee was the paragon, but Murphy went on to name other, more latter-day saints such as J. L. M. Curry, Lucius Quintus Cincinnatus Lamar, Charles Brantley Aycock, Hilary A. Herbert, and Andrew Montague (the Virginia governor), men who illustrated that the ideal of paternalism lived on after slavery had died.[20]

The new synthesis would also be effected in culture generally, and specifically in education. The masses, Murphy predicted, would be caught up in the burgeoning common school system in the South. New England, the North, and the West had long since established more or less comprehensive systems of elementary education. The South had been peculiarly laggard in that area. Almost as if to celebrate the beginning of a new century with the beginning of a new cultural era, the South after 1900 finally realized the ideal of mass education that had been preached for two generations.[21] Thus it was that great flocks of white youth were being ushered into the persisting high culture of the Old South through the schoolhouse doors. In the schools they found teachers and administrators who were not common folk like themselves, but rather the vestigal remains of that Old South aristocracy. The schoolhouse was staffed by the sons and daughters of the Old Regime. And in that place they brought the lasting values of the Old South to the children of the New.[22]

What was happening in a broad way at the base of the educational pyramid was also happening in a more exclusive and more concerted way in the colleges and universities, particularly those of antebellum origins. If the boy was a South Carolinian, for instance, and not already bent toward a technical education, he would probably go to the state university in Columbia rather than to either the technical school at Clemson, the military school in Charleston, or one of the small denominational colleges that dotted the state. If he went to the University in Columbia in or after 1909, he would encounter as his president Samuel Chiles Mitchell.

Mitchell, born in 1864, was out of the slaveholding aristocracy of Mississippi. He had attended Georgetown College in Kentucky and the University of Chicago to earn his degrees and had risen through the academic ranks to become a professor in Richmond College (later the University of Richmond), an eminent institution sponsored by the Virginia Baptists. Mitchell himself had caught the fever of idealism, in a major degree perhaps during his stay at the University of Chicago. He came to South Carolina convinced that the regeneration of the South depended upon a return to the quest for ideas, for ultimate values, as well as a more effective engagement by the University in the things of this world.[23] Under his aegis, the state university turned from a rather pedestrian traditional pursuit of the classics to a quest for the golden fleece. Or, rather, fleeces, the truths of life. The search advanced dialectically, in part, because most of the student body was divided into two debating societies—the Clariosophic and the Euphradian. The debating halls rang with cracked-voice adolescent oratory searching for the eternal verities lying enfolded in such ideas as "loyalty," "courage," "honor," and "love." The fever of idealism was catching, and for a time it seemed as if the south side of Columbia had moved back to pick up where Carolinians had left off in the 1850s when the fleece had definitely been sighted and, it seemed, almost grasped. There in the background was Medea—alias Southern womanhood.

Mitchell was, in essence, a more secular Edgar Gardner Murphy. He moved with sure foot and great energy to press the University into the living age. He expanded the offerings of the school to include such practical curricula as engineering and business. He inaugurated extension courses and an evening school by which the University reached out to touch palpably South Carolinians, old as well as young, far beyond its walls. He encouraged his professors to speak to the people on every possible occasion. He, himself, became very nearly notorious in that activity, once giving a talk to an audience of textile mill workers in Greenville on "Mirabeau, the Foremost Figure of the French Revolution." Mitchell was ardently for prohibition, child-labor reform, and compulsory education, and he was sympathetic to Negroes. In South Carolina, however, he found it necessary to repress somewhat expressions of his interest in these areas in order to be effective in others.

For four years Mitchell led the University to reach out into the state as never before to bring into the cultural communion all of the white people. Then entered the devil in the form of the Radical racist snake, Governor Coleman L. Blease (called Coley [ko-li] by his many enemies as well as his many friends). In 1913 Coley fired Mitchell amidst a general assault upon the alleged aristocracy of the University and its "diplomatized mollycoddles." Blease inaugurated a new fashion in political leadership in South Carolina—the demagogue, the extravagant, flamboyant, voluble, one-man band, full of sound and fury meaning very nearly naught. Coley's function was, ultimately, to occupy a public office and to entertain. His fulminations against the aristocracy and the University came to nothing. The University mustered its many friends and alumni in the legislature not only to survive, but to prosper as a Conservative stronghold long after Mitchell had been driven from the state.[24] Like so many institutions generated and regenerated in the South in the early twentieth century, it continued to run in the quasi-popular style of its original momentum, even after it forgot why it was doing so.

THE INDUSTRIAL REVOLUTION IN THE SOUTH: FOR WHITES ONLY

By 1900 there was clearly under way a movement toward industrialization in the South. As Murphy and many others understood, this was not a new beginning but the revival of an old one. It was a renaissance and an extension of something that had begun before the Civil War and was on the verge of success in 1861. "It is but one reassertion of the genius of the old South," Murphy insisted. The largest industry in the South by 1910 was textiles—almost wholly cotton textiles. The movement had begun in the antebellum period, revived in the early 1880s, and boomed in the late 1890s. In the South in 1880, there were 161 textile mills employing 17,000 people. In 1900 there were 400 mills with 98,000 workers, and in 1904 the number of mills had swelled to 550. In 1907 there were 600 mills with 125,000 workers. By 1910, South Carolina was second in the nation only to Massachusetts in the number of spindles running, and North Carolina was fourth.[25] The boom in mill building peaked after 1907 when, apparently, surplus labor had been absorbed. Murphy saw the mills as potentially a great liberating force for the region. In 1904 he maintained that textiles held the promise of effecting an "industrial rescue" from oblivion of a multitude of Southern whites among "the great army of non-participants." However, as the mills were then operating, they were not living up to their potential for good, especially in their employment of children. "The factory system, as a system, betrays a tendency to hold its humbler industrial forces in a state of arrested development; which from the broader social standpoint, and in relation to the larger life of democracy, means an arrested participation," he explained. "Here is an eddy in the fuller and freer current of democratic life; here, in the industrial imprisonment of the child, is a contradiction— however temporary—of those positive and deeper forces which are claiming the human possibilities of the individual—however lowly—as elements in the power and happiness of the State."[26] Murphy, himself, was a pioneer in promoting legislation to regulate the labor of children in the textile mills. But his work was not so much against the factories and the owners as it was for the children and the South.

Murphy asserted in an elaborate but abstract way that the South should accept the textile revolution, but Broadus Mitchell, in 1921, was the first to attempt a specific description of what it actually was in the region and to offer an explanation of how it got that way. Mitchell was the son of Samuel Chiles Mitchell. He was a pioneer economic historian, and another of those young scholars who emerged into the academic limelight from the graduate school at the Johns Hopkins University. As Mitchell declared in the preface of his book, *The Rise of the Cotton Mills in the South,* he tried to catch "the spiritual aspects" as well as the material aspects of that phenomenon. In that endeavor, he avowed, he owed most of his interpretation to his father, who held that the region lost the struggle for national eminence because it opted for slavery instead of liberty, state's rights instead of nationality, and for agriculture alone instead of industry smoothly integrated with agriculture. His study, he confessed, was "little more than illustration" of his father's analysis of the Southern experience.[27]

The younger Mitchell contended in this work that Southern leadership, imbued with a sense of paternalism, had created the textile mills of the South in order to save the mass of whites from poverty. The movement began with the loss of the presidential election in 1880, he explained. The South had rested all of its hopes upon a Democratic victory in that year. With the defeat came a realization that the future prosperity of the region would have to be found outside politics. Thereafter, the South turned in upon itself, and found there the path of progress. By "conscious teaching" the leadership produced a "social regeneration" in all places during the turn-of-the-century years. "When the South, after 1900, did embark on an educational campaign, the fervor previously given to industry received new expression," he declared. "It was 'Real Reconstruction' reaching another task."[28]

Broadus Mitchell applied to the textile experience much the same idea of homogeneity that Murphy had adduced in explaining the "new democracy." It was a fact vital to the textile revival, Mitchell argued, that the Southern white population was "homogeneous." They moved with a whole spirit. "No people less homogeneous, less one family, knit together and resolute through sufferings, could have taken instant fire, as did the South, at such appeals." The textile industry throve "within the Southern family. It made for an intimacy which at first rendered impossible and which continued to retard division between factory owners and workers according to economic interest."[29] The mills, then, represented a kind of new economic democracy in which great profits and high wages were not the ruling incentives. Rather was the mill the symbol of the Southern community in harmony with itself and with the real and modern world. Masters, trained to care for slaves on the plantations of the Old South, now brought capital and a kindly management to the white workers in the factories of the New. Less gifted whites brought labor and loyalty. In the mills of the South, management and labor gathered familiarly around the "coke box." The workers called the manager Mr. Frank, or "Cap'n," or Colonel, and he called each by his given name of Will, or Jim, or Carter, and all felt secure. This socially gentle weave of the new economics and traditional hierarchy was the combination that offered, Mitchell implied, high promise for the future of American life.

Whereas slavery had squeezed the less fortunate whites out of society, Volksgeistians now insisted that the textile mills were an instrument for bringing them in again. In the early colonial South, all whites had been very much alike. But increasingly slavery had divided the whites into two distinct classes, and the lower class, the "poor whites," deprived of "participation in the larger life of the section," had become non-participants. As Mitchell interpreted the process, "the pressure of slavery, if it worked to bring a small number of whites to the surface, gave to masses an impulse ever downward." But "when the 'poor whites' entered the mills, they reentered the life of the South." The mills had "opened the way" for the lower orders again to be integrated into an organic and very viable Southern culture.[30]

In truth, textile mills were, at first, very much family and community affairs. They were owned and operated by people who felt themselves an integral part of the local Anglo-Saxon community. Owners and managers were seldom off to socialize in Newport, Rhode Island, or the Virginia springs. They worked hard with their heads, and probably with their hearts too. As people will do, they mixed their material ambition and their hunger for power with a measure of *noblesse oblige,* and their lives were thus made better than bearable. They lived well, and they thought well of themselves and their work. Also, at first, they lived in the community with their people. Uppers were separated from lowers by all the social lines, but not ordinarily by spatial ones.

In the factory, both the reality and the rhetoric worked to keep white body and white soul somehow together for a remarkably long time. In the imagery of paternalism, the owner-manager was the father of his workers, a role prescription easily filled. Sometimes, the manager was in fact in some way the blood kin to some of his workers. Ultimately, all were brothers and sisters, fathers, sons, and daughters in, if not under, the skin. Adult children of respectable farmers fleeing agricultural recession and depression did not scruple at taking cash-paying jobs in the mills. And Southern society had never been so stratified that talent could not crash the class lines, if such they might be called, and old families often willingly accepted new blood . . . especially if it were red and rich.

Not all of the South was rice-country South Carolina or sugar-growing Louisiana where the best lands were limited in quantity, engrossed early, and gave rise to great and exclusive families. Nor was it even Old Virginia, where intermarriage between the great families proceeded so long that eyes crossed, hearing grew faulty, and noses lost their points. Outside of the old settled areas intermarriage ran up and down the scale of land and slaveholding. A pretty figure and a vivacious manner, male or female, coupled with respectability, could occasionally marry slaves and land, and all of his or her kin were then akin to the land and slaves. On the slave frontier (moving as it did through upcountry South Carolina and Georgia, across the great rich middle belt of Alabama, into the delta of

Mississippi, and out onto the rich flat lands of Arkansas and Texas) where life and love were not so much settled, if the poor did not marry rich, the respectable middling folks sometimes did. William Faulkner was right again. Thomas Sutpens did appear on the slave frontier; they rose from rags to riches; and they did marry Ellen Coldfields. Consequently, Miss Rosa Coldfield, her sister, was also married to the land and slaves, and no more divisible from them than she was from Henry and Judith, the children of the marriage. White Southern society in 1900, in the mass and spread over the whole geography from ex-slaveholding Delaware to the outer limits of Austin, Texas, was not so much a class society as it was one of twenty million personal dots hierarchically and organically arranged in thousands of community clusters, each person, each dot self-consciously occupying one special place in the array and highly conscious of the other dots and of the particular forces that fixed each in its certain place. It is often convenient, perhaps even necessary for communication, to use the term "class" in talking about the white South, but that society is not even nearly describable by two or more neat lines drawn horizontally across the whole population.

Winners in the marketplace and at the marriage altar did not dissolve family ties. Economic and social elevation was not a license to forget your family, even in its farthest reaches. On the contrary. Even in the hierarchical ordering, where some whites were distinctly superior to others, there was, nevertheless, a sense of kindredness, a *Gemeinschaft,* among all the whites, just as the Volksgeistians would have it. In 1900, white Southerners were, in essence, very much alike and becoming more so; and clearly they were more like one another than anyone else. The curious fact that academicians attempted to blink away that truth and soon came to assume that mill workers were "poor whites," with overtones of "poor white trash," was but another manifestation of the notorious tendency of the turn-of-the-century intelligentsia to lose sight of the great middle class of yeoman farmers that had existed in the antebellum period and afterward, and to flatter themselves that they as moderns were creating something grand out of what had been, theretofore, merely a remote potentiality. Whatever the myth, the workers in the mills were not, in the main, poor whites. They were the yeoman farmers of the Old South and their children translated into the industrial situation. Metaphorically, they were indeed the loyal men who had ridden around the Yankees with J. E. B. Stuart, charged with Pickett at Gettysburg, and, surrendered with Lee at Appomattox. They were those men and their wives and children translated down through time into the factory. If they were duty-bound to the leadership, they were also duty-due. Deference, after all, is only one side of a two-way street. It has its price, however willingly paid. Southern whites who deferred to their betters got something from their betters in return. Indeed, the stuff they traded, recognition of the alleged personal superiority of the elite, was clearly so valuable, so far beyond mere material price, that they eventually got whatever they thought they wanted . . . which was, in reality, not much. But for our purposes, for the mill towns, let us say simply that the workers, like vassals in the feudal order, got maintenance and protection—including in the latter an ostensible respect for their women.

Thus it was that Southern whites at large in the early twentieth century moved toward a sense of community, a sense of community that seeped sweetly and generally through the South in the 1920s and 1930s. Aristocrats and commoners, men and women, adults and children, were all caught up neatly, happily in a seamless and comfortable web of social orderliness, admittedly often more apparent than real, but nevertheless real in a significant degree. By the ordinary measures of man, they were a happy people because they felt that they knew who they were, where they were, and why they were there. Not many people, in not many cultures, for very long have had that feeling of surety. It marks a people, it marks a person, and one does not easily surrender the feeling.

Playing the role of protector of the common whites did not mean, of course, that either mill owners, regular Conservatives, or Volksgeistian Conservatives were anti-Negro. Indeed, they wanted to conserve the Negro and include him in their systems. "Place" was all important to them, and another true task of leadership was to find the proper place and realm for black people in God's steadily unfolding world. Enlightened textile leaders and their philosophical friends had no difficulty at all in finding the Negro's proper calling and in urging him to take it. His future was in the cotton fields. Again it was almost a divine Providence, as mill owner James Orr pointed out in 1901, that the South had been given mills where the white folks could spin and weave the fibers that black farmers would coax from the good earth.[31] This fortunate and natural division of labor was the key to economic progress in a biracial order, a happy prospect that was not lost upon the philosophers, and one they hastened to exhibit to the intelligence of the North.

Blacks for the land, whites for the factories. If the upper side of progress lay with the whites in the factory, that was all right because so too did the upper side of brotherhood lie with the white brother. He was the older, the stronger, the more advanced. But in the Volksgeistian view, between black and white, it was ultimately not really that one was better than the other. It was that they were different. It was not, either, that the sable fellow was being given an inferior place. It was only that he was being given, as Murphy with wonted and succinct elegance phrased it, "another place."

True paternalism would tame the factory system and harness it to Southern progress, but it would also save America, and the world. Volksgeistians saw an industrial system in the North and in Europe that was literally tearing civilization asunder. The rich were getting richer and the poor poorer; there was a dangerously rising alienation between the few of the classes and the many of the masses, between capital and labor. Excessive materialism, impersonality, and inhumanity was the bitter social fruit of the factory system. Hard as steel and fully as unfeeling, the industrial revolution was conquering the world, pressuring itself into every crevice of human existence. The factory system was like a runaway engine pulling a train with all humanity aboard, racing faster and faster toward some sudden and disastrous halt. In Europe, masses of people were frankly embracing class consciousness and hence social divisiveness, swelling socialist numbers into political pluralities in France, Great Britain, and Germany. Even in America, in 1912, Socialist presidential candidate Eugene V. Debs mustered more than a million male votes in his support. Most awful in all of this was the destruction of orderly society and the orderly evolution of society. Strikes, riots, and gutted factories were our promises. Socialism, communism, anarchism, sabotage, and assassination were the ultimate results of the rise of the factory Leviathan unrestrained. It had already begun in America. The bomb in the Haymarket riot in 1886, the general violence in the Homestead and Pullman strikes in 1894, the special violence of the Wobblies (Industrial Workers of the World), and the assassination in 1901 of President McKinley by an anarchist whose very name was unpronounceably alien were all plain forewarnings of an unredeemed America. The politics of "grab" in the post-Civil War era, and the more recent pursuit of a scheme of amoral laissez-faire had not worked, and disaster was in the offing.

In the crisis the South now offered the great saving ideal—paternalism. Paternalism, the key idea that had risen out of the ordeal of slavery, was to be infused into the new industrial order. With a selfless, enlightened leadership at the throttle, the train would be controlled, its progress would be slower, safer, and rendered totally beneficial. The factory system under the captaincy of the paternalists would carry us all smoothly into the happier land of God's promise. The whites first, but all in a train. And all finally together. The South had risen again, ran Volksgeistian thought, not merely to survive as an eddy in the backwater of American life, not as some insignificant and dependent part of a greater whole, but indeed as the very soul and spirit of that progressively rising order that was the new American nation.

OLD SOUTH IDEALISM BROUGHT INTO THE NEW

Volksgeistian Conservatism had its roots in nineteenth-century European idealism and, often, specifically, in Germanic idealism. No doubt, it received much of its impetus from continuing importations across the Atlantic either directly by Southerners visiting the Continent and attending European universities, or indirectly through such institutions as Johns Hopkins. But it was also indebted to the domestic variety of idealism, imported in the antebellum period, turned into a flower of local growth, and still alive, however precariously, during the Reconstruction era and afterward.

The antebellum South's becoming idealistic in this vein represented a profound alteration in its thinking from Revolutionary times. Speaking in the broadest, most general terms, thought in the South in the mid-nineteenth century slipped from a largely realistic, rationalistic world-view to one that was Platonic, idealistic, romantic, and transcendental, but one that included also a subordinate rationalism.[32] The declining world of Thomas Jefferson affords an accurate index to the change. In the South, by the late 1850s, Jefferson and his thought were either ignored, misused, or in outright disrepute among high thinkers. It was perfectly symbolic of the reality that on the eve of the Civil War beautifully rational Monticello was being used by a careless tenant as a hay barn.[33] Before the war, Southern thinking was moving with supple muscularity toward the creation of a philosophy that would organize their peculiar world by including both slavery and race. Southern intellectuals appropriated much of European idealism, and, specifically, much of that was Hegelian. Slavery was an idea and so was race. What mattered in slavery was not the practice of this or that slaveholder so much as the ideal of slavery itself—perceived in its true God-given nature uniquely by Southerners and progressively unfolding. What really mattered in race was not this or that specific Negro so much as it was the idea of "Negro." The two ideas combined neatly, and they were laced into an Hegelian progression to predict the attainment of new heights of freedom. For Negroes in America, perfect slavery was perfect freedom; crimes against Negroes arose only from an imperfect slavery. For whites in the South, perfect mastery was perfect freedom, and crimes arose only from a failure in mastery. If all this was not totally clear in 1861, it seemed surely to be headed in that direction.

The loss of the war damned the philosophy, and it damned no less the philosophers. How could it, and they, have been so wrong? With the end of the war, Southern intellectuality very nearly ceased to be. There was no strong current to swim either with or against. It is a useful hyperbole to say that the great mass of Southern whites in Reconstruction did not think at all. Minds numbed by a bloody civil war and crushing defeat, emotions shocked by alien invasion, occupation, and "black" Reconstruction, Southerners at large seemed incapable of philosophizing deeply about their experience. Anyone reading the literary remains of those people gathered in the archives of the land will be struck—and depressed— by one overwhelming fact: the South was physically and mentally devastated by the war. Southerners were reduced to the material and elemental. Quite literally, they were most concerned with food for their bellies and the bellies of those they loved. Reconstruction for Southern whites was a monstrously physical time, an animal time.

In this respect, Margaret Mitchell in *Gone with the Wind* was profoundly historical. Melanie Wilkes never surrenders the pure values of the Old South, but Melanies after the war were few and far between. Distressingly close to the common experience was that of Scarlett O'Hara. Fleeing a burning Atlanta and returning in the middle of the night to Tara, the once splendid and now ruined plantation, she and her dependents are on the verge of starvation. In the film, Scarlett (played by Vivien Leigh) discovers the remains of a slave garden, scrambles about frantically in the dirt, unearths a radish, and gnaws at it hungrily. She bends over retching, then lifts her face, dirt-stained and tearful. She struggles to her feet amidst the desolation of the plantation, fists clenched, grimly determined, looking to the sky: " . . . as God is my witness," she declares, "the Yankees aren't going to lick me. I'm going to live through this, and when it's over, I'm never going to be hungry again. No, nor any of my folks. If I have to steal or kill—as God is my witness, I'm never going to be hungry again."[34]

Scarlett was a metaphor for the New South that grew directly out of defeat in the war and did not wait for Henry Grady and other later prophets windily to announce its coming. That first New South, reflexively and without thought, put matter over mind and called it good. The roots of the immediately postwar New South ran shallow and visible on the earth of the Old. Those roots were manifested in manias for slaves and land and wealth, and then for more slaves, and more land, and more wealth— palpable things that you could see and touch and count, things that translated easily into earthly pleasure and power. Again, Scarlett illustrates the history well. In April 1861, lounging on the veranda at Tara with her suitors the Tarleton twins, she carries in herself the blood of her mother, "a Coast aristocrat of French descent," and her "florid Irish father." A belle of sixteen, she holds her "small white hands folded in her lap," and she wears twelve yards of fine muslin in her dress, the gift of her father's wealth. "Her manners had been imposed upon her by her mother's gentle admonitions and the sterner disciples of her mammy; her eyes were her own." Those green eyes, in "the carefully sweet face," were "turbulent, willful, lusty with life." They gazed upon the Tarleton twins, nineteen, six-two, lean, hard, sunburned, gay, and arrogant. "They laughed and talked, their long legs, booted to the knee and thick with saddle muscles, crossed negligently." In the yard were their horses, "big animals, red as their masters' hair; and around the horses' legs quarreled the pack of lean, nervous possum hounds." The twins were infinitely more physical than mental, and that quality had just led to their expulsion from the state college in Athens. Previously they had been expelled from the state schools of Virginia, Alabama, and South Carolina. The Tarleton twins were perfectly identical, and "their bodies" were "clothed in identical blue coats and mustard-colored breeches." Each was totally infatuated with Scarlett, and each pursued her ardently. But miraculously, neither was jealous of the other. Scarlett could have them both. She played them as a conductor plays an orchestra, first one, then the other, then both together, and she got what she wanted—two superbly physical male animals, as spirited, as strong, as perfectly obedient to her will as horse and hound, two men for the price of one.[35]

Excessive materialism—the prime sin of the New South—was, of course, plainly evident in the prewar South. There were, as the contemporary writer William R. Hundley labeled the type, "Southern Yankees" before there was any war at all.[36] Yet the war and the defeat did turn Southern Yankees loose as never before. Apparently, there is always an urge among the defeated to take on the imagined winning attributes of the victors, if only to beat them in the struggle next time. It should occasion no surprise that Southerners in defeat became somewhat Yankee, that some became totally Yankee, and that a few became more Yankee than the Yankees themselves. The lesson of the war for that first New South was that quantity (men and matériel) did, after all, beat quality. Scarlett and the great mass of Southerners learned that lesson well, and neither they nor their progeny ever totally forgot it. Scarlett was one of those who learned it early and practiced it to perfection. She began to build her fortune, most successfully by using convict labor, white as well as black, at the cost of ten cents a day, to produce lumber for the rebuilding of Atlanta. Forsaking the ideals of the Old South, Scarlett exploited her white brothers and the advantages of her sex, freely associated with the Yankees for profit, indulged in a soul-less materialism, and wallowed in the pleasures of the flesh with the highly physical Rhett Butler (Clark Gable in the film). Rhett Butler, an aristocratic South Carolinian by birth and breeding, was himself nearly all body, carrying within only a hint, a mere flicker of soul somehow surviving from his low-country Carolina past.

Ultimately Scarlett reaps as she has sown. Her daughter, ironically named Bonnie after the "Bonnie Blue Flag" of the Confederacy, is as beautiful, selfish, physical, and as empty as each of her parents. Bonnie is killed by a beautiful brute, her pony. Bonnie's neck is broken in a fall taken by both animal and mistress when she tries to jump him over a high bar. Rhett brutally kills the pony, in the film with a blast of his shotgun. He then goes away because he is seemingly only the shell of a man, however handsome and attractive the shell, and, frankly, he did not "give a damn," not for Scarlett, or the Confederacy, or the South, or anything else.

The South in Reconstruction, again like Scarlett, did not so much surrender thought as postpone it in favor of eating. Many eminent Southerners were not at all slow about going into business with Yankees in the first years after the war. Later, there would be time to think. "Food! Food!" says Scarlett to herself, "Why does the stomach have a longer memory than the mind?" She acts first to save the body. "I'll think of Mother and Pa and Ashley and all this ruin later—," she decided. "Yes, later when I can stand it." At the very end of the novel, Scarlett is twenty-eight and the year is 1873. Melanie dies and Scarlett at last can marry the man she has always loved, Ashley Wilkes, that masculine remnant of Old South aristocracy. She finds, finally, that she does not want him. "He never really existed at all," she declares, "I loved something I made up. . . ." She now sees in Rhett a flash of the virtue that she had imagined in Ashley. She has images of Tara, of her head against her black mammy's bosom, of getting Rhett back. "I'll think of it all tomorrow, at Tara," she decides in the last lines of the book. "I can stand it then."[37]

There were a few Southerners who did think deeply about the meaning of the war, defeat, occupation, and black Reconstruction even as they lived in the midst of those experiences. Some of these concluded that these scourges were signs from God that they had been wrong in slavery, wrong in the presumption that they had somehow discovered God's plan on earth for His people. The idea of the organic society had been a gross error, mocked in Reconstruction by the inversion of the hierarchy. In the black belts of the South the Yankee victors had put the blacks on top, put hands where heads were supposed to be, and they had made hands of heads. Black men in the state house and white men at the plow was the reality, and in some states and communities there was no end of that new order in sight. The Old South way of life seemed outside the pale after all; it was not the way of God. There was a mood of terrible vacuity among Southern whites after the war. It was worse than if the South had simply died; it was, indeed, as if it had never lived.

Some of the most thoughtful ascribed the fall of the South to the surrender of white men to the sex of black women. Flesh had smothered soul. "It does seem strange that so lovely a climate, and country, with a people in every way superior to the Yankees, should be overrun and destroyed by them," wrote low-country aristocrat William Heyward to a friend in 1868. "But I believe that God has ordered it all, and I am firmly of opinion . . . that it is the judgment of the Almighty because the human and brute blood have mingled to the degree it has in the slave states. Was it not so in the French and British Islands and see what has become of them."[38]

A very few Southerners, a corporal's guard persistently philosophical, explained defeat as simply the turning down of the great wheel of progress in another grand cycle. Defeat was not at all a judgment by God that the Southern people had been wrong. It was, rather, a part of the process of purification of his people for the next surge upward.

Soon after Redemption, and especially in the 1880s, intellectuality in the South began slowly to revive, and with it came the philosophical consideration of the meaning of slavery, the war, and defeat. There was in that decade a rising idea that the South had not, after all, been spiritually wrong, either in the war or in slavery. What had been interpreted as punishment for error was actually God testing and purifying his people. The life and labor of the Old South was not only valid, it was valuable because it had generated the virtues that brought the white people of the land through to the modern South.

THE NEW ORTHODOXY

Volksgeistian Conservatives differed from regular Conservatives in regard to their attitudes toward both blacks and whites. Racially, Volksgeistians sought to put blacks aside upon the assumption that thus freed they would rise within their separated sphere as high and as fast as they should. Regular Conservatives, on the other hand, would hold Negroes within the organic society and keep them in the super-subordinate place where they found them. Conservatives assumed that there was no such thing as God-given "black soul" and hence no black culture that whites needed to respect. Indeed, it was as if black people were white people in arrested development, and black culture at best was but a perpetually imperfect imitation of white culture.

In regard to the white world, the primary difference between Volksgeistians and regular Conservatives was that the Volksgeistians had more
faith in the capacity of the mass of whites to rise to the behavioral and
moral traditions of the white elite. Volksgeistians seemed to envision an
eventual melting upward of the white mass into a total cultural assimilation with a persisting and evolving Old South aristocracy—a *Herren-
volk*—and they seemed to expect in the result something like the arrival
of God's chosen people at a new high of earthly attainment. In their view,
the paternal energies of the white elite were turning and should turn to
raise up the whites of the lower orders. Regular Conservatives did not
have such great faith in the capacity of the mass of whites for elevation.

The result of these differences was that the array of institutions generated in the South in the early twentieth century—the institutions that
were to rule the South through most of the century—were a curious mix
of attitudes that were both inextricably interwoven and contradictory. In
race relations, mainline Conservatism evolved to build what might be
called the "new orthodoxy." The new orthodoxy retained much of the
Volksgeistian emphasis on the ineradicable separateness of black people
and set them aside at a great distance from whites. It also retained the
extreme reduction of black people that Radicalism had effected. But even
as resurgent Conservatism ruled blacks down and out, even as it insisted
upon their inferiority and wide separation from the white world, it maintained its faith in the organic society and insisted that black people
remain within that society. Congruently, it demanded that blacks strive
to attain the whiteness that they would never be allowed to possess. After
1915 Conservatives struck paternal postures as evidence of their sympathy
with the efforts of blacks to help themselves, but those postures yielded
little of substance to benefit black people.

On the white side of the line, the Volksgeistian legacy took the form
of a persisting suggestion that the South supported a superbly refined all-
white democracy, both in politics and beyond politics. Even after Volksgeistian Conservatism as a system of thought had rather totally passed
away in the 1920s, the institutions that Volksgeistians had helped to create rolled on, for examples, in the public schools and in medicine. These
institutions, headed by the elite, continued to do the real work of raising
up all white people together that the Volksgeistians had envisioned and
to lend the appearance of truth to the suggestion of democracy. In reality,
however, regular Conservatives never gave up the idea that theirs was
properly an organic society and that leadership was necessarily the work
of the elite distinctly separated from the masses. In the twentieth century,
in their view, Southern society was a pyramidal hierarchy with blacks
lumped indiscriminately together on the bottom and whites carefully

arrayed on the top. Individual whites found specific places in a functional and harmonic order ranging from the lowest to the highest, and most whites were expected to remain in the places to which they were born. Individuals might move up—or down—by dint of their talents, virtues, and industry, but they did so within the everlasting pyramid. Thus, there was a rhetoric that preached equality of opportunity for whites and there was a measure of truth behind the rhetoric, but power remained decidedly hierarchial.

This transition from one Conservative order to another was not unlike that which occurred in the last generation of slavery. In 1889, as in 1831 after Nat Turner's insurrection, the white elite began to perceive black people as shockingly threatening to themselves. They moved to adjust to the threat with the result that not only did race relations change in essential ways, but so did the structure of white society. The fabric of Southern society un-wove itself. Some of the old threads were lost, others changed color and texture, and some from the world outside the South were imported. After the Atlanta riot the reweaving of Southern society began, and by 1915 the new fabric was visible.

Like the reconstitution of Southern society that had occurred in the last generation of slavery, this new order after 1915 had its hard side and its soft side. The hard side, the fruits of Radicalism, were represented in institutions that kept black people down. The soft side, in part the fruits of Volksgeistian Conservatism, accorded black people in their place a degree of independence and a vague, romantic affection. In a world largely invisible to whites, black people were able to gather the strength to survive in a universe that was at best non-caring and at worst destructive. White people at large simply lost awareness about black people, and in the new orthodoxy there was a passion among whites not to see a race problem. Our blacks are good blacks, so ran the thought, if outsiders would simply leave them alone. As in that earlier reconstitution of Southern society, what had begun as a reaction against blackness ended as an assertion of whiteness. The focus of conscious interest in white minds passed from the black mass to the white mass. In the antebellum order it had been the white elite that counted. In the new order it was white people all together that counted. Blacks stood at the bottom of society, and they all looked alike. Whites stood at the top, and each individual white looked different. Blacks were all right in their place, and white Southerners were beautiful wherever they were.

At one level the Volksgeistian system provided Southern whites with a positive image of themselves; at another it functioned as simply one more Southern philosophical accommodation to existing realities. In the early twentieth century the factory had already come to the South in a significant way, and it was, relative to general economics in the South and the nation at large just then, a tremendous success. Mill owners and managers had already turned their institutions into practically all-white enclaves. At least in their own minds, they did see themselves as the paternalists of legend, and, as yet, workers seemed more respectful and grateful to their employers than otherwise. In race relations, blacks were already separated from whites and were becoming, in the cultural sense, progressively blacker. Separation—and disfranchisement also—was explained by the Volksgeistians as merely another curve in the path of progress and, hence, totally acceptable. Militant white supremacy was rationalized as but a transitional phase, a necessary discomfort that would fade away when it had run its course. In one sense the Volksgeistians were arch accommodationists in a specially sophisticated style. A true soul was duty bound to oppose the unreal and to struggle for the ideal, and to do so vigorously for a time. But if one did not overcome obstacles, it meant that he battled for an idea whose time had not yet come. His duty was then to seek another more satisfying front upon which to spend his energies. Thus, Volksgeistian Conservatism was a way of absorbing, intellectually, realities that one could not avoid; it was a lubricant to ease the white South into the twentieth century.

CHAPTER VII

Legacy:
Race Relations in the
Twentieth-Century South

At its worst Volksgeistian Conservatism was a justification, an intellectual legitimation of a sad racial plight. In that it contended that whites could do nothing essential about blacks but must leave them room to find their own genius and salvation, Volksgeistian Conservatism sanctioned a white withdrawal from blackness both in the body and in the mind. A logical result of such thinking was the promotion of the invisibility of black people, the further removal of white people from the possibility of recognizing the equal humanity of blacks, and, finally, the loss of the black problem in the white mind. Volksgeistian Conservatism licensed the turning of the white elite away from its hereditary interest in blacks, and it encouraged them to channel their interest instead toward their white brothers and sisters. The fear and hatred engendered by Radicalism shifted, too, from blacks to the alien enemy—to Jews, Catholics, and the Communist threat from abroad.

The white South in the 1920s and 1930s became, in both its mind and body, what it had been seeking to be since the 1830s, a relatively solid, unitary, most-together place. It was precisely this fact that made it possible for Wilbur Cash, who had been born in 1900 and matured in the 1920s to write such a book as *The Mind of the South* (1941). It was not possible for close students of Southern culture to write such a book earlier, nor to be totally comfortable with that one since. The profound fissures that had existed in the South before those years—between black and white, between the slaveholding elite and the non-slaveholding mass and, subsequently, the social heirs of each, Conservative Democrats and Radical Populists, between racial Conservatives and racial Radicals, and between men and women—were not dissolved, but they were covered over by a heavy plastering of myth, troweled smoothly on by an elite

determined to make it seem that there were no cracks in the structure
that was their world and never really had been. Out of that labor of
mythologizing the past and imagining the present, they brought forth a
most peculiar phenomenon. In the South, white leadership adduced a silver age without there ever having been a golden one. They imagined a
past that never was.

THE WHITE SOUTH LOSES THE BLACK PROBLEM

The most striking aspect of race relations in the South since the Radical
era has been the inability of white people to grab hold of and securely
retain an appreciation of the realities of black existence. Radicalism
served to disengage white people from black people with unprecedented
totality, practically to finish, in fact, a move toward unreality in race relations that had begun in the last generation of slavery and was signalized
by the creation of the Sambo stereotype. It is ironic that, after such a great
display of strength, by 1915 Radicalism had lost its hold on race relations
and had died as a system of thinking about black-white relations. With
that death went the death of the image of the Negro as beast. Of course,
various ideas and attitudes of Radicalism persisted and evolved (such as
an association of black people and super-sexuality), but Radicalism as a
thought-set passed away and was soon lost to living memory. In spite of
its short life, Radicalism had possessed great power, especially in the
black belts. It had done its work there most effectively, more effectively
in fact than its authors ever appreciated. In the black belts, it left black
people in a society in which ruling institutions had been reshaped in an
ethos that presumed their eventual demise. Those institutions persisted
even though that assumption was forgotten by the society as a whole. The
result was that black people lived in a world in which powerful forces
worked automatically day by day to depress the quality of their lives.
Moreover, Radicalism, by its very death, contributed to the continued
reduction of black people because, as Radicalism dissolved, its absence
induced Conservatism to flow quietly and gently back into the land, to
fill young minds, and, in essence, to freeze race relations at the low levels
generated by the Radical rage.

   Individual Radical leaders lived beyond 1915, of course, and many of
them continued to think, talk, and do battle as before. Shaking hoary
heads, waving palsied hands, and crying out in reedy voices, like so many
aging Cassandras, they warned of the race war to come. Most alarming
to them was the apathy of uncommitted youth, and the tendency of these
to lose sight of the black menace. Speaking in upcountry South Carolina

in 1909, that unhappy and wrinkling warrior Ben Tillman struggled to muster troops for the new fight as he had for the old in 1876. "Under the lead of those editors who were many of them in knee-breeches when we were in the throes of the Reconstruction era," he charged, "the rising generation has been taught that we have no race problem and there is no possible danger from negroes now...."[1] Tillman was undeceived by accommodationist dissembling, and he remained a Radical until he died of a stroke in 1918. So too did other Radical leaders keep the faith. Tom Watson passed away in 1922, having been elected to the United States Senate for the term 1921–27. The governor of Georgia appointed Rebecca Felton to fill the office until a special election could be held. Walter George was elected, and he very graciously allowed the still lively Felton, then aged eighty-eight, to occupy that seat for two days before appearing to take the oath himself. One can only imagine the sense of satisfaction Rebecca Felton must have derived from being the first woman ever to take a seat in the upper house of the highest legislature in the land. She died in 1930, and so too did James K. Vardaman, in his case after nearly a decade of mental illness. Tom Dixon lived on until 1946, but was virtually an invalid during the last ten years of his life. Radical leaders persisted, and often they thrived in the areas of their lives that lay outside of race, but like trees that fall in the deserted woods, their Radicalism tumbled and crashed where there was no ear to hear, no eye to see, and no one to care. They continued to preach a race war, but nobody came.

The very success of the Radicals in their first great effort promoted their failure in this last campaign. Conservatism had been practically muted in the black belts, and there were no whites willing to give vigorous battle. But most of all, Radicalism was defeated by the fact that its basic assumption was grossly in error. Black people were not retrogressing, and they were most definitely not going to disappear. Indeed, as the census of 1900 clearly showed and that of 1910 confirmed, the number of black people, like that of white people, was steadily increasing decade after decade. Intelligent young Southerners, noting those statistics, seeing blacks all around, and not having matured in the world to which the Radical leadership had matured, simply had no faith in the dissolution of black people. Blacks were here to stay, they thought, and, further, that fact did not demand much attention because blacks would stay in their places. The new generation took Booker T. Washington at what they thought to be his word: that he spoke for all Negroes, that all Negroes were happy in their then low estate, that they were content to put down their buckets where they were and work with what they had, and that they were to be, essentially, hewers of wood and drawers of water.

Throughout the South the new generation of white people, the generation that was born about 1900 and came to maturity in the 1920s and 1930s strangely lost the Radical idea of race, but they lived with the fruit of their Radical fathers' thought. Their racial patrimony, however unwillingly bequeathed, dwindled from a Negro dead and dissolved to a Negro felled and fixed in a new low of super-subordination. The base line of the new orthodoxy, the anchor that held it firmly to earth, was the reality of Negro life. Negroes in the mass in the black belts were undeniably low. To white people in the new order, it seemed that a simple recognition of material and moral realities argued that blacks were indeed what whites assumed them to be. In white minds, the fact supported the idea, and the idea supported the fact. The power of white people in the South was not without limits, but at the local level it had terrific force to press black life downward and outward.

White-hot Radicalism melted white people away from racial realities so thoroughly that they were unable to re-establish relatively effective contact with blacks for some two generations afterward. The image of the black beast had been born suddenly and grew prodigiously. Everywhere was the potential rapist, waiting for the unwary prey—to rape, mutilate, and murder. It was indeed a system to raise emotional fevers and breed insanities. The horror of the black image in the white mind was soon matched, and overmatched, by the real horror that was inflicted upon blacks by whites in riots and lynchings. Ultimately they turned and walked away, and they did not look back. There followed a decade of relative vacuity, a racial hiatus. Whites were certainly not talking much about black people, and, apparently, they were not thinking much about them either.

What came out of the hiatus was still another image, another stereotype of the Negro—the neo-Sambo. Neo-Sambo, the Negro who appeared in the white Conservative mind in the 1920s and after, was substantially diminished from the 1890s' version. Strangely he had somehow lost his progressive capacity. His engine in the model described by Booker T. Washington had somehow lost power. The sage of Tuskegee had died in 1915, and there was no longer a single conspicuous person who seemed to have a license to speak for blacks or to lead them. Instead there were many lesser leaders and in the South they seemed to voice only fading echoes of Tuskegee. Neo-Sambo did not press forward as a separate finger of the social hand. Indeed, it seemed to whites that he hardly thrust forward at all, but he did continue to be unthreatening. Like the original Sambo, he was docile, subordinate, pliable, conforming, and loyal. What had changed was that blacks, male and female, were allowed to gain a species of adulthood and a measure of independence within a separated world not permitted in the pre-Civil War model. These qualities would be handy to Southern whites if blacks were a permanent presence, and if they were to remain essentially "out there" rather than to be invited "in here." Blacks had learned to survive in the world without the constant and immediate supervision afforded by slavery, and they were marginally useful. They could be released after work on Saturday to do whatever marvelous things it was they did on Saturday night, and usually they could be trusted to show up again Monday morning, if only in jail. In the eyes of white people, blacks did retain some of the qualities of children, but they were child-like young adults rather than the raw children of the Sambo model. They were naïve, physical, easily frightened, sometimes innocently wise, usually harmless, and frequently amusing. They often engaged in "antics," guffaws, knee-slaps, jumps, and turns.

Some few exceptional black people were comfortably mature, much above the common type, and they usually became the local leaders by white designation. Often the local leader was a minister, undertaker, restaurant owner, landlord, storekeeper, or hip-pocket banker. His money came from the hands of black people who worked for the whites, and he drew a measure of insulation and hence of independence from that fact. Whites in the know quoted him as the authority on all things black. Whatever the words, the message was always the same: "He says that black people like it down there, and they always behave that way." The mass of blacks in their separate communities could be safely left to the management of these local leaders who understood them so well and explained them in confidential voices to interested whites.

The black leader had an elevated status only in his local world. If he left home he melted into the black mass. In the eyes of the whites, all Negroes looked alike unless they knew them very personally, and, in the opinion of whites, all could be treated essentially alike. Black people who resisted the neo-Sambo role were either exiled, jailed, killed, or they became, quite simply, "invisible." The new image of black people was suggested accurately enough by characters who appeared in the world of white entertainment—first on the stage, then on the radio, and finally on film. The black person in the abstract often was the singularly talented entertainer, dancer, or musician who, it seemed, had no other life than that of delighting white people. Beloved among whites were such characters as Amos and Andy, the Kingfish, Aunt Jemima, Stepin Fetchit, Buckwheat of "Our Gang" comedies, Scarlett O'Hara's Mammy, and Jack Benny's man Rochester. Among the favorites in a different, more serious vein, was George Washington Carver of peanut butter semi-fame. Credits were given by whites to black talent, but it was always discounted even as it was awarded.

In the 1920s, 1930s, and on into the 1940s, neo-Sambo washed over the black beast in Southern white minds, rendering Marcus Garvey merely pretentious and ridiculous, obscuring W. E. B. DuBois and the NAACP, fading to fleeting shadows the image of the black beast rapist, and totally erasing any active memory of Nat Turner and black men in the Union Army during the Civil War, black rebels against white rebels, double rebels, ready, willing, and able to shoot down white men upon the field of battle. Again in the mid-twentieth century, as in the last generation of slavery, white Southerners were insisting that their Negroes were good Negroes, and there was really no Negro problem at all as long as Negroes remained in the place made for them, and misguided and ill-intentioned whites left them alone.

THE PARANOID STYLE
IN THE TWENTIETH-CENTURY SOUTH

After the end of the Atlanta riot, white Southerners positively needed not to see the black beast rapist anymore. Collectively, they pushed him below the threshold of consciousness, and with him lost the white beast also. With both, they lost the Negro problem and, in the process, very nearly the Negro himself. Certainly the fear of blackness in the South did not die, and could not die. It simply went underground and was displaced. Southerners came to fear hidden blackness, the blackness within seeming whiteness. They began to look with great suspicion upon mulattoes who looked white, white people who behaved as black, and a whole congeries of aliens insidious in their midst who would destroy their happily whole moral universe. The continuous search for invisible blackness, the steady distrust of the alien, and the ready belief in the existence of the enemy hidden within gave rise to a distinctly paranoid style in Southern white culture in the twentieth century.

This paranoid style certainly had roots in the late slave period when Southerners argued that slavery was absolutely right and insisted that it was firmly endorsed by all significant parties, including God. Yet they felt the peculiar institution so peculiar, so grandly different from everything else in the world as to be endangered by anything foreign. The result was that the South closed itself off in vital ways from the outside world, and it persecuted vigorously those suspected of internal subversion. The United States mails, for instance, did not run in the South when they carried abolitionist literature, and more than a few itinerant merchants departed with a tarred skin and a coat of feathers. Southern paranoia had its modern beginnings in late slavery, but its continuous history began with the Radical era. It had its genesis in the Radical . red-hot fights of that age when Radicals drew a clear, fir. those who were on the right side of the race line and th black, who were on the wrong side. This extreme intolerance among their white brothers was so strong as to breed a new ᴀ blackness in the South. Whites who sided too closely with bla   ᴄ, as the phrase went, "white niggers." One could be perfectly whiᴄ genetically and yet be black morally. Clearly, about the turn of the century, there was a rising frequency in references to the behavior of certain whites as being Negro-like. In North Carolina, in the white supremacy campaigns of 1898 and 1900, for instance, there was a marked upsurge in the tendency to read out of the white community and into blackness those whites who consorted, politically or otherwise, with Negroes. Very often those who drew concerted fire were thought to have committed acts of sexual transgression.

By about 1900 blackness and whiteness became a matter not just of color or even blood, but of inner morality reflected by outward performance. Black people could seldom rise near to white values and white culture, but they ought to strive to do so. On the other hand, white people could easily descend into blackness, and some did. In the very midst of the whites, there were unseen "niggers," men with black hearts under white skins who might marry their daughters, who might by that fact quietly, insidiously rape them, and spawn a despicable breed. Increasingly in the early decades of the twentieth century, it was the unseen enemy that Southern whites came specially to fear.

White skin might also hide African ancestry. Southern whites of the Radical persuasion became very fearful of mulattoes passing for white. At this time, the white elite in the lower South were well into a changeover from a view that prevailed among them up to about 1850 that recognized mulattoes, and especially free mulattoes, as a useful group somewhere between black and white to one in which mulattoes and blacks were lumped together in an essentially undifferentiated mass. The "one drop rule" that relegated all to the same caste was rapidly becoming universal. One drop of black blood made anyone all black. In Radical eyes all mulattoes shared fully the bad characteristics ascribed to blacks, even though they possessed certain attributes special to themselves.[2] Southern whites became deeply suspicious of dark strangers, sometimes even expelling such a person from their community on the ground that he was attempting to pass for white. Prospective brides and grooms, applicants for admission to schools, fraternities, and sororities, and people in general with whom one's children might come into intimate contact came to have their ancestries closely scrutinized.

By the 1920s Radical frenzy had been replaced by a steady, quiet, yet alert fear that the attack would come not openly and violently from without by people obviously black, but unseen and insidiously from within, by people with apparently white skins. Your very neighbor might be a Negro, they whispered in their minds, your son or daughter might unwittingly marry one. The unseen Negro might be genetically black in some slight degree, or he might be pure white. The phenomenon is delicate and difficult to define, but it left its mark on Southern thought and behavior. It is evident in the vigil that resurgent Conservatism maintained against alien incursions into local affairs. The latter was often manifested in the fact that, when there was a serious disturbance among black people in any locality in the South, whites usually insisted that it arose not from any intrinsic failing in the Southern social order, but rather from the machinations of evil outside forces—the Germans in World Wars I and II, Communists after the Russian Revolution in 1917, and Jews, Catholics, and labor organizers all along. Figuratively, Southerners after 1915 were constantly casting quick glances over their shoulders and nightly passing broomsticks under their beds to detect the hidden enemy. This curious phenomenon, the emergence of the alien rather than the black as the ultimate menace to Southern civilization, appeared powerfully in early form in the case of Leo Frank. The affair began with the murder of a thirteen-year-old girl, Mary Phagan, in Frank's pencil factory in Atlanta in 1913 and ended with his death by lynching in Marietta in 1915.

Leo Frank was Jewish and in 1913 he was twenty-nine, five feet six inches tall, a thin, intense man with protuberant eyeballs behind thick lensed glasses. He had grown up in Brooklyn, graduated from Cornell University as a mechanical engineer, and came south in 1907 to manage the four-storied factory near Five Points in downtown Atlanta. The factory belonged to the National Pencil Company, a venture owned mostly by an uncle who lived in New York. Frank ran the factory efficiently, and the company profited steadily. In 1911 he married Lucile Selig, eight years his junior and the daughter of a settled, well-to-do Jewish family in Atlanta. The Seligs drew their money from making and distributing disinfectants, detergents, and other chemical products. In 1913 Leo and Lucile were living with her parents. Leo was well respected in the Jewish community. He was of German derivation, American-born, and college educated. Soon after he came to Atlanta he was elected president of the local lodge of B'nai B'rith.

Mary Phagan was the very child of the New South. She was born near Marietta, about eighteen miles northwest of Atlanta. Her parents had been tenant farmers, but when the price of cotton dropped to disastrous lows, the Phagans, like many other farmers in the region, were squeezed off the land. One day the parents and their six children simply left Marietta and walked to Bellwood, a mill village on the outskirts of Atlanta. John Phagan, the father, began working in the mill, and so did his older children—at 5 cents an hour. When John died, Mrs. Phagan married another mill worker. By 1913 Mary had a job in the pencil factory in Atlanta, commuting into town from Bellwood on the trolley, and earning 12 cents hourly. For ten hours a day she worked at a machine pressing erasers into brass rings fixed to the tops of pencils. On Saturday morning, April 26, 1913, Mary ate a breakfast of leftover cabbage and bread and took the streetcar downtown. She intended to collect her pay at the factory, knowing that Frank always did his books there on Saturdays. She expected to stay downtown to watch the Confederate Memorial Day parade along Peachtree Street. The widow of General Stonewall Jackson was to review the two hundred veterans of the rebel army who would march in the procession. A working child taking a holiday. Mary was small, four feet ten inches tall, and she weighed 105 pounds. She was an attractive girl. She had filled the role of "Sleeping Beauty" in the church play some two weeks previously, and she was rapidly becoming a young woman. Had she lived, two weeks later she would have been fourteen.

Mary entered the factory building and climbed the stairs to the second floor. She found Frank in his office, a space closed off by partitions from the machinery that filled the room. "I came to get my pay," she said. "I was out Tuesday, but I have Monday coming." Frank found her pay envelope and put $1.20 in it. Mary took the envelope and left. Frank thought he heard a thumping noise. He looked across the factory room, saw nothing, and returned to his books. It was then about 12:00 noon. It would later be established by medical examiners that Mary Phagan had died at 12:30. There were a few workmen servicing machinery on different floors, and some people came and went during the day. Frank went home for lunch about 1:20 and returned at 3:00 to work until 6:00. He left the night watchman on duty. Then he went home again and read, while Lucile, other members of the Selig family, and guests played bridge.

About 3:00 a.m. Sunday, the night watchman at the factory discovered Mary's body. She lay face down on a trash pile in the basement. The watchman telephoned for help, and the police came. Mary had been bitten on the shoulder and neck and beaten, but the cause of death was probably strangulation. Still wrapped around her neck was a cord, so tightly drawn that it had cut the flesh, and Mary had bled profusely. Her tongue protruded. A piece of her underclothing was also wrapped around her neck and partially covered her face. There had been, apparently, an unsuccessful attempt at rape. A door affording a rear exit from the base-

ment stood open, bloody hand prints smeared over it as if the murderer
had fled by that way.

The police immediately arrested the night watchman. Shortly after
7:00 Sunday morning the officers went to Frank's house. From the start
they were hostile, and within two days they had arrested him for the murder. Frank's trial was probably the most celebrated ever to occur in Georgia. Hugh M. Dorsey, the state's prosecutor, wanted to be governor, and
this was his chance.[3]

It was hot in Atlanta when the trial began late in July; the courthouse,
near the state capitol, caught the sun from early morning. Daily the tem-
perature hovered at 90°. The doors and windows of the courtroom on the
first floor were thrown open. The large blades of an overhead ventilator
swung lazily around and palm fans fluttered against the too still air. The
courtroom itself, the corridors, and even the yard around the windows
were filled with people, men and women, red-faced and perspiring. The
air was laden with an angry, violent mood insisting that Frank be convicted. Now and again the crowd shouted, "Hang the Jew, or we'll hang
you."[4]

Prosecuting attorney Dorsey was alive to the spirit of the mob and the
political advantage of giving them what they wanted. The press, the pulpit, and the politicians had all painted a picture in which an innocent
virginal Southern girl had been outraged by an alien Jew. He was college
educated, wealthy, and, they suggested, unscrupulous in using his power
to abuse sexually the girls and young women held virtually captive in his
factory. Dorsey felt certain that he could give the people a conviction.
His key witness was a black man, Jim Conley, who worked as the
sweeper in the pencil factory. Conley at first told police that he had not
been at the factory on Saturday and that he knew nothing. Several days
later the police discovered that he had lied. After repeated questioning
and some beating, he broke down and confessed more and more of the
"true" story. He admitted to previous lying, layer upon layer of it, and
finally came to a story that depicted Frank as a man who had engaged in
various "crimes against nature" with women in his second-story office
while Conley locked and guarded the front door to keep visitors away.
Frank was a monster who had performed unspeakable acts of sexual per-
version. On at least two occasions, Conley had entered the room while
Frank and his lover were still in suggestive positions. He was not, as Conley reported Frank saying of himself, "built like other men." Conley
swore that Frank had killed Mary when she resisted his advances and
then asked him to help dispose of the body. Together they carried her to
the basement. Frank intended at first to have him burn the remains. He
also had Conley pencil two notes constructed to look as if Mary had writ-

ten them just before she died. The notes accused the nightwatchman of the assault. However, Conley refused to attempt to burn Mary's remains without Frank's help. Thus, the body was found hours later in the basement with the notes near by.[5]

In the South in 1913 white people did not believe that black people ordinarily would tell them the truth at first questioning. Black people would lie, and whites would need to break through the lies to get the truth. Dorsey put his star witness on the stand and led him through confessions of his lies. Then the prosecutor had him tell the final story. The defense made the mistake of attacking Conley's credibility by going through the same routine in greater depth. It almost became a litany of lying as Conley confessed to having told one untruth after another. The all-white jury followed the proceeding with seemingly great satisfaction, nodding assent as Conley confessed to each lie and even repeated the performance of hanging his head in shame as he had done when the police had found him out in his mendacity. However, when the defense lawyers came to the crucial element—that Frank was the man who had killed little Mary Phagan—they were surprised to find themselves unable to break his story.[6] He was the chastened Negro, telling the truth at last. Ironically, the more the defense exhibited Conley as a liar, the more thoroughly the jury believed the final, and unbroken, lie. In the white mind, that last story had to be the absolute truth, and a black man's testimony in these circumstances was more valuable than the purest gold.[7] Diogenes had found his man.

Frank was, of course, convicted. He was sent to the state penitentiary in Milledgeville. In prison he was attacked by an inmate who cut his throat. He was saved from bleeding to death by another prisoner who happened to be a physician. In 1915 Governor John Slaton, a lawyer by profession and deeply disturbed by the blatant inequity of the trial, decided to commute Frank's sentence at the risk of ruining his own political future. Word of his intention got out. Several automobiles full of men went from Marietta more than one hundred miles to the prison in Milledgeville. The men broke into the compound, seized Frank, and took him away. They brought him to Marietta, near the site of Mary Phagan's birthplace. They stood him on a table, put a rope around his neck, and kicked the table away. The fall tore the stitches that had closed his neck wound. He bled profusely, and died.[8]

Leo Frank was lynched just as the murderer of Mary Phagan would have been lynched had he been black. But he was lynched upon the testimony of a black man, and that testimony was rendered in such a way as to compel white prejudice to judge it true. The awful irony in this case is that it was probably the black man himself who committed the deed.

Conley drank heavily, and on the morning of the murder he had attempted to borrow money for drinks without success. Most likely, he killed Mary simply for the $1.20 she carried in her pay envelope. Neither the money nor the envelope was ever found. Jim Conley's subsequent behavior suggested that he was mentally deranged. Later, in a confused relationship with a woman whose lover he wanted to become, he apparently admitted the crime.[9] In retrospect, it seems clear enough that Frank was innocent.

In the Frank case, white Atlanta, white Georgia, and the white South at large were stoutly and steadfastly determined not to see a black beast rapist when they had one right before their eyes. They were rapidly losing the capacity to cope with the omnipresent threat, and they were determined to substitute menaces more manageable. Leo Frank was killed as a surrogate for the black beast rapist. He was in a sense a scapegoat at least twice removed from the real cause of his death. He stood for the alien menace to the South, and the alien menace stood for blacks. Specifically, in the first connection, Frank represented the penetration of the South by the industrial revolution in a new and frightening way. He was a rich Jew, managing a factory mostly owned by his New York uncle. Little Mary Phagan was Southern, white, and an innocent virgin. She was born in the country and killed in the city, in a Yankee-owned factory, fighting to preserve her purity against a bestial Jew. Such was the menace to the South at large, and the South turned its anger away from blacks and toward those alien forces that seemed most threatening to its essential virtue. The cry thus shifted from "the blacks are raping our women" to "the imperialist mills are raping our women" to "the Jews are raping our women."[10]

It was appropriately symbolic that the film *The Birth of a Nation* was shown in Atlanta during the fall of 1915 after Frank was lynched. It was even more symbolic of things to come that the "second Ku Klux Klan" was organized in Atlanta that same year, and its regeneration was celebrated by burning a huge cross on top of Stone Mountain. However, in personnel and motive, the second KKK was most definitely not a continuation of the first. Indeed, it began primarily as a business venture, and its creators virtually sold it to other, more aggressive entrepreneurs in 1920. Like the original Klan it featured the idea of white brotherhood and relied upon regalia, rituals, and exotic titles for a part of its appeal. The gigantic difference was that the second Ku Klux Klan featured a hatred of Jews and Catholics that obscured its anti-Negro animus. This is not at all to say that black people were left out, but the fact was that in the 1920s the great mass of white people in the South did not think that black people were a problem. Those who looked for devils in the

South in the 1920s and after were forced to look elsewhere. They found them in the relatively small and relatively visible Jewish and Catholic populations. The second KKK was not, of course, an exclusively Southern phenomenon. Under the banner of native Americanism, it spread north and west, and gained such power as to influence the elections of one governor and several senators in a number of states, outlaw parochial schools in Oregon, and influence a presidential nomination. Eventually, in the 1920s, the Klan came to claim Indiana as its special stronghold, electing one of its own leaders as lieutenant governor of that state.[11]

The relative decline of blacks as objects of hatred by the second KKK and the taking up of Jewish people as a special target was something new. Before the twentieth century, there was no extraordinary anti-Semitism in the South. There were scattered references to Jews having killed Christ and to the venality of Jewish shopkeepers, but these slurs were more than balanced by numerous friendships and a great deal of respect between Jews and Gentiles, and by a large number of Jewish people (such as Judah P. Benjamin, a member of the Confederate cabinet) who shared fully in the Southern world-view. However, early in the twentieth century the rhetoric of anti-Semitism emerged and in some quarters rose to furious levels, for instance, in Tom Watson's journals. Nevertheless, even after the Frank case and the emergence of the Klan, Southern white Gentiles made a distinction between Jews of Old South and New South origins. The latter were often of the more recent migration from the Slavic countries; the former were British, German, and Sephardic in their ancestry.

New-coming Jews were insidious to the virtue of Southern women, and so too was the Catholic church. Tom Watson, in and after 1907, turned his venom upon Catholics. By 1912 he was accusing priests of using the confession to seduce attractive young women. By his questions, the priest learned which of his penitents were most vulnerable. Watson imagined the scene:

> Remember that the priest is often a powerfully sexed man, who lives on rich food, drinks red wine, and does no manual labor. He is alone with a beautiful, well-shaped young woman who tells him that she is tormented by carnal desire. Her low voice is in his ear; the rustle of her skirts and the scent of her hair kindle flames. She will never tell what he says or does. She believes that he cannot sin. She believes that *he* can forgive her sin. She has been taught that in obeying him, she is serving God.[12]

Another "white nigger," another rape, another secret outrage.

Southerners came to associate the hidden enemy at home with the overt enemy abroad. And they tended to associate both with their otherwise good Negroes. During World War I, the enemy was, of course, the Germans. Sarah Patton Boyle, whose lineage laced neatly back to the First

Families of Virginia and whose father was the Episcopal priest in Virginia most conspicuously concerned with missionary work among blacks, was a child during the war. She lived at that time on the family farm in the heart of the black belt relatively near the coast. She heard rumors that the Germans were landing agents from submarines to go among the Negroes and stir up insurrections preparatory to an invasion. Sarah secretly dug a cave in a hillside near her house. She intended to hide there with her family when the blacks insurrected at the instigation of the Germans.[13]

After the Communist revolution in Russia in 1917, the white South had another and very durable unseen enemy to combat. It did not improve their sense of security that the Communist International soon adopted a program for American blacks inspired by their own expert in racial and ethnic affairs, Josef Stalin. After the revolution, Stalin would solve the race problem in America by setting aside certain states in the deep South for exclusive occupation by blacks. In Communist America, as in Communist Russia, the race problem was expected to achieve first a geographical resolution and then a political one. After World War I was over, the Communist menace became the most popular menace in the South just as it did in America at large. Moreover, often enough, the visible Communists happened to be Jewish. Sometimes, almost as a bonus, they might also be labor organizers. When the Scottsboro case broke in 1931 the South had a perfect opportunity to exercise its paranoia. In this affair, nine young black men were accused of raping two white women hoboing on a freight train in northern Alabama. The Communist party in America made a *cause célèbre* of the case. In the Southern mind, the involvement of the Communists and a leading lawyer from New York named Leibowitz, who was Jewish but not a Communist, represented the nightmare come true. The Alabama Department of the American Legion deplored the "horde of Communists" who flooded the state and incited riot among the blacks by their defense of the "negro rapists" in the Scottsboro case. It is virtually certain that the charges were not true, but, as in the Frank affair, that hardly seemed relevant. Eight of the nine young men were convicted immediately and sentenced to death in the electric chair. Prolonged court action saved the lives of all the "Scottsboro boys," but a generation before such a resolution would have been most unlikely.[14]

During World War II, the Germans came to the fore again as the hidden enemy. And again, the white South associated the threat with black insurrection. Curiously, this time it was thought that maids in the white homes of the South were organizing so-called "Eleanor Clubs" in a conspiracy to raise wages and "bump" ladies off the sidewalks of Southern towns. Allegedly, somehow inspired by liberal Eleanor Roosevelt, black women were organizing to walk up and down the sidewalks of the

South rudely shouldering against white women as they went about their business. Perhaps the simple desertion by black women of white people's kitchens for well-paying factory jobs inspired these rumors.

Easier to understand was the idea that the Germans had organized "Swastika Clubs" among blacks to insurrect at the right moment to make a Nazi invasion of America successful. "Hitler has told the Negroes he will give them the South for their help," one informant reported to sociologist Howard Odum. Closely associated with the Nazi threat was the "ice pick rumor." Appearing throughout the South was the same basic story that the Negroes were buying up all the ice picks in preparation for an attack on the whites during the first blackout or at some other signal occasion.[15] All of this seems rather ridiculous, but what followed had no humor in it.

When the Cold War came on, Southerners were ready for it. They seemed almost to welcome the combat. With the Russians in possession of transoceanic aircraft, rockets, and atom bombs, it seemed fully possible that the outside enemy might very quickly become an internal one. What had been invisible suddenly became very visible. When the cold war warrior Senator Joseph McCarthy of Wisconsin first appeared, he had hearty approval in the South. The civil-rights movement was already gathering headway. Southern whites were quite ready to believe that any agitation on the part of black people was not the result of local conditions, but rather of alien agents—of whatever color—in the pay of Russian Communists. Many Southerners, and perhaps most of them, firmly believed that Martin Luther King and the whole civil-rights movement were instigated and paid for by Communist agents. Without interlopers and provocateurs, their blacks would be good blacks.

THE UNREAL SOUTH

It is ironic that at the turn of the century, just when other Americans were entering an identity crisis, Southern whites were emerging from one. Even in the first decade of the century, Southerners were coming to very definite conclusions about their own essential nature. They were deciding that they were a specially spiritual people with a high sense of ideals and personal honor. Symptomatic of the South's rising appreciation of itself was the fact that there were now beginning to appear "Southern" textbooks, written in the South, published in the South, and used by Southern students in a growing network of public schools. Professor J. G. de Roulhac Hamilton began to collect manuscript materials relating to Southern history at the University of North Carolina in Chapel Hill, while some ten miles away in Durham in 1907 the first course in Southern history was taught by William K. Boyd in John Spencer Bassett's Trinity College. Southerners were putting themselves together again, and the South was rising—at the very least, in its own eyes.

The rise in the Southern sense of self had much to do with the use it made of its past, most especially its Confederate past. One of the most interesting and revealing carriers of the Southern revival was the Kappa Alpha Order. The order was first organized in Washington College in Lexington, Virginia, in 1866 by students, some of whom were Confederate veterans. In its first two generations, it was a highly idealistic activity. It was formed for the purpose of preserving what those young men considered to be the virtues of the Old South. Foremost among these was "honor," followed closely by veneration for Southern ladyhood. Both of these were overlain with a heavy blanket of Christianity. "Order" was precisely the appropriate term to describe the character of this specially Southern fraternity in its first phase. It was built upon a regimen, a strict code for living in society in such a way as to purify the body and refine the spirit. Initially the KAs were not unlike the orders of the medieval church, such as, for example, the Knights Templar. KAs should not curse, drink, or otherwise defile their bodies, and they should pray. The early KAs saw themselves as something very much like Christian knights.

In the 1890s the KAs suffered schisms over several issues. Until that time the fraternity had accepted new chapters only if they were located in Southern schools. The question arose: should the order accept Northern chapters? Could a Northerner naturally possess the virtues that the order required? Did one actually have to be born into the *Volksgeist* of the white South to possess the ideals requisite for membership? Ultimately, the answer was that Yankees could not, indeed, be properly endowed, and the order remained distinctly Southern. The single exception was the West. It was decided that certain Western areas were sufficiently Southern to host the order. In 1895 a chapter was organized at the University of California in Berkeley and another contemplated at Stanford.

Kappa Alphas also split over the proper ranking of Robert E. Lee in the hierarchy of Southern leaders. Actually, Lee himself had been the president of Washington College when the order was founded. The late commander of the Army of Northern Virginia apparently never noticed the order, and the order in return was less than enthusiastic about Lee. Instead, the KAs raised up T. J. "Stonewall" Jackson as their pre-eminent hero. Jackson had died of wounds received in the war, and was famous for his piety. The KAs painted Jackson as a Christian knight martyred fighting for the liberty and honor of the Southern people. By the 1890s

Lee too had died, and the order finally decided to elevate him to the saint-hood also. The myth arose that Lee had somehow inspired the genesis of the order. In the early twentieth century, young KAs were encouraged to show the same sense of honor and duty, of *noblesse oblige,* in their lives that the great general had shown in the war.[16]

In moving to welcome Lee to the hall of Southern fame, the KAs were only doing what leading Southerners were doing. It is highly significant that Robert E. Lee became the great war hero of the South only in the 1890s. Before that time Jackson and Davis were the idols. Jackson was, of course, a candidate easily elected. His dashing generalship, chalking up victory after victory with his small, tough army corps, his tragic death, shot by his own men while bravely scouting the front lines, and his quiet Christian faith were the very clay of which mythical heroes are made. By the 1890s, Davis was dead, and, interestingly, as he receded from the public consciousness, Robert E. Lee came to the fore. Lee emerged, even over Jackson, as the personification of all that was great and good in the Civil War. His sense of honor, courage, loyalty, and care for his people were the great spiritual values of the South. Those values were also universal, of course, and they could exist among individuals in the North as well as in the South, KA opinions to the contrary notwithstanding. The two sections could reunite upon those qualities, erase the hatreds of the Civil War, and in union give birth to the new nation. Lee memorialized, in effect, became a bridge upon which North and South could meet again, embrace, and recognize their natural brotherhood. In the turn-of-the-century years, the special elevation of Lee and his association with Jackson, displaced the symbols of slavery, secession, and treason and focused attention on the totally virtuous Army of Northern Virginia.

The whole effort was abetted by the organization of Confederate veterans and their descendants. Veterans of the Confederate army organized themselves soon after the war, and they continued their associations through the decades. Most conspicuous in these organizations were the late soldiers of the Army of Northern Virginia. By the turn of the century, however, their ranks were sadly thinned, and it fell to their sons and daughters to continue the tradition. Associations of sons and daughters of the Confederacy became perpetual in the ensuing decades of the new century, marking the graves of their fallen fathers with maltese crosses, cleaning the grave sites, erecting statuary, and celebrating Lee's birthday every January. For a time after the war, annual memorial services had been held in the graveyards of the valiant dead on the anniversary of the surrender at Appomattox. By 1900 those services had been moved out of the cemeteries to the public parks and squares, and the dates chosen tended to coincide with the first rush of spring in the particular part of the South in which they occurred. Thus, the death of the Confederacy came to be associated with a perpetual rebirth of life, a resurrection. The dead had not died in vain, and the South was, indeed, risen again.[17]

The tragic truth was that, as whites discovered a mythical past for themselves in the 1920s and 1930s, they practically lost all understanding of race as a primary determinant of Southern culture and any real appreciation of the Negro. Tillman's nightmare had come true—the young South went to sleep at the Radical rack and let the Negro get away. The escape of black people from the white mind was amazingly total, and the Negro practically disappeared as anything more than a cipher in Southern white calculations. Negroes, for instance, were almost left out of History. Where they did appear, there were no problems. Slavery was a sort of boarding school for blacks; it was necessary, but it was also for the most part a fortunate connection and an enjoyable experience. Booker T. Washington might get a nod in history schoolbooks written for consumption by Southern whites, but barely more than George Washington Carver got for peanuts. Ulrich B. Phillips did publish his central theme essay in 1928, and historians should have taken that as a cue to keep Negroes and race relations to the fore in writing Southern history, but they did not. In scholarly writing, racial determinism was swept rather quickly and easily aside by other prime movers and particularly by economic determinism employed in varying strengths—up to and including industrial. After World War I, a heavy reliance upon the economic explanation swept through American historical writing like influenza. It was not the presence of the black man that made the South the way it was, ran the interpretation, it was cotton and commerce, railroads and factories, and, finally, greedy men and voracious monopolies. The Negro, much like his white contemporary, was a pawn in the economic game. Nat Turner and Frederick Douglass were all but lost to living memory, and W. E. B. DuBois was vaguely up North somewhere. The Negro had so lost power in the conscious mind of the South that he could no longer even qualify as a devil.

As Radicalism faded away, a bland Conservatism came to life and power again. The new Conservativism of the 1920s and 1930s was much more complacent than any had ever been before, with the possible exception of a few years in the 1880s. It was tepid rather than warm, tinted rather than colored, and its action was very slight. Paternalism toward neo-Sambo was its heaviest burden, and that burden was light, almost a pleasure to carry, hardly more than a miniature flag on one's lapel. Anybody who thought about black people at all in these years was able to find some black person to patronize—the cook, the laundress, the janitor at the office. Southern whites drifted into a racial dream world in which there really were no problems—that is, if Yankees, Germans, and Communists would simply leave the blacks alone. As Southerners saw it, they were married to their black people, and they took care of them—in sickness and in jail. The new Sambo was built up not only day by day in face to face encounters, but also by an intricate network of persisting beliefs and institutions that tied all tightly together. In a large measure, the image was maintained by the very distance that separated the races and the invisibility of black people to white. But, further, it was sharpened by the sheer power of whites to make visible blacks seem to be what they wanted them to be. In the first half of the twentieth century, Southern whites had great power to hold blacks in place and to enforce upon them prescribed behavior in the presence of white people. It was very clear that white people would use that power just as they wanted. They used it in a series of riots as black soldiers came home from France after World War I, and afterward in scattered violent forays. But they developed a method whereby they could see themselves both as the good parents of blacks and yet do the violence necessary to keep blacks in place. White people proved again and again that they were perfectly capable of descending from the racial dream cloud upon which they preferred to ride, exercising whatever ruthlessness was necessary to repress the imagined outbreak, and then climbing back on the cloud and pretending they had never left. Our Negroes are good Negroes, they would say to one another, it was aliens, outsiders who caused this late unpleasantness. It was an aberration now gone forever, and, hence, in effect it never happened.

Black people were lost from the textbooks; they dropped to the lower rungs of even the Ku Klux Klan's list of devils; and they very nearly evaporated from politics. The one place they did appear prominently was in the rhetoric of a whole genre of politicians who might be called "Dixie demagogues." Extreme racism had been aggressively preached by the Radical politicians, of course, but there was a difference between these people and those who came later. There can be no doubt that Tillman, Felton, Watson, Smith, and Vardaman believed what they preached about black people. The next generation of politicians, however, saved their race-baiting for election day. They raised cries of "Would you want your daughter to marry one," knowing full well that such an event was highly unlikely—in the South impossible by law, and in the North improbable by custom. These people represented a low in Southern politics, probably the lowest ever. They were essentially dishonest and negative. They did nothing socially, and they really did nothing politically. Their prime function, it seems, was simply to be colorful and to entertain. Gene Talmadge, Governor and later Senator from Georgia, was famous for his red galluses (suspenders). Robert Rice Reynolds, Senator from North Carolina, was known for his silver shirt. Ellison D. "Cotton Ed" Smith, for thirty-six years a Senator from South Carolina, had cotton white hair and campaigned from a cotton float drawn by farm mules. Theodore Bilbo, first a Governor of and then a Senator from Mississippi, was best known for his colorful and often profane language. Most of all it seems that the function of the Southern politician in this era was to entertain in a flamboyant manner, and race-baiting was but a familiar, favored, and, most of all, a safe song to sing. Politics in the South in the 1920s and 1930s were simply romantic. They were unreal. The one politician who was real, perhaps all too real, was Huey Long, and he was killed, shot down by his own people heading north and running for national power.

During the 1920s and 1930s, even as they lost their grasp on the real world, it seemed the whole of the white South came together as never before. As they slipped further away from an understanding of blacks, they found themselves as a people separated from the nation. They were bound together very much by a common perception of a past that featured a valiant soldiery and a tragic and honorable end. But also in these decades the Old South rose again. It was as if the Army of Northern Virginia had labored first and made legitimate the resurrection and laudation of the antebellum order. It became permissible, even creditable, to have owned land and slaves, and it was as if in the 1920s and 1930s everyone in the white South somehow retroactively acquired slaves and plantations. The great mass of yeomanry in the Old South, the plain folk, virtually disappeared, and the best efforts of historian Frank L. Owsley of Vanderbilt University and his very capable and energetic students seemed unable to raise them to lasting historical recall. The poor whites, often denominated "poor white trash," were remembered, but they dwindled to an insignificant few, a token few who, it seemed, in some miraculous way, left no descendants at all. White families, rather, remembered their fallen soldiers and faithful black servants. Blacks in the war were loyal to white masters because understanding whites in slavery were kind to blacks. There was no problem with race in slavery, and there was no problem with race in the conscious mind of the white South in the 1920s and 1930s.

Along with identification by the white mass with planters and slaveholders came an identification with the Confederate army. Retroactively, everyone joined that mighty band. The Confederate army of myth was built, of course, upon the reality of Lee's Army of Northern Virginia, and while that army lost physical battles, it won an unbroken series of spiritual victories right up to and including that one at Appomattox. In the early decades of the twentieth century, it seemed that everybody in that Confederate army enjoyed a constant progression of promotions. At the end of the war, there appeared to have been a whole flock of "boy colonels" and not a few generals in their mid-twenties. They seemed a virile, romantic breed, siring a massive progeny. And in the twentieth century, if one could not be a lineal descendant of a Confederate colonel or general, he or she could at least sing "Dixie" and verbally endorse the courage and nobility of the men in gray.

The myth of a whole South fused in its finest hour into the Army of Northern Virginia was promoted in formal history. Douglas Southall Freeman, another of those great deans of Virginia journalism, wrote a four-volume biography of General Lee in the war, and then did another three volumes on Lee's lieutenants.[18] The Army of Tennessee was all but forgotten. No one seemed easily to recall that it had retreated not only through and out of Tennessee, but also through Mississippi, Alabama, Georgia, South Carolina, and into North Carolina, finally to surrender so that in the end its very name mocked its failure. It had suffered defeat in Kentucky and never once crossed the Ohio. It came as something of a surprise to young Southerners to learn eventually, that there were other armies of significance in the Confederacy besides that of Northern Virginia and other generals of worth besides Lee and Jackson. It was even more shocking later to learn that there were deserters from the Confederate army, and a mild surprise that behind the armies there had been a Confederate government with a president named Jefferson Davis. It was almost as if the Army of Northern Virginia was out there disembodied, a spirit-fed army, that had no need of a great clanking, faction-ridden, dissident government to give it sustenance. Jefferson Davis, after all, was treason and best forgotten in the effort at reunion, while the Army of Northern Virginia was courage. The very thing that made the war so bad also made it so good. It was terrific courage, a capacity for fighting hard and dying bravely that bound the Union and Southern armies together even in most awful and bloody combat. The soldiers on each side could recognize the virtue of the other and so could their sons and daughters, and finally their grandsons and granddaughters—of spiritual as well as physical descent.

In spite of the boom and bust in world economics and politics, the 1920s and 1930s was a grand era for the South. Southern whites looked backward and somehow felt all together, warm, and secure. The Old South that might have been had been truncated, its heart had stopped in 1865, and then started again. It was as if the South of the twentieth century were a child, an embryo, frozen in its early youth and later warmed to life. In the freezing it had somehow stepped out of time and lost its place in the flow of the larger world. Southerners had lost the beat of time as other Americans knew it, and, by the 1920s, they had largely lost inclination to find it again. From the late 1880s into the 1910s, they had tried economic reform through political activity, alternating through several cycles with racial reform. Neither had worked, and, in the 1920s and 1930s, they tried nothing. Nevertheless, what the South had lost in action, it gained in a sort of contented, even defiant resignation. The South felt that it knew what was important, and it could live in peace throughout its days. It had earned its silver hair with honor, and it could observe its own existence with equanimity. The South might finally die, felled by the material Leviathan, but it would die differently as it had lived differently—safe in its own mind with the idea that it had marked the world with courage and grace. There, in the mind, all was woven together with the smoothness, the sheen, the toughness of silken cloth. The South was a fine spun living dream, and, in the decades of the 1920s and 1930s, the dream waxed rosy, romantic, and unreal.

SOUTHERN WHITE LIBERALS IN THE
TWENTIETH CENTURY

The recognition of the race problem in the South and moves to do something about it constitute another story and a very complex one. Moreover, it becomes one that cannot be told exclusively in terms of the South because not all, or even the great majority of black people in America were located in the fifteen ex-slaveholding states. In the 1960s perhaps slightly less than 50 percent were so located. In two generations, black people had moved out of the South and spread themselves across the nation from Boston to Chicago to Oakland, California. Particularly did they move into urban and industrial areas, a migration that was strongly promoted by the industrial needs of the military in World Wars I and II. The migrants were for the most part country-born and country-bred, but they lived their mature lives in the city. There, of course, they encountered a radically different environment from any they had known before. But they did meet the old and all too familiar prejudice. Ultimately, they responded to racial prejudice in the North and West as they had responded to it in the South by building up rather solid fortresses in the black community, especially in families, clans, clubs, and churches, wherein they might survive.

The story of race in America in the twentieth century is necessarily a national one, but it is also international. In 1941 the United States found itself locked in a bitter struggle against the fascists in Europe and the Japanese in the Pacific. The help of the Negro tenth of the American population was clearly a necessity. What had begun in World War I was repeated and multiplied in World War II as hundreds of thousands of black people entered war industries all over the nation. Black leadership was alive to the possibilities of the situation. In 1941, on the eve of America's entrance into the war, A. Philip Randolph, president of the Brotherhood of Railroad Sleeping Car Porters, organized a march on Washington to insist upon the opening up of economic opportunities to blacks. President Franklin Roosevelt, fearful of a show of division in the face of the coming war, struck a compromise in which Randolph called off the march in return for the establishment of a Fair Employment Practices Committee that would promote jobs for blacks in war industries.[19] Government contracts, then and thereafter, were a vast part of the national economy, and each contract contained fair employment practices provisions that opened jobs for black workers. Compliance was less than enthusiastic, but the war itself strained the manpower of white America to the limits, and it soon became highly acceptable for blacks, and white women as well, to enter jobs previously denied them. Also women and blacks enlisted in support units of the military in vast numbers, freeing white soldiers and sailors for front-line duty. As the war ground on and the number of casualties rose, black leaders agitated for the deployment of black troops under black officers on the front lines. At the beginning of the war, white America was firmly fixed in the opinion that black men would never make reliable combat soldiers. However, as the fighting took its toll, white soldiers barely eighteen years old were dying on the battlefront, and white men up to the age of forty-five were being drafted. Finally, the military yielded, most conspicuously, perhaps, in sending the all-black 92nd Division against the Germans in Italy and in transferring the 99th Pursuit Squadron to engage the Luftwaffe over northern Europe.[20]

The hot war with the Germans and Japanese had hardly ended before the Cold War with the Russians commenced. That struggle was more totally global than the earlier one, and it lasted much longer. Even as the Cold War began, the empires of the old order were breaking up, and out of those empires new nations emerged. The vast majority of people in the new nations were non-white. This "Third World" became vital in the struggle as the Russians attempted to recruit them to their side with the idea that Communism was not only anti-imperialist but also anti-racist. The United States, offering itself as both the modern exemplar and the champion of democracy, was faced with the problem of wooing the non-white people of the Third World into the anti-Communist camp while racism ran riot at home. It was fortunate that Harry S Truman, the senator who had been most involved with the FEPC, was then President. Truman had already in 1946 set up two commissions to study aspects of race relations in America. One concerned itself with the area of higher education and the other with civil rights. In 1948 the President proposed to Congress sweeping legislation looking toward racial equality. Also, as commander-in-chief of the army and navy, he ordered the military to desegregate. In 1951, during the Korean conflict, American forces found themselves suddenly thrown back from the Yalu River by masses of Chinese troops just entering the war. The American lines were so thinned by losses that the army was forced to use black support troops—cooks, stevedores, teamsters—to fill up the ranks of combat units. They discovered that not only did black troops fight as well as white troops, but that in the crisis black and white troops on the front lines fought well together.[21] From that time forward the services enlisted black men and women with increasing eagerness. While relations between blacks and whites in the service have often lacked harmony, the number of black people in the armed services has risen progressively, and black representation in the officer corps has increased dramatically.

Meanwhile, the NAACP was at work pressing toward, among other things, the end of segregation in the public schools. In 1954 when the Supreme Court handed down the Brown decision prescribing integration, four other such cases were pending, and three of the four were backed by the NAACP through the Legal Defense Fund. An alert and active black leadership and the real power of international politics were working in tandem to change race relations in America. The first hard thrust would come in the South, most especially in the deep South, and from a liberal element among the whites as well as from a progressive element among the blacks.

From the time of the Montgomery Race Conference in 1900 there persisted among Southern white Conservatives a thin thread of organized interest in black people. The Conference in dissolving itself resolved to have yearly meetings thereafter. That first meeting was, of course, a practical failure, and the annual meetings anticipated did not materialize. Even so, there was an echo of the idea in the yearly sessions of the Southern Sociological Congress that began in 1912. These gatherings, made up primarily of university professors, continued to track the problem of race relations in the South. In 1919 a permanent organization was established as the Commission on Interracial Cooperation. The Commission was organized in Atlanta and had some of its roots in the "Reconstruction" work that followed the Atlanta riot of 1906. More immediately, the Commission was a response to a rise in racial tensions and violent outbreaks all over America in 1918 and 1919 as a result of the rapid changes engendered by the war. Under the headship of William W. Alexander, a 1912 graduate of Vanderbilt's divinity school and for some years a practicing minister, the Commission functioned, for the most part, as an organization for investigation, study, and publication in race relations. In the 1930s, however, it took an important step toward activism when it employed Jessie Daniel Ames, a Texas women's rights leader, to organize the Association of Southern Women for the Prevention of Lynching. In that decade, Jessie Ames traveled from state to state, turning women's clubs and women's movements previously successful in the fight for suffrage into anti-lynching organizations. When a crime occurred that might result in lynching, local women would pressure local officials to act vigorously to prevent it. White women in the Association declared pointedly to white men that they did not want protection in this way. Ironically, Ames was a personality much like Rebecca Felton, but she delivered a message to white men that was precisely opposite to that of the fire-eating Georgian. She was a very strong woman who labored to maintain a household and rear three children after her husband's early death, and she was not very respectful toward men as men. She was forceful, a superb organizer, and highly effective. Also active in the Interracial Commission was Willis D. Weatherford. As a young man, Weatherford had been eminent in the YMCA. Even in the first decade of the century, he had worked to create and focus interest in the race question in YMCAs on the campuses of Southern colleges and universities. In 1910 he published a book, *Negro Life in the South,* designed to be used as a basis for discussion by such groups. Because of the work of Weatherford and others, during the first half of the twentieth century, campus YMCAs were one of the few places in the South where organized and liberal discussions of the race question could occur.[22]

In 1944 the Interracial Commission dissolved into the Southern Regional Council, an organization that expanded its interest broadly to include many other concerns of the South. While the Council as such was not an activist group, members often were active as individuals and pressed the organization to take direct action, especially in combatting segregation. In the postwar era, the Council became an important collector and dispenser of material relating to Negroes and race relations in the South and in America.[23]

The New Liberals, the native white Southerners who participated in the breakup of the neo-Conservative order in the middle of the twentieth century, were, for the most part, decidedly not organized. Their rebellions against the rigid racial establishment were mainly individual, scattered, and evolved over the decades. The New Liberals, like the old Liberals of the 1880s, were born Conservatives who somehow came to perceive black people in an image different from that of the mass of their contemporaries. Very often the generation of a new perception began with paternalism in the Conservative mode. For all its evils, paternalism led, at least, to contact with black people, and it sometimes happened that contact led to the racial re-education of white people. Once engaged, some white activists passed beyond paternalism to recognize the full humanity of blacks.

Much of the paternalism that initially motivated New Liberals to make contact across the race line had a decidedly Christian character. For decades the Southern Theological Seminary in Louisville, Kentucky, nourished an underground concern for black people that manifested itself in the covert teaching of young black ministers in something of a shadow school for blacks alongside the apparent one for whites. In addition, in the 1930s and especially in the 1940s, the attitude of the seminary was manifested more openly in a remarkable series of theses and dissertations that dealt very boldly with churchly problems of race in the South. Beyond the seminaries, in virtually every denomination there were professional churchmen who kept up long-running contacts with blacks for the sake of Christ and salvation. Also, there were always laymen who never quite accepted the idea that God had made Christians in two colors for eternal separation and discrimination. There were some other Southern Christians who began with that understanding as it related to earthly life, but finally came to feel that the racial order in the South was wrong.

Religion sometimes moved Conservatives to racial liberalism, but there was another prime mover that could appropriately be called empathy. It was almost as if some few Southern whites had the sensitivity and imagination necessary to put themselves in the place of black people and to understand something of the burden that color carried in the South. George Washington Cable had that quality; it made him a pioneer prison reformer in New Orleans, the translator of Creole culture for Anglo-Americans, and a champion of racial equity. Perhaps the best example in the twentieth century of one able to make the intuitive leap to a more equitable racial posture was Lillian Smith, the Georgia author. Born in 1897, Smith was the daughter of a prominent Methodist layman. In the early 1920s she had gone to China as a teaching missionary, and later in the decade she ran a summer camp and school for girls at her retreat in the Georgia mountains near Clayton. Progressively, the school came to teach a liberal message, racial and otherwise. In 1936 with the aid of friends, Smith established the *North Georgia Review,* a magazine devoted to literary art, social criticism, and humanism. That journal was bold and aggressive in racial matters, and so was Lillian Smith. In 1944 she published the novel *Strange Fruit,* an indictment of the sexual exploitation of mulatto women by Southern white men of the elite class. The book sold three million copies. It was banned in Boston because of its explicit statements about sex, and it underwent a withering fire in the South. Smith never flinched but rather continued the assault. In 1955 two young men burned down her house. In that fire she lost most of her papers and other personal treasures. Ultimately, her voice was stilled only by death in 1966 after a long and hard-fought battle against cancer.[24]

Finally, scores of academicians emerged from scholarly retreats to urge the restructuring of race relations in the South. Many of these people were moved by paternalism, by a Southern Christian faith, and by a sensitivity that led to sympathy and action, but also many of them seemed to be moved most essentially by a fundamental rationalism—a sort of philosophical intellectualism that put great faith in research and reason while it damned irrationality and illogic. These people did not set out to become Liberals. Rather they were committed to the pursuit of truth through conventional methods of scholarship, and that pursuit led to an appreciation of the racial realities. In the 1920s and 1930s, and on into the 1940s, the Liberal syndrome in this vein touched several disciplines and many schools, but sociologists and historians seemed particularly affected, as did certain schools that emphasized the liberal arts.

It was no accident that, among academicians, the New Liberals initially emerged in such schools as, for example, the Universities of Virginia, North Carolina, and South Carolina rather than in Virginia Polytechnic Institute, North Carolina State University, or Clemson College. New Liberalism in academia came out of the special retreats of racial Conservatism, and, in each state, one of the resorts of Conservatism was the campus of the state university that was devoted more or less intensively to the liberal arts. In terms of race relations, the more technical schools went Radical, and even those schools where the technical and liberal arts curricula were joined tended to have their Liberalism muted. Naturally not everyone who went through racially Conservative schools in the middle decades of the century was much concerned with race. Indeed, probably the great mass of students and most professors hardly gave the matter a scholarly thought. But they did afford environments not deadly hostile to inquiry into racial matters, and the venture came to be made with as much objectivity as faculty and students could muster. Once they began the inquiry, they sometimes learned much of the truth; and they were bound to tell it. When they told it, they easily won election to a difficult and unfavored office.

Academic Liberals tended to group together, and they flowed through certain channels. One clear, direct current ran from Emory University to the University of North Carolina. Howard Odum, for example, as a young student in Emory College in 1901 and 1902 took Latin at the feet of Andrew Sledd shortly before Sledd's forced departure for having written in the *Atlantic Monthly* that, among other things, lynching was a crime. As a Latinist, Sledd was reputedly partial to that early egalitarian Cicero. Cicero and the writers of his time were much concerned with the "freedmen" of the late Roman Republic. Their writings were full enough of expressions by those lately slaves that they were forever grateful to their erstwhile masters for raising them into civilization, and that they did not want to "marry their daughters." Odum passed on to take a doctorate at Columbia University and later settled himself as a professor in the University of North Carolina. Along with Rupert Vance he created the Institute for Research in the Social Sciences, and together they led in winning international fame for the University as a center for regional studies—their own Southern region being, of course, the pilot and model study of the type. The Institute fostered a host of scholars and sociological studies of Negro life and race relations in the South. Guy B. Johnson, Guion Griffin Johnson, John A. Wooster, and Arthur Raper were among those who made signal contributions in the field. Wooster, for instance, did a deep study of the black people in the Sea Islands of South Carolina, the black population in America culturally closest to Africa. Raper published in 1933 the only close study of lynching that has been done in the last two generations.[25]

Among historians, Fletcher M. Green, long-time professor at Chapel Hill, followed the path that Odum took from Georgia to North Carolina. Green took his bachelor's degree from Emory in 1920 and his doctorate at the University of North Carolina in 1927. He, too, joined the coterie of scholars in the Institute for Research in the Social Sciences. As a professor of history in the university, he directed the work of more than a hundred doctoral students. The dissertations of nearly all of these related to the South, and almost all of those included some consideration of Negroes and of institutions, such as convict leasing and the lien system, that touched black people most intimately. Two of Green's students were among the very first white scholars to begin to put black people back into the mainstream of history as understood by whites. Vernon Lane Wharton, a native of Mississippi, finished his dissertation and published it in 1947 as *The Negro in Mississippi, 1865–1890*. George Brown Tindall, a native of South Carolina, finished his dissertation in 1950 and published it in 1952 as *The Negro in South Carolina, 1877–1900*. Wharton's and Tindall's were the first studies by white scholars that depicted the experience of black people in and after Reconstruction realistically, with objectivity, and commanded both the attention and the continuing respect of scholars in the field. The history of black people, virtually lost to white historians in the late 1890s and early 1900s, was re-found.

A decade after Fletcher Green, C. Vann Woodward made the same trek. Born and reared in the black belt of Arkansas, Woodward took his first degree at Emory and in 1934 moved on to the University of North Carolina to take his Ph.D. in 1937. His primary scholarly ambition in those years was to write the biography of Tom Watson, the Georgia Populist and 1896 vice-presidential candidate. In his biography of Watson there was the strong suggestion that Watson tried to cope with the real economic problems of the nation in the 1890s but that the interests of big business did him in. Watson was painted as rising above the common posture in racial matters, reaching across the race line to preach to black people that blacks and whites together were held down in the ditch by the forces of big business who used the cry of race to divide, dupe, and control them. Watson was defeated, and in the early twentieth century, driven somewhat mad, became a rabid racist. Woodward seems to have sensed in the 1930s that there was a strong connection between the race problem and the industrial revolution, and that, indeed, something had gone horribly wrong in race relations in the South in the 1890s.[26]

In the fall of 1954, in a series of lectures at the University of Virginia in Charlottesville, Woodward defined rather precisely his conception of what had gone wrong. In the previous spring the Supreme Court had rendered its decision in the Brown case. Early in 1955, those lectures were published as *The Strange Career of Jim Crow*. The author dedicated his work "to Charlottesville, and the hill that looks down upon her, Monticello." Woodward's book became, as Martin Luther King, Jr., called it, the historical Bible of the civil-rights movement. It sold more than half a million copies in the generation after its appearance, and it has been not only read, it has been widely taught in the universities, colleges, and public schools of the land. It is highly pertinent that the book opens with the point that things have not always been the same between blacks and whites in the South, that there has been after all a history of race relations in which things did evolve over time. Moreover, the book makes the signal point that there has not been a single mind of the South in regard to race. Rather there have been several minds.[27]

The Strange Career of Jim Crow was a synthetic work. It drew heavily upon Wharton's and Tindall's books and upon Woodward's own previous studies, especially his biography of Tom Watson (1937) and his extensive and deeply researched *Origins of the New South, 1877–1913* (1951).[28] It also pioneered the field of race relations in American history. Wharton's and Tindall's books were conceived as histories of black people rather than as histories of race relations. In his own previous writing Woodward had treated the history of race relations as some very important half-remembered thing. Then in the fall of 1954, after the Brown decision the preceding spring, it was as if he suddenly recalled what he somehow already knew, that there had been, indeed, a history of race relations in the South, that things had not always been the same. Woodward was the first to grasp firmly the idea that the story of race relations in the South and in America had been diverse and evolutionary, and that it had not frozen with the end of either slavery or Reconstruction into an absolutely monolithic, rigid, and lasting pattern. He opened a new field of study in American history.

More immediately, in the lectures at Charlottesville and in the book, Woodward offered an interpretation of the origins of segregation and the history of race relations in the South that was much needed. What the Woodward thesis of the origins of segregation said to that Virginia audience and later to Southern whites at large was that they could accept the Supreme Court decision and desegregation without violating their Southernness. If a Southerner was heir to the Populistic tradition, he and she had a history that allowed them to reach boldly across the race line to promote the common good. If a Southerner came from the Conservative tradition, he and she had a paternalistic history that made it encumbent upon them to deal with black people with consideration and care. Extreme racism in the South was the result of not coping with the real problems of the 1890s and afterward. It was understandable that the South should have made a scapegoat of the Negro but it was an error that could be corrected by Supreme Court decisions, by laws, and, most of all, by a re-appreciation of true Southern values by Southern whites. It was a hopeful message to a people in emotional distress; it was an invitation to a cool, rational, and humane perspective on desegregation.

THE THREE FACES OF EVE

In the early 1950s, in the very midst of the rising furor on race in the South, an attractive woman of twenty-five entered the office of Corbett H. Thigpen, a psychiatrist on the faculty of the Medical College of Georgia. Eve, as they then chose to call this young woman, was the soul of Southern ladyhood. She was demure, sweet, very responsible, and mannerly. She was married and the mother of a three-year-old daughter, Bonnie. Eve had been suffering from severe and prolonged headaches, fainting spells, and, more recently, blackouts. She was distressed that her marriage was in danger of dissolution; she was Southern Baptist and had reneged on her pre-marital promise to have her child reared in the Catholic faith of her husband. Finally, she sought psychiatric help. Over the months, Eve's condition grew worse. Added to her previous ills, she began to hear voices when no one was there. During one interview she showed signs of extreme pain, alternating with a blank look, and ending with a slight shudder. Then, as Thigpen later reported, "she relaxed easily into an attitude of comfort the physician had never before seen in this patient. A pair of blue eyes popped open. There was a quick reckless smile. In a bright unfamiliar voice that sparkled, the woman said, 'Hi, there Doc!'" The psychiatrist suddenly found himself talking to another person in Eve's body. That person was apparently the polar opposite of the first Eve. She was sexually provocative, an exhibitionist who smoked, drank, and used racy language. She was frankly physical and hedonistic. "I like to live and she don't," she declared of Eve. Marvelously, Thigpen called the first woman Eve White and the second Eve Black. Beneath the extravagant differences, the two women shared an inability to bring sexual relations to a consummation. The doctor concluded that Eve White was "frigid," and Eve Black, in spite of her apparent sensuality, always eluded her would-be lover, if need be finally by dissolving herself and letting a bewildered Eve White emerge to face the persistent male. Eve Black had been with Eve White from early childhood and knew her intimately, but Eve White did not know that Eve Black existed. Even as a child Eve Black would sometimes "come out," as she called it. Occasionally, she would do bad things that Eve White did not recall and for which Eve White's parents would punish her. As therapy proceeded, Eve Black began to come out more frequently, learning that she could harass Eve White, weaken her, and take over the mind and body. She confessed that it was she who had caused Eve White's recent headaches, and the voices that Eve White had heard were hers. By the time she revealed herself to the psychiatrist, she felt that she could emerge almost at will. "I'm getting stronger than she is," Eve Black insisted. "Each time I come out she gets weaker." If that continued, she thought, "then the body will be mine." The struggle for control tended toward all or nothing, and Eve Black was winning—there was no middle ground. Finally, Eve White attempted to slash her wrists with a razor and was stopped only by Eve Black's emergence after a hard struggle. "I think she meant business," declared a thoroughly shaken Eve Black.

After more than two years of treatment, and again during an interview with the psychiatrist, a third person suddenly appeared, one who chose to name herself "Jane." She was superbly balanced, intelligent, responding to every situation with a rationality that was almost uncanny. "All her behavior was constructive and socially acceptable," Thigpen asserted. In a word, Jane was sane. She knew nothing of what had gone before; she thought of herself as having been born the moment she appeared before the psychiatrist. All Jane knew was what the doctor told her plus what she learned from the two Eves as she observed and heard them after her own emergence. She was an avid student of their histories and a fast learner. Soon she developed an extraordinary sophistication and vocabulary, well beyond the capacities of either Eve White or Eve Black. Seemingly Jane's stability was made possible by Eve White's recalling more and more of her childhood. It was finally Jane who, under hypnosis and in yet another, a fourth, voice, recalled the traumatic event some twenty years before that had educed a lasting Eve Black. When she was a little girl, Eve's grandmother had died. Her mother, a person of strong religious convictions, felt that touching the face of the dead was the best way of dealing with grief over the death of a loved one. It was, to her, a way of saying good-by in this world and an expression of faith in reunion in the hereafter. At the funeral, she forced little Eve to touch her grandmother's face. Under hypnosis, Jane recalled the scene: "Mother ...! Oh, mother ... Don't make me.... Don't.... Don't.... I can't do it! I can't do it!" Then Jane screamed, as Thigpen reported, like a "banshee." When Jane emerged from this sequence, she had mutated into a fourth personality—still recognizably Jane, but warmer, more comfortable and real. Thus, it was only after more than two years of working to get well and in the process of generating still another personality that the funeral episode was recalled. Eve had repressed the memory of that experience and the memory of her great revulsion against the act her mother had forced her to commit. Behind that episode she recalled other events— her mother gave birth to twin girls several months before the grandmother's death; she had experienced a profound envy over a cousin's new doll and suffered feelings of neglect, and, finally, she had been haunted by the knowledge that a strange man had drowned in a ditch filled with stagnant water near her home.

At first, as Eve Black and Jane One had become stronger, more and more they controlled the body and the conscious mind in which all three personalities existed. Eve Black had very little sympathy for Eve White, but she did not wish her ill. Most of all, Eve Black simply wanted full access to the mind and body so that she might live as she chose. Significantly, Jane One was more fond of Eve Black than she was of Eve White. Finally, both Eve White and Eve Black weakened as Jane Two came to the fore. During this stage Thigpen and his associate in the case, Hervey M. Cleckley, published the story of Eve in a book entitled *The Three Faces of Eve* (1957). The book led to a motion picture in which Georgia-born Joanne Woodward played Eve and Lee J. Cobb played Thigpen. In the film, in a last interview with the psychiatrist, Eve Black, who was so beautiful, and who had been so full of fun and life, fell sad. She knew that she was dying, that she would not be allowed to come out again, and she said goodbye to her friend the physician. It is a unique death scene and one of the most moving sequences in American film. When both Eves had died, Jane Two confessed to missing Eve Black most, and suggested to Thigpen her impression that he shared her sentiment.[29]

The story of Eve is a nearly perfect allegory for the mind of the white South in race relations. There was a time in the youth of the South in which its potentialities for development were various; it might have become many different things. But then it chose to walk a certain path, and that path led eventually to the practice of acts that were unnatural and repulsive to Western civilization, specifically the acts of slavery and its concomitants. In another time or place those acts might have been totally acceptable. But in Western society in the last generation of Southern slavery such was not the case. The South did not cope at all well with the experience of slavery, or with its memory. When slavery had passed, the South quickly repressed the memory of the horrors of that stage of its life, smoothing over the fault line with layer upon layer of the plaster of myth. In the 1880s, the era in which the Bourbon Democracy had ruled politically, Eve White came out in race relations in the South in the form of mild paternalism. The white South in the 1880s was unreal. It was a castle built upon a geological fault line, shatterable by the first strong shock. That shock came in the late 1880s and early 1890s in waves of economic, political, and psychic distress that brought forth Radical racial personalities in the very minds and bodies that had previously housed Conservative personalities. The extravagantly wild and murderous South of the 1890s and early twentieth century, physical, destructive, and sex-ridden, was unreal too, as unreal as Eve Black. Like Eve Black, when the South as Radical began to see the real horror of its acts, when it could no longer sustain the role and carry it to the murderous end implied, it dissolved itself and brought forth its more responsible—almost super-responsible—other self. The Janus face turned. The mind of the South in the 1920s and into the 1950s effectively lost the memory of its Radical personality, and it made slavery seem a beautiful thing. It coped with neither. The saccharine sweet South that showed its face to the world in those decades was Conservative and unreal, fully as unreal as Eve White in the early 1950s. An alert contemporary might have sensed difficulty. There were headaches, fainting spells, blackouts. No one is that good. "Maybe she is too good," was what Eve White's perplexed and desperate husband Ralph had said of her trouble.[30] In the late 1950s and early 1960s when the pressures became too great, when the sober, responsible South-as-Eve-White could not cope, the South-as-Eve-Black was loosed again. One can easily see her in the mad, wildly angry face of a woman in the crowd at Little Rock's Central High School, in the opened jaws and bared fangs of the police dogs set loose in Birmingham, and in the hysterical shooting of three civil rights workers in Mississippi and the mangling of their bones. Again in the later 1960s and on into the 1970s, when the South as "bad" could no longer maintain itself, when it could not live with what it had done and was doing, it dissolved . . . gave way, and the South as good, as "white," cycled to the fore. This time, as before, the South as white gained national approval and applause simply because it had ceased being horrid. Southerners came to dominate the field of Christian evangelism; Southern girls became Misses America; Jimmy Carter became President; and in 1981 the center point of the "Moral Majority" for all America seemed to find its locus in Lynchburg, Virginia. But no one is that good.

The story of Eve works as an allegory for the South because Eve was herself so very Southern. In her life and in her personality she recapitulated her culture, as, indeed, did her psychiatrist. She was so feminine, almost an exaggeration, a caricature of femininity, and he was so masculine. In the South, the absoluteness of the race role plays directly into the absoluteness of the sex role and roles of good and bad. Eve was wholly white racially, visibly she was thoroughly female, but she had difficulty being totally good. If she could not be totally good, she would be totally bad. In the South, a "good woman" (white) cannot be a little bit bad, or a little bit masculine, anymore than she can be a little bit black. At the other pole of race and sex, a black man is termed, in the lowest parlance, as either a "good nigger" or a "bad nigger." Probably no white Southerner has ever said the sentence: "He is a so-so nigger." Southern culture is deeply purist and intolerant of mixtures; indeed, it abhors a mixture—racial, sexual, or moral. Margaret Mitchell, a Georgia woman born to the generation previous to that of Eve, in the 1930s caught magnificently in fiction the extreme forms of Southern white womanhood encompassed by the two Eves. Scarlett O'Hara was virtually Eve Black. She was a "taker," physical, sensual, sexual, hedonistic, socially irresponsible, and, when the consequences of what she had done began to intrude upon her desires, she dissolved herself with the phrase, "I'll think of it all tomorrow." Melanie Wilkes was Scarlett's opposite. Melanie was a "giver," idealistic, spiritual, and totally responsible. Scarlett, like Eve Black, wanted no children; while Melanie, like Eve White, wanted children and hazarded everything, even her own life, for their lives. Eve White's daughter Bonnie, unlike Scarlett's Bonnie, was at the very center of her life . . . and, perhaps, of her death also. At the spiritual level, Scarlett was death and destruction; Melanie was life. But yet, from another perspective, each embodied the seed of the opposite quality; physically, Scarlett was always living, and Melanie was always dying. In the body, Scarlett still lived when Melanie had died, and in life there is hope. Margaret Mitchell left us with a suggestion that Scarlett would follow Rhett to Charleston and through him reclaim the spiritual qualities that were her natural heritage and would make her whole.

The South is a land of extremes, all linked together in tight tension. Extremes of one sort support and maintain extremes of other sorts. Extremes in the same category constitute a whole, and each extreme gains definition and clarity by reference to its opposite. Whites are made white by blacks, men are made men by women, and good is made good by bad. It is totally understandable that Eve should have appeared in the South and been a Southern white woman, that both Eve White and Eve Black should exist in one mind and one body, and that only one side could manifest itself at a time. It is also understandable that Corbett Thigpen chose to call one personality Eve White and the other Eve Black. Finally, there is an instinctive rightness in Jane's affection for Eve Black and her sense that Thigpen too was fond of Eve Black. They were fond of her, probably, in the same way that the South and all America were fond of Scarlett O'Hara. All America remembers, loves, and, indeed, relishes, Scarlett. Not many Americans even remember Melanie Wilkes, and if they do, they merely admire her. They adore Scarlett—perhaps, because she was "bad," and hence more real. She was a bad white woman in an America filled with white women striving to be good, whose society insists with double strength that they be extra good, and who, at the same time, resist not the tendency of the role but the extremity of the role as assigned. "Bad" Rhett Butler, appealing as he is and even as played by Clark Gable in the film, runs a clear second to Scarlett because he is a man. Men do not have to be as good—or, for purposes of negative identity, as bad—as women, and hence Americans did not find him so powerfully useful. Melanie is a good white woman, almost too good, and not nearly so valuable in affording definition as is her opposite. In real life as in fiction, Ashley Wilkes, the good white man, has virtually no use at all because white men do not need to be any better than they are.

The use of *Gone with the Wind* by America is a reflection of the use of the South and its culture by America. America relishes a bad South because it gives definition to a good America. The good South, itself, loves, protects, and will not surrender the bad South because, perhaps, it fears that without the bad South there would be no South at all. The "real" South, the "ought to be South," so to speak, lies somewhere between the good and the bad—in the person of, symbolically, some sane Jane. We sighted Jane in the Liberals in the 1880s, and again in the Southern academy in the 1920s, 1930s, and 1940s. She strove powerfully to come to the fore in the fall and winter of 1954 and 1955. Lamentably Jane represents a balance that the South has not been able to achieve in well over a century of striving.

In the mind of Southern whites for something over six generations, there has been a tendency to look at black people in essentially two ways. Blacks are either children and loved, or beasts and hated. As we have seen, there has been a trend for the mass of white people in the South to oscillate between the two extreme views without any substantial mediation between the two. The charge that Atticus Haygood leveled against his fellow whites in 1895 remains true: that they unrealistically expected the Negro to be "an angel in ebony" and when that proved not to be the case they lost all hope. Extreme racial views in the South are congruent with extreme views of sexuality and of good and bad. Southern white culture, Southern white personality, and Southern white ideas on race, sex, and morality are inextricably intertwined. To change the one is, inevitably, to change the other and, ultimately, the whole structure. Racial Liberalism, then, involved a threat not only to the racial establishment, but to traditional ideas about sex roles and ideas about good and bad as well.

Thus, when the sons and daughters of Conservatism—when Lillian Smith, C. Vann Woodward, and others—crossed over the bridge that their various traditions afforded to become the New Liberals, they were playing with fire and wind. The transition was never sudden, and it was never easy. In order for an individual white person to let black people go, to free black people from the tyranny of a white imagination that would make of them either angels or devils, the white person, in a sense, had to die, had to cease to be in an important way what he or she had been. Just as Eve White and Eve Black had to die so that Jane could come to the fore, so too with the Conservative and Radical mentalities in the Southern white mind. Southern white identity at any given time was intimately bound up with the Southern white image of the Negro, however unreal that image might have been. To let that image go, to see black people as people, was a precarious and exceedingly dangerous venture that exposed the individual to alienation from his natal culture and to the loss of his sense of self. It was a matter of declaring, essentially, "I am not going to be me anymore." That seemingly wonderously complete and whole Southern person, in his own conscious mind so happily superior, had to be roughly brought down from his cloud and footed securely on earth. He had psychologically, quite literally, to be "born again." In their minds, Southern white people have used black people to make themselves whole, to supply their missing parts, good or bad, and to smooth over the crudely sewn seams of their lives. To surrender the use of blacks was to give up a rather handy, attractive, seemingly necessary suit of mental clothing. Having blacks vulnerable led to needing blacks vulnerable, and to surrender the manipulation of black people in this fashion has proved to be a highly hazardous undertaking for Southerners. To yield the crutch gracefully requires an extraordinary effort, a capacity to risk the destruction of one's sense of self, to risk appearing and possibly being less of a man or less of a woman, and, equally frightening, less than purely good. A very large part of the race problem in the South resolves itself into the question of how one takes the racism, the unreality of seeing blacks either as child or beast, out of the Southern mind without killing the Southerner. How does one excise an integral and functioning part of the body and yet preserve the life of the patient? Ultimately, it would profit the Southern white Liberal little to save the whole world, if his own soul went floating in the doing.

The South at large has never been receptive to racial Liberalism, and it was not receptive to the New Liberalism in race in the mid-twentieth century. The most the New Liberal could hope for was permission to breathe, and often enough even that seemed precarious. The attitude of Southern society is easily comprehensible. In part, the South depended for its sense of identity upon images of blackness that Liberalism tended to dissolve, and it worshipped at the shrine of stability. Liberals made the paranoia of Conservatism seem not paranoid. There were indeed enemies of good order in their very midst, previously hidden, now shedding their disguises. Native white Liberals were the weak link in the solid chain of racism in the South. They looked like the other links, and seemed decidedly strong ones, by class, by education, dress, manners, family name, and in every other way. But their very Southerness made their defection all the more pernicious. The white Liberal who was deeply and persistently Southern was, indeed, a powerful foe against racial orthodoxy. He or she would not simply go North and do other things as did Cable, nor die as did Haygood, nor fall silent as did Sledd and other critics of the racial establishment. With undeniably legitimate Southerners persisting in asserting that things were not good, that, in fact, things were bad, then with black people reinforcing that assertion with legal actions, boycotts, and demonstrations, and, finally, with various persons and elements in the national government joining in, racial orthodoxy in the South was soon sorely embattled.

Clearly, the New Liberals began their conversion as Conservatives in pain and seeking relief. Like Eve White, they were inwardly unhappy with themselves and their society. Things were not right racially, yet rebellion in the South, seemingly like everything else, is very difficult. Ultimately they resorted to radical measures—shock treatments—in efforts to alter both themselves and their society. They suffered the results, and they struggled to hold their balance. Lillian Smith launched in

Strange Fruit both the boldest and most pointed indictment of the goodness of the "good white men" of the elite class yet made. Effectively, she
chose inter-racial sex as her weapon. The South counterattacked with
charges that Lillian Smith had sold out to the North, that she was bad,
and, finally, with whispers that she was not a woman to men. When Lillian Smith died in 1966, she was still struggling to find her way back to
some seat of soul, some method that would allow her to let black people
go and preserve her sense of self. Lillian Smith felt literally the fires of
Southern censure as they burned, not merely a cross in front of her home,
but the home itself.

William Faulkner could not be labeled a racial Liberal, yet he too
shared the plight of the Liberal who remained in the South and criticized
the people who determined its racial establishment. Faulkner remained,
not just in the South, but even on that little postage stamp of geography
in north-central Mississippi he knew best. There he made his criticism to
Southerners who never seemed to understand—at least not in his lifetime—the significance of what he said. Faulkner was critical of the South
for its failure to rise to its potential, for its rape of the land, this Southern
Garden of Eden, and the license it gave to the practice of inhumanity by
man to man. The South, he declared, had not met its history. It had not
coped with its past.

Faulkner was critical of the South for what it had become; C. Vann
Woodward defended the South for what it might yet be. *The Strange
Career of Jim Crow* was a prescription for the racial salvation of the
South, but it was an invitation that the South did not accept. In 1952 he
had written an essay entitled "The Irony of Southern History." In 1960
he re-published that essay in a book he called *The Burden of Southern
History*. Woodward pointed out that Southerners had shared the common lot of mankind in ways that other Americans had not. Southerners,
unlike other Americans, had known military defeat, occupation by an
alien army, and reconstruction, and they had known poverty and guilt.
These experiences had set them upon common ground with the great
mass of humanity in the world, and conditioned them to serve all by turning American power to the service of humanity.[31] Woodward and Faulkner shared a faith that somewhere in the history of the South lay the
source of its problem. Faulkner declared that the South had not met its
history, not coped with its past. Woodward was trying to find that history, not just in slavery or civil war, but in Reconstruction and after, in
defeat, occupation, and poverty. Finally, both men shared a driving necessity to restore that Southern Eve to the garden, to say to the white South:
"Yes, you are worthy too." Faulkner said it simply by not letting the
much-abused body die; Woodward said it by active search and exhorta-

tion. Southerners deeply needed affirmation from Faulkner and Wood-ward, and whoever else might offer it with eloquence, art, and conviction, because, after 1955, Sambo was not saying it anymore. Indeed, in the next decade Sambo virtually evaporated.

BLACK BREAKOUT

Sambo did go, and that, more than Northern re-entry into the race prob-lem and Southern liberal defection, bent the back of Southern Conser-vatism for a time. Before Montgomery in 1955, white people, at the sight of black bumptiousness, had been able to come down from the cloud for quick, firm, and violent sorties against assertive blacks. They could beat or lynch a black man, either with or without the help of the police, for what they considered to be the black man's insanity or even his simple stupidity in trifling with their property, lives, or women. But they did these things with the certainty that when the job was done, they could climb back up on the cloud and sail smiling and smoothly on. It was a sort of calculated insanity, a controlled fury that was compartmentalized and sharply focused. Perhaps whites were capable of the most awfully extravagant violence precisely because its object was limited. It was almost as if Southerners sometimes said to themselves, "Today I'm going to go deliberately crazy, but tomorrow I will be sane again."

The game of black balk and white bust, so familiar to the white South in the process of keeping black people under control, suddenly stopped on a city bus in Montgomery, Alabama, in December 1955, when a black woman named Rosa Parks refused to yield her seat to a white person. She would not move and the driver would not move the bus until she yielded. Myth has sometimes painted Rosa Parks as simply a black woman of mid-dle years, making her way home from work as a seamstress in a down-town department store. She was tired, she had suffered a lifetime of dis-crimination, and when the demand came from the driver, she simply refused. She was all of that and she did refuse, but she was also an active member of the local NAACP, she had been trained in leadership in an Association school near Monteagle, Tennessee, and the local chapter had been planning to stage just such a demonstration using a younger black woman before that woman became pregnant. Rosa Parks did do it on her own, but it was not exactly unplanned. What flowed out of her action was a boycott of the city's buses that had been long and carefully consid-ered. Within hours of the incident local black leaders had asked the twenty-six-year-old minister of the Dexter Avenue Baptist Church, Mar-tin Luther King, Jr., to lead them. After a night of soul-searching, he agreed, and shortly an organization was launched to boycott the buses and provide transportation for black people about the town using privately owned vehicles. The movement began with the objective of asking for equal accommodations with whites, not integration. Shortly, it moved on to realize that separate would always be unequal in a white-controlled city in a white-controlled state. For a year, the blacks fought, and in the end they won. The buses were desegregated. Out of the struggle came the method that would tear at the structure of institutional discrimination in the South with great effect—the non-violent demonstration. Also out of the struggle came the prime organization in using the method, the Southern Christian Leadership Conference, and its charismatic leader, Martin Luther King.[32]

With the emergence of Martin Luther King, Jr., and the Southern Christian Leadership Conference, the lodestone of black leadership moved from North to South. During the turn-of-the-century years it had centered on Tuskegee with Booker T. Washington. After Washington's death in 1915, leadership moved North and found its center in the NAACP with headquarters in New York. In 1955 it came to the deep South again, and it drew its primary strength from roots that had not been specially tapped by either Washington or the NAACP. Whereas they had been carefully secular, black leadership in the first phase of the civil-rights movement drew its power from the church.

After Montgomery there was a pause in the civil-rights movement. The Supreme Court had made its decision, but neither Congress nor President leapt to enforce it. Those schools that wanted to desegregate did so. Those that did not had trouble. Most conspicuous among the latter was Central High School in Little Rock, Arkansas. Those were the Eisenhower years, and the President was neither outstanding as a friend of black people nor vigorous in the exercise of central power. Finally, Eisenhower did order federal intervention in Little Rock, but only after it appeared that the authority of the national government was being challenged. The conflict ended in the closing of the schools. In February 1960, the movement of the waters quickened rather suddenly again when, in Greensboro, North Carolina, several students from the state's black A & T College sat in at the lunch counter of the local Woolworth department store. Among those students was Jesse Jackson, soon to become a minister and one of Martin Luther King's immediate lieutenants. Black students were getting restless, and, almost certainly, if they had not sat-in in Greensboro first, they shortly would have done so in any one of a score of other towns. After the Greensboro demonstration, the sit-in movement spread all over the South. Presently, black students were joined by white students. Out of this came another key organization, the Student Non-

Violent Co-ordinating Committee, commonly called "Snick" for its initials, SNCC. Sit-ins were followed by "ride-ins," which became the specialty of an inter-racial group formed in the war, the Congress of Racial Equality. Soon the movement spread to include the registration of black voters, a move fraught with difficulty for white people in the black belt areas. There, majority rule meant black rule.

Such organized and persistent demonstrations from black people were revolutionary in race relations in the South, and, ultimately, in the nation. Brief and violent sorties by whites did not suffice to destroy rebellions as they had in the past. Rosa Parks did not leave the bus quietly; the students did not shuffle away from the lunch counter; and they sat-in again and again. Moreover, the persistent Christian nature of the demonstrations shamed the opposition. Doubtlessly racial extremists would have preferred violent protests from blacks that they could have met with furious and unrestrained violence. But the facts that the demonstrators often came directly out of the black churches; that they were led by ministers, and that they did such things as stand, hold hands, and sing "We Shall Overcome" as if it were a hymn and they were Christians in the lions' den reached the whites where they lived. Southern whites saw themselves as specially Christian people, and they could not turn a deaf ear and an endlessly violent hand to these people who behaved so much, it seemed, as Christ would have behaved in their situation. The movement built and maintained a communication with the whites and with the white elite, whether the whites willed it or not. Whites had long heard what they wanted to hear from black people, and they had heard it from whomever they chose to hear it. The message that they had heard was that black people liked it down there. Now the message from blacks jangled back along white nerves to an unhappy, resistant, but hearing white mind. "We don't like it down here," it insisted. "We don't like it at all." White people did not respond positively and say, "Of course you don't, who would?" What the movement accomplished in the white mind was, rather, confusion, doubt, anger, and resentment. But most of all it accomplished the nearly total destruction of neo-Sambo. The traditional idea—applied in this case to say that "our" blacks would be happy blacks if Martin Luther King, the agent of the Communists, had not stirred them up—became absurdly weak when white people saw that many trusted local black leaders (heretofore trusted by them as their fathers had trusted Booker T. Washington and his clones) were not only in the opposition, but helping to lead it. They would have preferred to believe that the demonstrators were all imported from the North, but there were among them too many familiar faces to allow that self-deception to persist for long. Furthermore, there were too many native whites among the demonstrators. All the old devices of control, thoroughly tried, availed naught in the decade after 1955, and die-hard racial Conservatives knew not what to do. Their arsenal of violence was, after all, relatively thin, and when no weapon seemed successful in quelling the rebellion, the firing grew hesitant and half-hearted. With the March on Washington in 1963, with the opening of public accommodations equally to all persons by the Civil Rights Act of 1964 and the polls and politics by the Voting Rights Act of 1965, the fight went out of the Conservatives. They fell silent, and seemed to yield, at least to the law of the land.

There can be no doubt that the Southern white psyche in 1965 had reached a new low. The Southern sense of self had been brought from the heights to nearly nothing with defeat in the Civil War a century before. During the next forty years, Southerners slowly regained the sense that they were specially spiritual relative to Northerners. In 1912 they helped elect what was at least a Southern-born President to the White House, filled his cabinet in 1913, and rose to prominent chairmanships in the Congress. There was a complacency about the white South in the 1920s and 1930s that passed into anxiety in the 1940s, and became hysteria in the 1950s and early 1960s. The Southern psyche was long driven to seek respect from the North and love from the Negro. Southerners might survive a lack of respect from the North, but they could not survive continuing manifestations of hate from black people. Blacks were too numerous, too close, and, traditionally, too necessary to the Southern sense of self. Whites might go on and become what they would become and blackness need not ever be a vital part of their lives again. Or blacks might jerk the invisible string and whites respond, not in any certain style, but variously and with biases unpredictable and especially their own. Blacks do have a rather miraculous power over Southern whites, not to control them, but to upset them and drive them to frenzy.

The agony in the Southern white mind at the prospect of a black invasion of white culture was still building in 1964 and 1965 when a shadow of relief appeared. Black people were finding that there was a difference between sitting in and being in. A legal and a physical revolution, putting black bodies among white bodies in either token or massive numbers, had not produced a revolution in white attitudes. Indeed, many blacks found that being close to whites was much more painful than being away from them. The closer they got, the greater the pain. The white South, grudgingly, under pressure from court orders, television cameras, and the ultimate police power, accommodated black people in places where they had never been before. In particular, local business interests concerned themselves with projecting to the rest of the nation that the accommodation had, indeed, been completely made. The message of each was that their community had adjusted to the new reality, that peace and good order did prevail, and that outside commerce and industry could now safely invest in that locality.[33] But all of the physical evidences of a change in race relations did not mean that the white mind was revolutionized. Bodies were more easily mixed than minds. The white mind was, as I have said, shaken, but it was not converted. Probably the sum total of white prejudice remained largely unchanged by physical integration alone, and white words, looks, and deeds—often subtle, sometimes thoughtless, and even unintentional—cut like razors. Many black people, especially children, were not prepared for such emotional mayhem. Psychologically wounded and bleeding, some black children among the first integrated came reeling back out of the schoolhouse doorway to a black world that seemed somehow blessedly sweet.

> Holy Mother Blackness,
> Take me
> Make me . . . whole,
> Save my soul.

There is a paradox in race relations in the South and in America. It is that black people have to get out of white society in order to get into it, and they have to get into it in order to get out. They have to get into the society to get a minimum of those palpable things that people need in order simply to survive—material goods, education, government, a minimum of justice, law, and order. But yet because white people are prejudiced and have the power to manifest their prejudices in a multitude of ways, they have to get out, to withdraw to themselves in some degree, to maintain a sense of worth and self-esteem. In 1965, having gotten in as far as they had and having the promise of further entry by the law of the land, having suffered the slings and arrows of white prejudice as they had, and having the surety of further hurts by the laws of inertia and momentum, some black leaders began a move to pull black people away from white people. This separatist effort had a vast impact on the civil-rights movement. In the next five years conspicuous leadership in the black world changed hands from those who had led the fight to get in to those who led the fight to get out. Black leaders in the civil-rights movement had not been very old, but the new leadership was very young. Stokeley Carmichael, H. "Rap" Brown, and Huey Newton were now the names at the forefront. It was a quality of leadership vastly different from what had gone before, and they advocated very different programs under slogans of Black Power, Black Separatism, Black Nationalism and Black Is Beautiful. Black Separatism, the withdrawal, had the effect of ending the intimacy between black and white activists that had obtained during the civil-rights movement. In 1966, SNCC, by then under the direction of Stokeley Carmichael, dramatically expelled its white membership.[34] The assassination of Martin Luther King, Jr., in 1968 symbolized, horribly, the fact that the civil-rights phase of the Black Revolution was over. No single person was widely recognized as King's successor, and there was no one organization that headed up black leadership. Furthermore, goals, like leadership, became diffused, diverse, and sometimes unclear. "Burn, baby, burn" was understandable as a reaction against the past, but it was not a very clear prescription for a livable future. It was almost as if the resources for a drive to get in had been exhausted, and the only way to go now was out. More positively, in the process of withdrawal DuBois's concept of black soul was revived. The Harlem Renaissance, black culture, the African past, and slavery were re-discovered, raised up, and drew vast interest among black artists, intellectuals, and youth. In the late 1960s integration in the older sense of the term had lost meaning and power as the cutting edge of the Black Revolution.

Even as Black Separatism was getting under way, another highly important phenomenon occurred. In the summer of 1965 a riot broke out in Watts, a large and sprawling section of Los Angeles occupied by blacks. In twenty days of burning, smashing, looting, and sniping, some two hundred city blocks were laid waste. In a sense black people took charge of their homes and neighborhoods—mostly white owned—and they burned them down. The usual, and probably accurate, interpretation was that black people not just in the South, but all over America had been promised a better life by the civil-rights movement, and those things had not been forthcoming. Somehow, the nation had lost sight of the fact that the promise of equality and a better life for black people applied not only to black people in the South, but to black people in the North and West as well, and that these were rapidly becoming the majority of the Negro population in America.

There had been race riots before, of course, but the new riot was basically the doing of black people, and they attacked not so much white persons as white property inside the black ghetto. Harlem, apparently, had established the model in the 1930s, and, indeed, there was such a riot in Harlem in 1964. But Watts compelled attention because it was the first dramatic exportation of the model. The camera eye of the nation switched rather rapidly away from the South to the North and West as city after city, even Washington, burned and smoked in imitation of Watts. The meaning was as obvious as the fire and smoke: the racism and its physical results that white America had, heretofore, preferred to see and attack in the South was not merely Southern. Indeed, perhaps in its most awful modern manifestations it was Northern and Western as evidenced in the inner cities where black ghettoes were deteriorating materially, socially, and morally, with devastating effects upon the lives of millions of individuals. White racism clearly was national, and black protest must be made national also. In the South, protest could take form in nonviolent assaults upon legal segregation and disfranchisement. In the North and West, other targets would have to be chosen, and other means of assault devised. For some ten years, from Watts in 1965 to Chelsea, Massachusetts, in 1975, urban racial violence in the North and West gave demonstration after demonstration that white racism and the white South were by no means co-terminal, and that the Black Revolution begun in the South had become national.

THE CONSERVATIVE RESURGENCE

Southern leaders in the mid-twentieth century had great difficulty understanding that black people had been treated unfairly. They were convinced that blacks were innately inferior to whites, and segregation was not only necessary and fair, it was a triumph of statesmanship as well. They understood that not every American agreed with them, but the Brown decision in May 1954 left them shocked and disbelieving. Surely the North could not be so mean. Southern leadership had, indeed, honored the implicit bargain struck two generations before with the decline of Populism. The South had surrendered claim to substantial economic and political power in the nation in return for social and racial autonomy at home. Probably no state had honored that bargain more faithfully than Mississippi. In 1954 it was both the blackest and poorest state in the nation. With the organization of a White Citizens' Council in Indianola in July 1954, it was also the first to offer organized and conspicuous defiance to the High Court's ruling.

In May 1955 the Supreme Court handed down orders for the implementation of its decision. Primary responsibility was lodged with local school boards, while federal district courts were charged with overseeing the process. Some Southern leaders saw great relief in the arrangement. There was no prescribed timetable, and district judges were virtually always fully established members of the local ruling elite. "Thank God," declared Georgia's lieutenant governor, "we've got good Federal judges."[35] Hope rapidly faded as district judges, almost to a man, interpreted the High Court's prescription for "deliberate speed" to mean "begin now." Lower courts repeatedly smashed state laws mandating segregation and quickly brushed aside delaying tactics by local school boards.

Segregation was ultimately broken not by white people in general, nor even by federal judges in particular. It was broken by the first black child to walk through the doors of the traditionally white schoolhouse. It was further broken by the tens, thousands, and millions who followed that first one. Behind those children stood black families, black communities, and a black leadership. That action, and the actions after 1960 of other blacks who "sat-in" at lunch counters, on buses, and elsewhere evoked the violence that brought traditional segregation to an end. Probably, the crucial turn came when a black student, James Meredith, insisted upon entering the Law School of the University of Mississippi in September 1962. In the struggle that followed, 320 federal marshals supported by soldiers fought a minor war to keep Meredith in school. When the dust settled, the campus resembled a war zone.[36] Leaders in other Southern states, many of which were vying with each other for new investments in business and factories from the North and abroad, carefully avoided repeating the Mississippi experience. Desegregation came, but it did not end either discrimination or racism. Indeed, segregation was but an out-work in the front-line defenses of the Southern racial establishment. Hardly had that outwork succumbed before relief appeared on the hori-zon in the form of the self-segregation of black people and the rise of blatant racism outside the South.

Die-hard racial Conservatives in the South were delighted to see a vig-orous racism in the North and West, and they often worked diligently to show that it more than matched their own. George Wallace came out of the deep South in 1968 and 1972 to win amazingly high percentages of votes in several Northern states in the Democratic presidential primaries. In 1968, for instance, he shocked the liberal nation by garnering 40 per-cent of the Democratic primary vote in sometimes famously progressive Wisconsin, home state of Senators Robert La Follette and William Prox-mire. Southern Conservatives at large were greatly relieved to see racism everywhere but at home. They suddenly recognized racism with surprise and delight not only in the North, but in South Africa, Russia, and, finally, even in mother England. By comparison, Southern racism appeared to be of the mildest sort, and even to approach the benign. Again, the myth began to rise that Southern white people understood black people better than anyone else. Hence race relations in the South were better, so ran the thought, and more susceptible to easy improvement.

Racism in foreign parts was a great comfort to Southern white Con-servatives, but more important to them, as always, was what black people at home seemed to be doing. Black separatism was, of course, sweet music to their ears. The very best people, the ruling elite, the most exquisite and untouched among Conservatives, and their sons and daughters carefully nurtured in racial hothouses developed a strangely Mona Lisa cast to their smiles as they looked at Afro hairdos, dress, and dance. There grew up in the South a sort of two-part harmony in the dialogue between the Conservative elite and the more extreme black separatists. "I'm black," declares the Negro. "Yes," replies the Conservative, "indeed you are." "And I am beautiful," concludes the black. "Yes," responds the white, "Yes, you are." The Conservative then turns to his Liberal white friends with a look that says: *(sigh)* "See, I told you so. Negroes are different; they have a very special and a rather appealing thing, don't you think?" Beneath this is written in a hand quivering with relief: "THEY DON'T WANT IN, NOT REALLY THEY DON'T."

For roughly a decade after 1965 black separatism had great strength. Because of that fact, black culture today is stronger than ever before, more sophisticated, and self-conscious. Black people as a whole people are not, and now show little promise of ever again being willing to surrender totally their destiny to predominantly white culture. By the late 1970s, however, separatism had lost power. In the early eighties young black people as individuals evinced an obvious desire to get a fair share of the good things of American life, not to settle for being out and beautiful, but rather to insist upon being in and affluent.

Things have changed in this last generation, and they are better. Black people in the South and in America are better able to live the life they were previously led to idealize but denied the means to achieve. There is more freedom. There are black legislators, black mayors, black Congressmen, and even judges, sheriffs, and generals. There are black lawyers, professors, physicians, teachers, and ministers who have graduated from superb and heretofore all white schools and serve white clients. Clearly, many more are coming. But, it is also clear that the "in" phase of the Black Revolution has reached a high tide and is receding. Counterforces against the further integration of black people are rising in an often hostile and always power-packed white world. Prejudice in white minds is still rampant and discrimination, visible and invisible, witting and unwitting, exists on every hand. Nevertheless, among whites awareness of prejudice and feelings of guilt about discrimination are diminishing. The very success of some blacks in taking advantage of opportunities afforded by an America officially committed to racial equality in its fundamental legal and social constitutions is serving to diminish the reservoir of white guilt upon which so much of the progress of the civil-rights movement was built.

Conservatives in the early 1980s seemed bound for the promised land of racial unawareness. One can almost hear the click as black people in the white mind slip snugly back into that comfortable slot defined by things that white people need from blackness. Conflict gives way to complementarity, fear slides to love; a happy face rotates to the fore, locks in place, and, behold, again there is no race problem. One might well begin to look in the white mind for the recurrent Sambo, some neo-neo-Sambo to replace the image of the black militant in the style of either Martin Luther King, Jr., or Stokeley Carmichael. A decade or so after Nat Turner came Sambo. A decade or so after Reconstruction saw his pale revival. A decade after the Atlanta riot neo-Sambo appeared. Perhaps, a decade or so after the Chelsea riot we shall get the new stereotype. Perhaps, in that brave new world, the Conservative mind of the white South will generate for itself yet another racial soma pill in the form of a new model Negro. Last time they drove the model into place with rope and faggot. This time, it might be that they will pull him there bound in fur-lined manacles and with chains of gold. They need him, and they will pay a certain price to get him. Indeed, they might well come to see all the physical and emotional pain preceding the achievement of the new plateau of inter-racial peace as worth while. If one shares in the pleasantly complete logic of the very best Conservatives in the late 1890s, if one were, say, a providentially long-lived Edgar Gardner Murphy and could see the seeming conflict as in reality a divinely organized and inscrutable machine working to wear the hard rocks of life into the finely smoothed stones of God's current wish for man, the new separatism and the awful violence that have been our national lot of late could be as warmly welcomed as a second coming. Indeed, it has within itself the promise of still another redemption for the South and of paradise regained. Southern blacks are finding their proper places, it declares, and Southern whites are becoming once more—a beautiful people.

Conclusion

THE GREAT CHANGEOVER:
An Interpretation of White Culture and
Race Relations in the American South

Between 1850 and 1915 white culture and race relations in the South underwent a drastic and fundamental change. During this time the South switched from a racial pattern in which black people were firmly included in the society by way of slavery to one in which they were effectively excluded. The changeover was a complex movement in itself, but it was integrally tied to a larger and even more complex transition in the whole of American society and, indeed, in the Western world. At the heart of the change stood the industrial revolution, pioneered in the first half of the nineteenth century by the textile industry in England, Belgium, and New England. Earlier, in the seventeenth and eighteenth centuries, the American South had developed plantation slavery to contribute significant quantities of tobacco, rice, and sugar to world commerce. In the first decades of the nineteenth century it expanded the vast productive power of plantation slavery to supply most of the cotton that fed the mills of Manchester, Ghent, and Lowell.

Because of the climatic requirements of the cotton plant, the lower South in particular became the great cotton-producing area of the United States. Slaves from the upper South poured southward in and after the 1820s, and the lower South soon outstripped the world in cultivating the fleecy staple. The planter elite in the lower South came to presume that their place at the very fountainhead of the industrial revolution gave them great power. James Henry Hammond of South Carolina spoke well the sentiments of his class when he declared on the floor of the United States

281

Senate in 1858 that "Cotton *is* king," and asserted that "no power on earth" dared make war against it. In 1850 Southern blacks were bound intimately to the industrial revolution through the institution of slavery. By 1915 they were no longer centrally involved in that process, and, as technology progressed, increasingly marginal in their participation in it. Both in slavery and afterward, blacks in America generally have been steadily and firmly excluded from enjoying an appreciable share of the benefits of industrialization. In the economic sphere, the story of race relations in the South and in America at large in the twentieth century is the story of black people struggling to re-enter the industrial revolution and win a larger portion of its abundant material rewards.

Culturally, the story of race relations during the changeover transcends economics and is vastly more complicated. However, the process might be roughly schematized in the form of a triangle (See Figure). At each corner stands one of three important groups of people in the South: the white elite, the black mass, and the white mass. In 1850 the white elite, comprised of some 10,000 large slaveholders and their professional allies, had built a strong connection with the black mass through slavery. It was through the device of plantation slavery that they gained and held the power to control society. Especially in the lower south, the white elite strengthened its hold over the black mass by a cautious alliance with free people of color of the greatest affluence, sophistication, and status. The

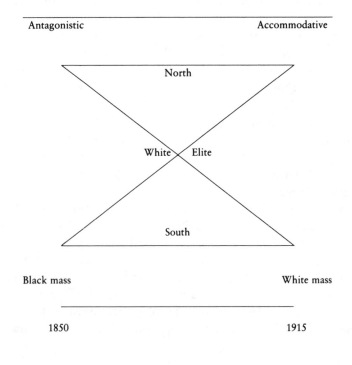

power line in the triangle, thus, ran from the white elite to the black mass. On the other side, the white elite maintained a rather tenuous, uncertain connection with the white mass. The prime objective of the elite on that side was to neutralize the mass of white people, to keep them in place in the system and to minimize their capacity to damage the sources of power of the white elite. Most critically, the white mass must not be allowed to tamper with the institution of slavery.

By 1915 the white elite had largely abandoned the black connection. In that process, beginning in the 1850s in the lower South, it turned away from its alliance with the free mulatto elite and moved to the relegation of all people of any color to the black mass. Simultaneously, the free mulatto elite was, of its own volition, moving away from its semi-alliance with the white elite toward a firm and lasting alliance with the black mass. That engagement was greatly advanced in Reconstruction and reached a consummation in the 1920s in the era of the Harlem Renaissance.

On the other side of the race line, in 1915 the white elite was busy bonding itself to the white mass. Over three generations the crucial line of power in the triad shifted from that which joined the white elite to the black mass through the institution of slavery to that which joined the white elite to the white mass through institutions that were, in the broad sweep of Southern history, essentially new. The end result was a culture in the South in which black people were practically excluded from influence upon the ruling power, and ruling power was devoted almost exclusively to the benefit of white people. The third possible power line in the schematic, an effective and durable alliance between the black mass and the white mass, has never occurred in the South.

Race relations in the South over the last century and a half have not been purely a Southern matter; they have also steadily involved the North and the nation at large. At the same time that it undertook to adjust race relations at home, the white elite has been forced to adjust relations between North and South. In that process it moved the South from a position of increasing antagonism toward the North during the last generation of slavery to one of accommodation in the twentieth century (See Figure p. 282).

In pressing that early antagonism to the extreme of war, they overplayed their hand and lost. Southern leadership lost power in the nation, and they lived for a time in an economic and political colony, a South nearly totally at the mercy of the imperial nation. They were forced to negotiate successive settlements from weakness rather than strength. By the early years of the new century, however, they had brokered out an arrangement in which they settled for markedly less wealth in the South and less power in the nation in return for a high level of power for themselves at home. Because politics both at home and away no longer carried great power, politics and politicians became less important. Southern politics rapidly degenerated into something very close to entertainment, and politicians often became more showmen than statesmen. They were, figuratively, the new minstrels, white men in white face displacing white men in black face, each attesting in very different ways to the same fact that black men were powerless. By the second quarter of the century, remnants of the slaveholding elite had passed away, and the white elite, no longer based on a single institution, would be found somewhere among the array of lawyers, businessmen, bankers, industrialists, ministers, newspaper editors, professors, educators, writers, intellectuals, dentists, and physicians, as well as large farmers and locally powered politicians, and the wives, mothers, and daughters of all these. The white elite varied widely in its constituency from one community to the next. In one it might center in the Men's Bible class in the First Baptist Church, in another the country club. In the Old South, the ruling element in the white elite had been powered by slavery; in the twentieth century they were powered by a capacity to organize and stabilize the white community, and either to exclude alien influences or tame them.

In the last quarter of the twentieth century it appears that the Southern white elite has managed superbly its campaign to retain local power. The all-white alliance in the South—in spite of the civil-rights movement, in spite of the drive by blacks for a fully equal participation in education, politics, and economics and the successes that they have achieved— remains in place and secure. Moreover, with well over fifty million people, the white South is gaining power in the nation, slowly and subtly in economics and politics, but rapidly and markedly in religion and race.

The Southern share of religious power in America is on the rise and already no less than astounding in its magnitude. On Sunday mornings from Castine, Maine, to Coos Bay, Oregon, it is easily possible to tune one's television set to a Southern evangelist. Indeed, in those still most segregated hours in America, if the set is on and the dials are turned, it is almost impossible not to hear Jerry Falwell from Lynchburg, Virginia, the Louisianian Jimmy Swaggart, Jim Bakker from Charlotte, or Oral Roberts from Oklahoma. Billy Graham, first and most famous, has achieved invasions of the North that Robert E. Lee might well envy, having stormed Washington several times and occupied the White House once or twice. The power of Southern evangelists in national religion is vast, not always recognized, and when it is recognized not usually welcomed. It smacks too much, for instance in the "Moral Majority," of St. Augustine presuming after all to bring the City of God down to Rome.

On the other hand, the rise of the South again to leadership in matters of race is recognized and, nearly universally, approved. In the twentieth century, it seems clear that the white South and the white North, in spite of their real cultural differences, have reached a practical congruence in their behavior in regard to black people. In all regions, when black people in large numbers have become relatively assertive in their pursuit of a fair share of the good things in life, white people have proved themselves ready for violence. Racially speaking, Chelsea in 1975 was not many miles from Birmingham in 1963. In a dozen years, the North had clearly lost legitimate claim to moral superiority in passing judgment on race relations in the South. Thereafter, an embarrassed North virtually ceased to shout "racist" at the South. By the time Alex Haley's *Roots* as book and film had run its course in 1976 and 1977, the North seemed to lose any inclination to pass judgment at all. There had been a horrible racism down there in the South back then, ran the response to that work, but there was none in the nation now and hence no reason why white people should feel guilty. The racist South had been cursed, whipped, and cured, and white America thereby cleansed and forgiven. In the new dispensation, Southern white leaders were seen to have some special affinity for dealing with black people, and it seemed best to leave local racial matters again in their hands. Most recently, one hears much about how the South has better relations between the races and hence should point the way to national progress in the future. Thus, within the twentieth century, the needle of leadership in matters racial in the nation has swung full compass and found no solution. The *style* of race relations in the South is certainly different from that of the North, but it is not at all clear that it is better.

Economic power, also, is moving southward—to centers such as Atlanta, Miami, Houston, and Dallas, not only in the form of sophisticated new factories, but even in the more vital spheres of communications, image-making, money, banking, and credit. That power is national, but it is also distinctly international and promises, vaguely, therein to bypass the North and West. The "Sunbelt" phenomenon as economics is new and real, and the end effect seems to be an evolving Southernization of national business as it operates in the South rather than a nationalization of Southern culture by way of business.

In politics, the South has recently produced a President who took office from the South and returned to the South when he had served his term. Even with that President's defeat in his bid for re-election, the South switched parties and maintained a measure of power in Washington. The most conspicuous new ambassadors of the region in the nation's capital are Republicans, and, at least presently, they are generally in tune with the rest of the country. These Republicans pose no threat to the traditional balance in the South; there is virtually no reason to expect that they will attempt to bring black power into play again. On the contrary, there is no history among the best known and most powerful of Southern Republicans in Congress that would lead one to suspect that they might favor black people in any substantial way. The long-sought two-party South has arrived, but it promises no revolution in either race relations or Southern culture, and it offers no invitation to the North to attempt again to reconstruct the South in its own image.

As the Southern white elite works to accommodate itself to Northern desires at the national and international level, local power is more assuredly in their hands. They can yield or not yield, as they choose, a great deal to black people without significantly threatening their power at home. After their momentary fright in the 1950s and 1960s, the Conservative elite in the South has come to realize that the civil-rights movement has resulted in no great revolution in race relations. In spite of strenuous efforts to do so, it has not pushed the power line back again toward an alliance between the white elite and the black mass, and there is no compelling evidence that the white mass and the black mass might soon combine against the white elite. The revolutionary but tentative experiments of Reconstruction and the Populist era on that bottom line were repeated with much the same result. Things are better, and blacks are more free in this last quarter of the twentieth century; but while the white elite might not have everything just the way they want it all the time in relations with black people, they generally have them so. On the other hand, over time they virtually always get exactly what they want from the mass of white people. The self-conscious all-white communion is still in place in the South, and, sadly, it is spreading to cover the nation. The Black Revolution appears to have been literally that, a revolution of awareness on the black side of the line not the white. Indeed, the Black Revolution seems, in a very large way, a reflection of the realization by black people that the all-white system still lives and grows and that the heartland of white exclusiveness remains intact.

There are, essentially, no such things as "black" people or "white" people. The overlapping of physical traits between the so-called races is so great that it is impossible to define a certain line to divide one group from another. Undeniably, there is a black culture and a white culture, but there is nothing in the physical structure of a person who seems to be white that precludes his or her being culturally black, any more than there is anything in one's physical structure that precludes one's being Moslem, Buddhist, or Chinese. Yet, it has happened that the power in the South has perceived a necessity for designating some people as black and keeping those people firmly separated from others called white. Physical separation has promoted cultural separation, and yet the separation has never been so great as to prevent a steady stream of interaction in which each culture took rather liberally from the other. The struggle to maintain distance in the face of inevitable and ongoing kinship has created a profound tension in Southern society. It is a tension that ramifies into areas of Southern life that seem to have nothing to do with race, and it is a tension that all America has come to share. The simple fact is that white America is married to black America by the space of national geography and by centuries of time. More importantly, they are married because each has given to each so much, and taken so much. Culturally, black America is so much white; and white America, in its stubborn and residual racial egotism, resists the realization of how very deeply and irreversibly black it is, and has been. The struggle against that awareness, the rage against the realization of their blackness and its legitimacy is the struggle of white people in race relations. To recognize and respect the blackness that is already within themselves would be to recognize and respect the blackness that is within the nation, and, functually, to surrender the uses, physical and psychological, that they have learned to make of blacks as a separate people. It is an unhappy world that white America has made, and it is unnecessary. Ultimately, there is no race problem in the South, or in America, that we, both black and white, do not make in our own minds.

Notes

I. SLAVERY AND AFTER, 1831–1889

1. Evarts Boutell Greene and Virginia D. Harrington, *American Population before the Federal Census of 1790* (New York: Columbia Univ. Press, 1932), 136–40, 125–26, 173; Abbott Emerson Smith, *Colonists in Bondage: White Servitude and Convict Labor in America, 1607–1776* (Chapel Hill, Univ. of North Carolina Press, 1947), 335; Peter H. Wood, *Black Majority: Negroes in Colonial South Carolina from 1670 through the Stono Rebellion* (New York: Knopf, 1974), 36.
2. Dumas Malone, *Jefferson and His Time*, 4 vols. (Boston: Little, Brown, 1948), 1:20–21.
3. Malone, *Jefferson*, 1:222; Carl L. Becker, *The Declaration of Independence: A Study in the History of Political Ideas* (New York: Knopf, 1956), 212–14.
4. Malone, *Jefferson*, 1:413–14.
5. Eugene A. Berwanger, *The Frontier against Slavery: Western Anti-Negro Prejudice and the Slavery Extension Controversy* (Urbana: Univ. of Illinois Press, 1967), 7.
6. Arthur Zilversmit, *The First Emancipation: The Abolition of Slavery in the North* (Chicago: Univ. of Chicago Press, 1967).
7. Winthrop D. Jordan, *The White Man's Burden* (New York: Oxford Univ. Press, 1974), 201, 205–14.
8. Paul J. Staudenraus, *The African Colonization Movement, 1816–1865* (New York: Columbia Univ. Press, 1961), 23–35, 251.
9. Herbert Aptheker, *American Negro Slave Revolts* (New York: International Publishers, 1943), 298–300.
10. Joseph B. Robert, *The Road from Monticello: A Study of the Virginian Slavery Debate of 1832* (Durham: Duke Univ. Press, 1941), 31–32; Alison Goodyear Freehling, *Drift Toward Dissolution: The Virginia Debate of 1831–1832* (Baton Rouge: Louisiana State Univ. Press, 1982).
11. Bureau of the Census, *Negro Population in the United States, 1790–1915* (Washington, D. C.: Government Printing Office, 1918), 57.
12. Clement Eaton, *The Freedom of Thought Struggle in the Old South* (Durham: Duke Univ. Press, 1940), 113–14; John Hope Franklin, *The Free Negro in North Carolina* (New York: Russell & Russell, 1943), 223; Francis Butler Simkins and Robert Hilliard Woody, *South Carolina During Reconstruction* (Chapel Hill: Univ. of North Carolina Press, 1932), 383.

13. Ulrich B. Phillips, *American Negro Slavery: A Survey of the Supply, Employment and Control of Negro Labor as Determined by the Plantation Regime* (New York: Appleton, 1918), 497–98.

14. Howell Meadoes Henry, *The Police Control of the Slave in South Carolina* (Emory, Va.: n.p., 1914); Benjamin F. Callahan "The North Carolina Slave Patrol" (Master's thesis, University of North Carolina at Chapel Hill, 1973). There does not exist any comprehensive history of the patrol. The discussion in the text is drawn heavily from these two very detailed studies for South Carolina and North Carolina. I am especially indebted to Benjamin Callahan for the many references he made to the patrol in other Southern states.

15. James M. Merrill, *William Tecumseh Sherman* (New York: Rand McNally, 1971), 133–35.

16. Francis Butler Simkins and Robert Hilliard Woody, *South Carolina During Reconstruction* (Chapel Hill: Univ. of North Carolina Press, 1932), 381–83, 55; Joel Williamson, *After Slavery: The Negro in South Carolina during Reconstruction 1861–1877* (Chapel Hill: Univ. of North Carolina Press, 1965), 197, 198, 47.

17. Donald G. Mathews, *Religion in the Old South* (Chicago: Univ. of Chicago Press, 1977), 137–250.

18. William Sumner Jenkins, *Pro-Slavery Thought in the Old South* (Chapel Hill: Univ. of North Carolina Press, 1935).

19. Stanley M. Elkins argued otherwise in *Slavery: A Problem in American Institutional and Intellectual Life* (Chicago: Univ. of Chicago Press, 1959), esp. pp. 82–139.

20. Lawrence W. Levine, *Black Culture and Black Consciousness: Afro-American Folk Thought From Slavery to Freedom* (New York: Oxford Univ. Press 1977), 90–101.

21. The phrases are derived from David Riesman with Nathan Glaser and Reuel Denney, *The Lonely Crowd* (Garden City, N.Y.: Doubleday, 1953), 22.

22. Kenneth M. Stampp, *The Peculiar Institution: Slavery in the Ante-Bellum South* (New York: Knopf, 1956), 30–31.

23. Barbara Welter, "The Cult of True Womanhood," *American Quarterly 18 (Summer 1966):* 151–74.

24. David Donald, *Charles Sumner and the Coming of the Civil War* (New York: Knopf, 1960), 288–97.

25. Clement Eaton, *Jefferson Davis* (New York: Free Press, 1977), 3.

26. John Lide Wilson, *The Code of Honor: or Rules for the Government of Principals and Seconds in Duelling* (Charleston: Thomas J. Eccles, 1838 (rev. ed. 1858), 13, 16.

27. James Marion Sims, *The Story of My Life* (New York: Appleton, 1884), 88. For a thoroughly researched and highly thoughtful inquiry into the place of honor in the evolution of antebellum Southern culture, see: Bertram Wyatt-Brown *Southern Honor: Ethics and Behavior in the Old South* (New York: Oxford Univ. Press, 1982).

28. John Lide Wilson, *Cupid and Psyche: A mythological tale, from the "Golden Ass" of Apuleius. . . .* (Charleston: n.p., 1842).

29. John Lide Wilson, *Abstract of a System of Exercise and Instruction of Field Artillery, and the Exercise of Heavy Artillery in Battery and Some Directions for the Laboratory, Together with the Sword Exercise . . . , for the use of the South Carolina Militia* (Charleston: n.p., 1834), 57. I am indebted to William Henry Longton for first bringing John Lide Wilson's work to my attention. See: William Henry Longton, "Some Aspects of Intellectual Activity in Ante-bellum South Carolina, 1830–1860: An Introductory Study" (Ph.D. dissertation, Univ. of North Carolina at Chapel Hill, 1969), 379–81.

30. Economic historian Gavin Wright caught admirably the material basis for the sense of power and euphoria that came to Southern leadership in the 1850s. In that

decade, for instance, he found that the value of slaves doubled while their numbers increased only 10 percent. In 1860 the average slaveholder was five times as rich as the average Northerner. In the South as a whole, almost a quarter of the whites belonged to slaveholding families, and in the lower South, the Cotton Kingdom, almost half did. It was but symptomatic of the Southern sense of self that James Henry Hammond of South Carolina could declare on the floor of the United States Senate in 1857, "Cotton *is* King." Gavin Wright, *The Political Economy of the Cotton South: Households, Mobility, and Wealth in the Nineteenth Century* (New York: Norton, 1978), 35–42, 88, 154.

31. Ira Berlin, *Slaves without Masters: The Free Negro in the Antebellum South* (New York: Pantheon, 1974), 316–18, 341–44; Joel Williamson, *New People: Miscegenation and Mulattoes in the United States* (New York: Free Press, 1980), 65–67, 75–76.

32. Williamson, *New People,* 63, 71, 73–75.

33. Richard C. Wade, *Slavery in the Cities: The South, 1820–1860* (New York: Oxford, Univ. Press 1964).

34. Edward A. Pollard, *Black Diamonds Gathered in the Darkey Homes of the South* (New York: Pudney & Russell, 1859). 54–58, 22; Jack Pendleton Maddex, Jr., *The Reconstruction of Edward A. Pollard: A Rebel's Conversion to Postbellum Unionism,* James Sprunt Studies in History and Political Science, vol. 54 (Chapel Hill: Univ. of North Carolina Press, 1975), 24–27, 34–35.

35. Pollard, *Black Diamonds,* 54.

36. Dorothy Ann Gay, "The Tangled Skein of Romanticism and Violence in the Old South: The Southern Response to Abolitionism and Feminism, 1830–1861" (Ph.D. dissertation, University of North Carolina at Chapel Hill, 1975), 133–65, esp. 147–48, 150–51.

37. Stampp, *The Peculiar Institution,* 322–82.

38. Ella Gertrude (Clanton) Thomas diary, May 2, June 24, 1855, Ella Gertrude (Clanton) Thomas Papers, Duke University, Durham, North Carolina.

39. Williamson, *New People,* 64–65, 118.

40. Ibid., 42–59, esp. 55–59, 67–68.

41. Mary Boykin Chesnut, *Mary Chesnut's Civil War,* C. Vann Woodward (New Haven: Yale University Press, 1981), 168–69.

42. The story of the Townsends, black and white, is contained in the Townsend and Cabaniss Collection, University of Alabama, Tuscaloosa.

43. For a deeply researched and highly provocative view of how the slaveholders made their world and how that world was flawed, see: James Oakes, *The Ruling Race: A History of American Slaveholders* (New York: Knopf, 1982), esp. the Epilogue, "The Slaveholders' Revolution," 225–42.

44. S. W. Ferguson to Theodore G. Barker, January 7, 1876, Martin Witherspoon Gary Papers, South Caroliniana Library, University of South Carolina, Columbia.

45. Joel Williamson, *After Slavery: The Negro in South Carolina During Reconstruction, 1861–1877* (Chapel Hill: Univ. of North Carolina Press, 1965), 408–12.

II. BLACK LIFE IN THE SOUTH, 1865–1915

1. For an excellent and exhaustive description of black people in transition from slavery to freedom, see: Leon F. Litwack, *Been in the Storm So Long: The Emergence of Black Freedom in the South* (New York: Knopf, 1979).

2. R. B. Anderson to his wife, Sep. 11, 1865, R. B. Anderson Papers, Southern Historical Collection, University of North Carolina at Chapel Hill.

3. Ralph Ellison, *Invisible Man* (New York: Random House, 1952).

4. Charles N. Hunter to H. Schuyler (Rector of Trinity Church, Trenton, N.J.), Feb. 20, 1902, Charles Norton Hunter Papers, Duke University, Durham, N.C.

5. Lawrence D. Rice, *The Negro in Texas, 1874–1900* (Baton Rouge: Louisiana State Univ. Press, 1971), 246–50.

6. Franz Fanon, *The Wretched of the Earth* (New York: Grove Press, 1963). There is no modern study of violence among black people in the South in the post-Reconstruction decades. Highly suggestive is an article by Sheldon Hackney examining aspects of Southern violence between 1920 and 1964. Blacks in the South, Professor Hackney concluded, were much more likely (by a ratio of about two or three to one) to be involved in homicides than whites in Western civilization, in the North, or even in the South. Sheldon Hackney, "Southern Violence," *American Historical Review* 74 (Feb. 1969): 906–25.

7. James A. Whitted to Charles N. Hunter, Nov. 24, 1890, Hunter Papers.

8. Osborne Hunter, Jr., to George T. Wassom, Oct. 20, 1886, Hunter Papers.

9. Maggie Whiteman to George T. Wassom, Oct. 21, 1886, Hunter Papers.

10. G. W. Murray to Whitefield McKinlay, Nov. 14, 1898, Whitefield McKinlay Papers, Carter G. Woodson Collection, Library of Congress, Washington, D.C.

11. Booker T. Washington to T. Thomas Fortune, Nov. 7, 10, 1899, Booker T. Washington Papers, Manuscripts Division, Library of Congress, Washington, D.C.

12. For a comprehensive and exhaustive treatment of black thought in this era, see: August Meier, *Negro Thought in America, 1880–1915: Racial Ideologies in the Age of Booker T. Washington* (Ann Arbor: Univ. of Michigan Press, 1963).

13. Louis R. Harlan, *Booker T. Washington: The Making of a Black Leader, 1856–1901* (New York: Oxford Univ. Press, 1972), 204–21.

14. Ibid., 308–9.

15. W. E. B. DuBois, "Strivings of the Negro People," *The Atlantic Monthly* 80 (Aug. 1897): 194–98: *The Conservation of Races*, American Negro Academy, Occasional Papers, Paper No. 2, 1897.

16. Meier, *Negro Thought in America*, 178.

17. Ibid., 178–79.

18. Ibid., 181–83.

19. For a close description of the connection between the abolitionists and the NAACP see: James M. McPherson, *The Abolitionist Legacy: From Reconstruction to the NAACP* (Princeton Univ. Press, 1975), esp. 385–93.

20. Charles W. Chesnutt to Hugh M. Browne, June 20, 1908, Chesnutt Collection.

21. The distance, and the lack of distance, between Washington and DuBois, has been carefully measured by Louis R. Harlan in the second and final volume of his deeply researched biography of the Tuskegean. Louis R. Harlan, *Booker T. Washington: The Wizard of Tuskegee, 1901–1915* (New York: Oxford Univ. Press, 1983), esp. 84–85, 174–75.

III. BLACK IMAGES IN SOUTHERN WHITE MINDS

1. Harold W. Mann, *Atticus Greene Haygood: Methodist Bishop, Editor, and Educator* (Athens: Univ. of Georgia Press, 1965), *passim.*

2. Atticus Greene Haygood, *Our Brother in Black, His Freedom and His Future* (New York: Phillips, 1881), *passim.*

3. Mann, *Haygood*, 190–91.

4. R. M. Johnson to A. G. Haygood, Feb. 12, 1885, Haygood Papers.

5. Atticus G. Haygood, "The Negro Problem: God Takes Time—Man Must," a typescript for *The Methodist Review*, Sep.–Oct. 1895, Haygood Papers.

6. Arlin Turner, *George W. Cable: A Biography* (Durham, N.C.: Duke Univ. Press, 1956). Much of this material is from Cable's unpublished "My Politics," George

Washington Cable Collection, Tulane University, New Orleans. See also: Louis R. Harlan, "Desegregation in New Orleans Public Schools during Reconstruction," *American Historical Review* 67 (April 1962): 663–75, esp. 671–72; John W. Blassingame, *Black New Orleans, 1860–1880* (Chicago: Univ. of Chicago Press, 1973), 112–22; and Roger A. Fischer, *The Segregation Struggle in Louisiana, 1862–77* (Urbana: Univ. of Illinois Press, 1974), 119–32.

7. Newspaper clipping, folder labeled "Racial Problems," Rebecca Latimer Felton Papers, University of Georgia, Athens.

8. William M. Baskervill to George Washington Cable, December 5, 1888, G. W. Cable Collection, Tulane University Library, New Orleans.

9. Clarkson's story can be traced in the voluminous James S. Clarkson Papers, Manuscripts Division, Library of Congress, Washington, D.C.

10. Allen J. Going, "The South and the Blair Education Bill," *Mississippi Valley Historical Review* 44 (Sep. 1957): 267–90.

11. Richard E. Welch, Jr., "The Federal Elections Bill of 1890: Postscripts and Prelude," *Journal of American History* 52 (Dec. 1965): 511–26, esp. 524. See also: James M. McPherson, *The Abolitionist Legacy: From Reconstruction to the NAACP* (Princeton: Princeton Univ. Press, 1975), 128–37.

12. William F. Holmes, "Whitecapping: Agrarian Violence in Mississippi, 1902–1906," *Journal of Southern History* 35 (May 1969): 166–67.

13. William F. Holmes, *The White Chief: James Kimble Vardaman* (Baton Rouge: Louisiana State Univ. Press, 1970), 134–45.

14. Bureau of the Census, *Negro Population in the United States, 1790–1915* (Washington, D.C.: Government Printing Office, 1918), 558.

15. Tillman gave this speech many times. This particular version is from the *Congressional Record*, 59th Cong., 2d sess. (Jan. 21, 1907) 41: 1441.

16. One close student of lynching thought in 1905 that interest in the subject had increased markedly only after about 1891. James Elbert Cutler, *Lynch-Law, an Investigation into the History of Lynching in the United States* (New York: Longmans, Green, 1905), 155.

17. A study published in 1905 indicated that of the 2,060 blacks lynched in the twenty-two years, 1881–1903, only 34.3 percent were accused of assaults or attempted assaults upon females. Ibid., 171, 174, 175.

18. The *Chicago Tribune*, beginning in 1882, was the pioneer in collecting statistics concerning lynching. In the 1890s Tuskegee Institute followed suit, significantly backdating its count to begin with the year 1889. Finally the NAACP picked up the count in its publication, *Thirty Years of Lynching in the United States, 1889–1918* (New York: NAACP, 1919), 30, and supplements published through 1931.

19. Atticus Greene Haygood, "The Black Shadow in the South," *Forum* 16 (Oct. 1893): 167–75.

20. George Harvey, "The New Negro Crime," *Harper's Weekly* 48 (Jan. 23, 1904): 120–21.

21. It is striking that from neither the Conservative nor the Radical camp was there a multi-authored widely accepted *Summa Theologica* of racism as there had been at least two such grandly synthetic statements defending slavery published in the last decade before the war: William Harper et al., *The Pro-Slavery Argument* as maintained by the most distinguished writers of the Southern states.... (Charleston, Walker, Richard & Co., 1852); and E[benezer] N[ewton] Elliott et al., *Cotton Is King, and Pro-Slavery Arguments....* (Augusta, Ga.: Pritchard, Abbott & Loomis, 1860).

22. Nathaniel Southgate Shaler, "The Negro Problem," *Atlantic Monthly* 54 (Nov. 1884): 703.

23. Nathaniel Southgate Shaler, "Science and the African Problem," *Atlantic Monthly* 66 (July 1890): 42.

24. Nathaniel Southgate Shaler, *The Neighbor: The Natural History of Human Contacts* (Boston and New York: Houghton, Mifflin, 1904), 34, 134, 136, 148–49.

25. Phillip Alexander Bruce, *The Plantation Negro as Freeman* (New York: Putnam, 1889), 129, 256, 83, 84.

26. Frederick L. Hoffman, *Race Traits and Tendencies of the American Negro,* Publications of the American Economic Association (New York: Macmillan, 1896), 52, 55, 60, 95.

27. Ibid., pp. 220, 229, 230, 217, 230–31.

28. Ibid., pp. 329, 312.

29. *The National Cyclopaedia of American Biography* (New York: James T. White, 1930), Vol. A, 345–46; Hugh C. Bailey, *Edgar Gardner Murphy: Gentle Progressive* (Coral Gables, Fla.: Univ. of Miami Press, 1968), 46; Walter F. Willcox in Joseph Alexander Tillinghast, *The Negro in Africa and America,* Publications of the American Economic Association, 3rd Series, Vol. III, No. 2 (May 1902): 1–231, printed by Macmillan, New York, p. i.

30. *National Cyclopaedia,* Vol. 7, 474; *America's Race Problems: Addresses at the Annual Meeting of the American Academy of Political and Social Science,* Philadelphia, April Twelfth and Thirteenth, MCMI (published for the Academy by McClure, Phillips & Co., New York, 1901), 198–99.

31. Hilary A. Herbert, "The Race Problem at the South," Publication of the American Academy of Political and Social Sciences No. 309. Undated. Hilary A. Herbert Papers, Southern Historical Collection, University of North Carolina at Chapel Hill.

32. Rebecca Latimer Felton, *Country Life in Georgia in the Days of My Youth* (Atlanta: Index Publishing Co., 1919), 58, 60, 62, 72, and *passim.*

33. John E. Talmadge, *Rebecca Latimer Felton: Nine Stormy Decades* (Athens: Univ. of Georgia Press, 1960), 20, citing *Atlanta Journal,* Nov. 11, 1928. See also: Scrapbook 24, p. 33; Scrapbook 32, p. 7, Felton Papers.

34. *Country Life,* 85–86, 88–89.

35. Talmadge, *Felton,* 22–136, *passim.*

36. Rebecca L. Felton to W. H. Felton, March 15, 1893, Felton Papers.

37. Leonidas F. Scott to R. L. Felton, May 30, 1894, Felton Papers.

38. Rebecca L. Felton to the Atlanta *Constitution,* December 19, 1898, clipping in Scrapbook 24, pp. 76–77, Felton Papers.

39. Clipping, Felton Papers.

40. Rebecca L. Felton to the Atlanta *Constitution,* Dec. 19, 1898, Scrapbook 24, pp. 76–77, Felton Papers.

41. The account that follows draws heavily upon a close reading of the Benjamin Ryan Tillman Papers in the Robert Muldrow Library, Clemson University, Clemson, S. C.. General biographical information is drawn from Francis Butler Simkins, *Pitchfork Ben Tillman: South Carolinian* (Baton Rouge: Louisiana State Univ. Press, 1944).

42. Printed "Inaugural Address," Dec. 4, 1890, John [?] H. Woodrow, State Printer, Columbia, S. C., Tillman Papers.

43. B. R. Tillman to John M. Nicholls, Sep. 29, 1891, Letterbooks, Tillman Papers.

44. Quoted in the Charleston *News and Courier,* July 7, 1892. For similar expressions, see Tillman's own letters to _____. _____. Hall, June 1, 1892, and to William J. McPherson, July 1, 1892, Tillman Papers.

45. D. H. Thompkins to S. G. Mayfield, April 18, 1893, Tillman Papers.

46. Cutler, *Lynch-Law,* 183.

47. Simkins, *Tillman,* 296; George Brown Tindall, "The South Carolina Constitutional Convention of 1895" (Unpublished master's thesis, University of North Carolina at Chapel Hill, 1948), 66, 152–53.

48. *Congressional Record,* 57th Cong. 2d sess. (Feb. 23, 1903) 36: 2511–15.

49. Ibid., 56th Cong., 1st sess. (Feb. 26, 1900) 33: 2245.

50. Baltimore *American,* Jan. 5, 1907, cited in *Congressional Record,* 59th Cong., 2d sess. (Jan. 21, 1903) 36: 1044.

51. *Congressional Record,* 57th Cong., 2d sess. (Feb. 24, 1903) 36: 2564–65. See also: B. R. Tillman to _____ . _____ . Chandler, Nov. 25, 1911; B. R. Tillman to Sophia Tillman Hughes (his daughter), May 4, 1912, Tillman Papers.

52. B. R. Tillman to Captain Moorer, March 4, 1912; B. R. Tillman to A. E. Leland, Dec. 8, 1911, Tillman Papers.

53. Thomas Dixon, Jr., *The Leopard's Spots: A Romance of the White Man's Burden—1875–1900* (New York: Doubleday, Page 1902).

54. Raymond Allen Cook, *Fire from the Flint: The Amazing Careers of Thomas Dixon* (Winston-Salem, N. C.: John F. Blair, 1968), 3–6. Much of the following account of Dixon's personal life is taken from Professor Cook's study. He, in turn, was privileged to use "Southern Horizons," an autobiography Dixon wrote in his last years and never published.

55. Thomas Dixon, Jr., to Helen Dixon, February 26, 1927, Amzi Clarence Dixon Papers, Archives of the Baptist Historical Society, Nashville, Tennessee.

56. Cook, *Fire from the Flint,* 8–12, 20–21.

57. Ibid., 35–49.

58. Ibid., 50–52.

59. Mollie to "My dear Parents," [May?] 23, 1884, Dixon Papers.

60. Cook, *Fire from the Flint,* 55–56.

61. Ibid., 56–61.

62. Ibid., 61, 64–65.

63. Ibid., 63–64, 65–66.

64. Ibid., 67–73.

65. Ibid., 73–81.

66. Ibid., 90, citing the N.Y. *Times,* March 11, 1895, p. 8.

67. Ibid., 91.

68. Ibid., 91–95.

69. Thomas Dixon, Jr., to Marion Butler, December 16, 1896, Marion Butler Papers, Southern Historical Collection, University of North Carolina at Chapel Hill.

70. Thomas Dixon, Jr., to Marion Butler, April 19, 1898, Butler Papers.

71. Thomas Dixon, Jr., to Marion Butler, June 27, 1898, Butler Papers.

72. Cook, *Fire from the Flint,* 95–97.

73. Ibid., 95–97, 101–2.

74. Ibid., 105–12.

75. Thomas Dixon to Helen Dixon, February 26, 1927, Dixon Papers.

76. Thomas Dixon to Helen Dixon, March 2, [1927], Dixon Papers.

77. Thomas Dixon to Helen Dixon, January 10, 1929, Dixon Papers.

78. Helen C. A. Dixon, *A. C. Dixon: A Romance of Preaching* (New York: Putnam, 1931), 9–12.

79. Cook, *Fire from the Flint,* 28–29, 66.

80. Ibid., 38–40.

81. Thomas Dixon to Helen Dixon, February 26, 1927, Dixon Papers.

82. Cook, *Fire from the Flint,* 126, 131.

83. Ibid., 137–38, 149.

84. Ibid., 116, citing letter dated May 10, 1902, private papers of Clara Dixon Richardson.

85. Ibid., 153–56.

86. Ibid., 150–53.

87. Ibid., 161–68.

88. Ibid., 169–73.

IV. IN VIOLENCE VERITAS

1. For an excellent and exhaustive account of the kind of interracial violence that occurred in Reconstruction, see: Allen W. Trelease, *White Terror, The Ku Klux Klan Conspiracy and Southern Reconstruction* (New York: Harper and Row, 1971).

2. *The Caucasian,* Sep. 26, 1889.

3. Ibid., Oct. 31, 1889.

4. Ibid., Sep. 10, 1891.

5. The National Association for the Advancement of Colored People, *Thirty Years of Lynching in the United States, 1889–1918* (New York: NAACP, 1919); James Elbert Cutler, *Lynch-Law, an Investigation into the History of Lynching in the United States* (New York: Longmans, Green, 1905); Frederick L. Hoffman, *Race Traits and Tendencies of the American Negro,* Publications of the American Economic Association (New York: Macmillan, 1896).

6. Atticus Greene Haygood, "The Black Shadow in the South," *Forum* 16 (Oct. 1893): 167–75.

7. B. O. Flower, "The Burning of Negroes in the South: A Protest and a Warning," *Arena* 7 (April 1893): 630–40. Flower took his description from a local resident who also sent him a clipping from the St. Louis *Daily Republic.* See also: Robert Wilson Shufeldt, *The Negro a Menace to American Civilization* (Boston: R. G. Badger, 1907) 138–39.

8. Shufeldt, *The Negro a Menace,* 117–38, 224.

9. Albert Bushnell Hart, "The Outcome of the Southern Race Question," *North American Review* 188 (June 1908): 56.

10. George Brown Tindall, *South Carolina Negroes, 1877–1900* (Columbia: Univ. of South Carolina Press, 1952), 255–56, citing the Charleston *News and Courier,* Feb. 23, 1898.

11. *Congressional Record,* 57th Cong., 2d sess. (Feb. 23, 1903) 36: 514–15.

12. Helen G. Edmonds, *Fusion Politics in North Carolina* (Chapel Hill: Univ. of North Carolina Press, 1951), 99. The cartoon was described to Helen Edmonds by Young's daughter in an interview. The charge was made in the *Democratic Handbook, 1898,* 146, 147–48.

13. Joseph Marion King to Marion Butler, Oct. 25, 1898, Butler Papers.

14. Benjamin F. Keith to Marion Butler, Oct. 26, November 2, 1898, and a rough draft of his withdrawal statement, n.d., Butler Papers.

15. Ms. letter of recommendation, John K. Ruffin, March 21, 1898; Ms. Commission; Ms. petition by several dozen citizens of Wilson, May 26, 1898 (a typed copy); "Mamma" (probably Mrs. H. G. Connor) to Kate, Nov. 13, 1898, Henry Groves Connor Papers, Southern Historical Collection, University of North Carolina at Chapel Hill.

16. The account that follows relies heavily upon the superb and close study of Robert Charles and the riot by William Ivy Hair, *Carnival of Fury: Robert Charles and the New Orleans Race Riot of 1900* (Baton Rouge: Louisiana State Univ. Press, 1976). For a survey of the city before the riot, see: Dale A. Somers, "Black and White in New Orleans: A Study in Urban Race Relations, 1865–1900," *Journal of Southern History* 40 (Feb. 1974): 19–42. For Turner and the back-to-Africa movement, see: Edwin S. Redkey, *Black Exodus: Black Nationalists and Back-to-Africa Movements, 1890-1910* (New Haven: Yale Univ. Press, 1969). Edwin Redkey was the first scholar to give Robert Charles extended recognition. Before his book appeared, students could only read the sketch in John Smith Kendell, *History of New Orleans,* 3 vols. (Chicago: Lewis Publishing Company, 1922) 2: 538–40.

17. New Orleans *L'Abeille (The Bee),* July 25–28, 1900.

18. Hair, *Carnival of Fury,* 184–85.

19. The account of the riot that follows relies heavily upon the intensive research accomplished by Professor Charles Crowe and published in *The Journal of Negro History* in two articles: "Racial Violence and Social Reform—Origins of the Atlanta Riot of 1906," *Journal of Negro History* 53 (July 1968): 234–56; and "Racial Massacre in Atlanta, Sep. 22, 1906," *Journal of Negro History* 54 (April 1969): 150–75.

20. B. R. Tillman to Dr. W. A. Ross, October 6, 1913, Benjamin Ryan Tillman Papers, Clemson University, Clemson, S. C.

21. Dewey W. Grantham, Jr., *Hoke Smith and the Politics of the New South* (Baton Rouge: Louisiana State Univ. Press, 1959), 3–21, 25, 40–55.

22. Ibid., 131-42.

23. For a close view of how Hoke Smith worked to take advantage of both the corporate rule and race issues in and around Clarke County (Athens), see the correspondence of his chief manager in the area, E. K. Lumpkin, for the period June 15-Aug. 18, 1906. Judge E. K. Lumpkin Papers, University of Georgia, Athens.

24. Grantham, *Hoke Smith* 142–54.

25. C. Vann Woodward, *Tom Watson: Agrarian Rebel* (New York: Macmillan, 1938), 379, citing the Atlanta *Journal*, Aug. 1, 1906.

26. Raymond Allen Cook, *Fire from the Flint: The Amazing Careers of Thomas Dixon* (Winston-Salem, N. C.: John F. Blair, 1968), 143, citing the Atlanta *Constitution*, Oct. 31, 1905, p. 2.

27. Ray Stannard Baker, "Following the Color Line," *American Magazine* 63 (April 1907):564–66.

28. Ibid., 566.

29. Ibid., 568.

30. Baker, "Following the Color Line," 575–79.

V. THE INNER CIVIL WAR: THE CONSERVATIVE MIND CONFRONTS RADICALISM, 1889-1915

1. George Brown Tindall, *South Carolina Negroes, 1877–1900* (Columbia: Univ. of South Carolina Press, 1952), 56–58, 310, 286–88; B. R. Tillman to F. P. Colcock, May 30; June 3, 1913 (copies); B. R. Tillman to Mrs. Tillman, June 3, 1913 (copy), Benjamin Ryan Tillman Papers, Clemson University, Clemson, S. C..

2. The study of race relations in Tennessee after Reconstruction had been blessed by a rich flow of recent scholarship. For an excellent overview, see: Joseph H. Cartwright, *The Triumph of Jim Crow, Tennessee in the 1880's* (Knoxville: Univ. of Tennessee Press, 1977). For the story in Nashville, see: Howard N. Rabinowitz, *Race Relations in the Urban South, 1865–1890* (New York: Oxford Univ. Press, 1978), 283–98, 324-27. For a close description of how the black vote was reduced, see J. Morgan Kousser's superb study, *The Shaping of Southern Politics: Suffrage Restriction and the Establishment of the One-Party South, 1888–1910* (New Haven: Yale Univ. Press, 1974), 104–30.

3. Carl N. Degler, *The Other South: Southern Dissenters in the Nineteenth Century* (New York: Harper and Row, 1974), 270–315.

4. Quoted in C. Vann Woodward, *The Origins of the New South, 1877–1913* (Baton Rouge: Louisiana State Univ. Press, 1951), 340, citing *Proceedings of the Constitutional Convention of Alabama, 1901*, 3: 2837, 2841; 4: 4302–03.

5. Arthur Lincoln Tolson, "The Negro in Oklahoma Territory, 1889–1907: A Study in Racial Discrimination" (Ph.D. dissertation, University of Oklahoma, 1966), 117, 2.

6. Printed copy, "Republican Platform, adopted at the Tulsa Convention, August 1, 1907," 2-3, Coleman Collection, Oklahoma University Western Collection, University of Oklahoma, Norman.

7. Laura Clay to Benjamin R. Tillman, Dec. 31, 1906, Laura Clay Papers, University of Kentucky, Lexington.

8. Keith L. Bryant, Jr., *Alfalfa Bill Murray* (Norman: Univ. of Oklahoma Press, 1968), pp. 93–95

9. T. P. Gore, to R. L. Williams, Nov. 4, 1915, Governors' Papers, Oklahoma Archives, Oklahoma City.

10. Tom G. Taylor to R. L. Williams, Dec. 8, 1915, Governors' Papers. W. L. Garner, the representative from Choctaw County, made the same statement about the southeast. W. L. Garner to R. L. Williams, Nov. 6, 1915, Governors' Papers.

11. C. C. Hills (Washita) to R. L. Williams, Nov. 8, 1915; Lee Howe (Delaware) to R. L. Williams, November 11, 1915, Governors' Papers. See also: H. S. Sitton (Lawton) to R. L. Williams, Nov. 9, 1915, Governors' Papers.

12. Tolson, "The Negro in Oklahoma Territory," 150.

13. B. R. Tillman to J. R. Chandler, April 20, 1914, Tillman Papers.

14. B. R. Tillman to J. K. Vardaman, Oct. 8, 1913, Tillman Papers.

15. Ms., "The Race Problem in America" (probably written in 1916), "Speeches," Rebecca Latimer Felton Papers, University of Georgia, Athens.

16. In 1964, Richard C. Wade published the pioneer study of segregation in the immediately prewar South. He found that it was an urban phenomenon and came on strongly in the larger cities in the 1850s as the white elite moved to control blacks, slave and free, who were getting out of hand. See Richard C. Wade, *Slavery in the Cities: The South, 1820–1860* (New York: Oxford Univ. Press, 1964), 266–77. Ten years later Ira Berlin published an exhaustive and excellent history of free Negroes in the prewar South. He found that in the eighteenth century there were few places where free blacks and whites might come together in ways that threatened the whites. By 1860, however, there had been a proliferation of these places as public institutions for the infirm and the criminal were established by states, various private organizations were founded, and public carriers came into being. "As these institutions and facilities appeared and grew," he concluded, "whites applied their racial assumptions by systematically excluding Negroes from or segregating Negroes within them." See Ira Berlin, *Slaves without Masters: The Free Negro in the Ante-bellum South* (New York: Pantheon, 1974), 321.-22, 383. Leon Litwack, publishing in 1961, found that segregation was by no means absent in the antebellum North. On the contrary, he concluded that segregation was the general rule in the North, in spite of steady opposition from the black community and some significant success for those efforts in Massachusetts. See Leon F. Litwack, *North of Slavery: The Negro in the Free States, 1790–1860* (Chicago: Univ. of Chicago Press, 1961), 97–100, 103–12.

17. The separation of the races on the urban frontier in the South in the generation after emancipation has been thoroughly studied in Howard N. Rabinowitz, *Race Relations in the Urban South,* 182–97.

18. Louis R. Harlan, "Disintegration in New Orleans Public Schools during Reconstruction," *American Historical Review* 67 (April 1961): 633–75.

19. *Proceedings of the Constitutional Convention of South Carolina Held in Charleston, South Carolina, beginning January 14th and ending March 17th, 1868* (Charleston, Denny & Perry, 1868), 691–94, 702–6.

20. Barnas Sears to R. C. Winthrop, Sep. 18, 1870, J. L. M. Curry Papers, Alabama Department of Archives and History, Montgomery.

21. Barnas Sears to Robert C. Winthrop, January 8, 1874, Curry Papers.

22. *Acts of the General Assembly of the State of Virginia, 1899–1900,* pp. 236–37; *Code of Virginia* (1904), 681.

23. George N. Henderson to C. N. Hunter, Nov. 3, 1892, Charles Norton Hunter Papers, Duke University, Durham, N. C.

24. For one view of the separation of cultures, see: Joel Williamson, *New People: Miscegenation and Mulattoes in America* (New York: Free Press, 1980).

25. For some comprehensive displays of names borne by black people, see Herbert G. Gutman, *The Black Family in Slavery and Freedom, 1750–1925* (New York: Pantheon, 1976), esp. Chart 1 facing p. 86, and Charts 14 and 15 facing p. 180.

26. William Ivy Hair, *Carnival of Fury: Robert Charles and the New Orleans Riot of 1900* (Baton Rouge: Louisiana State Univ. Press, 1976), 11–12.

27. Ray Stannard Baker, *Following the Color Line; An Account of Negro Citizenship in the American Democracy* (New York: Doubleday, Page, 1908).

28. Rebecca Latimer Felton, *Country Life in Georgia in the Days of My Youth* (Atlanta: Index Publishing, 1919), 118.

29. For a very provocative discussion of this subject, see Carl Degler, *At Odds; Women and the Family in America from the Revolution to the Present* (New York: Oxford Univ. Press, 1980), especially his chapter entitled "Women's Sexuality in 19th-Century America," 249–78. Professor Degler argues that it was women, not men, who were the prime movers in the reduction of sexual activity in the late nineteenth century.

30. William Faulkner, *Light in August* (New York: Harrison Smith and Robert Haas, 1932), 439–40.

31. Thomas Dixon, Jr., *The Leopard's Spots* (New York: Doubleday, Page, 1902), 39–40.

32. Ibid.

33. Raymond Allen Cook, *Fire from the Flint;* 73–79, 81–83.

34. Ulrich Bonnell Phillips, "The Central Theme of Southern History," *American Historical Review* 34 (Oct. 1928): 30–43.

35. Clipping from the Springfield *Republican*, July 1, 1909, Jacob McGavock Dickinson Papers, Tennessee State Library and Archives, Nashville.

36. Asa H. Gordon to "My Dear Friends," n.d. (probably 1913), Bumstead Papers.

37. Roger L. Ransom and Richard Sutch, *One Kind of Freedom: The Economic Consequences of Emancipation* (Cambridge: Cambridge Univ. Press, 1977), 195–96.

VI. WHITE SOUL

1. Typescript, "Resolutions on 'Paris Lynching,' 1893," Edgar Gardner Murphy Papers, Southern Historical Collection, University of North Carolina at Chapel Hill; Hugh C. Bailey, *Edgar Gardner Murphy, Gentle Progressive* (Miami: Univ. of Miami Press, 1968), pp. 1–10.

2. "Race Problems in the South—Report of the Proceedings of the First Annual Conference Held under the Auspices of the Southern Society for the Promotion of the Study of Race Conditions and Problems in the South ... at ... Montgomery, Alabama, May 8, 9, 10, A.D. 1900" (Richmond: B. F. Johnson, 1900).

3. "The Montgomery Conference," *The Churchman* 81 (May 26, 1900): 634.

4. Bailey, *Edgar Gardner Murphy*, 48–52.

5. Edgar Gardner Murphy, *Problems of the Present South: A Discussion of Certain Educational, Industrial and Political Issues in the Southern States* (New York: Macmillan, 1904); *The Basis of Ascendancy: A Discussion of Certain Principles of Public Policy Involved in the Development of the Southern States* (New York: Longmans, Green, 1910).

6. Afflicted with rheumatic fever since childhood, Murphy's health failed rapidly. He died in 1913 at the age of forty-four. Bailey, *Edgar Gardner Murphy*, 65–108, 138–85, 213–14.

7. Murphy, *Basis of Ascendancy*, 79.

8. W. E. B. DuBois, *The Souls of Black Folk* (New York: A. C. McClurg, 1903), 52. Murphy expressed his philosophy of race most lucidly in his book *The Basis of Ascendancy*, published in 1910. As the title itself suggests, Murphy argued that the

basis of progress was racial self-consciousness. See especially pages 79–81, 201–4, 209–17, 242–48.

9. *Problems of the Present South,* 34–35, 273–74.

10. Ibid., 273, 279, 277.

11. Printed report of a speech given in New York, April 15, 1903, Murphy Papers.

12. Murphy, *Problems of the Present South,* 17.

13. Ibid., 156.

14. Ibid., 272.

15. Ibid., 281.

16. Ibid., 18–19.

17. Walter Hines Page, "The Rebuilding of Old Commonwealths," *Atlantic Monthly* 89 (May 1902): 651–61. "The Forgotten Man" was published in Walter Hines Page, *The Rebuilding of Old Commonwealths* (New York: Doubleday, Page, 1902), 2–35.

18. Murphy, *Problems of the Present South,* 14–19.

19. Ibid., 255, 263, 264.

20. Ibid., 21.

21. Ibid., 15–16, 31–32.

22. Ibid., 46–50.

23. Manuscript (apparently an address to the students at the University of South Carolina by Mitchell), n.d., Samuel Chiles Mitchell Papers, South Caroliniana Library, University of South Carolina, Columbia.

24. For a history of Mitchell and his presidency of the University of South Carolina, see: Daniel Walker Hollis, *University of South Carolina,* vol. 2: *College to University* (Columbia: Univ. of South Carolina Press, 1956), 241–60.

25. Monroe Lee Billington, *The American South: A Brief History* (New York: Scribner, 1971), 256; Laurence Shore, "Daniel Augustus Tompkins and Blacks: The New South Faces the Race Question," Honors Essay, Department of History, University of North Carolina, Chapel Hill, 1977, pp. 63–64, citing the Daniel Augustus Tompkins Papers, Folders 107, 115, 188, 191, and 274, in the Southern Historical Collection, University of North Carolina, Chapel Hill; Ben F. Lemert, *The Cotton Textile Industry of the Southern Appalachian Piedmont* (Chapel Hill: University of North Carolina Press, 1933), p. 121.

26. Murphy, *Problems of the Present South,* 102, 103–5, 125.

27. Broadus Mitchell, *The Rise of the Cotton Mills in the South* (Baltimore: Johns Hopkins Univ. Press, 1921), vii–viii.

28. Mitchell, *Rise of Cotton Mills,* 69–86, 89, 94.

29. Ibid., 90, 161.

30. Ibid., pp. 161, 162, 169.

31. Orr, "The Negro in the Mills," 846.

32. The changeover in philosophic systems has been closely studied in South Carolina by William Henry Longton in "Some Aspects of Intellectual Activity in Ante-Bellum South Carolina, 1830–1860: An Introductory Study" (Ph.D. dissertation, University of North Carolina at Chapel Hill), 1969, esp. pp. 272, 273.

33. For a very perceptive discussion of Jeffersonian thought in the Old South and the New, see: Merrill D. Peterson, *The Jeffersonian Image in the American Mind* (New York: Oxford, Univ. Press, 1960), 38–82, 211–16.

34. Margaret Mitchell, *Gone with the Wind* (New York: Macmillan, 1936), 422–28; Sidney Howard, *GWTW, The Screenplay,* ed. Richard B. Harwell (New York: Collier Books, Macmillan, 1980), 242–44.

35. Ibid., 3–5.

36. Daniel Robinson Hundley, *Social Relations in Our Southern States* (New York: Henry B. Price, 1860).

37. Mitchell, *Gone with The Wind,* 429, 428, 1037.

38. William Heyward to James Gregorie, Jan. 12, 1868, Gregorie-Ellison Papers, Southern Historical Collection, University of North Carolina at Chapel Hill.

VII. LEGACY: RACE RELATIONS IN THE TWENTIETH-CENTURY SOUTH

1. Pamphlet, "The Struggle of 1876," delivered in Anderson, S. C. Aug. 25, 1909, n.p., n.d., Benjamin Ryan Tillman Papers, Clemson University, Clemson, S. C.

2. For a description of the changeover from relative tolerance of mulattoes in the lower South to intolerance, see: Joel Williamson, *New People: Miscegenation and Mulattoes in the United States* (New York: Free Press, 1980), 61–109.

3. Harry Lewis Golden, *A Little Girl Is Dead* (Cleveland: World Publishing Company, 1965), 6–25, 36, 50, 54. Harry Golden, the Charlotte, N. C., journalist, did excellent historical detective work on the Frank case. This account relies heavily upon his book, and that of Leonard Dinnerstein, *The Leo Frank Case* (New York: Columbia Univ. Press, 1968).

4. Ibid., 90, 98–99.

5. Ibid., 62–65, 75–84, 115–26.

6. Ibid., 127–37.

7. For a rendition of this phenomenon in fiction, see: William Faulkner, *Light in August* (New York: Smith and Haas, 1932), 275–77.

8. Golden, *A Little Girl is Dead,* 284–93.

9. Ibid., 231–33.

10. Harry Golden described most of these connections in *A Little Girl Is Dead,* 209–10.

11. David M. Chalmers, *Hooded Americanism: The First Century of the Ku Klux Klan, 1865–1965* (New York: Doubleday, 1965), 3–5, 29–31.

12. *Watson's Jeffersonian Weekly,* Jan. 25, 1912.

13. Sarah Patton Boyle, *The Desegregated Heart: A Virginian's Stand in Time of Transition* (New York: Morrow, 1962), 14, 16.

14. Dan Carter, *Scottsboro: A Tragedy of the American South* (Baton Rouge: Louisiana State Univ. Press, 1969).

15. Howard Odum, *Race and Rumors of Race* (Chapel Hill: Univ. of North Carolina Press, 1944), 86–88, 97-104, 135.

16. Gary Thomas Scott, "The Kappa Alpha Order, 1865–1897; How It Came To Be and How It Came To Be Southern" (Master's thesis, University of North Carolina, 1968).

17. Susan Spear Durant, "The Gently Furled Banner; the Development of the Myth of the Lost Cause, 1865–1900" (Ph.D. dissertation, University of North Carolina, 1972); Gaines M. Foster, "Ghosts of the Confederacy: Defeat, History and the Culture of the New South, 1865–1912" (Ph.D. dissertation, University of North Carolina, 1982).

18. Douglas Southall Freeman, *Robert E. Lee, A Biography,* 4 vols. (New York: Scribner's 1942–45); *Lee's Lieutenants, A Study in Command,* 3 vols. (New York: Scribner's 1942–44).

19. Jervis Anderson, *A. Philip Randolph: A Biographical Portrait* (New York: Harcourt, Brace, Jovanovich, 1972), 252–61.

20. Richard M. Dalfiume, *Fighting on Two Fronts: Desegregation of the Armed Forces, 1939–1953* (Columbia: Univ. of Missouri Press, 1969), 92–103.

21. Ibid., 201–19.

22. George Brown Tindall, *The Emergence of the New South, 1913–1945,* vol. 10: *The History of the South* (Baton Rouge: Louisiana State Univ. Press, 1967), 175–77; Jacqueline Dowd Hall, *Revolt Against Chivalry: Jessie Daniel Ames and the Women's*

Campaign Against Lynching (New York: Columbia Univ. Press, 1979), *passim;* Morton Sosna, *In Search of the Silent South: Southern Liberals and the Race Issue* (New York: Columbia Univ. Press, 1977), 20–41.

23. Tindall, *Emergence of the New South,* 719–20; Sosna, *In Search of the Silent South,* 152–63.

24. Lillian Smith, *Killers of the Dream* (New York: Norton, 1949); *Strange Fruit: A Novel.* (New York: Reynal and Hitchcock, 1944); Sosna, *In Search of the Silent South,* 174–94.

25. Sosna, *In Search of the Silent South,* 42–59.

26. C. Vann Woodward, *Tom Watson: Agrarian Rebel* (1938) (New York: Oxford Univ. Press, 1963).

27. C. Vann Woodward, *The Strange Career of Jim Crow,* (New York: Oxford, 1955), vii–ix, 3–95.

28. C. Vann Woodward, *Origins of the New South, 1877–1913,* vol. 9: *The History of the South* (Baton Rouge: Louisiana State Univ. Press, 1951).

29. Corbett H. Thigpen and Hervey M. Cleckley, *The Three Faces of Eve* (London: Secker and Warburg, 1957), esp. 1–11, 23, 26–34, 97, 107–8, 143, 158, 221, 222–34.

30. Ibid., 15.

31. C. Vann Woodward, *The Burden of Southern History,* 2nd ed. rev. (Baton Rouge: Louisiana State Univ. Press, 1969), 187–211, esp. 190.

32. Eugene P. Walker, "Montgomery Revisited," a paper presented at the First Anniversary Meeting of the State Committee on the Life and History of Black Georgians, Feb. 9–11, 1978. See also: David Levering Lewis, *King: A Critical Biography* (New York: Praeger, 1979), 446–84; and Coretta Scott King, *My Life with Martin Luther King, Jr.* (New York: Holt, Rinehart and Winston, 1969), 108–15.

33. For a close study of this process, see: D'Etta Barnhardt Leach, "Desegregation in Charlotte, North Carolina: A Study in Business Leadership," (M.A. thesis, University of North Carolina, 1976). For the Greensboro story, see: William Henry Chafe, *Civilities and Civil Rights: Greensboro, North Carolina, and the Black Struggle for Equality* (New York: Oxford Univ. Press, 1980).

34. Clayborne Carson, *In Struggle: SNCC and the Black Awakening of the 1960s* (Cambridge: Harvard, Univ. Press, 1981), 235–42.

35. C. Vann Woodward, *The Strange Career of Jim Crow,* 3d ed. (New York: Oxford Univ. Press, 1974), 153.

36. Ibid., 174–75.

Suggestions
for Further Reading

FICTION

Fiction offers a superb way in which to study race relations in the complex weave of Southern culture. The very best Southern writers are, in a special sense, among the very best historians of the region.

On the black side, Charles Chesnutt was a keen observer and a fine writer who gave us novels that are both very informative and highly readable. In *The House Behind the Cedars* (Boston: Houghton, Mifflin, 1900),* he wrote a compelling story of the "plight of the mulatto." The scene is set in Fayetteville, North Carolina, and its environs, the area in which Chesnutt grew to young manhood, and the book deals with the problems that people of mixed blood encounter when they attempt to "pass" across the color line and live as whites. We are also fortunate that Chesnutt traveled through North Carolina in 1901 specifically to learn about the Wilmington riot of 1898, an outbreak of violence against blacks which he had not in any way anticipated in his supposedly racially moderate ancestral state. He incorporated his findings in his novel, *The Marrow of Tradition* (Boston: Houghton, Mifflin, 1901).* Although cast in fictional form, this remains the best account of the riot and its causes that we have in any published source. Moving up a generation, Richard Wright's *Black Boy* (New York: Harper, 1945)* displays in the form of his life's story the awful reality of black existence on the netherside of life in the modern South. Ralph Ellison's allegorical *Invisible Man* (New York: Random House, 1952)* is known as a classic in its field. Much of the novel takes place in the North, but early in the story Ellison— South Carolina-born, Oklahoma-bred, and once a student at Tuskegee—captures brilliantly the mood of the black enclave and its lord in his treatment of a Southern black school. Overall, *Invisible Man* illustrated vividly and with a deft ironic touch the virtual loss of the Negro by white America in the second quarter of the twentieth century.

On the white side, William Faulkner's novels are endlessly useful. The three greatest of these will at first seem difficult to a reader new to Faulkner, but persistence will

* Available in paperback.

produce perpetual and incomparable rewards. Indeed, for beginning to understand the complexities of Southern culture, no other three books could carry the student so far. In various ways, all three deal with race, sex, and violence—primary themes in the story told in this book. In Faulkner's world, the three themes are, perhaps, most tightly linked in the character Joe Christmas in *Light in August* (New York: Smith and Haas, 1932).* More broadly, *Light in August* is a novel precisely about the "organic society" that we described historically in this study. Faulkner tells about the organic society by giving us an intriguing array of characters who are actually displaced from that society. *Light in August* is the most readily comprehensible of Faulkner's more ambitious novels and is probably the place for the reader to begin. The story of Thomas Sutpen in *Absalom, Absalom!* (New York: Random House, 1936)* carries us to the cotton frontier in Mississippi in the 1830s and into the superstructure of white culture that was building in the last generation of slavery and dissolving during the Civil War and Reconstruction. Summarizing this book, Faulkner himself once simply wrote, "It's about miscegenation." But it is more than that. It is a book about the emotional violence involved in the rise and fall of lower South civilization in the middle of the nineteenth century. The most difficult of Faulkner's novels is *The Sound and the Fury* (New York: Cape and Smith, 1929).* The depth of sex roles in Southern culture, the South's pursuit of an idealistic world view (as seen in the character Quentin Compson), and the intricate nexus of relationships involved in love, sex, and marriage, family, clan, and community in the turn-of-the-century years in a region increasingly imperialized by an alien force are all met in this great American novel. All of Faulkner's major themes are recapitulated, seemingly, in his masterfully tight, crystalline long story *The Bear* (contained in a longer work, *Go Down Moses* (New York: Random House, 1942)*). Faulkner's so-called "age of genius" ended with the publication of *Absalom, Absalom!* in 1936, but he did go on to deal pointedly with the struggle between the white elite and the white mass in the South in the Snopes trilogy. Also in this later phase he reflected the profound confusion of the white South about black people and the North on the eve of the civil rights movement in his fascinating detective story *Intruder in the Dust* (New York: Random House, 1948).* Faulkner seldom missed in matters of basic historical fact, and he never missed in catching the values cherished by Southern culture. Even more vitally, he caught poignantly the conflicts between those values that threw individual Southerners into agonies. It is in his capacity to depict the Southern heart in conflict with itself that Faulkner offers students of history an invaluable gift.

Moving back into the 1880s, one might read a very sensitive white man's version of the plight of the mulatto in the New Orleans setting in George W. Cable's *The Grandissimes* (New York: Scribner, 1884). An early fictional announcement of Volksgeistian Conservatism is in Ellen Glasgow's *The Voice of the People* (Boston: Houghton, Mifflin, 1900).* More on sex and, very subtly, race roles and the apparent loss of the Negro by the white South can be found in Margaret Mitchell's marvelously famous *Gone with the Wind* (New York: Macmillan, 1936).* Within a decade of the appearance of that book, Mitchell's fellow Georgian Lillian Smith published her telling indictment of upper-class Southern white men for their use of black women in her novel *Strange Fruit* (New York: Reynal and Hitchcock, 1944).* The writing of fiction in the white South continues to change and flourish, but one of the marks that seem to distinguish the stream during the last generation is an astonishingly complete absence of race as a central element. Southern white writers who remain in the South appear to be vastly concerned with the Southern white world, and there is as yet no young Faulkner in sight to breach the color bar.

Even so, across the race line, among women writers, and Southern writers living outside the South, there is recent movement that quickens the pulse. Three authors stand out. Georgia-born Alice Walker's novel *The Color Purple* (New York: Harcourt Brace Jovanovich, 1982)* speaks in myriad ways not only to the race revolution, but to the sex revolution as well. Moreover, *The Color Purple* carries the white reader by imagination onto ground where he or she could never really walk. Josephine Haxton, who writes under the name Ellen Douglas, is white and a writer with deep roots in Mississippi soil. She has dealt knowingly, sensitively, and directly with race relations in her earlier work, but most recently she has published *A Lifetime Burning* (New York: Random House, 1982), a powerfully searching story about sex roles and a white family in dissolution as judged by traditional Southern standards. *A Lifetime Burning* is as tough and challenging as *The Color Purple,* and it approaches *The Sound and the Fury* in sheer literary ambition. These two novels, one by a black woman and the other by a white woman, say much about where things are in the South today, and they say something about where things in the South are going. In both areas they venture onto ground where historians seldom tread and offer insights not available elsewhere.

Living outside the South for a generation now, Virginia-born William Styron has created what might well be *the* novel of the last decade, *Sophie's Choice* (New York: Random House, 1979).* The protagonist, nicknamed Stingo, is also an aspiring writer, Virginia-born, and living in New York. He is financed in the pursuit of his art by a small legacy derived from the sale of a slave by his family in antebellum years, preserved over the generations, and finally passed on to him by his father. Through Sophie, the survivor of a concentration camp, he comes to know evil in the world— retroactively, the witting evil of a concentration camp commandant and, currently, the unwitting evil of Sophie's schizophrenic lover. Stingo can live with the evil in the world about him—a feat that Faulkner's protagonist, the suicide Quentin Compson, also an intensely thoughtful young Southerner gone north, was not able to accomplish. Interestingly, an earlier novel by William Styron, *The Confessions of Nat Turner* (New York: Random House, 1967)* dealt directly with the problem of slavery in the South, but suffered a barrage of criticism from those who felt, in the zenith of the "Soul Movement," that the white author presumed too great an awareness of the black consciousness.

THEIR OWN WRITINGS

Another very interesting way of getting into the history of Southern culture is by reading the writings of the participants. DuBois's *The Souls of Black Folk* (Chicago: A. C. McClurg, 1903)* is a sensitive and passionate rendering of his views in 1903 with considerable insight into how he got to that point. Against DuBois's credo stands Booker T. Washington's *Up from Slavery* (Garden City, N.Y.: Doubleday, Page, 1901),* a book that says fully as much between the lines as in them about the black experience in and after slavery. A fascinating, highly readable account of the civil rights movement in the deep South is Anne Moody's *Coming of Age in Mississippi* (New York: Dial, 1968).*

Two white Radicals describe themselves and their times well in two very different styles: Rebecca Felton left her memoirs under the title *Country Life in Georgia in the*

Days of My Youth (Atlanta: Index Publishing Company, 1919). Thomas Dixon's primal novel *The Leopard's Spots: A Romance of the White Man's Burden—1875–1900* (New York: Doubleday, Page, 1902) is essentially autobiographical and, unfortunately, almost unread. The neglect of Dixon's first novel can probably be explained by the fact that scholars have generally focused on his later work *The Clansman* (New York: Doubleday, Page, 1905),* the direct forerunner to the film *The Birth of a Nation* (1915). Edgar Gardner Murphy wrote elegantly of his own views in several places, but probably the most useful of his works for us is *The Basis of Ascendancy* (New York: Longmans, Green, 1910), published only three years before his death. Wilbur Cash's *The Mind of the South* (New York: Knopf, 1941)* is, of course, a landmark in the evolution of Southern culture. Like Ellison's *Invisible Man,* Cash's book signaled the fact that Southern white folk had lost contact with black folk and that trouble was brewing. Finally, two books that touch Southern women intimately in the middle of the twentieth century are Lillian Smith, *Killers of the Dream* (New York: W. W. Norton, 1949)* and Corbett H. Thigpin and Hervey M. Cleckley, *The Three Faces of Eve* (London: Secker and Warburg, 1957).

WHAT HISTORIANS SAY

Race relations in the South have attracted the attention of a host of talented scholars. There are hundreds of books that deal wholly and directly with the subject, and there are thousands that touch the subject in part. What follows is an array selected, not to cover this vast topic comprehensively, but to offer the reader the most direct and the most readable books through which he or she might pursue specific interests.

Slavery

Race relations in the South were profoundly marked by slavery. The first leading professional historian in the field was Ulrich B. Phillips whose book *American Negro Slavery* (New York: Appleton, 1918)* grew out of work in which he had been engaged for a generation previously. Phillips looked upon slavery as a benign institution and his interpretation informed white America's understanding of that history for nearly two generations. The shift to a view of slavery as exceedingly cruel came with the civil rights movement after World War II. The signal modern response to Phillips came from Kenneth M. Stampp in 1956 in his book *The Peculiar Institution* (New York: Knopf, 1956).* In the wake of that work came a continuing stream of superb studies, each with its own special perception of slavery. Winthrop Jordan in *White Over Black: American Attitudes Toward the Negro, 1550–1812* (Chapel Hill: Univ. of North Carolina Press, 1968)* was the first to offer a deeply psychological interpretation of what has happened between whites and blacks over a broad geography and a lengthy period of time. In this vein *The Crucible of Race*—the parent book of *A Rage for Order*— is very much a sequel to *White Over Black.* In mood it is perhaps closer to no other work. Much of Winthrop Jordan's material related to colonial Virginia; in 1974 Peter Wood showed us strikingly different elements in South Carolina in *Black Majority: Negroes in Colonial South Carolina from 1760 through the Stono Rebellion* (New York: Knopf, 1974).* This book also gave us much substance to support an impression that historians had been building for some years, namely, that it is useful sometimes to make a distinction between the lower South where blacks were so often in the majority and the upper South where so often they were not. The understanding of this difference was promoted greatly by Ira Berlin's deeply researched, superbly organized, and very readable *Slaves Without Masters: The Free Negroes in the Antebellum South* (New York: Pantheon, 1974).* This highly significant geographical cleavage in Southern culture during and after slavery was also a major theme in Joel Williamson's *New People: Miscegenation and Mulattoes in America* (New York: Free Press, 1980).* *Slaves Without Masters* and *New People* both looked at the issues of miscegenation and mulattoes on a large scale. Two fine books bring the focus down to the living level. Gary B. Mills has chronicled the very human story of a Louisiana family of mixed blood who rose to the status of large slaveholders in *The Forgotten People: Cane River's Creoles of Color* (Baton Rouge: Louisiana Univ. Press, 1977). Michael P. Johnson and James L. Roark have done the same for a South Carolina family in *Black Masters: A Free Family of Color in the Old South* (New York: W. W. Norton, 1984).

The slave regime has been treated from virtually every perspective one could imagine, but clearly one of the most brilliant and provocative is offered by Eugene D. Genovese in a sequence of books. Especially notable are his first book, *The Political Economy of Slavery* (New York: Pantheon, 1965), and his more recent volume on the lives of black people under slavery, *Roll, Jordan, Roll* (New York: Pantheon, 1974).* The pioneer work on the latter topic, and one of lasting value, is John Blassingame's *The Slave Community* (New York: Oxford Univ. Press, 1972).* One specific community is offered in Charles W. Joyner's intimate, informative, and highly engaging *Down by the Riverside* (Urbana: Univ. of Illinois Press, 1984). Two very strong books on the black experience in slavery are Nathan I. Huggins, *Black Odyssey* (New York: Vintage, 1979)* and Vincent Harding, *There Is a River* (New York: Harcourt, 1981). Various important aspects of race relations in the Old South and the white culture that grew out of that order are well treated in: Edmund S. Morgan, *American Slavery, American Freedom: The Ordeal of Colonial Virginia* (New York: W. W. Norton, 1975)*; Donald G. Mathews, *Religion in the Old South* (Chicago: Univ. of Chicago Press, 1977); Albert J. Raboteau, *Slave Religion: The "Invisible Institution" in the Antebellum South* (New York: Oxford Univ. Press, 1978)*; Bertram Wyatt-Brown, *Southern Honor* (New York: Oxford Univ. Press, 1982)*; Gavin Wright, *The Political Economy of the Cotton South: Households, Mobility, and Wealth in the Nineteenth Century* (New York: Pantheon, 1974); and Richard C. Wade, *Slavery in the Cities: The South, 1820–1860* (New York: Oxford Univ. Press, 1964).* Finally, the most recent broad study of slavery proves that we have not yet arrived at the definitive book on that institution. It is James Oakes's deeply thoughtful *The Ruling Race: A History of American Slaveholders* (New York: Knopf, 1982).*

After Slavery, 1865–1915

Until recently, race relations in the fifty years after emancipation seem to have attracted fewer scholars than slavery. However, the balance now seems to be shifting. In particular, the writing of black history has reached a new high level of scholarship. In 1980 Leon F. Litwack's feeling and detailed story of emancipation, *Been in the Storm So Long: The Emergence of Black Freedom in the South* (New York: Knopf, 1979),* won the Pulitzer Prize in History. Reconstruction, like slavery, got a re-examination during the civil rights movement. The single book that gives a succinct, balanced overview of blacks in the Reconstruction South is John Hope Franklin's *Reconstruction: After the Civil War* (Chicago: Univ. of Chicago Press, 1961).* However, W. E. B. DuBois's *Black Reconstruction* (New York: Harcourt Brace, 1935)* remains intriguing as an object of the history of its own time as well as an interesting history of a previous era. These are overviews. If the reader wants an in-depth history of one state, South Carolina is an excellent candidate. There are, happily, several excellent studies of South Carolina from its beginning to the present, but two books that mesh well together and carry the reader from 1861 to 1900 are Joel Williamson, *After Slavery: The Negro in South Carolina, 1861-1877* (Chapel Hill: Univ. of North Carolina Press, 1965)* and George B. Tindall, *South Carolina Negroes, 1877-1900* (Columbia: Univ. of South Carolina Press, 1952).* Similarly, the study of the black world in one key Southern city, New Orleans, during the Reconstruction era is superbly rendered in John Blassingame's *Black New Orleans, 1860-1880* (Chicago: Univ. of Chicago Press, 1973).* An early, complex, and lasting account of the thinking of Booker T. Washington and W. E. B. DuBois is August Meier's *Negro Thought in America, 1880-1915: Racial Ideologies in the Age of Booker T. Washington* (Ann Arbor: Univ. of Michigan Press, 1963).* The definitive biography of Washington is Louis R. Harlan's masterful work in two volumes: *Booker T. Washington: The Making of a Black Leader, 1856-1901* (New York: Oxford Univ. Press, 1972)* and *Booker T. Washington: The Wizard of Tuskegee, 1901-1915* (New York: Oxford Univ. Press, 1983). Louis Harlan's second volume, like Leon Litwack's book, won a Pulitzer Prize. Finally, two outstanding works reach back into slavery and up into freedom to deal with the vital subjects of family and folklore in black life. These are Herbert G. Gutman's *The Black Family in Slavery and Freedom, 1750-1925* (New York: Pantheon, 1976),* and Lawrence W. Levine's *Black Culture and Black Consciousness: Afro-American Folk Thought from Slavery to Freedom* (New York: Oxford Univ. Press, 1977).*

Excellent broad coverage of the Southern scene during two generations after the war is offered in two books: Kenneth M. Stampp's *The Era of Reconstruction, 1865-1877* (New York: Knopf, 1965)* and C. Vann Woodward's *Origins of the New South, 1877-1913* (Baton Rouge: Louisiana State Univ. Press, 1951).* The student can learn more about white leaders in race relations by reading William F. Holmes's fascinating biography of James K. Vardaman, *The White Chief* (Baton Rouge: Louisiana State Univ. Press, 1970); Hugh C. Bailey's *Edgar Gardner Murphy, Gentle Progressive* (Miami: Univ. of Miami Press, 1968); Dewey W. Grantham's *Hoke Smith and the Politics of the New South* (Baton Rouge: Louisiana State Univ. Press, 1959);* and C. Vann Woodward's classic biography *Tom Watson, Agrarian Rebel* (New York: Macmillan, 1938).*

Violence has been central to race relations in the South. The story of Robert Charles and the New Orleans riot of 1900 is beautifully wrought by William Ivy Hair in his *Carnival of Fury* (Baton Rouge: Louisiana State Univ. Press, 1976). Violence in the Reconstruction period is fully treated in Allen W. Trelease, *White Terror: The Ku Klux Conspiracy and Southern Reconstruction* (New York: Harper and Row, 1971). An interesting book, and another artifact of its time, is the NAACP's own account of lynching, *Thirty Years of Lynching in the United States, 1889-1918* (New York: NAACP, 1919).

Four very fine studies that offer insights into special aspects of race relations in the postwar South are Joseph H. Cartwright, *The Triumph of Jim Crow, Tennessee in the 1880's* (Knoxville: Univ. of Tennessee Press, 1977); Howard N. Rabinowitz, *Race Relations in the Urban South, 1865-1890* (New York: Oxford Univ. Press, 1978);* J. Morgan Kousser, *The Shaping of Southern Politics: Suffrage Restriction and the Establishment of the One-Party South, 1888-1910* (New Haven: Yale Univ.

Press, 1974);* and Roger L. Ransom and Richard Sutch, *One Kind of Freedom: The Economic Consequences of Emancipation* (New York: Cambridge Univ. Press, 1977).*

The book that opened the ground for the study of race relations in the South is C. Vann Woodward's *The Strange Career of Jim Crow* (New York: Oxford Univ. Press, 1955).* This is a fascinating work, and it is perhaps the ideal point at which to start any study of the subject. Three highly significant books that followed not only dealt with the story of race relations in the South in the turn of the century decades, but also expanded their scopes to include either the North or the Union of South Africa as well. The first of these was George Fredrickson's excellent *The Black Image in the White Mind* (New York: Harper and Row, 1971),* which covers the whole of the United States. His *White Supremacy* (New York: Oxford Univ. Press, 1981)* ambitiously and profitably compares race relations in the South with those in South Africa, as does John Cell's *The Highest Stage of White Supremacy* (New York: Cambridge Univ. Press, 1982).

Legacy

The full history of the South from 1913 to the end of World War II is contained in George B. Tindall's comprehensive *The Emergence of the New South, 1913–1945* (Baton Rouge: Louisiana State Univ. Press, 1967).* George Tindall's volume brings the History of the South series up to 1945. The next volume will be written by Numan V. Bartley, a close student of race relations in the South over the last three decades who will certainly do justice to that subject on the larger canvas.

For an intriguing account of the Leo Frank case, the scholar ought to read the detective-story-like rendering by journalist Harry Golden, *A Little Girl is Dead* (Cleveland: World Publishing Company, 1965). The Scottsboro case is dramatically told in Dan Carter's *Scottsboro: A Tragedy of the American South* (Baton Rouge: Louisiana State Univ. Press, 1969).* The horror story of the induction of the disease syphilis into black prisoners in Alabama for experimental purposes is well told by James H. Jones in his book *Bad Blood* (New York: Free Press, 1981). The Greensboro sit-in in 1960 is done with a masterful hand and sensitivity to the larger scene by William Henry Chafe in his *Civilities and Civil Rights: Greensboro, North Carolina, and the Black Struggle for Equality* (New York: Oxford Univ. Press, 1980).*

Useful insights into the sources and nature of Southern white liberalism in the mid-twentieth century are offered in three excellent studies: Jacqueline Dowd Hall, *Revolt against Chivalry: Jessie Daniel Ames and the Women's Campaign Against Lynching* (New York: Columbia Univ. Press, 1979); Morton Sosna, *In Search of the Silent South: Southern Liberals and the Race Issue* (New York: Columbia Univ. Press, 1977); and Daniel J. Singal, *The War Within: From Victorian to Modernist Thought in the South, 1919–1945* (Chapel Hill: Univ. of North Carolina Press, 1982). Extremes of bigotry are described in David M. Chalmers's *Hooded Americanism: The First Century of the Ku Klux Klan, 1865–1965* (New York: Doubleday, 1965). A fine way to get into the civil rights movement is through David Levering Lewis's easily readable *King, A Critical Biography* (New York: Praeger, 1979).* An earlier struggle by a black leader working from the underside of life is sensitively portrayed by Nell I. Painter in *The Narrative of Hosea Hudson* (Cambridge: Harvard Univ. Press, 1979). Hudson left the farm and went to the city, finally to become an iron worker, a union leader, and a Communist organizer; another black working man named Nate Shaw stayed on the farm to organize agricultural workers and ended in jail after a shoot-out with the "law." Theodore Rosengarten has chronicled Shaw's story in yet another fascinating book, *All God's Dangers* (New York: Vintage Books, 1974).*

Taken all together, the literature on race relations in the South is marvelously rich, and it is an excellent device by which to study not only relations between blacks and whites, but also the history of America at large.

Index

311